The Granada Woolwich, decked out for its first anniversary celebrations in April 1938.
(From BFI National Library Special Collections – Sidney Bernstein Collection.)

Right: the usherette is taken from the opening programme for the Granada Kingston
in 1939 (courtesy of John Platford).

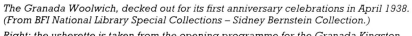

THE GRANADA THEATRES

The Granada North Cheam, June 1964. (Photograph by Photo Coverage.)
Opposite: the Granada Welling, February 1938. (From author's collection.)

THE
GRANADA
THEATRES
●●●●●●●●●●●
ALLEN EYLES

CINEMA THEATRE ASSOCIATION
Distributed by **BFI PUBLISHING**

 Publishing

First published
in September 1998 by the
Cinema Theatre Association
34 Pelham Road
London N22 6LN

Distributed by
BFI Publishing
British Film Institute
21 Stephen Street
London W1P 2LN

The CINEMA THEATRE ASSOCIATION was
formed in 1967 to promote serious interest in
all aspects of cinema buildings, including
architecture, décor, lighting, music, film
projection and stage facilities. The CTA
campaigns for the preservation and, wherever
possible, the continued use of cinemas and
theatres for their original purpose, and
maintains an archive of historical material.
Visits to cinemas and theatres in the UK and
overseas are regularly organised, as well as
lectures, talks and film shows. The CTA
publishes the annual magazine *Picture House*
and the bi-monthly *CTA Bulletin*, a members'
newsletter.
(Enquiries/Membership Secretary:
Neville C. Taylor, Flat One, 128 Gloucester
Terrace, London W2 6HP.)

The BRITISH FILM INSTITUTE exists
to encourage the development of film,
television and video in the United Kingdom,
and to promote knowledge, understanding
and enjoyment of the culture of the moving
image. Its activities include the National Film
and Television Archive; the National Film
Theatre; the Museum of the Moving Image;
the London Film Festival; the production and
distribution of film and video; funding and
support for regional activities; Library and
Information Services; Stills, Posters and
Designs; Research; Publishing and Education;
and the monthly *Sight and Sound* magazine.
(Membership details:
Membership Department, South Bank,
London SE1 8TL.)

ISBN: 0 85170 680 0

Cover design and design
consultant: Malcolm Johnson

Printed in Great Britain by
The KPC Group
London and Ashford, Kent

The KRASZNA-KRAUSZ FOUNDATION
provided a grant for the research of this book.
The Foundation, created by the late Andor
Kraszna-Krausz, exists for the appreciation,
promotion, improvement, development and
maintenance of the art and science of
photography, cinematography, television
and their derivatives. It seeks to achieve this
by encouraging a high standard of art and
technique in these arts and sciences.

Contents

Acknowledgements

At one time I was happily beginning work on the story of Odeon as the follow-up to my circuit histories of ABC and Gaumont-British. That was before I met Brian Gauntlett. The veteran Granada manager-showman strong-armed me into writing about his circuit first, putting at my disposal his own extensive scrapbooks and offering to introduce me to many of his old colleagues. Brian remained on hand to offer encouragement, answer questions, dig out illustrations, and comment on the text. I hope this book measures up to his expectations.

Other Granada Theatres veterans who reminisced about their time with the company for my benefit were Alex Bernstein, Ivan Cluley, Jeff Curtis, Barry Haigh, Bob Morgan, George Mullins, John Platford and, not least, John Young. Many of them were also helpful in supplying further old company material for information and for illustrative use.

On top of Brian Gauntlett's persuasiveness, what attracted me to writing this book on Granada was the knowledge that the British Film Institute's National Library held the business records of Sidney Bernstein, the head of Granada, plus company scrapbooks containing flyers, hanging cards and other promotional material, other scrapbooks of advertising and events at various Granada cinemas, and files on other areas of company activity. These were donated to the BFI by Granada following the death of Sidney Bernstein and are available as a BFI Special Collection for inspection by appointment. I sampled them in writing *Gaumont British Cinemas* and realised that they would require a daunting amount of time to explore in detail. Fortunately, the Kraszna-Krausz Foundation provided a grant specifically to enable this material to be properly researched and I am most grateful to its Trustees for their support.

The BFI collection by no means provides a complete history of the company but it does offer numerous insights into company policy, once confidential information, and much fascinating detail — as well as much trivia. A few seemingly minor files were in too fragile a state to be inspected. Janet Moat, Special Materials Librarian, and her assistant, Saffron Parker, were most helpful in providing access to this material. Also at the BFI National Library, David Sharp kindly facilitated the copying of other reference material.

I have not been able to locate many early photographs of the circuit's cinemas. But a further incentive to undertake this book was the survival of thousands of negatives of the cinemas from the Fifties onwards taken by Granada's official photographer, Photo Coverage, and carefully preserved by the company's present owner, Stephen Scrase, who has made the substantial number of contact prints credited to Photo Coverage in this book. (Unfortunately, some of the negatives have suffered chemical decomposition and are no longer printable, so it has not been possible to include quite every view that I would have liked.)

Although many of my own colour photographs appear in this book, something of better quality was needed for the front cover and John D. Sharp has kindly supplied an historic image of the Granada Tooting which

he took while the building was still a cinema. In handling the front cover design and processing my page layouts, Malcolm Johnson has shown a dedication beyond mere professionalism and it has been a pleasure to work with him.

As with my Gaumont and ABC books, John Fernee read the entire text closely, discussed many points with me, and continually stoked up my enthusiasm. Richard Gray, chairman of the Cinema Theatre Association, kindly read the pre-war chapters of this book and provided some most useful comments. Tony Moss, president of the CTA, not only wrote the chapter on the organs but also went through the full text and made some excellent points. Another CTA committee member, Les Bull, contributed some valuable reminiscences, while David Trevor-Jones commented on some of the earlier text. Elain Harwood read the pre-war chapters and offered valuable observations and additions. Besides Brian Gauntlett, John Young valiantly perused the entire text while Bob Morgan vetted the chapter covering his years with Granada.

Some of the information in this book came from the post-war files of the architect David E. Nye, which were collected by Richard Gray and now reside in the CTA Archive. Richard Gray also provided me with items concerning Theodore Komisarjevsky's relationship with Granada which he discovered in the Harvard Theatre Collection in the United States. And David Eve kindly photocopied some useful items of Granada history which he saved from destruction in a clear-out.

Among other CTA colleagues, Giles Woodforde advised on the printing arrangements for this book and much is owed to Jeremy Buck as Sales Officer for his expert distribution of my previous two CTA books to members, which ensured their financial success and made this one possible. At BFI Publishing, John Atkinson has provided sterling support in arranging trade sales and promotion.

Among others to whom I am indebted in various ways are John Billington, Arthur Hawkins, Colin Jenner, Ian Johnson, Charles Morris, Keith Skone, D.W.C. Sparke, Terry Staples and Martin Tapsell. The following CTA members (or friends of members) kindly offered information, reminiscences and/or illustrations: Louis Barfe (Surbiton), Tony Duggan (Hillingdon), Ken George (Lewisham), Peter R. Godwin (Great Munden), Richard Hawkins (Gosport), Mike Ostler (Grays), Alan Scott (Sevenoaks), Neville C. Taylor (London), D. W. Vaughan (Hornchurch), G. Warne (Bexley) and Trevor Williams (Worcester Park). My apologies and thanks to anyone whom I may have inadvertently omitted.

Much initial research into programming was undertaken at the Wandsworth Local History Library, consulting local press advertising for four Granada theatres in the area. I am grateful to the librarian, Tony Shaw, and his assistant, Meredith Davis, for their co-operation. One particularly elusive date was researched for me with great thoroughness by Miss J. Walsh of the Ewell County Information Centre, Ewell Library, Surrey.

Introduction

As a youngster, I lived within walking distance of the Granada Tooting – to many eyes, the greatest cinema ever built in Britain.

Was I impressed?

Yes and no. I found the Granada intimidating. My first visit was on my own in the early Fifties, to fill an empty afternoon. I bought the cheapest ticket for a Foreign Legion romp called *Ten Tall Men* with Burt Lancaster. I remember being hastened across the baronial main foyer to the mirrored back wall where caped usherettes in blue and gold processed me into the auditorium and whisked me down to the front stalls. It was pretty full and I was placed in a side seat close to the screen, from which I dared not move despite the awkward angle. The dire Gene Autry supporting feature, *Beyond The Purple Hills*, confirmed to me that there was better value in the repertory double bills at the tiny Vogue cinema round the corner where you could sit much further back with a straighter view of the screen for the same money or less.

Moved shortly afterwards to nearby Streatham, I concentrated on the cinemas there and those along the main roads to Brixton and Croydon. The Granada Thornton Heath became the best place to see the Gaumont release (as Streatham's Gaumont had yet to recover from war damage). This Granada was a less ostentatious, more relaxing hall than Tooting.

Here I saw CinemaScope for the first time: *King of the Khyber Rifles*. The screen looks small in the photograph on page 9 but the effect of that wide image and the enveloping stereophonic sound from halfway back in the stalls was truly sensational. The impact quickly wore off, although to this day I always derive an added pleasure from watching films in 'scope.

In the mid-Fifties, I chose a visit to the Granada Tooting as a birthday treat from Mrs. Peters, the lady upstairs at the house where I'd lived before. I had somewhat selfishly selected a western called *Rough Company* and we sat in the best seats for the afternoon show. It was an excellent film in early Cinema-Scope but I remember thinking that the sparse audience detracted somewhat from the enjoyment.

Some time later, I went back for a show that included a revival of the British comedy, *Appointment with Venus*. The place was packed but the reels were screened in the wrong order. I attended a Sunday revival of the Hollywood war drama *Twelve O'Clock High* and the projectionist sought to enhance the flying sequences by playing the mono sound of planes droning across the sky through the stereophonic speakers and then switching back to the speaker behind the screen whenever anyone spoke.

Against such lapses, I later sat gripped through a perfect presentation on the enormous CinemaScope screen of that black-and-white masterpiece *The Hustler*. I was so transfixed I never noticed whether there was a crowd around me or not.

My friend Tom Vallance saw the Granada Tooting in its heyday and to him it was "a truly palatial building which, despite its size and grandiloquence, always seemed warm and inviting" – a quote from the reminiscence he contributed to *Picture House* (issue 19, Winter 1993/94). He recalls its significance as a home of live shows, but he too found it "cold and unwelcoming" when its audiences dwindled.

Sadly, the partnership between audience and building was let down by a fickle public. The patrons dropped away but the building remained as the finest example of the full-scale picture palace in this country – and, along with sister theatres at Woolwich and Clapham Junction, one worthy to stand comparison with the best American examples on which the Granada style was loosely modelled. Even the less elaborate "standard" Granadas built by the circuit were extraordinarily opulent and spacious for the neighbourhoods in which they appeared.

"We sell tickets to theatres, not movies," said Marcus Loew, head of Loew's Theatres. It was a philosophy adopted by Sidney Bernstein, head of Bernstein/Granada Theatres. Loew had built up one of the leading chains of movie theatres in the United States, including many spectacular buildings, before his death in 1927. Bernstein, who only really took off in 1930, matched his achievement with some of Britain's most striking cinema buildings. Others believed in the drawing power of particular cinemas, with patrons returning week after week, but none as

The Granada Tooting, seen in Spring 1939 with queue and its American style vertical sign lit up. (Photograph by John D. Sharp/Tony Moss Collections.)

Sidney Bernstein as depicted in a 1928 trade journal (left). Cecil Bernstein in 1934 (courtesy of Alex Bernstein).

much as Sidney Bernstein. (A survey published in 1946, the peak year of attendance, showed that twenty-three per cent of frequent picturegoers generally went to the same cinema regularly, and a further ten per cent also generally attended a particular cinema when the film appealed to them.)

Bernstein had fixed ideas on design. Bernard Levin in *The Times* (24 December 1993) declared: "Anyone who knew Sidney knew also that he was the most complete and intense architect manqué there has ever been"; and, "If his feet, when he was young, had not been turned towards the cinema, he would indeed have been an architect, and I believe a great one. He supervised, down to the tiniest item, the building of Granada cinemas..."

Denis Forman, in his vivid portrait of Sidney Bernstein in *Persona Granada*, declares that he was no conceptual architect: "He would have to call in Lutyens or Komisarjevsky to supply the great design. But when it came to a layout and interior fittings of a kitchen, a cinema or a lavatory there was no one to touch him. He was, in fact, a jobbing architect of genius." (Sidney certainly took great care to ensure that his cinemas' toilet facilities were the best anywhere, but he spent the absolute minimum on exit corridors.)

Richard Gray, who interviewed the late architect David Nye for an article in *Picture House* (no. 22, Summer 1997), wrote: "Nye remarked that while Bernstein could intelligently discuss plans when looking at them the wrong way up, he 'didn't have much idea about design, quite frankly', a somewhat surprising statement considering Bernstein's patronage of the greatest cinema decorator of the day, Theodore Komisarjevsky. For the interiors at North Cheam, the Russian designer produced rough drawings which Nye's draughtsmen would then work up for use by the fibrous plaster contractor when making the decorative mouldings."

Certainly, it was Bernstein's good judgement in selecting Komisarjevsky that ensured his theatres stood out from the competition.

And in management, publicity, programming, branding and general showmanship, the Granada circuit made its mark more distinctively and incisively than any other group. Sidney Bernstein gained an influence out of all proportion to Granada's share of the British exhibition market. Despite the sale of shares to the public, it remained essentially a privately run business until the Sixties, dominated by Sidney Bernstein, and Britain's most important independent cinema circuit. Granada did not grow at the speed of Odeon or reach the size of the other two major circuits, Gaumont and ABC, but it seems likely that Bernstein did not want the company to become too large for him to continue exercising personal control. (The success of Granada Television finally took the company out of family hands.)

Although Bernstein dominated the chain – not only determining its direction but taking an obsessive interest in the details of its operation – he did not run the cinemas single-handed. He was often absent – on extended holidays and business trips, working for the Ministry of Information during World War Two, as a film producer immediately afterwards, and later setting up in commercial television in Manchester. But he set the style of operation, he was still kept informed, and he was apt to ask probing questions over the smallest details.

It is easy to gain the impression that Sidney Bernstein was directly responsible for all his company's accomplishments. But those who worked for the company identify many others who had key roles.

In particular, there was Sidney's quieter younger brother, Cecil. In *Persona Granada*, Denis Forman declares: "In their business life... the two were as close as identical twins with an almost extrasensory power of communicating with each other. In their private lives there was no such bond. [...] But if one of them were to step into the shadow of a cinema which could be for sale, see a preview of a 'smash', hear of a threatened bankruptcy, he instantly became part of the business unit which was the sum of the Bernstein brothers, thinking and acting as one person."

It was Cecil who immersed himself in the film trade, knew everyone, and smoothed the feathers sometimes ruffled by Sidney's autocratic ways; Cecil who had the feel for popular mass entertainment that the more patrician Sidney lacked; Cecil who was a leading light in the Cinema and Television Benevolent Fund (its president for an exceptionally long period, 1970-1981) and, among other details, saw that the small distributor was always paid first.

And there were various other long-term associates. Take the financial advisers. The earliest was E. G. (Ernest George) Bygrave, a director of the theatre company until circa 1950. Then there was Maurice King, prominent in the drinks business, a director of Granada Theatres from the Thirties well into the Sixties. Halford W. L. Reddish and Richard J. Willder were other long-term directors. And Joe Warton, who began as an office boy and rose through the ranks, became the financial brain in the Fifties and through the era of greatest expansion into television.

"Sidney was a brilliant man, but deeply controlling and deeply autocratic", declares his nephew Alex Bernstein. "Someone once said of him that he had a whim of iron – quite true. Sidney used to tell a story against himself. Someone met him and said, 'You're one of the Bernstein brothers – tell me, are you the nice one or the nasty one?' Sidney said he knew which one he was."

The Granada Thornton Heath – not one of the original Granadas but the former State, taken over in 1948 and soon renamed. The exterior dates from 16 February 1960. Interior view, with festoon curtain raised, was taken on 11 January 1955. The CinemaScope screen is slightly angled towards the circle. A small-size circuit-style chandelier has been installed in the ceiling. One of the stereophonic speakers can be seen mounted on each side wall at the edges of the picture. (Photo Coverage.)

"What Sidney was good at – unlike many people – was working with a very small, good team. And the people that built Granada were Sidney as the leader (no question about that); and my father [Cecil] who was very close to him and a very shrewd businessman; and Joe Warton, who was the financial brain."

Bob Morgan, booking controller for many of the later years, recalls: "Cecil was a lovely man. He could be very nasty, he could be very difficult. Basically he was overshadowed by Sidney. Cecil loved movies. He called me Bob. Sidney called me Mr. Morgan."

This book is much concerned with the design of the Granada Theatres and here, undoubtedly, Sidney Bernstein had the final word. He had old-fashioned tastes in design and believed that people wanted architecture with marble columns, gilt and mirrors and this would ensure that his cinemas were profitable.

Not for him, in 1930, the atmospheric fantasy interior or streamlined exterior of the New Victoria. He found what he liked in the work of Komisarjevsky and stuck with it, repeating decorative schemes over and over. This, of course, also saved considerable time and money. He permitted modern exteriors, as at Woolwich, but continued to insist on neo-classical interiors rather than the streamlined look of most cinemas built by the major circuits, even after it was clear that audiences were just as happy sitting in plainer, less elaborate surroundings.

He retained organs long after they were passing out of favour and was drawn into public debate over them with Oscar Deutsch of Odeon, who thought they were not worth a penny of extra business.

An American influence permeated all Sidney Bernstein's ideas about cinema operation and showmanship. He frequently visited America and cultivated the Hollywood studio heads, but he also looked at the way the movie theatres were being operated. He called his cinemas "theatres" as the Americans did, although he was far from alone in that and most of his buildings were equipped for theatre use and did present live performances (Deutsch's Odeons were called "theatres" even though they usually had no live show capacity at all). Bernstein's theatres showed "programs", not programmes. They had fin signs reminiscent of the verticals on American theatre facades, and chaser lights and changing neon patterns attached to the main name signs, all a rarity in Britain. Bernstein mixed music hall and film in American-style cine-variety longer and more extensively than any other circuit did in Britain. He used the American showman Phineas T. Barnum (1810-91) – American promoter and hoodwinker, author of the saying "There's a sucker born every minute" – as his somewhat curious model of showmanship, and placed a portrait of Barnum on the wall of every manager's office – "to remind us all", he said, "that we are in

show business." (This same reminder was later placed in the offices of bemused television executives and motorway service area managers.)

For many years, each of his cinemas advertised itself as "The Service-With-A-Smile Theatre". What was this but an early form of the "Have a nice day" American philosophy of pointed friendliness to customers? It was reflected in cinema category boards which were not allowed to state "Open" at a certain time but had to say "We Open". Similarly, it was "We Close" rather than "Close". Similarly, it was "Doors Open" at a certain time rather than "Close" or "National Anthem". Sidney insisted on music being played in the foyers of his cinemas. He wanted a distinctive, friendly, welcoming approach. When Granada opened a chain of sweet shops, what were they called? Miss Candy, after the American word for confectionery. A chain of fast food shops was named Havasnack (Sidney wanted to make it Havasnak which would have made it more American still). A shortlived car wash venture was called Supawash.

"Do things differently": that was the Granada approach, says Sidney. He set it up himself, but he set a company philosophy, an outlook, and any new ideas by others would be tailored to fit.

This is not to say that Sidney Bernstein thought up all these touches himself, but he set a company philosophy, an outlook, and any new ideas by others would be tailored to fit.

Denis Forman writes of two things he learned for certain in his early days at Granada Television: "that Sidney had a talent amounting to genius to ensure that every bit of credit for Granada's success reflected on him personally." Forman refers to two histories of Granada Television that were completed, rejected as unworthy by Sidney Bernstein and suppressed, because, Forman believes, others were given too much credit.

Curiously, Sidney did not take credit on the two films he produced in partnership with Alfred Hitchcock. But then nobody else received credit either.

Sidney ensured that Granada were the best employers in the exhibition business. He recognised the cinema trade union, the National Association of Theatrical and Kine Employees, from the first, accepting its terms of pay and conditions. However, Alex Bernstein remarks with a laugh: "He was very good at recognising trade unions, but very good at fighting them once they were recognised."

Sidney and Cecil Bernstein required, says Bob Morgan, "a standard of excellence. Whatever you did you had to do well. They would back you in public. What they said in private is another matter, but never ever did they let me down. They were good employers." Sidney in particular would always ask questions, hold a post-mortem. "Even on holiday, Sidney kept an eye on the business. You were never out of Sidney's care."

A long-time projectionist, Barry Haigh, notes that Granada employed a handyman to fix the arms on the seats and the flush in the toilets while his counterparts at a nearby Gaumont had to do such chores as part of their job. "I thought it was the best circuit to be with. You used to hear terrible things about guys who worked for ABC. The Odeons seemed to be all right, but the Granadas seemed to be top of the range." As personnel manager, former manager George Mullins was allowed to bring in pensions for the part-time cleaners (which usefully encouraged them to stay with the company).

Like many wealthy men, Sidney Bernstein was fanatical about saving money. "The Bernstein system of running a cinema chain was enshrined in a bulky procedure manual which was followed to the letter by every cinema manager," notes Denis Forman. "It told him how to indent for lavatory paper, how much to pay the cleaning ladies per square foot and what a uniform could cost for a small, medium and outsize commissionaire. If a form of expenditure was not in the manual it could not happen without reference to head office. This system was perfected and replicated over some four dozen cinemas until the Bernsteins were satisfied it was virtually spend-proof."

And Forman again, on travelling with Sidney in a car around 1950: "Frequently we would stop at a cinema. If it was a Granada, Sidney would carry out one of his surprise inspections, prizing open ashtrays, flushing lavatories and inspecting the usherettes' fingernails whilst the manager stood two paces behind him, the old hands taking the bombardment of quick-fire questions with robust good humour, the younger men rigid with terror."

John Platford, an organist with the circuit over a 35-year span, recalls a story told about a Bernstein visit to Clapham Junction: "An office assistant left in charge of the theatre one morning had the team enter the building for a tour of inspection. All went well until Sidney Bernstein wanted to enter a locked room. 'I don't have the key, Mr. Bernstein,' said the assistant. 'I want to see inside that room,' Mr. Bernstein said. The assistant, heart in hand, charged the door and it burst open. 'Thank you,' he said. The team left and a fortnight later the assistant was promoted to assistant manager at another site."

Barry Haigh recalls that each projector lamp carried a guarantee for 100 hours and he had to date stamp it when it was first used and send it back for replacement if it expired prematurely...

Against this, there are many instances of Sidney's personal financial generosity towards employees in difficulties and there is no doubt that he and the other head office executives inspired loyalty in their managers and staff. Granada paid its staff better than the trade norm and there was rarely any need for the unions to intervene. The circuit usually promoted from within, and (with rare exceptions) never recruited managers who had trained with and worked for the three major circuits. Granada managers were required to fill in much less paperwork than their counterparts on the big chains. Although they did have to write a weekly letter describing audience response and other happenings, first to Sidney in the Thirties and later to Cecil, these were not a waste of time: they would be read and often draw a response.

Despite the tight control, managers were encouraged to exercise any flair for showmanship. However, they were discouraged from submitting their publicity stunts to the trade papers so that rival cinema managers could see them. Instead, stunts were reported in the circuit's own newsletters, logged and cross-referenced for the benefit of other Granada managers, while small monetary rewards were made.

Sidney was apparently known to some of his friends in the Thirties as "the low highbrow", a description he found "not unreasonable". Within Sidney Bernstein lurked both a businessman and a man of culture, a left-winger and a man of wealth. When the two aspects came into conflict in the operation of Granada, the businessman usually won.

To some extent Bernstein believed in improving the life of his patrons by both what they saw on the screen and the surroundings in which they sat. In an article on cinema decoration published in 1924, he wrote: "In so many lives that are drab and devoid of colour, the kinema brings a measure of illusion and forgetfulness. It has the complement of beautiful music [this being the 'silent' period], and let there be added to that in the theatre itself colour and form that are beautiful... Exhibitors must... reflect that for the poorer class of patron, as well as for those in more expensive seats, there is an inborn sense of beauty..." In a paper he delivered in November 1934, he said: "Every intelligent theatre owner wants films of a better quality and knows that, if he does not get them, his public will desert him. He knows, too, that a demand from the public for pictures will result in the production of better pictures."

Ways in which he tried to raise standards were by the questions he posed in his Questionnaires and by insisting that the names of the directors as well as the casts of films be displayed in the foyer. Some important documentaries and shorts were given their only widespread mainstream showings as supporting features in Granada theatres, and there is an impression that the circuit showed better quality films than its rivals. The foyers sometimes featured travelling art displays. But Denis Forman suggests that the credit which accrued to him from such gestures was in part a way of concealing his primary desire to make money. (Lest it be thought that Forman has written a work critical of Bernstein, quite the reverse is true and he is called "one of the most extraordinary men of our generation".)

Certainly, the Granada circuit showed many crude exploitation films in the best P. T. Barnum spirit, and played many "exclusives" rejected by the major circuits. Overall I have the feeling that the quality of films shown was actually slightly lower than at Odeons, Gaumonts or ABCs.

One of Sidney's great detestations was free publicity. He would not have manufacturers placing their names on their goods – unless they paid for it. He made projectionists remove the trademarks of film distributors from the beginning of films (although he had to relent where the bigger studios were concerned) and he took the name off the bonnet of his Rover car, replacing it with studs. In the restaurant kitchens he removed the name on the hot plates and he even had the name plate of the boiler manufacturer stripped off the set of one of the films he produced with Alfred Hitchcock.

Granada made as little use of distributors' posters as possible because their names were too prominent on them. The circuit created its own colourful posters and publicity displays through a fully-owned subsidiary, Posterprint, at Kingston, Surrey. An artist called John Barnet produced a high quality of output that more than satisfied managers.

The big Granadas were receptive to a variety of uses, not just films but live events for a day or a whole week – classical and pop concerts, ballet, opera, operettas, pantomimes, wrestling, even straight plays. With such diversity, which included nights of bingo before it took over full-time, these buildings became more than just cinemas, serving whole areas as cultural centres. True, the circuit's role was usually just to hire out the buildings and the increasing diversity of later years was caused by the shortage of popular films, but nevertheless Granada more than any other British circuit explored the full potential of its buildings. (The big irritation of full-time bingo is that it strangles all other uses of a building.)

Sidney Bernstein seems to have been blind to the lasting value of the cinemas designed for him by Theodore Komisarjevsky. His nephew Alex Bernstein declares: "I remember Sidney saying, 'You can't have any sentiment to bricks and mortar. Sentiment to people, but not to bricks and mortar.'"

Sidney was furious when local authorities and English Heritage saw fit to list some of his buildings, restricting his freedom to do what he liked with them. This may have coloured his judgement. But, despite himself, Sidney is left with more than the Granada Tooting as a lasting monument. No less than seven of the Granada Theatres have been listed – an extraordinarily

high percentage of the cinemas the company commissioned.

Of course, there was a lot more to these cinemas than bricks and mortar. There was the life they led, the ambience they created for audiences, the films and shows they played, and the job satisfaction they gave to staff. I hope this book gives some impression of both the architectural splendour and the life of these buildings as cinemas.

1 • Empires, Rialtos And Kinemas

When the first Granada opened in 1930, the Bernstein family had been established in the entertainment business for a number of years.

Alexander Bernstein and his wife Jane took their first tentative step into show business when on 21 August 1907 she signed an agreement with two experienced variety managers, Jesse Sparrow and Harry Bawn, leasing them land on which they put up a new music hall, the Empire at Edmonton, North London. The architect was Bertie Crewe. Although it has been suggested that, as a builder, Alexander Bernstein erected and outfitted the Empire, to anchor a shopping development on a site he had purchased two years earlier, the foundation stone laid on 16 September 1908 made no mention of Bernstein, giving the directors as Harry Bawn, Jesse Sparrow and two others, and naming the contractors as Kirk and Kirk. Although films were included in the programme, this theatre continued primarily as a music hall with Harry Bawn as managing director.

However, the boom in cinema construction and attendances encouraged Alexander Bernstein to invest in film exhibition. In 1912, in association with Harry Bawn, he took over Ye Olde Paragon Music Hall at Mile End, East London, and converted it to the Empire which, seating around 2,000, was one of the largest buildings of the period dedicated to showing films. He was proprietor and joint managing director with Bawn.

In April 1913, Bernstein opened his first purpose-built cinema, in the town where he lived – the Empire, Ilford, East London. With seating on a single floor, it claimed a capacity of 2,000 (*The Bioscope Annual*, 1915). This seems to have been a cheap and cheerful operation, prominently advertising that admission was just one penny (the price of the local newspaper).

It was followed by three other Empires. The Empire Kinema at Plumstead, near Woolwich in Southeast London, was another very simple affair – four walls and a roof. "If it is not a success, then we shall turn it into a factory", said Bernstein of both this and his Ilford venture. Plumstead had bench seating for approximately 900 (a maximum of 1,008 patrons was later permitted; *The Bioscope Annual* of 1915 gives a capacity of 1,800 although the *Kinematograph Year Book* of 1917 reduces the figure to 1,500).

The Empire Kinema at West Ham Lane (Stratford) opened in July 1914 and the Empire Kinema, East Ham, arrived around the same time. According to the *Bioscope Annual*, these two North-east London properties had capacities of 2,500 each. Equally suspect figures in the 1917 edition of the *Kinematograph Year Book* give seating figures of 2,000 and 1,400 respectively.

Bernstein first ran this small chain from his building headquarters, the Empire Works, further along from the Empire cinema in West Ham Lane at the corner with Church Street. He also started Film Agencies Ltd., a company which made and sold cinema equipment as well as booking and distributing films. Soon an office was established in London's West End off Charing Cross Road at 19 Cecil Court (this pedestrian passage was known as "Flicker Alley" for its concentration of film concerns).

Early Years

Born circa 1860, Alexander Bernstein was of Russian Jewish origins, having arrived in the East End of London from Latvia in the early 1890s with his brother Julius. He married Jane Lazarus, a tailor's daughter, in 1893 and, like many prosperous Jews, they moved out of the crowded East End and went eastwards to Ilford. They lived in a succession of houses in the area, increasingly larger and more lavish as he expanded both his various business activities and the size of his family. He was principally a builder with his own stone quarries in Wales. His eldest son was born on 28 May 1894 and named Selim A. Bernstein. Two daughters followed, Rae and Beatrice, then Sidney Lewis Bernstein on 30 January 1899 at Ilford. After Sidney, came three more sons – Cecil, Max and Albert – and two more daughters, Ida and Beryl. Selim served in the Middlesex Imperial Yeomanry in the First World War and was killed at Gallipoli on 8 September 1915.

Sidney left school in Ilford at age 16 to become an engineering apprentice for a company in Bow. He tried to enlist in the War but was declared medically unfit because of breathing difficulties resulting from an accident in a football match at school which had dented his nose. He was permitted to join his father's company, Film Agencies (in 1916? at age nineteen? –

FOUR STAR ARTISTES
in FOUR Special Photo-plays

Monday,
Tuesday,
Wednesday,
June
14, 15, 16.

MARY PICKFORD
in her great success
Rags
Our Mary is seen in her
finest character study

WILLIAM RUSSELL
in a thrilling super-play
Hearts or
Diamonds
Russell in a new breezy,
easy style picture

Thursday,
Friday,
Saturday,
June
17, 18, 19.

NORMA TALMADGE
in the dramatic success
The
Probation Wife
To secure love and wealth
she has to fight her way
through life

DOUGIE FAIRBANKS
as the man who cheers—in
The Habit of
Happiness
if you feel blue you should
see Dougie

MileEndEmpire
"Ye Olde Paragon"

FOR ONE WEEK
COMMENCING APRIL 26th

D. W. GRIFFITHS'
Stupendous Spectacle

Intolerance

LOVE'S STRUGGLE
THROUGHOUT
THE AGES"

Created by Griffiths—Producer of
Broken Blossom showing at the
Alhambra.

This production cost £150,000 and
took 2½ years to produce.

Showing THREE TIMES DAILY:
2.30 — 5.45 — 8.15

Double Orchestra
every performance.

EMPIRE KINEMA

Ilford Lane
(10 minutes from Broadway)

Far left: a starry week at the Mile End Empire, formerly Ye Olde
Paragon music hall.

Left: 1920 flyer for the Empire Ilford which may be a printer's
proof as the misspelling of "orchestra" has been corrected
(although errors over D. W. Griffith's name and his film Broken
Blossoms remain unnoticed). This shows the emblem used since
1915 (or earlier) for the Empire Kinemas and other Bernstein
companies such as Film Agencies,
with the name reversed out of a
blue band on a red circle (similar
to signs on the Underground).
Far left: the device appears in
the window above the entrance of
the Empire Ilford, seen circa 1925.
(All from BFI – Sidney Bernstein
Collection.)

Above: the Plumstead Empire,
renamed the Century, seen on
27 September 1956 when the
auditorium remained very basic
(both Photo Coverage).

Left: Alexander Bernstein.

sources and details vary), where he concentrated on booking the films, avidly attending the trade shows and the West End cinemas to see the latest product available.

In 1919, Alexander Bernstein's Empire Works built a new cinema, the Electric Theatre at Bournemouth, Dorset, for Capital and Counties Electric Theatres as a replacement for a 500-seater. Bernstein took a seat as a director of the company, perhaps having accepted shares in lieu of payment. The architect of the cinema was Cecil Masey, who had earlier worked on the Empire Edmonton under Bertie Crewe. The Electric would be counted as one of the Bernstein cinemas for most of the decade.

By 1920, Sidney was a director and general manager of Film Agencies. He was also the secretary of the West Ham Engineering Company, which his father ran with A. Simon and which was one of several companies based at the Empire Works in West Ham Lane. Another company in High Wycombe which manufactured cinema seats was taken over by Alexander Bernstein.

Much of Sidney's time was spent in devising prologues for major features in his cinemas, and his work extended to a special showing of the American spiritual drama *Earthbound* at the Royal Opera House, Covent Garden, using back projection. *Earthbound* then played the Empire Mile End.

At the end of 1920 a further Empire Kinema was opened at Willesden, Northwest London. Designed by Cecil Masey and built by the Empire Works, this was larger than its purpose-built predecessors, with 1,450 seats – but it was still on one floor. Film Agencies supplied the seating, other furnishings, the stage setting, the electrical installation and projection equipment. The make of projector was the Motiograph, for which Film Agencies was the British distributor.* A public drinking fountain was placed along the adjoining Ilex Road by the front right side exit as a memorial to Selim Bernstein (even in the 1950s managers had the unspecified responsibility of keeping it clean and in working order – but in 1998 it has been blocked up and abandoned).

When Willesden opened, the Bernstein circuit totalled eight cinemas. The Lyric at far-off Guernsey and the Electrodrome at Bow, East London, had recently been added while the Mile End Empire had been leased out and would never return to the fold. The Lyric did not last as one of the Bernstein theatres but the Electrodrome did, in some kind of a partnership arrangement with local entrepreneur H. Forrest and his successors.

For a short while, Sidney explored the idea of working in film production. He and Michael Balcon co-produced a promotional short, *The Story of Oil*, for the Standard Oil Company with Victor Saville directing. When Sidney sailed to New York on 4 June

1921 to explore the possibility of setting up a British agency to supply American studio equipment to film-makers here, he was already giving authoritative statements to the trade press. He told the *Kinematograph Weekly* (26 May 1921): "I have felt for a long time that one of the difficulties which the British producer has had to face is the lack of proper studio equipment. The Americans have all sorts of wonderful contrivances for lighting and studio effects of which, I am sure, the British producer has not heard – simply because there has been no one in this country to bring them to his notice. In addition to studying all the latest methods of film presentation in the American theatres, and the signing of agreements whereby my company will handle all the latest and best in theatre equipment, I hope to establish, on my return, a studio equipment department." It does not seem that he ever imported film-making equipment, but his visits to the huge American movie palaces of that time must have helped shape his own tastes in cinema design.

On his return, Sidney was appointed Director of Entertainment for the cinema circuit and such was his standing by this time that he was invited to set up a film show for prime minister Lloyd George in Scotland and then a Christmas show for the Royal Family at Sandringham that year. For both occasions, he selected Charlie Chaplin comedies.

Sidney Bernstein takes charge

When Alexander died in March 1922 after a long illness, Sidney became head of the family businesses at the age of twenty-three. As the eldest surviving son, he also took on the responsibility of looking after his mother and seven brothers and sisters.

One of Sidney's first acts was to recover the lease of the Empire Edmonton, which was doing badly. He closed the building for refurbishment, then re-opened it later in 1922, running it himself, still as a music hall. It was here that the celebrated Marie Lloyd gave her last performance on Tuesday 3 October 1922. According to one reminiscence, she was so ill after the first house that Bernstein and booking manager Leon Pollock advised her not to go on for the second show. But she refused to disappoint her audience and, after taking a tonic, gave a memorable performance. She returned home and retired to bed, dying two days later aged fifty-two. Elsewhere, she is said to have collapsed in mid-act. There is no dispute that Sidney ordered her dressing room to be permanently locked up and when this part of the theatre was demolished in 1933 he kept the star which had been pinned on the door.

The Empire Willesden offered films plus variety, changing programme mid-week. The cinemas at Ilford, Plumstead and West Ham seem to have changed programmes every two days.

---

* Film Agencies had its own factories which manufactured slides, tins, carbons, lamps, rewinders and transport cases.

The Empire Stratford (West Ham Lane) in the early 1920s.

The entrance of the Stratford (West Ham Lane) Empire, circa 1922, with a Jackie Coogan lookalike promoting a three-day run of the comedy drama My Boy. The timetable reveals the live act of Rene and Renard was part of the two evening performances, while Kagan, the French orchestra leader, was a further addition to the second evening show. The newsreel, the Topical Budget, was screened at the start of each show and again at the end of the evening. (BFI – Sidney Bernstein Collection.)

At Willesden and Plumstead, it was advertised that the orchestra played all day, but at East Ham only in the evening. The pedigree of the musical performers was worth promoting. At one theatre, "the famous French virtuoso" Kagan performed with his Wonder Orchestra from 2.30 to 10.30pm. At Ilford, patrons were reminded that the violinist conductor, List Nairne, who performed daily with his orchestra, came from the London Opera House, Kingsway.

The chain of Empires was augmented in November 1922 by a new Empire at Shrewsbury, Shropshire, which seated under 1,000 but also had variety acts along with the films. This was apparently a reconstruction of an older property and the owners, Shrewsbury Empires Ltd., asked Bernstein to manage it for them, appointing him a director as well as the company's consulting engineer. It was a long, narrow, straight-sided hall with a shallow curved ceiling and a small balcony far back. The Empire was later acquired by Bernstein and Shrewsbury became a Granada stronghold, The Empire turned into the longest survivor among the earlier Bernstein properties, continuing to operate as a cinema until January 1998.

Besides the full-time variety at Edmonton and the supporting live acts at Shrewsbury, music hall artistes were also engaged at this period for the Empires Willesden, East Ham and Ilford.

By 1923, the Bernstein organisation had outgrown its premises in Cecil Court and moved to 197 Wardour Street. During 1923, the Kinematograph Equipment Company was established to supply seating, easels, still boards and other items, also becoming the British distributor of Ross projectors. It remained a subsidiary company supplying Bernstein cinemas and others into the 1950s.

Sidney Bernstein contributed a short piece to the enlarged New Year issue (3 January 1924) of the *Kinematograph Weekly* in the "Showmanship for the Exhibitor" section, giving his views on decoration before he took up with Theodore Komisarjevsky. "To furnish a kinema in good taste should not be so very hard a task, yet how rarely does one see this successfully achieved," he began. "The first consideration to which theatre furnishers and decorators give precedence is how much decoration they can use, instead of pausing to work out the necessary minimum... Masses of gilded plaster, which usually comprise the imaginative compass of the theatre and kinema decorator, only distract and disturb the eye; and if the original designs of the architect be ill-conceived, all the applied decoration, and all the furniture in the world will fail to mend matters.

"If the intention be to have a 'period' kinema, it entails no more trouble to copy from the best contemporary designs, nor does it involve any increased expenditure. The recent innovations in theatre lighting which have largely been developed on the Continent should offer infinite scope for decoration. Concealed coloured lights thrown on to a neutral-tinted wall could not only be constantly varied, but would be a welcome relief from the usual decorative scheme...

"Soft and subdued colours and plain surfaces are soothing, and form an admirable setting for the varying phases of life depicted on the screen. They mellow scenes of garish display, and soften rugged pictures of poverty and distress. In so many lives that are drab and devoid of colour, the kinema brings a measure of illusion and forgetfulness. It has the complement of beautiful music, and let there be added to that in the theatre itself colour and form that are beautiful.

"Exhibitors must... reflect that for the poorer class of patron, as well as for those in more expensive seats, there is an inborn sense of beauty, and that in these competitive days audiences will go where they find conditions most sympathetic."

In 1925, Sidney Bernstein was one of the founders of the Film Society, established to show important foreign films that were not being picked up for commercial release and to revive others of distinction. Sidney's connections with the film trade were invaluable and he arranged the hire of the New Gallery in Regent Street from Provincial Cinematograph Theatres for the Film Society's Sunday afternoon shows. He found time to travel extensively in Europe and kept an eye open for new films that might be suitable for the Society. Sidney remained active in the Film Society until its screenings were stopped by World War Two.

Late in 1925, the Kinema at West Ham Lane (Stratford) was closed for refurbishment and re-opened as the Empire. It now had a new stage, seating and heating system, all at a cost of over £5,000. A policy was inaugurated of films being accompanied by three variety acts.

Around this time, Bernstein took over the Rialto at Enfield, North London, a former live theatre which had become a cinema in 1920. "Rialto" briefly replaced "Empire" as the favoured name for cinemas. At this Rialto, an American soda fountain was opened, offering ice cream sodas at fivepence (tuppence more for fruits on top), sundaes at eightpence, parfaits at one shilling, etc.

In 1926 the Rink cinema and skating rink at Leytonstone, North London, was acquired, and the following year it closed for substantial alterations. This was a most peculiar building – opened originally as a skating rink, then subdivided to include a large cinema on a flat stalls floor plus a small balcony with a projection room on stilts. The cinema was entered through the arcade of the adjacent Bearman's store while the skating rink was reached on Kirkdale Road on the far side. Cecil Masey drew up a scheme which converted the entire space to one cinema of 1,760 seats on one sloping floor within the old roof and walls. The projection room was moved forward. Although the company

Empire Shrewsbury. October 1961 exterior displays misspellings of Glynis Johns and Spider's Web on the canopy. Interior view dates from 20 September 1971. (Photo Coverage.)

The Rialto Enfield as it looked in the Sixties. The entrance (photographed in June 1964) was down a side road, visible from the main street. For many years there was a subsidiary entrance to the right on the corner of the market square. Foyer view dates from 4 December 1967 and shows a Komisarjevsky chandelier added, as does the view of the proscenium arch (probably also 4 December 1967) with reefer curtain not quite hiding the bottom of the screen. Note the ashlar treatment of the lower side walls, like that in the later Granadas. View of balcony (5 October 1965) shows another standard light fitting at the rear, the rather awkward placing of the side exit, and a heater attached to the wall high up. (All Photo Coverage.)

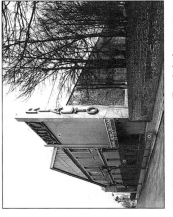

The Rialto Leytonstone. Top left: front entrance built into the corner of Bearman's store (January 1954). Left, cinema entrance at far end of arcade (14 March 1966). Above, top: auditorium in April 1949 – note art deco ceiling lights rather than standard Thirties fittings. Above, left: secondary entrance at the back (9 March 1965). Above, right: main foyer with entrance hall at back and doors to auditorium on right (14 March 1966). (All Photo Coverage.)

O UT of the converted shop of twenty years ago has arisen the mighty "movies" of to-day. True, the Kinema is still considered by some to be the cinderella of arts; but by most it is recognised as a new art dimension, a national power and the greatest of national recreations.

Only great and wonderful production has placed the Kinema in this position; mighty screen pictures have attracted the world's attention and the public's support.

Every year we have seen the screen's appeal increase but we forecast for 1927 the greatest "movie" year yet.

Never in our experience has there been a year with pictures ready for showing to compare with 1927—attractive, intelligent and masterly pictures produced not only in America, but in England, France, Germany and, in fact, the whole world.

Sidney Bernstein

STAGE

I N our search for perfect staging and a designer for a new stage set we found Mons. Theodor Komisarjevsky in the Russian City of Art—Moscow—as director of their world-famous Art Theatre. It took time to persuade this master of the theatre to come to England and design sets for Kinema stages, but eventually perseverance triumphed and his new masterpiece in stage craft is to be seen at the Willesden Empire Kinema.

The Semiloff method of stage lighting which makes colours resemble nature's wonder shades—as installed at the London Hippodrome—is another addition to our stage equipment.

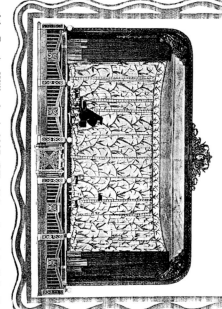

Two pages from the re-opening programme of the Empire Willesden in 1927. (BFI - Sidney Bernstein Collection.)

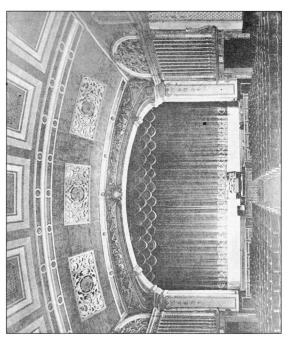

Theodore Komisarjevsky's interior decorations of the Empire Willesden (above) and West Ham Lane, Stratford (below), taken from a trade magazine.

formed to acquire the property was Empire Kinema (Leytonstone) Limited, this re-opened with the Rialto name in January 1927. It retained the two entrances. The one on Kirkdale Road now had an enlarged entrance hall taking patrons across part of the old skating rink floor. The display of an electric sign on the arcade entrance had to be negotiated with Bearman's.

In February 1927, Sidney announced plans to re-build the Empires at Edmonton, West Ham and Willesden, and to replace the Empire Plumstead with a new cinema. He also intended to build a cinema (or concert hall?) across the road from Sadler's Wells. In that same month, a new Bernstein subsidiary Empire Kinema (Lewisham) Ltd. was formed. Three months later it took control of the Lewisham Hippodrome in Southeast London from the current lessees, a company with the interesting name of Trans-Atlantic Productions headed by Albert de Courville and Joseph Horrowitz.

Enter Komisarjevsky

Early in 1927, Theodore Komisarjevky began his association with Sidney Bernstein by producing half-hour shows for the theatres. Born in 1882, Komisarjevsky had started his career in the Moscow theatre and moved to England in 1919, shortly after the Russian Revolution. He had produced several plays in the West End and staged a notable season of Chekhov plays at the small Barnes Theatre in 1925-26, also designing the sets.

Bernstein declared that "the music hall public is dying out" and so the Edmonton Empire would switch to films along with the Lewisham Hippodrome. He also had in mind considerable improvements to several cinemas, and appointed Komisarjevsky as head of "Art Direction" for the circuit with Cecil Masey as his architect. H. C. Fontaine was general manager.

Publicised as the "World famous director of the Moscow Art Theatre", Komisarjevsky first applied his hand to redecoration at the Edmonton Empire which closed in March for a little under four weeks to re-open as a cinema with thirty minutes of live variety three times daily in support.

In May, the Willesden Empire shut for five months of extensive alterations. The roof was raised by 24 ft. and a balcony of 786 seats added, along with a new ceiling. The balcony steppings were not in one long curve but followed an undulating line: a device unique to Masey's work and applied to later work for Bernstein. A Christie organ was installed, and Komisarjevsky devised a new colour scheme and new stage settings. Frank Dobson provided the sculpture on the outside. (According to a profile of Sidney Bernstein by Tom Driberg, he also employed such artists as John Armstrong, McKnight Kauffer and Oliver Messel in the Twenties and Thirties, but little is known of their precise undertakings.)

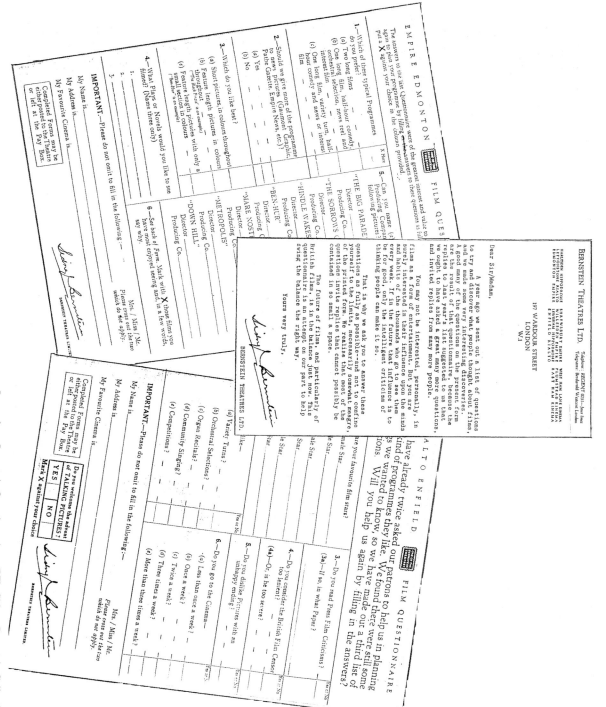

Pages from Bernstein Questionnaires. (BFI - Sidney Bernstein Collection.

The Enfield Rialto closed in July for a month while the stalls floor was raised in height by 4 ft. 6 in. at the stage end and 6 ft. at the back, and a new stage floor built. Two hundred more seats were added, and a new proscenium arch and "very novel colour scheme" were designed by Komisarjevsky. The cinema also gained new Ross projectors from Kinema Equipment, while work began on installing a Christie organ with a console in carved Japanese lacquer (this opened on 5 September with a special recital).

On a Saturday in September, Bernstein took over the Willesden Hippodrome, a music hall which was actually located in adjacent Harlesden in North London. According to press reports, he had two hundred workmen there on the Monday converting it to a cinema. It was re-opened the following Monday by the leading British star Betty Balfour. It now offered two films and variety acts in every programme. Komisarjevky provided new stage settings.

By November, the West Ham Lane Empire at Stratford had been thoroughly overhauled. The roof was raised by ten feet and a new ceiling and large stage installed; spring tip-up seats and an organ were introduced. The name was changed to Kinema. Komisarjevsky's decorative scheme which included grilles on the side walls was, by later standards, muted.

There was one reduction in the circuit: the Empire Ilford was sold off completely, to Sam Martyn. Circuit strength stood at eleven halls, including the Bournemouth Electric.

At this time Sidney Bernstein was also a director of Auto-maticket, which manufactured the press-lever ticket dispensing machines. And he found time for politics, representing Willesden Green ward on Middlesex County Council as an independent Labour member for five years.

Through Komisarjevsky, Bernstein also took an interest in live theatre, forming Sloane Productions in partnership with Arnold Bennett and leasing the Royal Court in Sloane Square in the autumn of 1927. They had some success with Bennett's play version of his novel Mr. Prohack, but the venture as a whole lost money and ended early in 1928. Komisarjevsky directed two plays in London that year and also a now lost film, a romance set in Paris called Yellow Stockings.

The Questionnaires

Sidney Bernstein was no ordinary cinema proprietor. He created the series of lengthy Questionnaires in which the audiences at his theatres were asked to name their favourite stars and to give their opinions about other matters. The first questionnaire was launched in 1927.

When one was issued in June 1928, a quarter of a million patrons were attending Bernstein Theatres each week and eligible to vote. The editing and tabulation took six months and

the results were not announced until April 1929. It was revealed that in answer to the question "Do you welcome the advent of Talking Pictures?", men were divided fifty-fifty while seventy per cent of women said no with only thirty per cent in favour. Over seventy per cent of those responding welcomed variety turns as part of the show and sixty-two per cent favoured happy endings. Betty Blythe was top female favourite for the second time (but tying now with Dolores Del Rio) and Ronald Colman again the top male star. The results were reported in all three evening papers and several of the national dailies as well as the trade press, greatly enhancing the prestige of the Bernstein theatres and, of course, the standing of Sidney Bernstein himself.

Showmanship

A rare "class" attraction of the kind seen in later years at Granada was a Russian ballet company which presented a "miniature" version of a show which had enjoyed "phenomenal success at His Majesty's" in early and mid-evening performances for a week at Leytonstone. Another cultural feast was a version of Pagliacci on stage at one of the Rialtos. In May 1929, the cinemas at West Ham, Leytonstone and Enfield featured short election addresses by local politicians in May 1929, each major party being allocated a different night. Jazz band contests and community singing were featured on special nights at some theatres.

There is at least one example of a Film Society choice subsequently playing a Bernstein Theatre. The German film Waxworks was booked into the Willesden Hippodrome in 1928 as an "exploitation offering" and a publicity handout refers to its having been shown by the Film Society before overcoming censorship problems to become a West End hit. This was probably a special case, the Hippodrome being such a poor performer that anything was worth a try.

Shows for children

Sidney Bernstein used his Film Society connections to launch regular shows for children. Terry Staples, in his book All Pals Together, refers to this as "the first British attempt at turning matinees into a social service rather than a money-making enterprise."

In a letter to the Kinematograph Weekly (17 May 1945), Sidney's younger brother, Cecil G. Bernstein, recalled that Granada "pioneered on a big scale" Saturday morning matinees in 1928:

"On March 16 of that year we launched our scheme at a luncheon at the Savoy Hotel, and, as then reported in the Kine Weekly, those present included Sir John Foster Fraser, Arnold Bennett, Miss Lena Ashwell, Sir Benjamin Goot, secretary of the

TO PARENTS AND TEACHERS

WE know that you do not really like the idea of your children going to see all the "grown-up" pictures so we have decided to give

Special Programmes for Children

starting on Saturday morning, March 31st, at 10.30

These performances will be in your own district—no heavy fares. You can rest assured that we shall show your children pictures that will really teach them something as well as entertain them—clean and healthy pictures that will do them nothing but good. Please encourage the children to come and make our experiment a permanent success.

PRIZES WILL BE GIVEN one for girls, one for boys—for the best letter I receive. What do you most want, a cricket bat, a paint box, a book of adventure? This is what I shall ask the lucky winners.

SPECIAL PICTURES FOR CHILDREN

Our programmes will include:—

Peter Pan, the story all children love

Nelson, showing the life of the great sailor from his boyhood

Excerpts from one of the Tours of The Prince of Wales

Betty's Day at the Zoo

Feeding Time at the Zoo

and many of the wonderful "Secrets of Nature" series. All programmes will have some comedy—a Felix, an Æsop Fable or one or two of the "Our Gang" series.

I shall be happy to receive any suggestions which will help us to make this scheme a success.

Miss J. M. HARVEY, Children's Film Section, Bernstein Theatres, 197 Wardour St., London, W.1. Telephone: Regent 0251.

CHILDREN! REMEMBER SATURDAY MARCH 31

On that morning there will be the first of some special programmes for you at this theatre—not stiff grown-up pictures which don't amuse you, but really jolly ones.

DON'T YOU LOVE THE ZOO?

—Yes, well, you'll see our picture of the animals' feeding-time there. Come and see Peter Pan, the story you all enjoy; then Nelson from the time he was a little boy—and, but there, I must not tell you all our secrets.

After the first four Saturday mornings write and tell me what you like best in the programme; address it to Miss J.M. Harvey, Children's Film Section, Bernstein Theatres, 197 Wardour St., W.1, or leave it at the theatre.

From leaflets promoting children's shows in 1928. (BFI – Sidney Bernstein Collection.)

Middlesex County Council Education Committee, Mr. (now Sir) Gordon Craig, and Miss J. M. Harvey, secretary of the Film Society.

"My brother, Sidney, outlining his scheme at the luncheon, explained how he had invited the Film Society to organise at our theatres special Saturday morning children's programmes consisting of films 'mostly of a travel and historical nature.' He added that he hoped the scheme would spread beyond our theatres and be generally adopted.

"The first of these matinees took place on March 24, 1928, at the Empire (now Granada), Willesden. The scheme met with immediate success, and in consequence we extended it throughout the circuit until at the beginning of the war we were playing to nearly 50,000 children a week. Long before 1939 we organised the children into the Granadiers Clubs."

In a paper Sidney Bernstein presented to the Conference on Films for Children, held in November 1936, he set out the reasons for arranging children's shows: they were a "nursery for film-goers" (where they should be encouraged to develop their critical faculties in favour of better films), they created goodwill among parents, they drew children away from regular performances where they were disruptive and where they paid half price for seats that might be sold to adults at full price.

He recalled: "In March, 1928, my own organisation made what was, I believe, the first serious experiment of its kind in the country. We do not claim to have been the first in the field but only to have tried to organise for the first time a planned series of children's performances at a number of cinemas.

"Miss J. M. Harvey, who was at that time Secretary of the Film Society and who had many contacts with the educational world, joined my organisation to take charge of the scheme.

"Our advertising was not confined to children. We circularised parents, and school authorities. Miss Harvey booked programmes which included Peter Pan, Cinderella, Nelson, Where The Rainbow Ends, the Rin Tin Tin films, Robinson Crusoe, The Thief Of Bagdad, Charlie Chaplin's film The Circus, The Wonderland Of Big Game, Dinner Time At The Zoo, the Secrets Of Nature series, and the Felix, Bonzo and Out of the Inkpot cartoons.

"The experiment was started at four suburban theatres in Willesden, Enfield, Leytonstone and Edmonton. Prices of admission were 3d. in the stalls and 6d. in the circle, and the programmes started at 10.30 on Saturday morning and finished at 12.30.

"At Willesden, on the first day, we turned away over two hundred children. Those who saw the show appeared to enjoy themselves.

"And yet attendance figures diminished from week to week. At the beginning of the summer, because of the holidays we had to suspend the scheme. We were not despondent however: Miss Harvey did not give up hope. She renewed her contacts with the Education Authorities, paying them almost weekly visits; she again approached the Press and succeeded in getting more valuable publicity. She again tackled the parents; and thanks to her efforts we resumed the shows in October, 1928, and continued them through the winter and spring of 1929. Still the matinees did not prove a success, and in the summer of 1929 we had to abandon the scheme.

"Now why was the scheme a failure as a whole?

"First, perhaps we aimed a little high in the programmes we chose: perhaps we were too anxious to do the children good.

"Another reason was that the local regulations regarding the admission of children to adult performances were not so rigorously applied as to-day. Why should children turn out to an early show on Saturday morning when they could see the ordinary adults' show – longer certainly and maybe better – in the afternoon, for the same money?

"The third reason for our failure was the most important. With the exception of Willesden, co-operation from outside was lacking. In Willesden, indeed, the education authorities were extremely helpful. Dr. Bridges, chairman of the Education Committee, appeared regularly at the matinees. His teachers gave their whole-hearted co-operation, and even the distribution of handbills in the schools was permitted.

"Indeed, in 1930, the Willesden Education Authority approached us and asked us to recommence our matinees. We did so, and for a time – but only for a time – with the schools co-operating even to the extent of selling tickets in the classrooms, we met with success."

Miss Harvey's position was head of the Children's Film Section at Bernstein Theatres. For that first well-publicised show, the large Empire Willesden was packed to capacity. Children were treated to Gaumont's recent production of *Robinson Crusoe* supported by the Topical Budget newsreel and two "interest" shorts. The second week brought a revival of the Betty Bronson *Peter Pan*. Soon after that children's shows were launched at Edmonton, Enfield and Leytonstone.

In his book, Terry Staples commented: "The Granada scheme differed in four ways from what was going on all around. First, the performances were not run for profit: a letter from Harvey to a local paper proclaimed, 'our books are open for inspection'. Second, they took place on Saturday mornings, not afternoons, even though this involved the expense of employing staff at a time when they would otherwise be off duty. Third, seeking public support, Bernstein launched the scheme at a special Savoy luncheon attended by influential journalists. He invited parents, schools and local authorities to co-operate – and some

did. For the audience, it was the fourth change that was the most important: the films were not derived from the cinemas' ordinary show. Instead, they were specially selected as offering 'clean, healthy entertainment'. This included an attempt to represent British culture where possible, rather than settle for the easy option of one hundred per cent Hollywood.

"For sixpence in the circle, or threepence in the stalls, Harvey's normal Granada matinees – all silent – consisted of a cartoon, a short and a feature. Foremost among the cartoons were two American series, Koko the Clown and Felix; but there was also a British series about Bonzo, a chubby, mischievous puppy. The shorts were largely animal documentaries, such as *The Wonderland Of Big Game* and *Dinner Time At The Zoo*. A British series, *The Secrets Of Nature*, focussed on smaller creatures such as bees, moths, magpies and those found within *An Aquarium In A Wine Glass*. Harvey's real challenge was to find features that would meet her proclaimed criteria, and she ranged over the past decade in her quest."

The Bernstein Theatres gave children sensational value for money: they were able, in fact, to see new releases as well as big hits of the past, including *The Circus*, *Oh You Tony*, *Where the Rainbow Ends* and *A Kiss For Cinderella*, although they might have found *King Of Kings* heavy-going. Saturday morning shows of the week's regular attraction (where appropriate) usefully reduced children's attendance at other performances.

Children's shows had been commonplace for years and the Bernstein Theatres had arranged earlier screenings on an occasional or irregular basis. They had never succeeded on a regular basis. When the Bernstein shows stopped during the summer of 1928, the stated reason was the undesirability of providing counter attractions to children's more healthy outdoor pursuits but it was probably in anticipation of a seasonal decline in attendances. A new season of children's shows started at the end of September. Terry Staples is inclined to blame the programming for their cessation in the summer of 1929. Perhaps Bernstein had, as he himself suggested, aimed too high and made the shows too educational?

The Denman deal

In March 1928, the Bernstein circuit was sold to a newly formed company called Denman (London) Cinemas. This was an extension of the Gaumont-British Picture Corporation empire.

Denman (London) Cinemas took a controlling interest (fifty-one per cent) in the principal Bernstein theatres, leaving the Bernstein family with the rest of the shares (forty-nine per cent). The deal was very attractive to Sidney Bernstein because he remained in charge as managing director with an annual salary of £5,000. Other directors were E. G. (Ernest George) Bygrave, the Bernstein company auditor and accountant, and, representing Gaumont, A. C. Bromhead (Chairman) and R. C. Bromhead. The money that Bernstein received from Gaumont for the shares (reported to have been £250,000) provided the basis for starting a new chain. Another factor in the sale was the benefit to his small group of being part of such a large and powerful new combine as GBPC, which also took over much of the administrative burden, including engaging variety acts and (for a while) film bookings.

The Bernstein cinemas taken over by Denman (London), all in North and East London, were primarily the East Ham Empire, Edmonton Empire, Enfield Rialto, Leytonstone Rialto, Plumstead Empire, West Ham Kinema and Willesden Empire. Bernstein's loss-making Willesden Hippodrome at Harlesden was also grouped with the Denman properties but went back to being a live theatre in January 1929 and was then taken over by the ABC circuit the following year. The Lewisham Hippodrome was included but remained a music hall until 1931 when it was modernised and very briefly operated as a Denman (London) cinema. The Electrodrome Bow seems also to have been part of the deal, although not publicly listed at the time. The Shrewsbury Empire was excluded and continued to be booked by Bernstein.*

The Denman (London) cinemas were never directly operated by Gaumont and would be fully re-acquired by the Bernsteins through Granada in 1965. The group was never expanded and all of Bernstein's subsequent new theatres – except for the building of a replacement cinema at East Ham and the Edmonton reconstruction – had no Gaumont involvement.

After the link-up with Gaumont, improvements to the theatres continued and in 1928 it was the turn of the East Ham and Plumstead Empires to be upgraded and their old-fashioned name replaced by Kinema. However, even into the Fifties, all expenditure on the fabric of the Denman properties above a very low limit had to be approved by Gaumont (later Rank).

At East Ham, new tip-up seats were installed and a new orchestra performed "non-stop" from 2pm to 11pm (Sundays from 5.30pm), with three variety acts in every show. "Everything big but the price" was the slogan at East Ham. The following year, in July, a £5,000 Christie pipe organ was inaugurated by Mabel Poulton. At Plumstead, the old bench seating

was replaced by 913 individual seats and the orchestra was enlarged. Around this time, variety was added to the film double-bills at Enfield and Willesden.

A new beginning

In March 1928, the same month as the Denman (London) deal took effect, Sidney Bernstein set about building a new circuit of his own. He opened negotiations for the Taylor's Depository site at 1 St. George's Street, Newington Butts, at the Elephant and Castle, South London. Discussions extended from March 1928 to April 1929. By this time, it seemed clear that Hyams and Gale would be first with a giant cinema in the area (the Trocadero in New Kent Road) and the idea was dropped.

In September 1928, Cecil Masey inspected a possible cinema site in Dover, Kent, where the population of 39,985 was inadequately served by the existing, locally run cinemas. The earliest surviving correspondence in the Bernstein papers over the site of the Granada Tooting dates from the following month.

For several months in late 1928 and early 1929, Bernstein Theatres booked films for the Pavilion at Dorking, Surrey, owned by H. Aron. This was a run-down hall and Bernstein declined a request to take over the management while Gaumont rejected a separate invitation to buy it.

In December 1928, the Bernsteins took over the Victoria cinema in Hoe Street, Walthamstow, North London, from R. Specterman and began laying plans for a super cinema on the site and adjoining property.

All Talking

By this time sound was coming in. Some kind of inferior talkie device was tried out at Walthamstow in February 1929 and at Plumstead in May. The first Bernstein theatre to introduce a major new sound system was the Rialto Leytonstone on 8 July 1929, using Western Electric apparatus to present Lola Lane in *Speakeasy* – "Hear New York City Talk!" "Perfect Talkies" came to the Willesden Empire two weeks later with the Al Jolson smash hit, *The Singing Fool*. Then it was turn of the Edmonton Empire on 12 August, followed by Shrewsbury in early September (with *Fox Movietone Follies Of 1929* and Movietone News) and by a more successful installation at the Victoria Walthamstow on 30 September. It was a cruel business: the entire orchestra was dismissed at Edmonton and Enfield, although at Shrewsbury the musicians were transferred to the café. A prominent sign on Enfield Bridge that once read "Pictures and Variety" now proclaimed "Talkies".

The lesser theatres had to wait and make the best of it. "Talkies? – No! But Always a Tip-Top Program", shouted a flyer for Plumstead after it had abandoned its earlier experiment with

* The Electric Bournemouth was still owned by Capital and Counties Electric Theatres and Sidney was a director of the company. But there appears to have been no close participation in booking or managing the theatre at any time. It seems to have been a problem and was unsuccessfully leased out in the late Twenties. In this period it was linked to a J. Bravery who ran cinemas in Poole. Sidney Bernstein was still a director in 1953 and regularly consulted, although he rarely attended board meetings.

THE FIRST BRITISH TALKIE "has the best of American Talkies beaten to a frazzle!" *Daily News*

Directed by ALFRED HITCHCOCK A NATIVE OF LEYTONSTONE possessing an uncanny instinct, first, f... the mind of the public and, second, for the ideal means of conveying his ideas. PRODUCED AT ELSTREE

Blackmail

DEMONSTRATES *the* BEAUTY *of* OUR ENGLISH TONGUE

PLAYED BY DONALD CALTHROP & ANNY ONDRA this Talkie version of Charles Bennett's great stage play packed The Capitol Theatre in London for weeks.

Also GEORGE LEMAIRE *of "The Dentist" fame—in his latest* TALKING COMEDY "The New Chauffeur"

BRITISH MOVIETONE NEWS is an entertainment in itself—always!

MONDAY NOVEMBER 25 FOR SIX DAYS

Rialto LEYTONSTONE

Left: leaflet promoting the talkies the Rialto Leytonstone in July 1929. Above: same cinema's handbill for a talkie directed by "a native of Leytonstone". Below: July 1929 newspaper advertisement for Enfield. The Rialto Talkies emblem bears a striking resemblance to the Radio Pictures trademark. (BFI – Sidney Bernstein Collection.)

RIALTO ENFIELD

Hear AL JOLSON—in The Singing Fool

Monday July 29

Open at 1.30 p.m.

TIMES OF SHOWING: 2.0 4.30 7.15 9.30: ONE WEEK ONLY

THE NEW ART

Rialto TALKIES

FOR THE NEW AGE

PICTURES WITH A VOICE

THESE CHANGING TIMES!

One of the greatest changes in our time has happened in the entertainment world.

The stage has actually moved to the screen to-day.

The great artistes of the Stage of yesterday have become the great artistes of the Screen to-day.

The addition of voice to the screen has conquered all its previous limitations and made it the greatest medium of expression the entertainment world has ever possessed

Hitherto these great artistes were excluded from the popular-priced suburban theatres because of the enormous salaries their talents command. The Talkies have altered this. Now, there is no great artiste whom the Rialto cannot afford to present

We have always endeavoured to provide the kind of entertainment we believed you most desired. The development of the sound picture has afforded us yet another opportunity to serve you, not only as we believe you wish, but in a far greater measure of variety and quality.

See and hear for yourself at Rialto, July 8th

[signature]

THE MIRACLE OF OUR TIME

Lend me your ears

Six months back a wave of "talkie" enthusiasm swept the country—everybody "talkied," some experimented—whilst Leytonstone picture-goers wondered and waited!

What did the Rialto do? Regardless of cost we investigated and experimented and have now attained Talkie perfection.

Therefore we break the silence to make our greatest offering yet to the cause of worth-while entertainment—Rialto Talkies, the golden voice of the silver screen.

On July 8th our priceless equipment made by the famous Western Electric Company will be ready. We promise you shall hear everything from every seat. In no other theatre in the world can you see and hear better.

Six months of intensive development has equalled six years of silent screen progress. The year-old Talkie—even the three-months-old talkie equipment—is now obsolete.

The cost has been great, the delay tantalizing, but we have the satisfaction that we have not taken your money without delivering the goods, have not let you share the cost and disappointment of experiment, have not broken faith with our generous Rialto public.

Now we bring to this theatre all those infinite creations of drama and music—the greatest of American, Continental and British productions—the world's greatest opera singers, musicians, tragedians, comedians—in fact there is no limit. The miracle of our time has happened. Perfect Talkies are here

Our equipment is really different. You may expect everything in perfect sound and picture presentation.

BERNSTEIN THEATRES PROMISE— YOU WILL NOT BE DISAPPOINTED

sound. (The American spelling of programme became a company rule from 1929.) "Hear a 100% Human Orchestra – Hear the £5,000 Wonder Organ", riposted the East Ham Kinema in answer to the recorded musical soundtracks playing elsewhere.

Denman takings

From surviving records of the Denman group in September 1930, the theatres rank in this order for the month's box-office takings (profit not indicated), with their previous positions in March 1930 and then September 1929 indicated in brackets:

1 Leytonstone Rialto (2, 1)
2 Willesden Empire (1, 2)
3 Edmonton Empire (3, 3)
4 Enfield Rialto (4, 4)
5 Plumstead Kinema (6, 7)
6 West Ham (Stratford) Kinema (5, 5)
7 East Ham Kinema (7, 6)

The Rialto Leytonstone took twice as much as the worst performing theatre. Both the West Ham and East Ham cinemas were still restricted to silent films in the spring of 1930 and offered seven variety acts. A single act spruced up the programme at Leytonstone and Enfield.

The West Ham Lane (Stratford) Empire as it looked, rebuilt and renamed the Kinema in the late Twenties. Compare with view on page 16.

2 • Start Saying Granada: Dover And Walthamstow

In January 1929, Cecil Masey reported favourably on the site at Dover. Contracts were exchanged and County Theatre Dover Limited was registered the following month to build the theatre. Work on the first new Bernstein theatre started in the summer.

Negotiations continued to obtain the largest possible sites in Walthamstow and Tooting for further new cinemas.

In August 1929, Sidney Bernstein was on the lookout for a site in central London on which to build his private dream of a concert hall.

In March 1930, Masey visited a possible cinema site in Southampton at Sidney Bernstein's request but declared it unsuitable. At the same time, Masey also came up with potential sites on his own which he brought to the attention of Bernstein and two rival concerns. Among others, sites that Masey suggested at Eltham, Southeast London, and at Colchester, Essex, were rejected by Bernstein in March 1930 (Masey designed the Regal on the site in Colchester for another client).

A further scheme that interested Bernstein was for a 4,000-seat cinema in Loampit Vale, Lewisham. Empire Kinema Lewisham Ltd. was formed and Sir Alfred Butt subscribed to the scheme. He later withdrew and Bernstein went into an equal partnership with Gaumont-British. In March 1930, Bernstein pressed Gaumont's C. M. Woolf for progress on the scheme. Seemingly dissatisfied with the response, he sold the Bernstein half-interest to a Gaumont subsidiary, Denman Construction, the following month.

Dover

The cinema was originally to be known as the County Theatre and Tea Room. The team was again Cecil Masey as architect and Theodore Komisarjevky as interior designer. For the first time the Russian was to have the chance to decorate an entire auditorium from scratch.*

* He was not the only theatre scenery designer to be let loose on cinema auditoria: the architect-promoter Edward A. Stone had cleverly decided that the French team of Marc Henri and Gaston Laverdet, who designed the sets for Cochran revues among others, had the right background to provide an "atmospheric" interior, just like a giant stage set, for the Astoria Brixton. This opened in August 1929 with an Italian garden theme. In 1930 the team worked for Stone on the Astorias at Streatham and Finsbury Park.

Sidney Bernstein may well have instructed Komisarjevsky to come up with a Moorish scheme for Dover. In a company booklet *This Is Granada* (undated, post 1974), Bernstein is quoted as once having told a reporter: "Every Easter and practically every summer I used to walk somewhere in Europe with a rucksack on my back, staying where I could, usually in small hotels. One Easter in the 1920s I took a ship to Gibraltar with the intention of travelling overland to Barcelona and then from there taking another ship to Majorca. This I did. En route from Gibraltar I arrived very late at night at the city of Granada. (I saw little of the place until morning – the morning incidentally after the night of the first snowfall that Granada had had for years.) The snow melted early in the day and I then discovered the city. It was wonderful. The Alhambra (the magnificent palace started by King Alhamar in 1238) was a rare, dazzling building in a wonderful setting. I was very impressed and the memory lingered on. I had fallen in love with it. At that time I was searching for a new name for our Theatres and I did not want cold initials or the usual names and decided that the word 'Granada' had all the theatrical and exotic feeling I wanted in a name. It represented the gaiety of Spain. So Granada it was."

Certainly the name fitted Komisarjevsky's design. In an article entitled "Decorative Problems" in *The Ideal Kinema* (13 February 1930), he explained: "... the masses who frequent cinemas usually come to the theatre tired out after hard work, probably in not too cheerful surroundings. The homes of many of these people are not very bright ... The picture theatre supplies these folks with the flavour of romance for which they crave. The richly decorated theatre, the comfort with which they are surrounded, and the efficiency of the service contribute to an atmosphere and a sense of well-being of which the majority have hitherto only imagined.

"In this auditorium I have endeavoured to give an impression of the Moorish style with[out] slavishly copying the original Alhambra Palace in Granada, as is so often done where Moorish treatment is concerned.

"I could have imagined the auditorium at Dover decorated by the Moors, but a modern artist must remember that one is living

From the publicity campaign for the opening at Dover. (BFI – Sidney Bernstein Collection.)

in 1930, and that one's immediate public lives in 1930 too! Working in this way on my decorative scheme for the 'Granada' auditorium I succeeded (my apologies for being immodest!) in producing an effect of architectural harmony of richness, and at the same time of restfulness. If I had, for instance, attempted to imitate the actual Moorish palaces and to enrich the walls with the genuine details of the Alhambra made in the genuine materials and used the actual colours of that building, I would never have been able to see my scheme realised.

"In the first place, because it would have been much too expensive, and then with the modern proportions of the building and other modern requirements, and without the Spanish sunshine and environment (at Dover!) it would not have looked at all Moorish, and would certainly not have justified the trouble and the expense incurred. The result would have merely seemed massy, ugly, and out of place, possibly similar to the incongruous 'Moorish' interior of the Pier Casino at Nice, or to the interiors of the various theatres and restaurants all over the world bearing the name of 'Alhambra'."

Komisarjevksy does not mention the highly elaborate and effective work being done in Spanish, Moorish and other styles in American atmospheric movie theatres.

Clearly, Sidney Bernstein's original name for the cinema, the County Theatre and Tea Room, was inappropriate. To judge by Komisarjevksy's remarks, the name "Alhambra" would have been too commonplace. There were already in England many Alhambra Theatres including the one in Leicester Square (later replaced by the Odeon) while an Alhambra cinema which depicted the Alhambra in Spain in panels on the side walls opened in Moseley Road, Birmingham, early in 1929. But there was not a "Granada".

And so the Granada name was chosen. Demonstrating already that flair for publicity which would become so characteristic, the Bernstein team plastered Dover with cryptic posters on hoardings and trams and press announcements reading: "Start saying Granada" "All roads lead to Granada" "Soon! Granada in Dover" and "Everybody will go to Granada." Then all became clear and the townspeople flocked to see their new cinema.

Although Bernstein may have hit upon the Granada name by recalling a walking holiday in Southern Spain, the fact is that, like Alhambra, Granada had been widely adopted as a name for cinema buildings in North America and was only new in Britain. (The huge Granada on Market Street in the centre of San Francisco had opened as far back as November 1921 with 2,734 seats. The Granada in Santa Barbara, California, dates from 1924, had a full Spanish decor, and is still open under its original name with curtains depicting a view of the town Granada from the hills. The 1926 Granada on Chicago's north side was a 3,400

The Granada Dover. Above, in 1946 as an ABC house (from author's collection). Below: the main foyer in 1930, looking back from the head of the stairs to the doors from the outer foyer.

seater with an Italian baroque treatment. In January 1929, a Spanish-style "atmospheric" Granada Theatre opened at Sherbrooke, Quebec, Canada, and retains the name as a multi-purpose hall to this day. There are many, many more examples.)

The debut of the Granada Dover, England, was delayed by problems dealing with a stream running across the site. This added six weeks to the construction schedule and it was a rush to open the cinema on time. One of those working on the building was W. T. Moore, who recalled (in a book of local history, *Picture Palaces Remembered*): "The opening was fixed for the afternoon of Wednesday 8 January 1930, and as I was over-seeing the marble work, I went in on the Monday, not emerging until the Wednesday, apart from a bite to eat. Sidney Bernstein and his wife were there, working for hours painting railings, assisted by Theodore Komisarjevksy, the designer. Through all that time, the stage acts and a troupe of dancing girls, together with Hedley Morton at the organ, and Leonardi's huge stage band of twenty musicians, were rehearsing. On the Wednesday afternoon the workmen left by the back door as the invited audience came in by the front door, with much of the paint still wet." The wet paint was a common feature of cinema openings, but it is interesting to hear of Sidney Bernstein's hands-on participation in the decoration.

Externally, the Granada was tastefully designed with a huge round-headed window above the entrance and a name sign mounted horizontally on the stonework higher up. The paybox was sited in the inner corner of the vestibule with doors leading off to the right into the spectacular double-height main foyer in neo-classical style, dominated by a crystal-glass chandelier. A stone staircase at the far side, flanked by two giant fluted columns with Corinthian capitals, led upstairs. To the left of these columns on the ground floor was a cloakroom and, to the right, a concessions counter.

Set in the middle of the side wall on the left were double doors to the stalls. At the top of the staircase was a large, round-headed mirror which reflected the chandelier. A wide gallery or promenade ran all around the foyer, the balustrades draped with tasselled Spanish shawls. The floor here was carpeted, unlike downstairs. The promenade on one side served as a balcony foyer with entrances at each end. Etchings and photographs of the Alhambra in Spain were placed on the walls.

This distinctive foyer plan became the model for later Granadas. Normally, the promenade led to a café-restaurant over the outer foyer but the tea room proposed for Dover was dropped.

Seating 1,717, the auditorium resembled an enclosed courtyard. had long, straight side walls with flat Moorish arches that had vistas of continuous countryside painted behind them.

There was a 35 ft. wide rectangular proscenium arch with a stepped edge. Grilles set within Moorish arches appeared on each side above exits, positioned diagonally across the corners of the auditorium. The righthand grilles covered the chambers of the Christie organ.

The auditorium was illuminated by suspended light fittings. Window-like openings, covered with decorative grillework, appeared on the lower side walls above the dado and were lit up (the only available visual records of the interior as it originally looked are of very poor quality, in contemporary magazines and publicity material). The balcony front and rows of seating were arranged in parallel, undulating lines – a device first seen at the Willesden reconstruction that was becoming a regular feature of architect Cecil Masey's work.

Although the Granada lacked a fly tower, there was a 15 ft. deep stage with lighting switchboard and dressing rooms on three levels for variety acts.

The frantic rush to open the cinema inspired an offbeat handling of the first night. *The Bioscope* (15 January 1930) reported: "For the opening ceremony... a film trade party travelled from London by a special 'Granada' Pullman... Punctually at the advertised hour, Knightsmith, the celebrated London toast-master, appeared on the stage before a packed house and announced, following a blast of trumpets, that he would introduce some of the leading people responsible for the erection of the theatre. Then the curtains parted to disclose the Architect, Cecil Masey, FRIBA; the Decorator, Theodore Komisarjevsky; the Clerk of the Works, E. H. Swann; the Musical Conductor, Leonardi; and others feverishly engaged with vast quill pens at a couple of bare tables on final details of the plans. Above them loomed a large blackboard, threateningly inscribed, 'The Granada must be opened by January 8th.' This amusing introduction not only succeeded in giving an entertaining twist to what is often a laboured ceremony, but also underlined the fact that the theatre had been completed, despite unusual constructional difficulties, in the remarkably short time of six and a half months." This tableau would become a feature of most of the later Granada openings, which would usually take place on a Wednesday.

The cinema opened with *The Last of Mrs. Cheyney*, which was followed from the next Monday by the smash hit *Bulldog Drummond*. Leonardi and His Band performed every day along with Morton at the organ. There was a 45-minute stage show in each programme including "West End Varieties" (i.e. performers of West End standing) and the Eight Granada Girls. The slogan on the opening programme was "A King Can Have No More". Max Miller appeared live on two separate weeks. You could "Phone Dover Six and Book Your Seat". While many

The Granada Dover. Part of the first floor promenade overlooking the main foyer and a poor view of the auditorium at opening (both taken from the trade press).

cinemas were playing off contracted backlogs of silent features as supporting features, the Granada boasted that only talkies would be shown, even on the one-day Sunday revivals.

There was a snag when the town's Sunday licences were not renewed in early October 1930. The Granada and all the other cinemas put on their lights and had staff on duty to tell patrons that they were closed on the instructions of their own council.

New films usually ran from Monday for six days with occasional split weeks. A contest for juvenile performers was held in December 1930.

The Granada seems to have been a success: a figure of 982,750 admissions in its first year was claimed. But prices were reduced from 12 January 1931. One shilling-and-threepence seats became one shilling; one shilling-and-sixpence seats were now one-and-three; and the two shillings-and-fourpence seats were substantially reduced, to one-and-six. (Matinee prices were sixpence, eightpence and one shilling.) Granada presented this as its "birthday gift" to the people of Dover, but the reason for reducing prices has always been a need to increase business. At the same time economies were made and patrons were getting less for their money: the expensive live shows were dropped, Leonardi and His Band moved to London, and only Ronald the Wonder Organist remained to support the films.

Confirmation of difficulties comes from Sidney Bernstein's willingness to let the theatre go. He entered into negotiations with an independent exhibitor, Nathan N. Lee, who formed a new company, Granada (Dover) Limited, to take it over on a long lease just three months later, from 12 April 1931, retaining the Granada name – Sidney Bernstein must have often regretted not insisting on a change of name. Nat Lee and his partners – A. Rosenberg, A. Curzon and S. A. Barry – soon installed their own manager, Sydney Sale.

Lee went into partnership with a man called Mistlin and they built and opened a large, new cinema at Hove, East Sussex, in July 1933. Quite naturally, it was named the Granada after the Dover cinema.

In June 1933, Sidney Bernstein received a letter from John Maxwell, head of the Associated British Cinemas circuit, asking if ABC could lease the Granada Dover. ABC already ran the smaller Plaza in the town. Bernstein wrote that he would only consider an outright sale of the property, and Maxwell responded the same day, asking for particulars. The company secretary, E. G. Bygrave, estimated that any sum over £57,840 would represent a profit for the shareholders of County Theatre Dover Limited, including £4,000 compensation to Nat Lee and his associates for terminating Granada (Dover) Limited's lease. The asking price was set at £65,000.

There is no evidence that Maxwell bought the Granada Dover

at this time. He seems to have waited and taken over Nat Lee and partners' interest in both the Granadas at Dover and Hove from the middle of 1935. When ABC bought the freehold of the Dover property is unclear, but the Granada Dover remained with ABC and never returned to the Bernstein fold. Both the Dover and Hove theatres retained the Granada name until the 1960s when they were renamed ABCs.

Sidney Bernstein later became well known for regarding the Granada name as his own private property, yet he was unable to stop other cinemas calling themselves Granadas. The large Granada at Dovecot, Liverpool, was built by a local company, The Granada Cinema (Liverpool) Limited, headed by builder C. J. Doyle and M. Wilkinson. Designed by A. Ernest Shennan and opened in December 1932, it was essentially modern in design. This was taken over by the ABC circuit in the middle of 1935, a week before the Dover and Hove cinemas, and retained the Granada name throughout its days as a cinema and for a few years as a bingo hall in the 1960s. Others seized on the name as ideal for enhancing their cinemas. The humble Granada at St. George's, a suburb of Bristol, was the result of a 1935 renaming of the St. George's Hall Cinema. Also in 1935 came the more impressive Granada at Parkhead, Glasgow, opened by prominent Scottish exhibitors Bernard and Alex Frutin. This 2,206 seater was a lively exercise in modern design that did at least incorporate some Spanish murals on the sides of the auditorium to justify the name. In his book, *100 Years of Glasgow's Amazing Cinemas*, Bruce Peter claims: "Shortly after it opened, the Granada was plunged into controversy when Sidney Bernstein, who owned a chain of lavish Granada cinemas in London suburbs, objected to the Frutins using what he regarded as his trade name. His attempt to get a court order against them was rejected; Bernstein's nearest cinema was three hundred miles away in Bedford!" The Parkhead cinema continued in business under the Granada name until 1971.*

Walthamstow

At Walthamstow in Northeast London, Theodore Komisarjevksy had the space to deliver a really spectacular and impressive cinema interior which made this the first major Granada. Cecil Masey was again the architect.

The cinema replaced the Victoria which had been built at right angles along Hoe Street, providing a site with a wide frontage. The

* Bernstein's most notable attempt to lay exclusive claim to the Granada name came when he sought to stop Ford using it on a range of cars. However, there is one instance in 1973 when Bryanston School was given permission to call its private cinema by the Granada name.

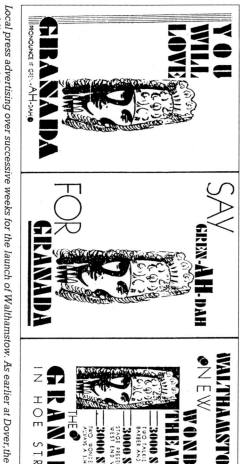

YOU WILL LOVE GRANADA
PRONOUNCE IT GREN-AH-DAH●

SAY GREN-AH-DAH **FOR GRANADA**

WALTHAMSTOW'S NEW WONDER THEATRE
THE ● GRANADA IN HOE STREET

3000 SEATS
TWO TALKIE FEATURES
BARBER AND HIS BAND

3000 SEATS
STAGE PRESENTATIONS
WEST END VARIETIES

3000 SEATS
TWO WONDER ORGANS
ALWAYS A 3-HOUR SHOW

GRANADA
WALTHAMSTOW
Monday, Sept. 22nd
FOR 6 DAYS

3,000 SEATS

TWO ORGANS

StageShow
BARBER & HIS BAND

Atlantic
JOHN STUART
JOAN BARRY
MONTY BANKS
FRANCIS LISTER
MADELINE CARROLL
DONALD CALTHROP
FRANKLYN DYALL
JOHN LONGDEN

Local press advertising over successive weeks for the launch of Walthamstow. As earlier at Dover, the public were advised to pronounce the name of the cinema "Gren-AH-dah" rather than "Gran-narr-dah".
Below: this view (24 July 1959) of the Granada Walthamstow shows the imposing frontage and the full height of the façade above the canopy (the apex was removed in 1960). (Photo Coverage.)

The Granada Walthamstow. The outer foyer, seen on 9 February 1966, with ticket windows on each side – the inner set of doors were removed by August 1968. The café-restaurant, seen on 31 March 1954. (Both from Photo Coverage.)

Granada extended much further back than the Victoria, which was completely demolished.*

Externally, the Granada Walthamstow enlivened a drab high street with its white stucco façade and Spanish treatment of the entrance block. This projected slightly forward and rose to a rounded peak in contrast to the pantiled low pitched roofs of the wings. Above the canopy was a tripartite window with spiral columns and a triple arch with cusped Spanish-style window heads. Two tall, narrow windows in matching style appeared on either side.

To the right of the entrance was a passage to the back of the theatre, built over at first floor level. To the left of the entrance was a much wider row of shops with the theatre restaurant placed above. At first floor level, spiral columns between the pairs of roundheaded windows made a link with the central section.**

Theodore Komisarjevsky outlined his approach to designing the interior of the Granada Walthamstow in the opening programme (reprinted in *The Ideal Kinema*, 9 October 1930). In adopting the Moorish style for the auditorium, as at Dover, he again pointed out that it was impossible to follow the methods or use the materials employed by the Moors, besides which the proportions of rooms and their arrangement were quite different to modern requirements. He declared:

"I have not attempted to copy any particular Moorish building when decorating the Granada Theatre, Walthamstow... I have endeavoured to give an impression of old Moorish architecture under modern conditions and surroundings. From my knowledge of the art of the Moors I have evolved in my modern imagination a *new* Alhambra for the auditorium and foyer ceiling, *not* true in detail to that of Granada but which seems to me to give at least an impression of the decorative art of the conquerors of Spain.

"For the large entrance hall I chose decorations in the 17th century Spanish Baroque style inspired by the work of the architects Juan de Toledo, Juan de Herrera and Mora who, under Philip II, built the royal palace of Aranjuez.

* This was not the only replacement cinema scheme in the area: the old Prince's Pavilion closed two months after the Victoria to make way for the new Dominion which opened three months after the Granada – but it was nowhere near as large or as well located, and markedly less popular.

** Cecil Masey came up with a very similar Spanish-American façade for the Regal Colchester, opened in 1931. Masey also used a Spanish-style design for the Regal Beccles, Suffolk, the same year and for the Avenue Northfields, West London, in 1932. In all these cases, Masey apparently designed the impressive interiors himself. Although some may have seen the hand of Komisarjevsky at Northfields, it is unlikely he would have worked without credit and Richard Gray points out to me that the auditorium decoration was "in the round" while Komisarjevsky's schemes were flat like stage sets. Masey's planning at the Avenue copied the Granada-style of low-ceilinged outer hall with ticket windows, leading into an inner foyer reminiscent of Walthamstow in its split level arrangement.

The Granada Walthamstow. Top: the main foyer, seen on 14 January 1966, with two of three round-headed mirrors on the side wall visible behind the Miss Candy counter. Below: rear of foyer with stairs that originally led down to the stalls and here (9 November 1973) lead to mini-cinemas under the balcony.

Top: this space in the main foyer above the stalls entrance was originally occupied by a grand piano (the marble-topped table was stolen in a "made to order" robbery some years back). Below: the passage extending from the back of the main foyer under the balcony has doors at each end and leading into the circle. Both views taken 9 February 1966. (All Photo Coverage.)

The auditorium of the Granada Walthamstow, taken on 24 May 1965. (Photo Coverage.)

"I am fully aware that learned specialists in matters architectural have no doubt claim to find in 'my Alhambra' traces of the palaces at Cordoba or even greater 'inaccuracies' and 'blunders', but I can assure these gentlemen that what they are pointing out I am already only too well aware of."

The Granada's opening had been set for Thursday 11 September when the Harold Lloyd film *Welcome Danger* would have been the first screen attraction. But the first night was postponed to the following Monday, when the film shown was *Splinters*.

The opening ceremony, copied exactly from Dover, again impressed trade reporters – and the local audience as well. At 8pm precisely, Knightsmith, the toastmaster resplendent in a red coat, extended a hearty welcome from the proprietors. Curtains parted to disclose a hive of activity and Masey, Komisarjevky and other key figures paused and looked up for a second as they were introduced before carrying on with their work. "I think the very novelty and form of opening appealed to Walthamstow mightily, judging by the enormous volume of their applause," said one trade observer, adding: "Then we settled down to one of the niftiest little programmes it has been my pleasure to witness. The pep these boys put into the stage show was amazing. It just went with zip! bang! from the moment the show opened, and you would have imagined that the theatre had run for a year instead of it being the opening performance. There wasn't a hitch anywhere – just perfect co-ordination and organisation."

The cinema seated 2,697 – nearly one thousand more than Dover. It had Ross projectors, Western Electric sound, and twin organ consoles.

There were stage facilities but no flytower. Granada promised "Always a three hour show" with two talkies, Barber and his Band (twenty musicians), "West End varieties" plus two organists. Once again it was claimed "A King Can Have No More". From June 1931, Barber and His Band were replaced by Leonardi who also performed at the Rialto Leytonstone each day.

The Granada had no car park of its own, and an arrangement was made with a nearby garage, patrons using vouchers priced sixpence obtained from the doorman.

The entrance hall was enormous. As at Dover, tickets had to be purchased in the outer foyer before patrons could pass through the inner set of doors to the entrance hall. This was in marked contrast to most cinemas of the Thirties where patrons would buy their tickets well inside the main foyer. Although Granada did not copy the American example of the external pay-box, there seems to be an American influence in positioning the ticket window in this and later cinemas so close to the outer doors.

The lofty, marble-floored entrance hall had roundheaded mirrors on the side walls between Ionic fluted pilasters, a central chandelier with glass beads and other similar light fittings elsewhere. Tables and chairs in this reception area were designed by Komisarjevsky. A central staircase straight ahead led down to the stalls. Wide staircases up on each side provided access to the balcony, with a space in the centre, over the stairs to the stalls, for a grand piano to be played to welcome patrons. At the higher level, a barrel-vaulted corridor extended the width of the auditorium to left and right, with more small chandeliers along the centre. At the far ends of this passage, patrons passed through doors and ascended a few steps to enter the balcony from the sides.

At Dover the balcony steps had been within the auditorium. At Walthamstow, the steps were in a passage outside the auditorium. Patrons entered through facing doorways surmounted by decoration in the form of a Moorish arch. Unusually, the gangway did not extend all the way across, the centre section being filled with a row of seats. The seats in the balcony followed wavy steppings as at Dover.

The side walls forward of the balcony carried richly detailed arches and grillework in Moorish style, while the proscenium arch was elaborately ordered. The side walls of the back circle were painted to resemble stone blocks with a decorative cornice and modillions.

The area of flat ceiling closest to the proscenium arch was decorated by a bold zig-zag pattern with a central light fitting and four others in each corner. These had five bulbs each. The ceiling over the rear balcony was covered in a criss-cross lattice pattern and recessed in three sections, each with a chandelier. These had eight bulbs each. Patrons underneath the balcony were not deprived of their share of splendour as recesses in the soffit enabled substantial chandeliers to be suspended over their heads.

3 • *The Phoenix Theatre*

At the same time as Walthamstow was being constructed, Sidney Bernstein embarked on what seems to have been a private enterprise, investing in the construction of the Phoenix Theatre in Charing Cross Road in the West End of London. According to Bernstein's biographer, Caroline Moorehead, he was approached by Bovis, the company which built the Dover and Walthamstow theatres, to save a scheme for a live theatre which was foundering. Sidney's enthusiasm had not been dulled by his losses at the Royal Court and he took on the project with Victor Luxemburg, calling on Theodore Komisarjevksy to handle the interior design and Cecil Masey to work with his mentor, leading theatre architect Bertie Crewe, on the exterior and shell of the auditorium. The design of the Phoenix Theatre deserves close attention because it was here, in the Italian Renaissance scheme devised by Komisarjevsky, that many of the features found in the later Granada cinemas originated.

Komisarjevsky declared that he chose the High Renaissance period before the transition to the baroque because it was lighter and more ornate than earlier years, and more suited to a place of entertainment. He readily declared that his ideas had come from the work of Raphael, Giulio Romano, Girolamo da Carpi, Giovanni da Udine and others, and that he had directly copied details from the courtyard of the Palazzo Boncompagni, built in 1538 at Bologna, for the coffered ceiling in the larger of the two entrance halls and the columns in the other. The designs for the fittings, carpets and upholstery were also taken from Italian originals. The Florentine velvet seats were in soft rose and gold colours. The furniture in the bars and foyers was also in 16th century Italian style.

The theatre opened to the public on 24 September 1930, barely two weeks after the Granada Walthamstow. It is worth noting that the other new live theatres built in London at this time – the Prince Edward, Cambridge, Whitehall, Saville – were aggressively modern in design, but Bernstein preferred a traditional look.

The largest entrance was located down a side street, Phoenix Street (from which the theatre took its name) but there was an 18ft.-wide curved corner frontage on Charing Cross Road at the opposite side of the building which had to make an impact to

advertise the theatre. Bertie Crewe designed a towering campanile with a beacon on top, but this was considered too brash by the authorities. Bernstein persuaded the eminent architect Giles Gilbert Scott, best known for Liverpool's Anglican Cathedral, to tackle the problem. The result was a tall, dignified frontage with a recess occupied by four slender columns with Corinthian capitals supporting an entablature, with the name sign above and a small balcony higher up. A projecting roof was covered in Italian pantiles. Bernstein liked this scheme so much that it formed the basis for several later Granada entrances. (The adjoining frontage of flats and shops on Charing Cross Road was rebuilt in 1933-4 in a streamlined style, rising above the theatre entrance and somewhat reducing its impact.)

Two entrance doors provided access to a small rotunda with a paybox on one wall. Here Komisarjevsky introduced a series of columns around the edge with a fleur-de-lys design in red and gilt and Corinthian capitals. A frieze carried an inscription in Latin in which the team behind the theatre identified themselves for posterity: HOC THEATRVM AUSPICE LVXEMBVRG BERNSTEIN – Æ DIFICATVM AB SCOTT CREWE ET MASEY – ORNAMENTVM EST AN ARTIFACE KOMISARJEVSKY. (Just in case of accident, the motto is said to have been displayed elsewhere in the building.)

The Phoenix Street entrance, in white glazed tiles, was much wider and livelier, with three arched windows, spiral columns between, double pilasters to each side, and a frieze across the top beneath a projecting roof. A small entrance hall was placed between two sets of heavy, glass-panelled wooden doors. This had box-office windows in the side walls with richly decorated pilasters and a coffered ceiling lit up from the rim. It was much more elaborate than the outer foyer at Walthamstow but conceived on similar lines. Beyond this lay a rather cramped rectangular foyer spectacularly dominated by a large expanse of coffered ceiling, again strongly illuminated by concealed lighting from the rim. Here, around the coffered area and over the stairs leading to the dress circle, were to be found chandeliers very close in design to those that would appear in the the "standard" Granadas. The walls above the stairs had round-headed mirrors that would also be a feature of Granada foyers,

The Phoenix Theatre, Charing Cross Road entrance, circa November 1982. Auditorium, circa August 1982. (Both adapted from colour transparencies by Allen Eyles.)

as they had been at Walthamstow. Further stairs led down to the stalls, with ashtrays mounted on the walls here and elsewhere in the same style as those in later cinemas.

The auditorium was tall and narrow, seating only 1,028; but in several respects it set the pattern for the later standard Granadas after Tooting. The basic treatment of the proscenium arch and front side walls with sets of three round-headed arches and a running frieze was adapted for the cinemas. Here the arches contained the boxes and were draped with red velvet (the main colours of the auditorium were gold and magenta); in the cinemas they were filled with decorative grillework. The shallow circular dome in the ceiling over the front stalls was repeated in Granadas, but usually flattened out. The main chandelier, hung from the centre of the dome, was almost identical to those seen later on. The side walls of the dress circle and balcony were plain, concentrating attention forwards – a principle of the cinemas.

The Phoenix site was far narrower and the auditorium much taller than in the case of any of the later cinemas. The provision of a gallery level at the Phoenix meant that there was more wall space to decorate higher up and copies of famous Venetian paintings were placed above the proscenium arch and boxes. This idea was adapted in later Granadas to a narrow frieze of small figures. The reproductions at the Phoenix were of work by Tintoretto (three panels), Titian (two), Giorgione, Pinturicchio and Filippo Corbizzin (one apiece), while a huge reproduction of Jacobo del Sellaio's "The Triumph of Love" appeared on the safety curtain (all these were painted from black-and-white photographs by Vladimir Polunin, a well-known Russian emigré like Komisarjevsky, an artist who taught decorative design at the Slade and who had previously worked with Diaghilev's Russian Ballet). It was extremely rare for the safety curtain to be painted as an extension of the decorative scheme.

Other features were not repeated in the cinemas, notably the ceiling of radiating mirrors at one end of the passage at the back of the stalls. In the standard Granadas, the decorative elements were spread over a much wider area. In concentrated sumptuousness, the Phoenix stands unique among Komisarjevsky's work.

Like almost every theatre built in the Thirties, the Phoenix made allowance for cinema use. In the West End, this was not only to provide an alternative if live shows failed: theatres of this size were in great demand for film trade shows during "dark" periods, and the Phoenix was particularly well located for the purpose. A projection room was provided above the gallery and three Ross projectors and Western Electric sound were installed – if not by the opening, then soon after.

The Phoenix's opening attraction was assured of success. Charles B. Cochran presented Noel Coward and Gertrude

Handbill for the run of Le Million.
(BFI – Sidney Bernstein Collection.)

Lawrence in the debut of Coward's *Private Lives*. Coward restricted the run to three months in London before taking it to Broadway for a further three months. Other less popular productions followed, and the theatre was set to go dark for two-and-a-half weeks before a new play opened. At the last minute, Sidney Bernstein and James V. Bryson, the head of Universal in Britain, hit on the idea of filling the gap with the British premiere of the René Clair comedy *Le Million* with English subtitles for a limited two week engagement, supported by an unadvertised MGM short, *Pip from Pittsburgh*. The French feature did so well that its run was extended for a full month, ending only when a transfer was arranged to the Rialto Coventry Street.

The Phoenix returned to live use, enjoying some success from June 1931 with the stage version of the hit film *Five Star Final*. But it also began to be used for cinema trade shows. The projection throw of 80 ft. was at a severe angle of 28 degrees, producing a keystone effect on the screen, which was itself an odd size, measuring 14 ft. 9 in. by 12 ft. 9 in. Only the Tivoli, among West End cinemas, had a slightly worse angle of projection.

In a 1944 profile of Sidney Bernstein, Tom Driberg refers to the Phoenix as his "blind spot" and adds: "It took £3,200 a week for thirteen weeks, but he lost most of his available cash in it. (The pressure of getting the theatre ready for the first night was such that he couldn't sit in it for the neurotic fear that the candelabra might fall on the audience.)"

Bernstein sold the Phoenix to Victor Luxemburg in March 1932, but continued to handle film bookings for a while and also arranged for a new, larger screen to be installed in the correct ratio. Luxemburg did not fare too well and the Phoenix was in the hands of the Receiver by December 1933. Some occasional film use followed, but it survives in 1998 as a live theatre, listed Grade II and essentially unaltered in its design, retaining even the decoration on the safety curtain.*

* A new cinema, the Curzon Phoenix, was added on adjacent property, using the Phoenix Street entrance. This opened in 1987 but patrons who passed admiringly through Komisarjevsky's foyer found themselves in a very plain and undistinguished auditorium. The cinema closed on 4 June 1998.

4 • *1931: The Flagship – The Granada Tooting*

The Granada Tooting opened on 7 September 1931, nearly a year after the Granada Walthamstow and the Phoenix Theatre. This day in September is a strong contender for the most notable one in British exhibition history, as not only did it see the debut of the Granada Tooting but also the opening of the Gaumont Palace Salisbury (now the listed Odeon) and the Paramount Newcastle (now the Odeon, unlisted).

The Tooting scheme had taken nearly three years to complete. This densely populated suburb of South London had been an attractive location for a number of reasons. It had no theatre or music hall. There were five cinemas operating but all dated from before World War One and their total seating capacity was only 3,000. In addition, being in the London County Council area, a new cinema would be able to open on Sundays, giving it a distinct advantage over adjoining districts like Wimbledon, Morden, Mitcham and Croydon where cinemas at that time were closed. Also, many of these areas, such as Mitcham and Morden, were rapidly expanding.

No large cinema had been previously built in Tooting for lack of a suitable extensive site. As elsewhere, Sidney Bernstein was prepared to take his time – as much time as it needed to buy up sufficient property to create a substantial site.

A row of six shops was acquired and demolished to provide the frontage on Mitcham Road, a main street near the centre of Tooting. It took eighteen months for local estate agents to arrange vacant possession of the whole site, which covered two acres.*

A cutting from a scrapbook at the local history library on Lavender Hill, Clapham Junction, indicates that the cinema replaced an historic area of old Tooting called Salvador:

"Salvador was, until a few years ago, a tiny village on its own,"

with its small beer house and one or two shops, and there were inhabitants who never went outside the little village from one year's end to the other... The little cottages had long gardens, which were cultivated to the last inch, and the beer-house, the Britannia, served the local community. The residents were never troubled with the traffic of Mitcham-road, and while Tooting was growing into a big town, Salvador remained just 'the little village'...

Today Salvador has been practically wiped out. Half of the houses and the quaint little alleys were cleared away this year for the great cinema which now stands on the site, and the tremendous Granada over-shadows the remaining cottages."

Did the Granada clear slums or did it destroy a picturesque enclave of country cottages? Even at the time, in October 1929, there were protests over the loss of housing but it was emphasised that generous compensation had been paid and, where required, equivalent or better accommodation for the displaced residents had been provided.

Houses were still being demolished in May 1930. Two went to provide an exit from the car park onto a residential street at the far side. Space was provided for 250 cars (as well as a pram park). Such a large car park would not have been essential if only local patronage was sought and indicates that the Granada expected to draw from a wide area (and was, perhaps, anticipating a future increase in car ownership).

First announcements of the project suggested a "mammoth" cinema which would seat 4,000 with standing for another 750. It would be in the Baroque style, resembling the Chicago Theatre erected by Balaban and Katz. (In fact, it seated nearly a thousand less and did not resemble the Chicago Theatre architecturally although its operating procedures, as suggested in the introduction, followed the example of American palaces like the Chicago.)

Construction of the Granada started on 19 August 1930. To acquire the freehold of the site had cost £31,000. The advance estimate of the cost of building the cinema was £119,000. According to one set of figures, the cinema cost £132,047 11s. 9d., including interest on capital, head office expenses and Western Electric sound equipment, but possibly excluding ventilation

* Elain Harwood provides details on an earlier, smaller scheme for part of the site: "A proposal by [architect] Stanley Beard for the front part of the site, made in November 1919, was rejected by the London County Council the following month. Beard made another application, which was approved in June 1925, for Mrs. Rose Lamartine Yates. It was for a hall similar in size to those built at Clapham and Wandsworth around this time, and had a capacity of 1,264. Long and narrow, it ran from Mitcham Road at the front to Salvador Place at the rear."

The Granada Tooting. The outer foyer with ticket window in the wall, seen on 16 June 1965. Two views of the main entrance hall plus the mirrored back wall at the top of the stairs, taken on 17 June 1965. (All from Photo Coverage.) For exterior photographs, see pages 8 and 217.

and film projection equipment. Another set of figures puts the cost of building at £102,251 7s. 0d. with fixture and fittings adding £43,525 19s. 6d., giving a total of £145,777 6s. 6d. Work proceeded so well that the Granada opened a month ahead of schedule.

Cecil Masey was again the architect and appears to have worked on early plans for the interior decoration. He originally devised a front elevation in moderne style. This was submitted to the London County Council for approval and a drawing was published in the trade press, suggesting that Sidney Bernstein had accepted it.* It seems fair to assume that he changed his mind and instructed Masey to follow the example of the Phoenix – but on a grander scale.

The entire interior design was provided by Theodore Komisarjevsky for a fee of £500. He sent his first sketches from Paris and was told he would not be needed in England until 10 November 1930. According to the *Kinematograph Weekly*, workmen were sworn to secrecy over the decorative style.

Masey provided à towering entrance block in white artificial stone that ensured the cinema was conspicuous from a distance along Mitcham Road and made a dignified impression. Its most distinctive feature was the set of four tall pillars with Corinthian capitals supporting the entablature with the main name sign displayed above it. A matching pilaster was set in each side wall. Floodlit from the canopy with no function other than to advertise the cinema, the tower had Spanish clay tiles on the roof. The overall design was very similar to that of the Phoenix Theatre's Charing Cross Road frontage except that there it was on a curve.

Floodlights on the canopy created a pattern of light and shadow in the recess behind the pillars. On one corner of the frontage, a vertical name sign was suspended with chaser lights around the

* Schemes in the London Metropolitan Archives have been examined by Elain Harwood who notes: "There are two main sets of plans, both undated, but one stamped with the London County Council's approval on 2 July 1930, the other in April 1931. The first scheme shows a car park coming out on Bickley Road to the south. The size and layout of the cinema are broadly similar, though two shops are shown on either side of the entrance which are by July omitted in favour of escape stairs from the café (amendment made in May). This is the scheme with the smaller, much slimmer entrance tower in the moderne style. There are also sections which show a heavy classical scheme. The side walls of the auditorium have two round arches with Corinthian pilasters, and these are in turn subdivided into three by smaller Corinthian pilasters. Further back at the edge of the circle are more pilasters, more akin to those eventually installed. The area under the balcony, shown with fat, heavy columns, is similar in both schemes, as is the position of windows at the top of the circle side walls, although these do not have the Gothic decoration found in April. Similarly, the section through the foyer and hall of mirrors has the same heavy classical treatment in July 1930, although the underlying drawing shows the same layout. The barley sugar decoration is shown in the April 1931 version."

edge and a pointed lower end, very much in the style used by American movie palaces like the Chicago Theatre although rather more modest in size. This type of sign was rarely seen in this country. The wide canopy stretched around the corner over the pavement alongside a private road, called Granada Street, leading to the car park at the rear. The external café entrance was set on the corner.

A wide set of steps led to a line of outer doors and into Komisarjevsky's domain. A low-ceilinged outer hall in Gothic style had ticket windows set into each side wall. It was necessary to buy a ticket before proceeding through the next set of doors.

One then entered the lofty main entrance hall (or "grand foyer") with its marble floor (this area was never carpeted downstairs in a Granada). Designed rather loosely in the manner of a medieval baronial hall, the foyer had a high ceiling with imitation oak beams and walls painted to resemble stonework. Six small Gothic-pointed mirrors were placed high on each side wall in the arches between pilasters which were decorated in an oak-leaf pattern with capitals of griffins playing the trumpet and harp. Higher up, where the side walls extended forward, heraldic lions were painted on a squared background, interrupted at intervals by small windows with stained glass in a diamond pattern lit up from behind, on one side by daylight. This was probably the largest such entry space in any British cinema to that date and could hold up to five hundred patrons waiting for seats. Komisarjevsky designed the Gothic-style tables and hall seats with high backs intended for display rather than use.

Patrons could take a staircase on one side, past a "pulpit" to the café which was set over the outer entrance hall and designed like a minstrels' gallery. Whereas most cinemas enclosed their cafes, Granada always preferred to leave them more open, directly overlooking the main foyer, to advertise their presence more clearly and tempt cinemagoers into using them.

At the other end of the hall, balcony patrons ascended a wide marble staircase with a stone balustrade on each side, arriving at a landing. Stalls patrons continued forward at ground level between the staircases. Both sets of cinemagoers passed four marble-like columns and came up against a mirrored wall that reflected the columns and the entrance hall, adding to the sense of space and depth. Stalls patrons turned to left or right as directed by staff, to enter the auditorium at the back or along the righthand side wall.

Circle patrons had the bonus of entering a hall of mirrors – a corridor under the balcony 150 ft. long and 20 ft. wide with over seventy mirrors in all along both sides, each under its own cusped arch. Every other mirror had a bracket holding a candle-shaped lamp to add to a castle-like atmosphere.

Off to the right of this hall of mirrors, halfway along, lay a short

The Granada Tooting. Top left: the hall of mirrors as it looked on 17 June 1965. (Photo Coverage.) Top right: 1931 view across circle shows repetitive design of ceiling coffering, undulating rows of seats and the side and centre entrances. (BFI Stills, Posters and Designs.)

Above: further photographs of the auditorium in 1931. In the view across the rear stalls. note the standing area on the far side – the exits to each side lead into the main foyer. (BFI Stills, Posters and Designs.)

flights of steps up into the centre of the balcony at the crossover which divided the rows of the most expensive front circle seats from those further back. At each end of the hall of mirrors were other sets of stairs that brought patrons into the balcony through loggias with stepped roofs set at an angle from the side walls. In most cinemas, circle patrons came up in the middle of the seating so that they had less distance to walk, but Granadas were always designed so that they entered at the sides. Tooting was exceptional in having the further access in the centre, presumably because the balcony here was so much larger than anywhere else. Patrons leaving via the hall of mirrors found exits on the other side that avoided the waiting throng in the entrance hall and provided quick access to the car park at the back of the building.

The auditorium lay at right angles to the entrance (the rear of the balcony extended on pillars over the carriageway at the side). The balcony had a massive span of 123 ft. The seating here was in undulating rows in the usual Masey style. Slips on each side added a few awkwardly placed seats in front of panels of medieval figures painted in oils by Alex Johnstone from small originals by Lucien Le Blanc.

The Granada was designed to seat 1,748 in the stalls and 1,354 in the balcony, a total of 3,102. With standing room in the auditorium and in the outer halls for 1,065, the theatre would have had a capacity of 4,167. In fact, the seating figure was slightly less – 3,086 – and standing room for 360 was allowed in the auditorium. The seats were in beige and green, the carpet in a rose colour.

The auditorium was extraordinarily rich in decorative features in an ecclesiastical, continental Gothic style. Komisarjevsky was attracted by the architecture of northern Italy in which the Gothic style of countries to the north had been reinterpreted with strong colours. Arches over the stalls side exits incorporated more images of medieval figures by Le Blanc and Johnstone. Further forward, the side walls carried backlit stained-glass windows with chandeliers in front that were later nicknamed "Christmas trees".

Suspended from the ceiling in front of the extremely wide proscenium opening of 58 ft. was a backlit row of cusped Gothic pendants in a wide curve like a crown. In the centre of the large orchestra pit, the console of the Wurlitzer organ ascended on a lift. The ceiling over the front stalls recalled the "atmospheric" style of American movie palaces, being painted to represent a cloud-flecked blue sky viewed between beams.

Over the balcony, a richly coffered ceiling had gold and blue as the predominant colours. Four chandeliers were suspended from the central recess, with a further chandelier on each side and flambeau-style fittings on the walls between a line of small false windows. The lower side walls of the balcony were painted to represent plain stone blocks.

The ceiling under the balcony was deeply recessed with much decorative moulding and chandeliers, enabling rear stalls patrons to feel they were also sitting in sumptuous surroundings.

In the plans, the manager's office was far too remotely placed at circle foyer level, requiring him to come down flights of stairs to reach the main foyer where he was most often required. While managing this theatre, John Young learned that the plans were revised during construction. A gents' toilet just outside the rear stalls in the passage from the main foyer was hastily turned into a ground floor office for the manager. Exiting patrons in search of relief would often open the door by mistake. The upstairs room was used as a general office.

The Granada Tooting was fully equipped for stage shows. The stage was 26 ft. deep (although 30 ft. and 35 ft. depth were claimed at opening) and 68 ft. wide, with a full switchboard. There were two screens, one larger and presumably intended for the expanding Magnascope system. These could be flown and the loudspeaker horn moved to one side on a track. Dressing rooms and three chambers for the organ were placed under the stage. There was a phantom grand piano cased in white and gold.

The projection throw from the back wall of the balcony was almost 170 ft. The operating box was equipped with three Ross machines, two Brenkert spots, and a Master Brenograph. The sound system was Western Electric.

There was a private view of the completed building for the press on 4 September 1931 and a cocktail party from 5 to 7pm on the opening day, 7 September. Sidney Bernstein lured the producer (Raymond Massey, better known as an actor) and the star (Godfrey Tearle) of the current production at the Phoenix, *Five Star Final*, to attend.

The *Kine Weekly* (10 September 1931) reported the opening Monday evening performance:

"Komisarjevsky... has visualised a temple of pleasure and has achieved a distinctive decorative scheme by adopting Gothic motifs, in which the main feature is obtained by the suggestion of huge stained-glass windows on each side of the auditorium. The effect upon the huge audience when the lights went up was remarkable, an enthusiastic round of applause swept the house.

"The opening proceedings, though essentially simple, were extremely effective. At seven o'clock 16 trumpeters of the Life Guards blew a fanfare from the steps of the brilliantly lighted façade. And thereupon the public streamed into the theatre, or away, as many as could be accommodated, for every seat had been booked well in advance, and over 2,000 people had to be turned away.

"The performance began with a brilliant lighting display, in

The Granada Tooting in 1931. (BFI Stills, Posters and Designs.)

which the electrical equipment of the theatre, in combination with Komisarjevsky's decorations, provided illumination effects of rare beauty.

"A novel item opened the programme, showing in shadow-graph the progress of the construction of the theatre and introducing the architect, and other chiefs of department who had contributed to its erection.

"At the conclusion, a backcloth was dropped, showing the completed theatre, and there was driven on the stage a baby Austin, the doors of which were opened by two of the most stalwart of the Granada's commissionaires. From the car there stepped forth a dainty kiddie, who was presented with a bouquet by a diminutive page and declared the theatre open.

"The remainder of the programme comprised an organ recital on the Wurlitzer by Alex Tayor, *Two Crowded Hours*, Michael Powell's British short feature, and *Monte Carlo*, the Paramount super.

"...Sidney Bernstein has decided to run an all-talkie programme with no variety, although lighting and musical interlude will play a definite part in the entertainment."

The Granada Tooting was certainly the most expensive, the most elaborate, the most stupendous cinema that Granada ever built. It offered the people of Tooting and the surrounding area an awe-inspiring temple of entertainment at a price within their reach. Like the Hyams brothers and the Greens of Glasgow, Sidney Bernstein believed that audiences wanted this kind of cathedral-like or palatial decor.

Other cinema operators shunned the past and sought a more modern and innovative look. Ernest Wamsley Lewis, who designed the undersea art deco fantasy setting of the New Victoria for William E. Trent and Gaumont/PCT, recalled: "I had been reported in one paper as an opponent of simpering cherubs, gilt and plush. Sidney Bernstein on the opening night said to me: 'People do not want this sort of thing; they want architecture with marble columns, gilt and mirrors. This won't pay.'"

Who was right? The New Victoria showed films for almost two years longer than the Granada. In 1973, they were the first two cinemas to be listed for their architectural merit. Both, in their different ways, are indisputably masterpieces of cinema design.

To the Bernsteins' undoubted annoyance, another large site was found for a rival cinema in Tooting. Five months after the Granada, an independent syndicate opened the Mayfair cinema in Upper Tooting Road with just under 2,000 seats. The Mayfair was not as well located as the Granada but it provided substantial opposition and once it passed into the hands of the major ABC chain fifteen months later it ensured that the Granada could never play any of that circuit's releases first run. However, given the huge population in the area, there was more than enough room for both cinemas to thrive for many years to come. Indeed, the Mayfair (later renamed the ABC) outlasted the Granada as a cinema.

A feature in the local *Mercury* newspaper (26 May 1933) reported that the Granada had a staff of eighty-five, including three engineers who attended to motors, lighting, batteries and other aspects of the electrical fittings. Three operators were in attendance in the projection room at all times. There were three projectors and one Brenograph, the latter the device for throwing effects on the screen such as twinkling stars. There were three men on the stage who arranged all the settings for the organ interludes and kept the stage clean. Forty attendants, who lined up for inspection by the theatre foreman before opening, looked after the 45,000 patrons who came in each week, working in shifts with none of the ladies putting in more than forty-two hours a week. For twelve hours after the end of the evening show, staff brushed, cleaned and swept the theatre, their work being inspected at 11am by the assistant manager and the house manager. A full-time painter and two carpenters were also employed, while a fireman was always in attendance, "just in case". There were two organists – at this time Harold Ramsay and an assistant.

According to John Platford, "When Tooting opened, heating and ventilation of buildings were in their infancy, so to advertise the fact that it had a heating and ventilation system to the public in the theatre, the plant manager was supplied with white overalls embroidered with MR. WEATHERMAN and encouraged to stay in the patrons' view as much as possible."

Tooting achieved national fame for its radio organ broadcasts. Among the many played by Harold Ramsay was a recital to a completely empty house between 6.10pm and 6.30pm on Christmas Day 1934.

A Lewisham postscript

The Granada Tooting was not quite the circuit's sole construction venture of 1931, as both Masey and Komisarjevsky were involved in work at the Hippodrome Lewisham. The largest live theatre in the London suburbs, it was closed as a music hall on 28 March to become a cinema five days later. Although this may not seem a significant period of time, it is reported that over two hundred men were employed to work night and day on a "transformation" and so quite a lot may have been achieved – but details are lacking.

Why Sidney Bernstein decided to turn the Hippodrome into a cinema at this moment is unclear. Perhaps it was losing too much money to carry on as a music hall. Perhaps he didn't care if Gaumont eventually built on their site in Loampit Vale as the Hippodrome was not in immediate competition, being some distance away at Catford. But why then did he sell the Hippodrome to ABC within days of re-opening it? The likely answer is that ABC, seeking an outlet in the area, made an irresistible offer. Bernstein may also have been anxious to reduce his overheads while building Tooting, as the transfer of the Hippodrome took place at the same time as he leased out the Granada at Dover. End of speculation.

A 3,050-seat Gaumont Palace Lewisham opened at Loampit Vale in December 1932. ABC lost interest in the Hippodrome when it acquired the nearby Prince of Wales in July 1933. The Hippodrome returned to music hall under a new owner with films on Sundays.

Another view of the huge balcony of the Granada Tooting, seen on 17 June 1965. (Photo Coverage.)

Leaflet promoting the re-launch of the Hippodrome Lewisham as a cinema. (BFI – Sidney Bernstein Collection.)

EWISHAM HIPPODROME

NOW BEING TRANSFORMED INTO A MODERN [TA]LKIE THEATRE WORTHY OF YOU AND YOUR FAMILY

A great change in entertainment has become necessary to progress with the swiftly changing times in which we live.

The stage has actually moved to the screen. The great artistes of the stage of yesterday have become the great artistes of the screen to-day. Now, we can bring to the Hippodrome the greatest of American, Continental and British productions with the greatest actors and actresses of the whole world.

A new model of the Western Electric sound equipment—in itself a guarantee of the reproduction of the living human voice without mechanical distortion—is being installed for the first time in England at this theatre. We promise you shall hear *everything* from every seat —you will not be able to see and hear better in any other cinema.

A continuous supply of film programs of an unusually high standard is ensured by the exceptional resources of our established organisation. All our films are selected with more than ordinary care by expert reviewers and never is cost allowed to be the deciding factor.

Upholstered balcony seating and lots of other improvements are being effected, improvements you may not easily notice but equally necessary for your comfort.

We look forward with pleasure to serving the public of Lewisham and district with generous programs of entertainment at modest prices of admission.

OPEN AT ONE O'CLOCK
SATURDAY, APRIL 4th
3 HOUR PROGRAM ALWAYS

...rnoons, before four
... 6d   Circle 1/-

Evenings: Balcony 6d
Stalls 8d & 9d; Circle 1/6

5 • 1933: Edmonton's "Symphony Of Simplicity"

After the opening of Tooting in September 1931, it was almost two years before the next major piece of building work was completed. This was a thorough reconstruction of the Empire Edmonton.

In 1932, some improvements were made to the Regal Watford, which had come under Bernstein Theatres management during that year. The Regal was the old Central Hall, opened in 1913 and recently re-named. It closed for over a month for alterations to be carried out around the clock from plans by architect George Coles and interior designer Theodore Komisarjevsky. The seating capacity was 1,286. No photographs appear to survive showing the final result. The connection with Bernstein Theatres lasted around three years and further changes seem to have been made in 1936 under new management.

In January 1933 the Bernsteins were involved in the opening of the Plaza Rugby (covered in chapter 11). In March 1933, Sidney Bernstein announced he was starting a circuit of twelve halls in smaller provincial towns and that the first of these would be at Shrewsbury where demolition work on the site had already started. Shrewsbury and two others, he declared, would open in 1934. His continuing enthusiasm for live theatre showed in his declaration that they would be putting on a live play every fourth week.

Empire Edmonton: "The Symphony of Simplicity"

The Empire Edmonton had been built as a music hall in 1908 and operated as a cinema from 1927, becoming one of the Denman group jointly owned by the Bernsteins and Gaumont-British. It was not an ideal shape for showing films and had a particularly cramped foyer. It faced competition from a huge new super cinema at a better location: the Regal, first announced by A. E. Abrahams in February 1932 though not completed until March 1934. Sidney Bernstein put Cecil Masey and Theodore Komisarjevsky to work on rebuilding the Empire, which closed in January 1933 for seven months. The new building retained the Empire name rather than being called Granada when it re-opened on 28 August.

The existing auditorium extended along the road at right angles to the entrance. Adjacent land was available at both ends of the rectangular site to add a new stage tower at one end and a new entrance at the other in matching red brick, cornice and stone pilasters. A new foundation stone was laid in early August by Jessie Matthews and Sonnie Hale. The frontage became approximately 220 ft. long while the depth of the site still averaged 80 ft. There was no space for a car park.

Only the original side walls and roof were retained. The old dressing rooms were demolished, including the one occupied by Marie Lloyd on her last engagement, from which she had been carried to her death bed in 1922. The new stage – 60 ft. high – and grid tower included ten dressing rooms and a room for the organist.*

A green and bronze canopy extended over the new entrance with film titles slotted in two lines on the front edge. A narrower canopy to shelter queues extended along the length of the side wall to the fly tower. A vertical downward-pointing arrow sign with the name Empire edged by light bulbs was mounted on the side wall towards the fly tower end while a horizontal neon sign spelled out the cinema name against the apex of the entrance block. Another horizontal name sign was mounted on the back of the fly tower.

Although the exterior remained old-fashioned, Theodore Komisarjevsky delivered an aggressively modern, "futuristic" interior. The stark, angular scheme – based on the Dutch cubism known as "De Stijl" – was in startling contrast to his use of rich ornamentation in traditional styles at other cinemas. Straight lines and squared corners and strong primary colours were evident everywhere. The lofty foyer had solid sides to the stair-case rather than the openness of balustrades. Tall mirrors were spread around the foyer and at the turn in the stairs to the circle. The walls were a silver grey hue with bright colours on the piers, staircase supports and front edge of the upper landing. The

---

* John Young, as the assistant manager in 1956 at the Empire, recalls that the red velvet armchair into which Marie Lloyd collapsed was kept in a dressing room named after her. Long-serving members of staff maintained that Marie Lloyd's ghost haunted the backstage area.

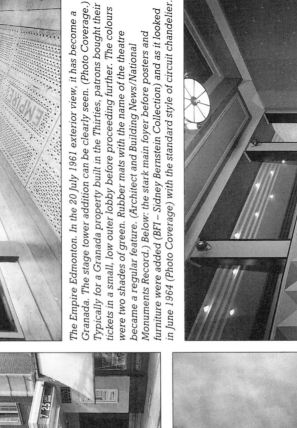

The Empire Edmonton. In the 20 July 1961 exterior view, it has become a Granada. The stage tower addition can be clearly seen. (Photo Coverage.) Typically for a Granada property built in the Thirties, patrons bought their tickets in a small, low outer lobby before proceeding further. The colours were two shades of green. Rubber mats with the name of the theatre became a regular feature. (Architect and Building News/National Monuments Record.) Below: the stark main foyer before posters and furniture were added (BFI – Sidney Bernstein Collection) and as it looked in June 1964 (Photo Coverage) with the standard style of circuit chandelier.

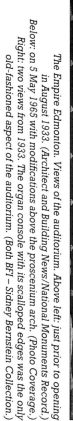

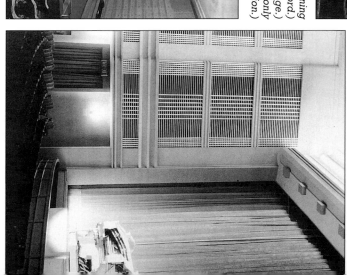

The Empire Edmonton. Views of the auditorium. Above left: just prior to opening in August 1933. (Architect and Building News/National Monuments Record.) Below: on 5 May 1965 with modifications above the proscenium arch. (Photo Coverage.) Right: two views from 1933. The organ console with its scalloped edges was the only old-fashioned aspect of the auditorium. (Both BFI – Sidney Bernstein Collection.)

mosaic work on the floor was also in strong colours. Globe light fittings provided a contrast to the straight lines.

The auditorium was long and narrow, with parallel straight sides except for the narrowing in towards the screen. The angular severity was relieved by Masey's undulating steppings in the balcony and the curve to the front of the circle and to the rows of stalls seating. All the seats were covered in a warm red pattern. The narrowing of the auditorium at the screen end was accentuated by a triangular laylight in the ceiling over the front stalls pointing at the proscenium arch and emphasised by parallel bands to each side. Further back, the ceiling formed a large flat rectangle of primrose hue with a stepped edge in orange and had long cylindrical light fittings of frosted glass with chromium-plated bands near each corner. Further back still, there were three deep recesses in the ceiling, each finished in a different colour: primrose, orange and green.

For the splay walls, Komisarjevksy designed sets of three identical grilles, slightly staggered, with a tubular lattice pattern in silver. The plasterwork was painted in different colours for each grille: green, primrose and orange. The side walls further back were finished in silver grey with, at balcony level, horizontal bands in orange interspersed with silver extending from the edge of the grilles. One awkward feature of the auditorium was that columns were needed near the far back corners to help support the balcony.

The large proscenium had a narrow surround, painted green. Three horizontal troughs casting concealed lighting upwards were placed above the opening. Three-colour footlights illuminated the main curtains. There were more than 500 extra seats in the new Empire, giving a total of 1,842.

A Magnascope screen was installed with masking that opened out to provide an enlarged picture for spectacular sequences. The screen and sound apparatus could be flown to clear the stage for live presentations. For details of the Wurlitzer, see the chapter on organs at the end.

The Empire boasted the first fog-catching device installed in a London cinema, fog being notorious for seeping into cinemas through the ventilation system.

The straight side wall with single line of seats facing across auditorium and central section of grillework protruding slightly. (BFI – Sidney Bernstein Collection.)

6 ● *1934: The First Standard Granadas And A Take-Over*

In March 1933, Sidney Bernstein announced the start of a new circuit of twelve cinemas. The only cinema built during 1933 was the Granada Maidstone, which opened early the following year. Costing much less than Tooting and Walthamstow and smaller in size, it provided the template for the "standard" Granada, two more of which were built during 1934 at Shrewsbury and Bedford, with six others following. Thanks to the decoration devised for their interiors by Theodore Komisarjevsky, they were spectacularly impressive when compared to other cinemas being built in towns of similar size. Repeating the decorative scheme (with slight variations) and also many of the exterior features offered opportunities for reducing costs and consolidating the circuit image, but this was rarely done elsewhere in the Thirties. In Granada's case, it seems that Sidney Bernstein liked what he saw at Maidstone and saw no reason to change it.

There is no indication that Bernstein actually had twelve sites lined up and confirmed when he made his announcement. The search certainly continued for suitable locations. A younger brother, Max Bernstein, checked out many possibilities. He inspected a site in Cheam, Surrey, in the summer of 1933 to see if it was suitable for a small cinema to take second runs (and, sure enough, Granada opened the Century Cheam Village in 1937 as a second-run house). Max also looked for sites in the Southgate district to link up with the planned extension of the Underground to Cockfosters. He recommended Southgate itself – but Odeon won the race to build here.

A site with a narrow entrance came up at 82 High Street, Bromley, Kent, but was not pursued – Odeon built on a similar site elsewhere in the High Street while Gaumont set up on a commanding corner location. A site at 324 High Street, Chatham, Kent, was offered in August 1934 – but Union nabbed that for its Ritz. Also in Kent, Sevenoaks was initially considered promising territory for a new Granada, then rejected after further consideration (although Granada would eventually take over one of the two modern cinemas that were built there – the Cinema/Plaza).

Many promoters courted Sidney Bernstein as a potential partner. There was the aptly named F. J. Partner who requested a meeting to discuss his ideas for a cinema in Banstead (never built).

One entrepreneur, seemingly the well-known Sokoloff, wanted Sidney to come in on a site that he had leased at Rose Hill, near Sutton, in Surrey; the details were passed to Gaumont and a G.-B. theatre was eventually built, although its construction was arranged by architect/promoter Harry Weston.

In the middle of 1934, Bernstein was looking closely at the Oxford Street Hippodrome as the site for a new super cinema in the heart of Manchester. In October, it was announced that Oswald Stoll had arranged to sell the live theatre and Granada would take it over from the following February for immediate demolition. This scheme went ahead – but with a surprise dénouement.

During 1934, it was decided to replace two of the Denman cinemas. At a press conference held on 20 August, Bernstein appeared with his fellow directors from the Gaumont side, Mark Ostrer and C. M. Woolf, to announce that two sister theatres, almost identical in construction and decoration, would be built at East Ham and Enfield to replace the Empire and Rialto. Both were to be designed by Gaumont's chief architect, W. E. Trent. An Enfield Granada would open in September 1935 and contracts for its construction were said to have been placed. The replacement Granada at East Ham would open a month later. Perhaps because of Gaumont's parlous financial condition, which reduced its own openings to a trickle, the Enfield scheme was abandoned. A new Granada did arrive at East Ham but not until November 1936.

The later months of 1934 saw several existing cinemas added to the circuit (see chapter 11), but there would only be a couple of further, minor take-overs during the rest of the decade. The emphasis was henceforth on new builds.

Granada Maidstone

The Granada Maidstone was the first completely new Bernstein theatre to open since Tooting and, as just mentioned, Komisarjevsky's decorative scheme set the pattern for many more that followed. It seated 1,684, with standing room for 180 (a capacity of 2,000 claimed for publicity purposes). With a population of 42,259, the town had four existing cinemas, all much smaller

GRANADA GRANADA

LOWER STONE STREET · MAIDSTONE

● Granada Facts

Maidstone workmen established a record in building the Granada. It was on August 1st, a mere five months ago, that they embarked on the task of erecting the building. Such a job as this usually takes nine months but they cut this time down by more than sixteen weeks working an ordinary eight-hour day. Of course, experts in certain crafts of building had to be recruited from outside. Their number, however, is trivial. Of the 152 men employed on the Granada, approximately 125 were drawn from Maidstone and district.

Maidstone can justly be drawn to this record of work achieved by Bovis, Ltd., a firm with international building experience, pay striking tribute to this record job of work achieved by Maidstone men.

In addition to the 152 men directly employed on the Granada, work has been indirectly provided for men and women. belonging to 49 different firms scattered throughout the world from Heckmondwike in Yorkshire to the maple forests of Canada.

For instance, the Granada building has used up 20½ miles of electric wire manufactured in Southampton ; 247 tons of steel work from Liverpool and Glasgow ; and 1½ miles of silk damask provided by Bradford.

Then there were :

751,000 bricks	(Peterborough)
27 switchboards	(Nottingham, Chelmsford, London)
252 Electric Switches	(London)
1½ miles of wilton carpet	(Heckmondwike)
1½ miles of underfelt	(Kidderminster)
1,250 square yards of linoleum	(Kirkcaldy)
500 lbs. of tin-tacks	(Birmingham)
508 tons of concrete	(Maidstone)
2 miles of webbing	(Dundee)
3,500 yards of canvas	(also Dundee)
6,300 square yards of ply-wood	(High Wycombe)
4,154 electric lamps	(Witton & Rugby)
18 tons of cast iron counterweights	(West Bromwich)
1,275 ash trays	(Birmingham)
4,300 yards of rubber nosing	(Malay States, via Edinburgh)
373 tons of cement	(Snofland)
42 tons of iron seat stands	(West Bromwich)
200 yards of stage flooring	(Maple forests of Canada)
20,000 feet of steel conduit	(Birmingham)
3 tons of asphalte	(Trinidad)

In striking contrast to all these British and Empire products there are only two items bearing a foreign label:
15 tons of marble (Rome & Verona, Italy)
5 cork bases for electric motors (Jerez, Spain)

The Maidstone Granada is a monument to British materials bought with British capital and handled by British workmen.

● To-day's Program

(JAN. 10, 11, 12, 13)

NEWS IN SOUND

ORGAN RECITAL

"Hello Everybody"
Organist: ALEX TAYLOR

CUCKOO IN THE NEST

A Gaumont-British Picture
Story by Ben Travers
Directed by Tom Walls

CAST:		
Major Bone	...	TOM WALLS
Peter Wyckham	...	RALPH LYNN
Marguerite Hickett	...	Yvonne Arnaud
Mrs. Spoker	...	Mary Brough
The Rev. Sloley-Jones	...	J. Robertson Hare
Noony	...	Gordon James
Barbara Wyckham	...	Veronica Rose
Mrs. Bone	...	Grace Edwin
Pinhorn	...	Mark Daly
Claude Hickett	...	Cecil Parker
Alfred	...	Roger Livesey
Gladys	...	Norah Howard
Landlord	...	F. Pettingell
Kate (the Wyckham's maid)	...	Joan Brierley

MERRY OLD SOUL

An Oswald-the-Rabbit Cartoon

REUNION IN VIENNA

A Metro-Goldwyn-Mayer Picture
Story by Robert E. Sherwood
Directed by Sidney Franklin

CAST:		
Rudolf	...	JOHN BARRYMORE
Elena	...	DIANA WYNYARD
Anton	...	Frank Morgan
Ilse	...	Una Merkel
Father Krug	...	Henry Travers
Fra Lucher	...	May Robson
Poffy	...	Eduardo Ciannelli
Kathie	...	Bodil Rosing
Musician	...	Morris Nussbaum
Musician	...	Nella Walker
Countess Von Stainz		
Count Von Stainz	...	Herbert Evans

● OUR POLICY

We built the Granada in the belief that Maidstone had need of a luxury theatre consistent with the Borough's ever increasing importance. Experts in science, engineering and every other sphere of activity associated with motion picture entertainment have contributed their quota that the Granada should be unsurpassed for luxurious comfort and outstanding programs. The resources at our command will always ensure that the pick of the world's best films will be available immediately they are released. The Management.

NEXT WEEK'S PROGRAM

● SUNDAY, JANUARY 14
Marion Davies
"Peg o' My Heart"

● MONDAY, JANUARY 15
FOR SIX DAYS
Jack Buchanan and
Elsie Randolph
"That's a Good Girl"
AND
Robert Montgomery
and Helen Hayes
"Another Language"

Program

The Granada Maidstone. Opening programme (courtesy of Les Bull). Left, exterior on 19 January 1961. The canopy has been modified to carry the then standard style of enamelled lettering. The café-restaurant sign is a larger, more elaborate replacement for the original one which stretched only above the four centre windows. All the shops are being used by Granada and the restaurant entrance lies beyond them. The main name sign is obscured by the entrance block. (Photo Coverage.)

1934: The First Standard Granadas And A Take-Over ● 55

The Granada Maidstone.
Left, the outer lobby (seen on 18 May 1954), with standard rubber mats and light fittings, plus box-office windows as usual in the side wall.
Below left, the main entrance hall in 1954. Note the sign to the café above the stairs. A few years later, the small concessions counter to the right of the stairs was replaced by a much larger one in front of the two pillars. Note the Granada News board on the wall to the right, a standard feature of the period.
Below right, this view (19 April 1971) shows the ceiling detail of the main foyer. The space over the outer lobby has been blocked off for several years.
Right, this 1954 view of the promenade at the head of the stairs shows hanging lights that were a standard circuit fixture and the original carpet design. Doors at each end lead up into the circle.
(All Photo Coverage.)

Workmen began erecting the new Granada in Lower Stone Street at Maidstone, Kent, on the first day of August 1933. The architect, once again, was Cecil Masey. The site for the cinema was on rising ground. The usual patriotic emphasis was placed on the maximum use of British materials. "The Maidstone Granada is a monument to British materials bought with British capital and handled by British workmen", declared the opening programme in which it was stated that the only foreign items needed were fifteen tons of marble from Rome and Verona and five cork bases for the electric motors from Jerez in Spain. These same items would continue to be imported for later Granadas.

The exterior of the cinema was largely faced in brick but, for the central feature of the imposing corner entrance block, Masey placed a recess in which he set a line of four stone columns with Corinthian capitals supporting a pediment, with two pilasters at each side. This same arrangement of pillars had, of course, been seen at Tooting and the Phoenix Charing Cross Road. At the back of the recess was a wall in brick with sets of ordinary windows on two floors. An area of plain brickwork above the pediment called out for a Granada name sign across it, but nothing would be placed here until the word BINGO appeared in 1971. The frontage was capped by a decorative frieze in stone just like the one at Dover. A Granada name sign appeared high up on the front wall of the auditorium block behind where it could be seen from the greatest distance although not from the street immediately outside. Because of the narrow pavement, there was a shallow canopy with two lines of changeable lettering mounted on the front and returns.

A long, two-storey side elevation on Lower Stone Street displayed a series of eight round-headed windows at first floor level, behind which lay a café-restaurant. At ground level was a series of shops. A small vertical sign marked the public entrance to the café-restaurant at the far end of the row of shops. On the other side of the cinema entrance lay a new side road called Granada Street. The side wall here had exits and four round-headed windows at first floor level.

Somewhere on the outside of the building, according to John Platford, were windows to the plant room, floodlit at night, so that passers by could see the heating and ventilation equipment and be reminded of the comfortable and hygienic atmosphere the theatre provided. The display was an advance on Tooting's Mr. Weatherman. The equipment was similarly displayed at two or more later theatres.

There was a short outer lobby with box-office windows in each side walls, on the lines of those at earlier Granada theatres but rather more compact and barely decorated. An inner set of doors admitted patrons to the two-storey foyer, dominated by a chandelier suspended from a saucer dome and by a grand stair-

case at the far end similar to the one at Dover. The stairs led up to a promenade under the balcony and to passages along each side leading back to the café-restaurant which seems to have extended over the entrance. It was Granada practice to have bare marble floors and staircases in entrance halls. However, carpet was laid in passages and along the promenades as well as in the auditorium. Little use was made of mirrors compared to the Phoenix (where they were needed to create an impression of greater space).

In the auditorium, the circle seating was in the wavy rows indicative of Cecil Masey's participation. Theodore Komisarjevsky adapted and simplified the Italian Renaissance style he had used for the Phoenix Theatre. There he had been confronted with a tall, hemmed-in space. Here he could spread his scheme across a much greater expanse.

Some of the light fittings were copied from the Phoenix, notably the large main auditorium chandelier with its outer ring of lights covered by crenellated shades and a smaller version of the same for the rear circle and foyer. Cylindrical or drum-shaped fittings were attached to the ceilings in the outer lobby and passages.

The large dome above the main chandelier at the Phoenix was replaced by a flat ceiling at the Granada. The radiating decoration of the dome was modified to a wheel-like pattern of slightly raised spokes. The intervening segments were decorated with six-sided shapes reminiscent of the old threepenny bit that looked as though they could have been created by a giant pastry cutter. The Phoenix's panels of classical paintings were replaced with a narrow frieze of allegorical figures at cornice level, carefully painted but barely visible from any seat – these showed matching scenes of a charioteer and running figures in clouds on each side wall, and figures apparently fighting each other in the central panel over the proscenium arch (the inspiration for these scenes is not noted anywhere).

In place of the three roundheaded boxes at dress circle level on each side at the Phoenix, Komisarjevsky provided three decorative grilles (all the same design) with a balustrade which projected slightly from the centre grille above a stalls exit. As at the Phoenix, the side walls of the circle were essentially plain, emphasising the richness of decoration further forward. They were painted to provide an ashlar effect, as were the side walls underneath the balcony, with grooves to suggest horizontal courses and vertical joints.

As always, the ceiling was stepped up over the rear circle to accommodate ventilation grilles at the front edge and to clear space for the projection beam. This ceiling was left plain in the first three standard Granadas.

The Granada Maidstone opened on Wednesday 10 January 1934

The Granada Maidstone. Top left, this view (19 April 1971) shows the wavy pattern of the seat rows and the plain side walls of the balcony. Speakers for stereophonic sound are evident, dating from the installation of CinemaScope in 1954. Audiences came up at each end of the cross-over. The ceiling was always stepped up over the rear circle to accommodate ventilation grilles at the front edge and to clear

space for the projection beam. This area was lit by small chandeliers in the same style as the main one and those in the foyer. Below left, the rear stalls in 1954, a relatively plain area with a small clock centrally placed on the back wall. Top right, auditorium on 19 April 1971. (All Photo Coverage.) Projection box view dates from Thirties (courtesy of Les Bull).

This May 1954 view across the auditorium of the first standard Granada at Maidstone slightly predates CinemaScope, for which the screen was brought forward. The organ console can just be seen behind the orchestra rail. The side walls have an ashlar treatment more pronounced to either side of the exit arch under the grilles. The frieze of figures above the proscenium arch and side grilles at cornice level has faded. (Photo Coverage.)

The Plaza (later Granada) Sutton. Exterior in Spring 1940 photographed by H. J. Stull. The vertical sign has been added in Granada lettering conflicting with the original style over the windows. Note the white bands on the tree trunk for the war time black-out.

Left, the huge café/ballroom above the entrance, seen on 25 March 1965. (Photo Coverage.)

Above top, the outer entrance hall (also 1965) with a standard chandelier out of place amidst the plain concentric curves of the ceiling. (Photo Coverage.)

Above, a March 1965 view of the main entrance hall shows bucket-shaped chairs by Komisarjevsky against the side wall and more of his standard light fittings. The doors to the left were later removed. (Photo Coverage.)

at 2pm. There was a full house with many unable to obtain admission. The programme opened with a newsreel and organ recital, followed by two big films, an Aldwych farce called *A Cuckoo in the Nest* with Tom Walls, Ralph Lynn and Robertson Hare and (after a cartoon) the Hollywood production *Reunion in Vienna* with John Barrymore and Diana Wynyard. The same programme continued until Saturday. The theatre was equipped for stage use, although it had no fly tower. There was an adjacent car park.

The Granada Maidstone would remain the town's outstanding cinema despite major improvements to two of the others at different times. It was not an immediate runaway success but it caught on in time and, if company publicity can be believed, there had been 2,233,546 admissions by its third anniversary.

Plaza Sutton

The Plaza Sutton was a venture by Lou Morris, one of several designed for the promoter by leading cinema architect Robert Cromie – others including the Capitol Winchmore Hill (1929), Playhouse Dewsbury (1931) and Princess Dagenham (1932). Morris was unusual in that he liked to open properties and then sell them very quickly at a profit and move on to new ventures.

The Plaza Sutton was one of his biggest undertakings, seating 2,390 (2,500 seats were claimed). Building work started on 15 February 1934 and, according to the opening programme, 450 workmen were involved. British materials were used exclusively, except for Swedish deal flooring and French asphalt.

Lou Morris had arranged to sell the Plaza to Granada before he opened it on Saturday 8 September 1934 as "The Wonder Theatre of Surrey". The first night programme consisted of a "screen novelty" (a short), the Laurel and Hardy comedy *The Private Life of Oliver the Eighth*, an organ recital, and the big film, *Catherine the Great*. Control of the Plaza passed to Bernstein Theatres on the Monday after the opening. Morris retained a small interest and a directorship in the Granada subsidiary formed to take over the cinema. There was no mention of it becoming a Granada theatre in advertising at this time.

The take-over, arranged just days before the opening, meant that the design of the cinema could not be adapted to the circuit style.

Robert Cromie provided the Plaza with a rather plain frontage. This was primarily in multi-colour facing bricks with Portland stone dressings to the columns between five tall windows. An up-to-date look was created by the style of lettering for the name, placed just above the windows, and by the two pairs of porthole-shape openings just above the canopy to each side of the main windows.

As at many other of his cinemas, Robert Cromie drew on a

talented team of interior designers, Eugene Mollo and Michael Egan, to add a modern, streamlined look to his architectural shell. The Plaza's outer foyer had a low ceiling of concentric circles rising to a centre point from which was suspended a large light fitting. There was an island paybox and stairs in each corner leading to the circle. Over the foyer was a huge café-restaurant with dance floor, probably the largest ever operated by Granada, with its own strikingly streamlined look and dramatic use of concealed lighting in troughs. There were large inner foyers at stalls and circle levels.

The auditorium was not one of Mollo and Egan's more forceful designs – far less elaborate than their work on Cromie's Regals at Wimbledon and Godalming or Ritzes at Chelmsford and Southend for the County circuit. It did have rounded corners and the comb-like plasterwork descending onto the proscenium arch characteristic of this team's work of the period, plus plain pierced grillework on the splay walls (similar in its horizontal banding to Komisarjevsky's work at Edmonton). The walls and ceiling had what was described in the *Sutton Advertiser* at the time as "a golden granular surface, shaded in parts of the building with rose". The paper continued: "The lighting of the auditorium is in amber, and much of it is from lamps concealed in the decorative scheme of the ceiling. There will be coloured lighting effects on the stage and the console of the Compton, the latest of its kind, will be illuminated in changing colours…"

The cove lighting across the ceiling made this the Granada theatre most dependent on concealed illumination. It was supplemented by direct illumination of the rear stalls and the rear of the balcony.

With a stage fully equipped for live shows, the Plaza would be one of the Granada theatres most extensively used for pantomimes, concerts and other live events.

The Plaza Sutton featured in a special Cinemas issue of the *Architects' Journal* (7 November 1935) where it was commended by the fastidious Julian Leathart in his article on "Structure and Facing," for having an elevation of charm with a design of extreme simplicity. The auditorium was commended for the ensemble design of the organ grille, proscenium and "reflecting" ceiling. No Granada was illustrated, although Sidney Bernstein was invited to contribute the foreword to the issue. He used the opportunity to vigorously attack the modern look in cinemas:

"Alas, the great modern artists – the Cezannes, the Monets, and the Piccassos [sic] – engendered an outburst of so-called modernism which, when interpreted by cinema decorators, follows neither the original conception of the artist, nor the basic laws of functional architecture. Rather it reveals itself as a fake art, trying vaguely to imitate the purity of African negro design; using great masses of paint, generally plastic, and crudely

The auditorium of the Plaza Sutton. View forwards dates from 27 April 1964, view to rear from 10 August 1971. (Photo Coverage.)

coloured, in an effort to conceal artistic ignorance and initial architectural errors. This school, which misrepresents the twentieth century, further illuminates its ignorance of design by such characteristics as hiding hundreds of electric lamps in cornices and corners, thus creating an atmosphere better suited to captive fish than films (with, incidentally, an excessive labour bill for maintenance).

"This is not an attack on modern architecture as a whole, but on cinema design in particular. Cinemas seldom fulfil the needs of their patrons for a sense of comfort, for change from the limitations of their home, for surroundings that will give them week by week an exciting and refreshing background to their entertainment.

"Most cinemas decorated in the alleged modern manner already look old-fashioned. Perhaps their architects were afraid that by taking lessons from Michelangelo, Wren, Inigo Jones and other great masters they would prove that they were just passengers in an age of mediocrity.

"All this may not prove, but certainly tends to support, my theory that cinema building can never be the work of one person. It must be the work of a group inspired by the idea of producing a theatre that is at once efficient in operation and appealing in appearance. This can be done without pandering to mass vulgarity.

"Experience has taught me that such a group must be comprised of the architect, the interior decorator, the electrical engineer, the ventilation engineer, and the owner, who must, because of his practical knowledge of theatre management, guide the experts in producing the theatre which his public will appreciate and which can be efficiently and economically run.

"The owner should guide the experts in creating an atmosphere of 'theatre,' by which I mean the combination of luxury and restfulness which patrons subconsciously demand.

"The owner's knowledge of staff routine, functional requirements, running costs and maintenance must harness the efforts of the experts into fashioning a building that is practically planned in every detail.

"Such factors in cinema construction would seem to be elementary; yet examine the greater number of cinemas in this country, and you will find them inefficient in practically every respect, and it is solely the enthusiasm of the public for films which has protected them from the fate they deserve."

After his association with Komisarjevsky and obvious preference for traditional styles (apart from the experiment of Edmonton), it is surprising that Bernstein was ever invited to write the piece, which went against the spirit of the issue. Indeed, after agreeing with his declaration that cinemas needed to be built by a team rather than one person, the editor of the magazine took issue with Bernstein in his preface:

"Mr. Bernstein, however, is on dangerous ground when he contends that 'the owner should guide the experts in creating an atmosphere of "theatre," by which I mean the combination of luxury and restfulness which patrons subconsciously demand.' The typical cinema owner does not know the real meaning of the words 'theatre,' luxury or restfulness. His idea of what the public wants is generally a combination of gin palace and fun fair. The public is conditioned to this style because the owners know of no other. It is time that some owners gave the architect his head."

That cut no ice with Sidney Bernstein. He liked what Theodore Komisarjevsky had provided and he stuck with it.

Granada Shrewsbury

The Granada Shrewsbury and the Granada Bedford opened a month apart at the end of 1934. Bernstein had been connected with Shrewsbury through his interest in Shrewsbury Empires Ltd, from when it had opened the Empire in 1922. The town's King's Hall and Central had also been taken over but the latter had been destroyed in a fire. A prominent site mainly occupied by the former Central and near the station, was obtained for the new Granada cinema, which was built through Shrewsbury Empires and would be held separately from the rest of the circuit for many years. Originally, local architect Arthur E. Williams was appointed to handle the scheme, but Cecil Masey took over.

The site had much the same shape as Maidstone, but ran downhill rather than uphill. Externally, Masey repeated his work at Maidstone – the only differences in the entrance block were that the back of the recess behind the columns was faced in stone rather than brick and the canopy was less substantial with just one line of lettering on the fascia. Here, unlike Maidstone, a large name sign was mounted on the brickwork above the pediment. Again, there was a long row of shops to the right with a line of round-headed windows on the first floor, some of which related to the café-restaurant which extended from above the entrance. Again, there was a side street with a further, shorter row of round-headed windows at first floor level.

The small outer vestibule and the double-height entrance hall followed the pattern of Maidstone, except at the far end of the foyer. Here, the arrangement was unusual. Because of the slope of the site downhill, far more than was needed for the rake of the stalls floor, patrons descended down flight of stairs at the back of the foyer. No staircase was needed here to reach the balcony. There were three round-headed arches across the end of the foyer and a short flight of three steps through the central arch led up to a passage that extended sideways in both directions, taking patrons to stairs up into the balcony.

Komisarjevsky's foyer decoration differed slightly from

The Granada Shrewsbury. Above, in this 1953 view, the oldest available, the name sign is in a distinctive design that was replaced within ten years by the regular italic block serif lettering. The sign on the far end of the building was also replaced while the small café sign gave way to one reading "Restaurant" placed nearer the main entrance. Below, the foyer in March 1957, with the restaurant area on the first floor (in use to judge by the coats on stands). The stairs leading down to the stalls are in darkness at left (note the etched pattern in the mirror above).
(Both Photo Coverage.)

The Granada Shrewsbury. The view (dated 13 May 1965) of the foyer looking towards the auditorium shows more clearly the pattern on the mirrors at the top of the roundheaded arches, with shields in the centre of two of them. This kind of elaboration was not seen in any other Granada.

Top right, the promenade just beyond the arches in the previous view, with doors into the balcony at either end (also taken in 1965). (Both Photo Coverage.)

Below left, this undated shot of the auditorium shows the sinuous curves of the balcony seating and the stage setting. Speakers have been mounted on each side close to the proscenium arch. (Courtesy of John D. Sharp.). View to rear is also undated.

Maidstone with a coffered look to the central ceiling recess while mirrors in the heads of the arches and over the staircases to the stalls had etched-glass patterns, some with crests in the centre.

With 1,525 seats in all, this Granada had a slightly smaller capacity than Maidstone. The balcony was entered at the sides by the central cross-over and the rows of seats displayed the Masey undulations. The decorative scheme of the auditorium was almost identical to Maidstone. The ceiling was dominated by the same circular pattern and chandelier. There was the same set of three decorative grilles on the splay walls with mock balustrading (which matched the real balustrading at first floor level in the foyer) and a painted impression of stonework below. But at Shrewsbury the pilasters between the grilles were richly decorated rather than left plain, the central section of balustrade did not project forward slightly to suggest a balcony, and the exits on each side were placed beneath the grille closest to the screen. In place of a frieze above these grilles, there were decorated ventilation openings. However, a frieze of figures did appear above the wide proscenium arch. A set of mock tassles filled in the top of the arch.

It will be remembered that Sidney Bernstein intended Granadas of this period to function as live theatres one week in four. The Shrewsbury theatre did not have a full-height stage tower because of local objections. There was flying space only at the front of the stage which had a sloping roof. There was storage space for sets under the stage. Although it proved too difficult to find enough attractions prepared to visit this slightly out-of-the-way location for live shows as often as every fourth week, Maidstone eventually become one of the Granada theatres most extensively used for live shows. A dressing room block seems to have been built onto the side of the auditorium, on the side road.

Shrewsbury was the only purpose-built Granada not to have an organ. The reason for this is unclear.

Granada Bedford

The Bedford Granada extended 120 ft. across a site in St. Peter's Street with a depth of 200 ft. to Lurke Street. The site had first been spotted and leased by architect/promoter Edgar Simmons. He formed a syndicate with John Ray (a builder), L. E. Ager and a Mr. Sado to buy the site for £21,000, planning a County cinema to follow the one he had built at Hertford. This alarmed Ernest E. Blake, best known as the head of Kodak in Britain, who operated the Palace and Empire, two small, old-fashioned cinemas in Bedford. Simmons offered to form a new company with Blake to lease the County when built, together with Blake's two cinemas. But Blake preferred to go into partnership with Sidney and Cecil Bernstein to buy the site from Simmons and build a Granada

Exterior of the Granada Bedford in 1934 and the restaurant, overlooking the main foyer at right, with windows to the street at left (taken on 6 March 1957 by Photo Coverage).

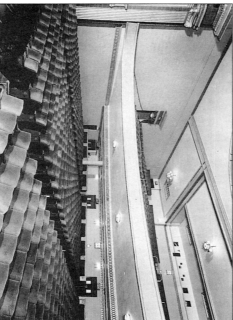

The Granada Bedford. Main foyer, entered by turning right from the outer vestibule (12 April 1965) and the rear of the auditorium (May 1950). (Photo Coverage.)

instead. Out went Simmons as an architect. In came Cecil Masey to review Simmons' scheme in April 1934. The partnership of William T. Benslyn and James Morrison were appointed to re-design the building, providing a shell to incorporate Komisar-jevksy's design for Maidstone. Bernstein Theatres also took over the management of the Palace and Empire before the Granada opened. This still left the independent Plaza (which became a Granada property, but not until 1969). No further new cinemas were built in the town until the multiplex era.

Construction started on 2 July 1934 and took five and a half months. Benslyn and Morrison, assisted by Robert Furneaux Jordan, decided to follow (or were obliged to follow) the external look established at the Granada Maidstone and Shrewsbury. However, they revised it to provide a front elevation of greater finesse and intricacy, overcoming the challenge of a straight frontage. The entrance block protruded very slightly and was faced in stone with four squared columns which engaged the wall behind and supported a pediment on which was mounted the Granada name. There were tall windows between the columns which lined up with four windows above the parade of four lock-up shops to the right of the entrance. The heads of the four windows were filled in with a fan-shaped decorative design while the words RESTAURANT – CAFÉ were mounted on the brick-work above. The café area of 77 ft. by 24 ft. was initially leased out but promoted in the cinema's advertising. The same fan decoration appeared over an arch to the other side of the entrance which had a brick infill and two small windows. This side of the building extended over a Granada Street leading to the car park at the back of the property. There was a secondary entrance to the front stalls off this private road as well as windows displaying the heating and ventilation equipment as at Maidstone.

Beyond the usual ticket hall, the main foyer, originally decorated primarily in green and gold, extended at right angles behind the row of shops rather than straight back as at Maidstone and Shrewsbury. It was narrower and longer than that of Maidstone with a grand staircase at the far end that had a long curving balustrade on each side and a large round-headed window at the top of the first flight of steps. Further steps to the right led to the restaurant, those to the left to the circle. The ceiling treatment of the foyer was different, with a small circular recess in the centre from which a chandelier was suspended.

The Bedford auditorium was publicised as being a replica of Maidstone's. It had 1690 seats, 996 in the stalls and 694 in the balcony – six more than Maidstone. In broad terms, the auditoria were identical. The variations are slight enough for a spot-the-difference competition. But here, for the record, are some of them. The architects at Bedford dispensed with serpentine rows of circle seating in favour of conventional straight curves. The

The Granada Bedford in May 1950. (Photo Coverage.)

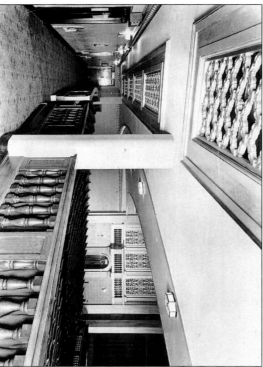

The Granada Bedford. Two further views of the auditorium in May 1950 (Photo Coverage). Note how plain these early standard Granadas looked at the back.

Above, this photograph (undated but almost certainly 1934) shows more clearly the frieze of figures high up and the design of the decorative grillework. A semi-circular spool-like pattern may just be visible within the segments of the ceiling decoration. The auditorium floor was covered in Wilton carpet of a cerise colour. The stage drapes were in old gold silk. A phantom piano linked to the organ is on the stage.

staircases into the circle again came up on each far side but here (as at Tooting and Walthamstow but for the only time in any of the standard Granadas) they were placed outside the actual auditorium, ending in a doorway set in each side wall facing the crossover. Vents in the rear corners of the balcony were placed in the ceiling rather than on the back wall. And, in the circular decoration of the front ceiling area, the space within the double outer ring was broken up into sections at Bedford.

The proscenium opening measured 54 ft. wide by 28 ft. high. The stage at Bedford was only 17 ft. deep, lacked a fly tower and was not fully equipped but could (and would) be put to full live use. The total cost of building and outfitting the theatre was given as £48,750.

The Granada Bedford opened on Saturday 15 December 1934. A fanfare of buglers from the Scots Guards was followed by the usual living tableaux of department heads at a long table, introduced to the audience by the toastmaster. Then the chairman of the County Council, Lord Ampthill, declared the theatre open. Before the big screen attraction, *The Thin Man*, came a short, the news, *The Private Life of Oliver the Eighth* (the Laurel and Hardy comedy that had been part of the first show at Sutton), and an organ recital (by Harold Betts).

This Granada got off to a good start, reporting £7,312 profit for its first year, exceeding the estimate in the prospectus. Variety was not generally featured, but organists such as Harold Ramsay and Reginald Foort were the star attractions when they played week-long engagements.

Twice in its lifetime, the Granada received giant screens. When the first of these – 25 ft. 6 ins. by 19 ft. 6 ins. – was installed in July 1937, it was said to be the largest in the Midlands. Later on, the Granada Bedford would acquire the second largest screen in the country.

7 • 1935: In And Out Of Manchester

It was to have been Granada's first venture in the North – a huge new cinema on a prime site in Manchester with a particularly elaborate interior design by Theodore Komisarjevsky lifting it well above the current series of standard Granadas, if not quite to the level of Tooting. Back in December 1934, Bernstein Theatres had clinched its deal to buy the Hippodrome in Oxford Street from Oswald Stoll and it closed on 2 March 1935 to be almost entirely demolished to form the site for the new super cinema. Jessie Matthews and Sonnie Hale laid a foundation stone on 2 September 1935. Work proceeded and then, to general surprise, it was announced that Bernstein Theatres had arranged to sell the cinema when completed to Gaumont-British and that it would open a month later as the Gaumont, not the Granada. Such switches were not unknown, but usually the big circuits took over cinemas being built by independents–in the way that Granada had taken over the Plaza Sutton.

In the case of Manchester, the official announcement given to the Press stated: "The deal has been governed by the fact that the Gaumont-British Picture Corporation have not hitherto possessed a key theatre in Manchester although they have key theatres in every other big city." The cinema was said to have cost £300,000. The price paid by Gaumont was not disclosed. (According to Tony Moss, Gaumont acquired the owning company, Granada Manchester Ltd., and Sidney Bernstein remained a director.)

The deal is not so surprising when the existing partnership of the two circuits in Denman (London) Cinemas is taken into account. They were in regular close contact and had a year earlier announced joint plans to build new cinemas at Enfield and East Ham. Gaumont certainly did need a city centre outlet and would have no difficulty programming it with its national release, while Granada may have had doubts about its ability to secure top product in competition with strong local exhibitors.

The capable architects of the building were William T. Benslyn and James Morrison, who had previously collaborated on the Granada Bedford. The tall frontage was clad in faience and had a rounded corner but did not look modern: the arches, balconies and other details were in Italian Renaissance style corresponding

to the interior (historian Richard Gray wonders if Komisarjevsky had some direct input here). There was no large window; the space above the main entrance was filled with an enormous advertising panel, 38 ft. high by 26 ft. wide, with a triple border in blue and green. This accommodated up to twelve rows of 18 in.-high letters which lit up in red, announcing the current attraction. The frontage really came alive at night, its shape accentuated by three lines of neon tubing on the canopy and two lines along the cornice. The main Gaumont sign above the panel was in red letters 4 ft. high, outlined in neon. In all, about 3,000 ft. of neon tubing was mounted on the exterior of the building. At the rear corner of the cinema down the side street, the heating and ventilation plant was again placed on public view.

The interior design by Komisarjevsky resembled that of Maidstone, Shrewsbury and Bedford but was far more lavish in detail. There was a vast double-height foyer with red non-Gaumont carpet and elaborate chandeliers. The side wall columns were richly decorated their full height. The balustrade design was distinctive and eye-catching. At the end, a curved grand staircase with gold-fluted walls led to a promenade which overlooked the main foyer for its entire length. Each arched recess was fitted with a mirror, facing the mirrors on the opposite wall of the entrance foyer – an adaptation of the hall of mirrors theme at the Granada Tooting.

The auditorium had three pierced grilles on each of the side walls, in rounded arches much larger than those at the standard Granadas so that one arch was actually within the balcony alongside the front rows of seats. The grilles had a new pattern of railings in dull gold. The first two grilles were illuminated from below by lighting concealed behind an extension of the balcony front. A fourth matching arch on each side faced the balcony cross-over and contained the main entrance/exit.

The ceiling had a coffered design with heavily moulded flower decoration, but no big central chandelier nor circular ceiling pattern – illumination came from a series of smaller fittings with ornate bases supporting an art deco "tray". The raised ceiling over the rear of the balcony had smaller, octagonal-shaped coffers.

The Gaumont Manchester.

Left: the exterior in October 1949. The advertising space between the two vertical signs had not been used since war broke out. (Courtesy of Derek Knights.)

Below: 1949 photograph of the huge foyer looking towards the outer vestibule with the street to the right. The armchairs are far too comfortable to have been designed by Komisarjevsky.

Lower left: the promenade overlooking the foyer (1949 photograph).

The wide proscenium was flanked by columns with gold high-lighted Corinthian capitals. As usual with Granadas, the walls to the back of the auditorium were plain, but looking forward – as audiences did – the general effect was sumptuous and fully the equal of the Paramount across the road.

Total seating capacity was a large (but less than colossal) 2,250. The stage was 23 ft. deep with a proscenium opening of 50 ft. The projection room extended over the rear balcony with a throw of 132 ft., using Ross machines adapted to Western Electric Wide Range sound equipment. In the basement was the Long Bar, the only part of the cinema treated in a contemporary style and at 60 ft. the longest licensed bar in the North of England, plus a buffet restaurant. Refreshments were also available from the balcony foyer, above the entrance.

The Gaumont Manchester. Undated views of the auditorium in the wide screen era. The front rows of stalls seating have been removed, and acoustic tiles and stereophonic sound speakers have been placed on the blank areas of the side walls.

For a later alternative view of the exterior, with the advertisement panel over the entrance reinstated, and for views of the grand staircase in the foyer (circa 1960) and of the auditorium to the rear (1949), see pages 75 and 149 of Gaumont British Cinemas in this series of circuit histories.

8 • 1936: Start Of "A New Chain"

At the beginning of 1936, Granada announced a new expansion programme: the company would be building eight new cinemas during the year. By September 1936, the number of forthcoming cinemas had shot up to fourteen. By October, another two had been added. They involved a number of architects who had not worked for Granada before as well one further assignment for Cecil Masey and three involving James Morrison (previously partnered with William T. Benslyn on the cinemas at Bedford and Manchester).

Only nine of the sixteen schemes went ahead. The Granada Wandsworth Road (Vauxhall) was completed during 1936; the Century Cheam and Granadas Woolwich, North Cheam, Greenwich, Harrow, Clapham Junction and Greenford all followed during 1937. The Granada Welling arrived in 1938.

Among the seven dropped was a Granada for Bow Road or Mile End in the East End of London. There seem to have been two schemes for this area, one replacing the circuit's Electrodrome and another elsewhere. Nicholas and Dixon-Spain were appointed architects for one of the sites (possibly both). The schemes had been dropped by September 1938.

Plans for a cinema at Plumstead Common swelled from seating 1,200 in January 1936 to 3,000 in October of that year before it was never heard of again (as co-owners with Bernstein of the smaller Kinema in Plumstead itself, Gaumont-British cannot have been enthusiastic about it). Granadas were also envisaged for Enfield Wash and Gidea Park (the latter seating 1,500), but further details have not emerged.

More is known about a proposal for a Granada at Woking, Surrey. Designed by James Morrison with 1,750 seats, a café-restaurant, car park, stage facilities and eight dressing rooms, it was said to be opening in the autumn of 1936 if plans were passed. At the same time, the Union circuit acquired a site in Woking and built the Ritz which opened in April 1937. Union's rapid progress may have prompted Granada to drop its scheme.

Two 1,500 seat Granadas at Woodford, Essex, and East Molesey, Surrey, were still under consideration when World War Two made further progress impossible. They were listed on company notepaper as being "under construction" although no work beyond fencing off the sites and displaying an announcement was carried out.

The Woodford cinema was apparently sited at Buckhurst Hill. The East Molesey scheme (sometimes described as being at Hampton Court) is better documented. The site had attracted a lot of interest towards the end of 1936. The owner – a Mrs. Marcus – talked to Odeon and Union as well as Granada, which offered cash to clinch the deal, subject to the "usual qualifications" about obtaining planning and licensing consent. Architects H. B. Horner and Leslie C. Norton received instructions to draw up plans on 21 October 1936 and made their first inspection of the site three days later. They started detailed planning of the cinema in November 1936 in parallel with their work on the site at Clapham Junction.

The architects developed at least two schemes for East Molesey, one of which provided 1,500 seats. By May 1937, Theodore Komisarjevsky had completed an interior scheme and was informed by Sidney Bernstein that this would be one of four cinemas opening between August and November of that year. When the Granada Clapham Junction opened in early November 1937, the Granada East Molesey was advertised as following shortly but Horner and Norton did no further work on it after 4 December of that year. In June 1938, a sign at the site declared that a Granada would be coming but a company official visited the area and reported that it offered poor prospects with many empty shops and flats and many houses for sale. This pessimistic view was reinforced by another head office inspection at the end of October 1938 which found "the place is very dead" and noted "an entire absence of mass population around the theatre", declaring that it would need a larger car park than the site allowed to draw in sufficient patrons with automobiles. In this respect, the best opportunity lay in drawing people from the Esher Road direction but the report warned that, once in their cars, patrons could decide to go to any number of cinemas. In 1946, the hoarding was still up, but used to display posters of programmes at the nearby Kingston Granada. The site was still held in October 1950.

Additionally, in 1936, Granada took over a huge site at the

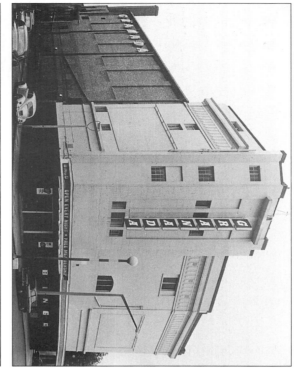

Granada Willesden, formerly the Empire. Exterior, circa 1970. The oldest brickwork on the lower side wall is darker and a line of windows has been filled in. The lighter brickwork above dates from the 1927 reconstruction, along with most of the lofty frontage. Note the two blank panels, once used for advertising the programmes, and, higher up, the decorative frieze which has been painted over. Patrons climbed steps to reach the paybox, then turned right to enter a wide foyer with a staircase at the far end leading up to a corridor under the circle. A tall mirror over the doors from the outer lobby created an illusion of a much larger space. In this 20 March 1957 photograph, the ceiling light fittings are in the Komisarjevsky style. The auditorium, seen left in January 1950, is modern but unremarkable, and has undergone a bizarre decorative treatment of diagonal lines, vertical stripes and fairground tent emblem above the proscenium arch. (Bottom left and top right from Photo Coverage.)

GRANĀDA

GRAND OPENING TO-NIGHT

WANDSWORTH ROAD at VAUXHALL

YOUR NEW WONDER THEATRE

WHERE THE CLOCK TOWER USED TO BE

TUESDAY, OCTOBER 13 at 7.30 p.m.

By SYDNEY HOWARD

FAMOUS BRITISH FILM STAR (In Person)

THEN DAILY FROM NOON

GRACIE FIELDS

QUEEN of HEARTS (U)

LEW AYRES

TRAPPED BY WIRELESS (A)

★ HARRY FARMER—The Radio Star at the MIGHTY WURLITZER ★

2,500 ARMCHAIR SEATS

ADMISSION PRICES:
STALLS: 6d. 9d. 1/- · CIRCLE 1/3, 1/6
Before 3 p.m.
ALL STALLS 6d. CIRCLE 9d. 1/-
REDUCED PRICES FOR CHILDREN
.... pass the door

BUSES: 77, 77a TRAMS: 26, 28

OPEN SUNDAYS at 5 o'clock
COMPLETE CHANGE of PROGRAM

Opening advertisement for the Granada Wandsworth Road. The earliest available photographs date from its re-opening in September 1949 after extensive war-time bomb damage had been repaired. These are featured in Chapter 13.

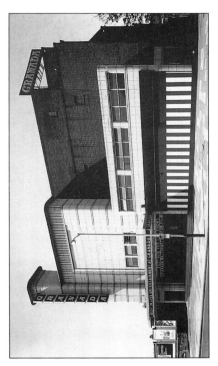

The Granada East Ham, little altered on 20 May 1975 when it was only in use as an occasional live entertainment venue. (Photo Coverage.)

corner of Holloway Road and Tufnell Park Road in North London for which they paid American architect C. Howard Crane the sum of £250 for design work on a cinema to seat 3,000. This site had been optioned as far back as 1930 by the Astoria circuit for an addition to their major halls at Brixton, Streatham, Old Kent Road and nearby Finsbury Park. In September-October 1936, Granada sold Crane's plans at cost to Gaumont Super Cinemas, the partnership of Gaumont-British and Hyams & Gale. The Gaumont Holloway opened to Crane's design in September 1938 and is operating today as the Odeon.*

Before any more new cinemas opened, Granada carried out a major remodelling of the Empire Willesden in ten weeks, just nine years after its last reconstruction. At that time, the balcony had been added and the exterior had acquired its ugly, top-heavy appearance. Now architect James Morrison gave it a more modern but undistinguished look, both inside and out, as Komisarjevksy was not brought in. This upgrading qualified the building to re-open with the Granada name on 21 September 1936, the first time it had been applied to a Bernstein theatre of the earlier era.

Granada Wandsworth Road

The first cinema to be opened by the circuit for nearly two years, the Granada Wandsworth Road was described as "the first of a new chain". Replacing the Clock Tower Cinema which Bernstein Theatres had booked for at least a couple of years before buying it for demolition, the theatre was launched on the Tuesday evening of 13 October 1936 by the comedian Sydney Howard, with Sally Eilers and Rod la Rocque also present. The usual routine of the curtains opening on a bare stage was employed, and the usual exaggeration of seating figures inflated 2,056 seats into 2,500.

There were hundreds of spectators outside the cinema and a full house inside. The film attraction was Gracie Fields' *Queen of Hearts*, which was playing at many other South London cinemas that week, supported here by a B feature *Trapped by Wireless* and an interlude on the mighty Wurlitzer.

The new Granada had nearly three times the seating capacity of its predecessor. It seemed out on a limb in the drab Wandsworth Road, amid working-class houses, gasworks, railway lines and industrial sites. "It will considerably brighten the two-mile road. And how Wandsworth Road needs brightening!" commented *The South London Press* (9 October 1936).

* Granada was still the landlord in the 1970s – booking controller Bob Morgan remembers being sent to assess its takings when a rent review was due. For the same reason, he also visited another Gaumont circuit cinema, the Grange Kilburn, which at some unknown point fell under Granada ownership although it was never operated by the company.

In fact, it was far enough away from other cinemas, including those of Wandsworth itself, to count as a solo situation, giving it access from the first to all the major circuit releases. But this did not count as an advantage in the long run, as it simply wasn't part of an entertainment or shopping centre and had to rely on a very local audience.

It was the only cinema ever built to the design of E. D. Lyons, L. Israel and C. H. Elsom, and was among the first works of the team who had launched their careers in 1934 by winning a competition for Wolverhampton Town Hall and Assembly Rooms. The front elevation, in rustic fletton facing bricks, had blue faience tiles in columns between deeply recessed windows and blue concrete paint on the sign and canopy. The extensive use of blue was somewhat unusual. Neon strips were placed in the horizontal string courses and on the vertical piers to dramatise the building at night.

The site sloped away and audiences had to descend a flight of steps to reach the inner foyer. This created a "rather depressing" effect, according to a former projectionist, Barry Haigh.

The main foyer and auditorium were arranged in the standard manner with a staircase at the far side of the inner foyer and a promenade under the balcony. Entry to the circle was through doors in the side walls rather than within the balcony.

The decorative scheme in the foyer and auditorium was completely different. Komisarjevsky was not involved. Presumably the architects were responsible for the pattern of coffered squares on the walls to each side of the proscenium opening: some of these contained the organ grilles, and Frank Dobson, a well-known sculptor who had been a member of the committee of the Film Society along with Sidney Bernstein, was commissioned to provide the decorative motifs of various musical instruments in gold leaf and Chinese lacquer – representing the different phases of organ music – that occupied eighteen of the red and silver panels on each side. (Dobson had contributed to the 1927 rebuilding of the Empire Willesden and also created a bust of Sidney, which was displayed outside his office in Golden Square, Soho, along with photographs of himself and Cecil Bernstein.)

Although there was a fully-equipped stage, this Granada did not feature any variety, not even on the opening night. Granada's publicity director, Ewart Hodgson, told *The South London Press*: "We want first to test the reaction of our audience before we decide definitely whether to put on stage shows or not. If they want stage shows, then they'll probably get them. If not..." It was, of course, cheaper to see if the cinema could operate without any variety. Amateur talent contests and stage novelties such as a dart championship contest were featured, but the live facilities seem not to have been put to full use.

Granada East Ham

The Granada East Ham was opened on the Monday evening of 30 November 1936 by the comedian Sydney Howard, six weeks after he had performed the same function at Wandsworth Road. Here he arrived in a gilded coach pulled by four horses, accompanied by the Mayor of East Ham. The usual trick opening ceremony took place with scarlet curtains parting to the sound of a trumpet fanfare to reveal a bare stage. Sydney Howard was an apt choice as he starred in the opening week's attraction, *Fame*. This had a co-feature, *The Singing Kid*, and variety featuring acrobats The Great Magyars, comedians Murray and Moore, the American dance company of Gracie Schenck, plus Bobbie Howell and His Band. There was also a Wurlitzer organ.

This was not part of the new circuit Granada was developing but a new hall for the Denman (London) circuit, co-owned with Gaumont, replacing the old Kinema which closed in late May 1936. Sidney Bernstein had been acquiring property behind the Kinema since February 1929 with a view to building a much bigger cinema. Architect W. Sydney Trent, working for his father, Gaumont chief architect W. E. Trent, discussed rebuilding with Sidney Bernstein in March 1933 and provided plans for his approval that same month. Apparently unhappy at the capacity shown, Bernstein turned to his own architect, Cecil Masey, who drew up plans in July 1933 to extend the existing building further back to St. John's Road behind, producing a seating capacity of 2,922 (1,548 stalls and 1,374 balcony), but this scheme foundered. Reconstruction, which had been scheduled to commence on 6 November 1933 with the first steelwork arriving the following month, was postponed. W. Sydney Trent worked on a new scheme. In August 1934 came the public announcement of the rebuilding of the Kinema along with the Rialto Enfield, with a new Granada to open in October 1935 at East Ham. Work finally started on 25 May 1936, with W. E. Trent designing the building and W. Sydney Trent taking charge of the interior decoration. This would be the only one of the Denman halls to be completely rebuilt.

Trent's main elevation offered a slimmer version of the tower he had provided for the Gaumont Bromley. The Granada name was set on each side of a vertical fin that projected above the flat top of the tower. The name was in red lettering on a white background, with red neon and three lines of green neon on the outer edge of the fin. The letters in the Granada name lined up between horizontal bands that carried neon tubes across the light-coloured tiles covering the tower and across the frontage above the main entrance.

The area above the entrance had a very slight recess but was curiously blank apart from a row of three small windows hidden from view by the canopy, suggesting that it might have been

The Granada East Ham. Foyer shots from time of opening. Note the armchair, clearly not by Komisarjevsky, and the wireless at the foot of the stairs.
The views of the auditorium show the different treatment

of the ceiling. View forward (displaying CinemaScope screen) dates from 20 January 1972, to rear from June 1960 (both from Photo Coverage). Two further photographs are in Gaumont British Cinemas, page 80.

originally designed to display programme information. As the cinema lacked a café (being outside a main shopping centre), no windows were required on that account. A two-storey extension of three shop units filled in the rest of the street frontage. A roof sign giving the Granada name faced east along Barking Road, mounted on the corner of the auditorium block. (The only other Granada property that seems to have displayed a roof sign was, apparently, Sutton.)

In August 1936, W. Sydney Trent produced various designs in a "modern" style that had been agreed with Sidney Bernstein. But Bernstein decided on a "classical" look. He disapproved of several submissions by Trent, who arranged for an outside company, Maples, to provide some further ideas. Sidney turned to Komisarjevsky, whom he had probably wanted all along, leaving Trent to complain in writing: "You took the matter out of my hands without either explanation or apology". Describing himself "in complete disagreement" with Komisarjevsky's scheme and hesitant about attending the opening, Trent informed Bernstein, "It must be made perfectly clear that I am not responsible for the interior decorations." Bernstein responded with a soothing letter. No one received credit for the work in the opening programme.

The interior of the cinema resembled a standard Granada but the variations in Komisarjevsky's decorative scheme were not an improvement.

There was a low outer foyer where payboxes were placed against the sides rather than as windows set into the walls. Patrons proceeded forward into the main foyer which extended off to the right. Access to the balcony was by a staircase at the far end. This led to a promenade at first floor level with doors at each end bringing patrons into the balcony as usual at the crossover. Mirrors on the back wall of the promenade lined up with mirrors on the facing wall of the main foyer, as at Manchester.

Although the auditorium fell short of Masey's figure, it still seated a hefty 2,468 (2,700 was claimed) – over a thousand more than the old Kinema, and the largest capacity of any Granada after Tooting, Walthamstow and Clapham Junction. The aim seems to have been to exceed the 2,408 seats of the local Gaumont hall, the Premier Super. The depth of the auditorium forced Komisarjevsky to vary his handling of the ceiling decoration. The main chandelier – of the usual standard Granada design but smaller in size – was placed further back with a reduced amount of decoration (here octagonally-shaped) above it. The rest of the ceiling was left plain except for coffering at the front and side edges. Two small chandeliers were suspended from coffers in each front corner. At the back of the circle on each side a further small chandelier was hung from a domed recess with rosettes.

The three pierced grilles on each splay wall were of a different (but similar) pattern to those in earlier Granadas, painted dark on a light background rather than the reverse. The pilasters between the grilles were not ornamented but left plain, and no figures appeared on the frieze. The grilles here stopped far short of the balcony front, adding to the expanse of plain side wall. All told, this was a thinner, weaker variation on the standard scheme.

One false economy was putting the sound system from the old Kinema into the new Granada. It was acknowledged to be very poor in a head office note in the autumn of 1938.

The Granada seems to have had limited parking facilities which were improved by the opening of a new car park for 200 vehicles at the end of 1938.

At this theatre, variety would heavily featured as a major part of the programme to overcome film booking problems and to compete with the East Ham Palace music hall.

9 • 1937: Add Seven

This was the peak year for the opening of new Granadas as part of the expansion announced in early 1936. Further locations were explored. In March 1937, Granada (Neasden) Ltd. and Granada (Ponders End) Ltd. were registered as subsidiaries, but no Granada cinemas ever materialised at Neasden (near Willesden) and Ponders End (near Enfield) although architects Nicholas and Dixon-Spain drew up plans for the latter site.

In the summer of 1937, Granada made a surprising announcement that it was planning a cinema with a seating capacity of 2,500 in far-off Swansea in Wales. This scheme was being designed by Lyons, Israel and Elsom (who had handled Wandsworth Road) but seems to have been quickly dropped.

At the same time, Granada revealed that it had taken over a scheme drawn up some time previously by American architect C. Howard Crane at Slough, Berkshire. This did come to fruition.

Turning to the seven cinemas that opened during this year, there could not have been a greater contrast than between the first two to be completed, the Century Cheam Village and the Granada Woolwich.

Century Cheam Village

This small cinema ("Intimate But Luxurious") was planned for second-run showings of "Great Films You Intended To See". Opened by Tom Walls on 22 March 1937, it seems to have been an experiment to find out whether this kind of cinema was viable. It also ventured into the art house market with foreign subtitled films.

Economically designed by James Morrison, the Century had a plain frontage that included a vertical name sign on one side. "Century" became the standard name applied to lesser cinemas. (Granada were not the first to use the name: a substantial and well-designed Century cinema had been opened in Clacton, Essex, in May 1936 by a small circuit called 20th Century Cinemas.)

The Cheam property had a simple but pleasing auditorium with a small balcony. It was said to seat 1,001, but the capacity was probably another exaggeration. There was a small car park. Morrison was also assigned to the company's full-size Granada at Cheam, being built out of the town centre on the London Road.

Granada Woolwich

The Granada Woolwich opened on 20 April 1937 with the usual rigmarole of the creative and building team pausing to be introduced while hard at work on the stage. The celebrity guests were Glenda Farrell and Claude Hulbert. Reginald Dixon, prominently billed as "The Ace of Radio Organists", was at the Wurlitzer. Will Hay, star of the opening attraction, *Good Morning, Boys!*, made an appearance on the second night and his comedy partner and co-star Graham Moffatt followed on the third.

The cinema was up against extensive competition in a major concentration of working class population in Southeast London, and this seems to have dictated a more lavish treatment than that applied to the standard Granadas. Komisarjevsky provided a variation on his Gothic treatment at Tooting.

With 2,434 seats, the Granada Woolwich was much smaller than Tooting and had slightly fewer seats than the recently opened Granada East Ham. By the mid-Thirties, the major circuits shied away from the period look; but big independent cinema operators like the Bernsteins, Hyams & Gale and the Greens of Glasgow still believed that highly ornate, neo-classical interiors in their really large cinemas would best impress the masses – as at the Hyams' State Kilburn (1937), Green's Playhouse Dundee (1936) and the Granada Woolwich. In each case, however, they chose a modern exterior.

At Woolwich, Sidney Bernstein probably knew that the Odeon circuit had acquired the site directly opposite and this may have influenced him to demand a striking front elevation – which was devised by Reginald H. Uren, although Cecil Masey was the over-all architect. As at the Phoenix, Masey seems to have been given outside help whether he wanted it or not.

When the Odeon opened six months after the Granada, it boasted one of George Coles' boldest and most eye-catching exteriors in cream-yellow faience. The Granada responded with a curved brick frontage that had a huge slab tower near the far end. This carried the name of the cinema vertically on the sides and encased a glass fin which lit up at night (the Odeon opposite boasted another fin, which lit up on its outer edge). The tower seems to have been suggested by Joseph Emberton's tower for

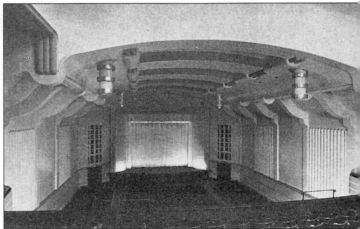

The Century Cheam Village. The exterior had not changed significantly when the view top left was taken on 8 December 1953. The canopy lettering was originally dark on a light background but this has been reversed. An advertising display blocks the central window above the canopy. The space next to the theatre had been used only for advertising hoardings since the cinema was built.

The entrance hall and foyer shots (also 1953) show the paybox in the usual position on a side wall by the front doors and rubber floor mats. The foyer may well have just been redecorated.
(All three: Photo Coverage.)
The auditorium shot is reproduced from a 1937 trade paper and shows the simpler kind of light fittings used, compared to Granadas.

Green's Playhouse Dundee, opened a year earlier (another case where a cinema architect collaborated with a noted outsider who provided the key exterior feature) – although Richard Gray points out to me that Uren was much influenced by the Dutch architect Willem Dudok. Elain Harwood notes some similarity to the tower built by Uren at Hornsey Town Hall, his first and most influential work. Gray suggests that this specifically *brick* fin was also probably inspired by Julian Leathart's Dreamland Margate.

The frontage at Woolwich was tied together by a very narrow canopy that carried programme details on its front edge and extended forward over the main entrance doors. Above the canopy, five tall recessed windows admitted daylight into the café-restaurant area while, at the top, the Granada name was wedged between two narrow bands of stonework in a manner reminiscent of the way the Gaumont Palace name had been placed at Wood Green, Lewisham and elsewhere.

"The Granada Woolwich London England – The Most Romantic Theatre Ever Built" claimed the front cover of the souvenir brochure, price tuppence. This Granada did not outclass Tooting – but it was very definitely in the same league, achieving the same awe-inspiring impact on cinemagoers. Were it not for Tooting, its auditorium would be the master achievement of the circuit.

Komisarjevksy called his interior scheme "Continental Gothic". He wrote an introductory essay for the brochure, entitled "Down the Centuries to Granada", explaining his choice of style. His concluding argument for adopting an ecclesiastical look is interesting. This is the entire piece:

"The style of decoration I employed for the Granada Woolwich is Gothic. The word 'Gothic' comes from the name of an ancient people known as the Goths. The Goths were direful, hairy, unwashed, bellicose ruffians. In their crude buildings we find the first suggestions of what is known nowadays as Gothic architecture. Various peoples in the East, less direful than the Goths and not so hairy and unwashed, stole some of their architectural ideas and embodied them in their own temples and palaces.

"The Mussulmans and the Byzantines adapted the eastern architectural achievements to their tastes and needs. The Crusaders on one side and the Moors on the other acquainted Europe with the beauty of Mahommedan buildings, and the medieval knights and barons, as well as the medieval churchmen, adapted the eastern architecture to their tastes and needs.

"Later on, when interest in Roman and Greek civilization was spreading throughout Italy, certain 'classic' elements began to be incorporated in the canons of medieval architecture.

"Everyone knows that there were no proper theatrical buildings at the times described, and it may seem absurd that I selected the Italian Gothic style, used mostly in churches, to decorate the interior of the Granada Woolwich.

The Granada Woolwich. Opening night advertisement – note the usherette with service with a smile motto. For an exterior see the opening page of this book.

Below: the island paybox with main entrance doors reflected in mirror behind and doors leading to foyer in background (11 June 1965, Photo Coverage.)

"I had to adapt to modern tastes and needs what the unshaven and unwashed Goths invented, and what the Mussulmans, the Byzantines, the medieval barons and priests and the Italians, adapted to their tastes and needs. It goes without saying that those people had not the slightest notion of the necessity of the air in public buildings being 'laundered in synthetic mountain streams' or having to feed the 'thousands of pipes and twenty thousand other parts' that go to make up the 'mighty Wurlitzer organ.'

"It was a laborious job to achieve all the necessary adaptations, but I thought it very worth while. The public that comes, as I hear, even from the Malay States to see the Granada Woolwich is, I hope, in agreement with me. If there are a few grumblers who think that a 'church style' doesn't suit a theatre, I'd like to point out to them that not only during the Gothic period in Europe, but before it in the Renaissance and Baroque times on the continent, the architectural decorations of churches did not differ greatly from those of places of amusement.

"Houses of worship were not intended to be like cold and dismal drill halls or mortuaries. They were not meant to depress people. Churches were designed for 'religious shows' which had the same origin as the shows of 'secular theatre.' The aim of ecclesiastical architecture was to attract people, to offer them not only rows of pews in which to say their prayers but romantic relaxation and artistic pleasure amid surroundings of hope, colourful beauty and harmony."

In her book *Sidney Bernstein*, Caroline Moorehead relates how Komisarjevsky and Bernstein did not like the original colour scheme: "Komisarjevsky had chosen a set of colours based on early church manuscripts with lines of gold, grey and red. At nine o'clock, two nights before the cinema was due to open, the two men went to watch the ceiling scaffolding come down. They stood together in the aisle, staring up at an overpowering impression of green. Finally Sidney said: 'Let's go.' They drove, in silence, to the Savoy where they ordered two large whiskies. They both knew that the ceiling was wrong. Next day, the scaffolding went back up; thirty-six hours later the Granada Woolwich opened, looking very different (and giving birth to the legend that Sidney disliked the colour green)."

In *The Picture Palace* (1969), the first British historical survey of cinemas, Dennis Sharp wrote of the Granada Woolwich, by then a bingo hall: "Externally this large building – seating 3,000 people – gives little indication of its exotic interior. It has a plain curved brickwork street frontage with a tower feature, a canopy and simple Granada lettering. The first visual shock comes to the patrons after paying their money and entering the foyer. Out of this space a staircase, decorated with golden gothic arches on the wall behind the landing and lit from concealed floods, leads up to the circle and restaurant. Once up at balcony level the patron could at one time either go into the restaurant or through the puce and pink Moorish 'hall of mirrors' (now a casino) to the auditorium, the decorative climax itself. Inside, the heavy arches are prominent and the complexity of colour, contour, lighting and detailing still draw the astonished 'ahs' and 'ughs' when the house lights go up. One unusual feature at stalls level is the carved wooden balustrade that runs around three sides of the auditorium for the use of standees. At one time, amid all this artificial splendour, Reginald Dixon rumbled out his popular melodies on the mighty Wurlitzer."

In his book *Cathedrals of the Movies* (1980), David Atwell comments: "[Komisarjevsky's] main entrance foyer is rather indeterminate, with an alarming mixture of modern and Renaissance motifs. It wants to be a baronial Grand Hall, but it does not quite succeed. A fine double-flight staircase with a delicate wrought-iron balustrade has Gothic arches on the landing wall and leads to a circle lobby which, as at Tooting, is in the style of a long cloister, though here suggesting the Moorish style rather than Gothic. It is also wider with an aisle, but its flat pitched ceiling, and mirrors to one side only rob it of the reflective impact of Tooting. ... Into the Venetian Gothic auditorium, and the space is closely modelled on Tooting. Slightly smaller, overall, the detail has become somewhat coarsened, perhaps through a need for more economy in 1937 than 1931, but it is still undeniably most impressive. The ceiling is not coffered, being divided by beams, and the side walls are dominated by great doorways reminiscent of the Porta della Carta at the Doge's Palace in the way they are handled, though there are stronger echoes of the 13th and 14th-century Gothic style, and motifs from the great portals of the cathedrals at Amiens, Bourges, Rouen and Lyons can all be identified. Lyons is the closest source but Komisarjevsky, with cavalier disregard for niceties of style, inserts a rounded Romanesque arch under the pointed canopy. The proscenium is narrower and more vertical in proportion, but the cusped pendants are similar to Tooting."

The entrance to the Granada could have been at the tower end of the façade: this would have provided more direct access to the auditorium, but the actual position enabled it to confront the Odeon entrance as directly as possible and led patrons through a more extensive foyer area.

In the low outer foyer, there was an island paybox rather than ticket windows in the side wall. The main foyer, to the right, had chandeliers in a very similar style to those at Tooting and medieval figures displayed in panels at the upper end of the "Grand Staircase", on each side. These were devised, like the similar figures at Tooting, by Vladimir Polunin. The inner hall stood in an awkward relationship to the auditorium. The stalls could be entered

Grand Staircase leading to the Hall of Mirrors

Café-Restaurant on the Foyer Balcony

On the Balcony overlooking the Foyer

The Hall of Mirrors

The Granada Woolwich. Images from the opening brochure (in author's collection): the main foyer with grand staircase; the café-restaurant over the main entrance with island paybox

just visible downstairs; figures attributed to Vladimir Polunin in panels at the top of the grand staircase; and the hall of mirrors.

The Proscenium from the Circle

A glimpse of Granada sple

In the Stalls

The Granada Woolwich. Further images from the opening brochure: the auditorium; the side wall decoration; the rear stalls area, showing the raised promenade along the side wall. Lower right: a later view of the balcony (22 June 1965, Photo Coverage.)

fairly easily through double doors to the left of the grand staircase. But this grand staircase was too short to match the epic
scale of the auditorium and took patrons in a roundabout route
to the balcony instead of leading them directly there as at
Tooting. Equally, patrons had to turn back to reach the restaurant
and Richard Gray in *Cinemas in Britain* (1996) points to the
"collision" between the foyer decoration and the streamlined
façade windows in the café area over the entrance.

Circle patrons arrived at a hall of mirrors underneath the
balcony and took the staircases at each end, entering the auditorium alongside the side walls. At Tooting and Walthamstow,
cinemagoers entered the balcony from outside – a slightly more
impressive arrangement.

The auditorium gives the impression of being much taller than
that of Tooting, partly because of the way the ceiling steps up
and is arched over the balcony. However, the balcony has far
fewer rows than Tooting and the auditorium, seen from the back,
lacks the overpowering scale of Tooting. Gothic panels placed
diagonally across the front corners of the balcony cover the
narrowing of the building but have less impact than the massive
arches at Tooting and are purely decorative instead of being
entrances. Cecil Masey's signature is in the undulating rows of
balcony seating.

Woolwich had a full working stage with a depth of 28 ft., a
proscenium opening of 48 ft., a height of 30 ft., and a grid height
of 65 ft.

Granada North Cheam

This Granada had what the *Kine Weekly* called "one of the
snappiest opening ceremonies ever staged" on the evening of
Wednesday 22 September 1937. "The band of the Royal Marines
played before the opening and provided a fanfare which
preceded the entrance of the Dagenham Girl Pipers, who piped
Jessie Matthews and Sonnie Hale on the stage through the
auditorium." Hale made a few light-hearted remarks and Matthews
declared the cinema open. In less than four minutes the first film
was on the screen. Shown that night were the Astaire-Rogers
musical *Shall We Dance?* and B feature *Clarence* with Lloyd
Thomas performing a novelty item on the Wurlitzer, fitting the
story of the theatre's construction in rhyme to a medley of
popular tunes.

The Granada stood on the London Road between Morden and
Epsom with Sutton the big entertainment centre close by to the
south east (where, of course, Granada operated the huge Plaza).

This was an instance of a cinema being built in anticipation of
a later development. Usually, this meant housing estates that
would provide a big enough audience base. At North Cheam,
the Granada anticipated an extension of the Northern Line Under-

*The Granada North Cheam. Exterior in Spring 1938.
Note the café entrance to the left of the main entrance.
A vertical name design was added over the exits at the
far end of the facade before the Second World War.
(Author's collection.)*

*View of ticket hall dates from 6 May 1965 and shows a
loudspeaker above the inner set of doors to greet patrons
with light music. (Photo Coverage.)*

For view of main foyer, see picture facing title page.

GRANADA · London Road GRANADA · London Road
NORTH CHEAM   NORTH CHEAM

NEXT WEEK'S PROGRAM

Monday, Sept. 27, for Six days

ELEANOR POWELL
JAMES STEWART, UNA MERKEL
VIRGINIA BRUCE
"BORN TO DANCE" Ⓤ

PAUL MUNI, MIRIAM HOPKINS
"THE WOMAN
BETWEEN" Ⓐ

At the Mighty Wurlitzer
LLOYD THOMAS
Famous Broadcasting Organist

Sunday, Sept. 26, from 5 o'c

Ray Milland, Dorothy Lamour in
"JUNGLE PRINCESS" Ⓐ
Edward Everett Horton
and the "Pixilated Sisters"
"LET'S MAKE A MILLION" Ⓤ

WHAT GRANADA STANDS FOR

We felt that the rapid expansion and ever increasing importance of North Cheam and the surrounding districts demanded a theatre of the calibre of Granada.

In the world of entertainment the name Granada has come to be regarded as a guarantee of outstanding entertainment and . . . Service With a Smile.

We welcome you.

THE WONDER THEATRE OF 1937

Program

GRANADA · SERVICE

HOURS OF OPENING   Weekdays: Continuous performance from 2 o'clock. Sundays from 5.30 (open 5 o'clock) with a complete change of program.

ADMISSION PRICES –
Stalls, 9d   1 - 1 3   Circle, 1 6   Loges, 2 -
Children accompanied by adults –
Stalls, 6d, 9d   Circle, 9d.   Loges, 1 -

BARGAIN MATINEE PRICES before 3.30 p.m.

CHILDREN'S MATINEES   Specially selected program at 10 o'clock every Saturday morning. Admission 3d. Tickets may be purchased in advance.

CAFE – Open daily from 2 o'clock; Sundays from 4 o'clock. Teas, light refreshments. Really good English food . . . perfect service . . . pleasant surroundings . . . and sensible prices.

MIGHTY WURLITZER ORGAN – Designed and specially built for the Granada, its versatility ranges from a full symphony orchestra to a Chinese tom-tom. There are nearly 2,000 pipes, the smallest half-an-inch in length, the largest 16, feet.

ORGANIST – At the console during this week is Lloyd Thomas, one of the greatest Cinema Organists in the world.

VENTILATION – Even the air you breathe is "laundered" in a synthetic mountain stream before it enters Granada. The Weather Control Station provides the theatre with two million cubic feet of washed air every hour. First it is drawn into a special chamber, then washed in the water purifier, then heated or cooled as necessary, and finally filtered through a screen. Believe it or not, a bucket of mud is extracted from the air even on the sunniest of days.

DECORATIONS M. Theodore Komisarjevsky, for many years director of the Moscow Art Theatre and now London's greatest stage producer, is the artist responsible for Granada's interior decorations. The style is Italian Renaissance.

CAR PARK with room for more than 300 cars. Nominal parking fees 6d for a car, 3d for a motor-cycle dispense with the irritating onus of gratuities.

CLOAKROOMS Free of charge for all patrons, in the main foyer.

EARPHONES For the hard of hearing, obtainable at the main foyer cloakroom without charge

TELEPHONE There is a public call box in the foyer

GRATUITIES – Are always embarrassing – please don't offer them. The staff are instructed not to accept or expect them.

SUGGESTIONS Tell us how we can improve the Granada. We welcome constructive criticism and will pay £1 for the first written suggestion adopted each week from now until the end of October.

INFORMATION Telephone SUTTON 122 day or night

TO-DAY'S · PROGRAM

(SEPTEMBER 23, 24, 25)

GRANADA SOUND NEWS

CLARENCE

A Paramount Picture
Directed by George Archainbaud

The Players: Clarence Smith ... ... Roscoe Ka...
Cora Wheeler ... ... Eleanore Whit...
Mr. Wheeler ... ... Eugene Palle...
Bobbie Wheeler ... ... Johnny Dow...
Violet Pinney ... ... Charlotte Wynt...
Mrs. Weeler ... ... Spring Byingt...
Della ... ... Inez Courts...
Dinwiddie ... ... Richard Pow...
Herman Tobias ... ... Theodor Von ...

ORGAN RECITAL

presented by
LLOYD THOMAS
The Famous Broadcasting Organist

SHALL WE DANCE?

A Radio Picture
Directed by Mark Sandrich
Music by George Gershwin

The Players: Petrov ... ... Fred Asta...
Linda Keene ... ... Ginger Rog...
Jeffrey Baird ... Edward Everett Hor...
Cecil Flintridge ... ... Eric Ble...
Arthur Miller ... ... Jerome Cow...
Lady Tarrington ... ... Ketti Ga...
Jim Montgomery ... ... William Brisc...
Harriett Hoctor

The Granada North Cheam. Facing page: opening programme
(BFI – Sidney Bernstein Collection); café-restaurant (which extended
behind the windows for the entire length of the frontage) and balcony
foyer with mirrors, both from Spring 1938 (author's collection). The
opening programme is set in the Rockwell typeface used by the
company in leaflets and brochures from this period to the early Fifties.
Rockwell is the typeface adopted for this book.

Above: the auditorium on 6 May 1965, showing the enriched ceiling
decoration (with some signs of water stains) and the new design of
side wall grilles (Photo Coverage).

The Granada North Cheam. Top: the ashlar effect is still retained in the plain areas of the splay walls but further back is replaced with a new pattern. Spring 1938 photograph.

View looking back dates from June 1964 and shows the decoration of the rear ceiling area (Photo Coverage).

ground from Morden to Sutton which never took place. The cinema entrance was even turned to face the proposed station site. Left in a somewhat isolated position, the Granada was never a top money-earner and its huge first floor café (75 ft. long by 23 ft. wide) was short-lived. The site as a whole was unusually spacious. The building was set back and there was room for over 200 vehicles in the largest car park on the circuit.

The building of this cinema was marked by tragedy. James Morrison was the architect. He had been an assistant on the Gaumont Palace Lewisham, then teamed up with William T. Benslyn to work on the Granadas at Bedford and Manchester, and other cinemas. Setting up on his own, he had handled the remodelling of Willesden, the new Century at Cheam Village and the aborted Granada Woking as well as North Cheam. But David Nye replaced Morrison in circumstances recalled by Richard Gray in his *Picture House* article "David Nye – Cinema Architect of the Thirties": "Nye had been called in by Bernstein following the suicide of the original architect, James Morrison, after the side wall of the cinema had been built in the wrong position and condemned by the local fire department. Nye did some replanning and, as the project was late due to Morrison's death, work proceeded at great speed to meet the deadline for opening on 22 September 1937. It was Nye's only major work for Bernstein; he described him as a 'frightful driver' (to completion) – one can only speculate if this characteristic may have had a part in the demise of poor Morrison. The façade at North Cheam was Morrison's authorship, with a resemblance to his Granada at Bedford."

Granada blamed a shortage of materials due to the rearmament programme for the delay caused by Morrison's death, then congratulated itself on taking only seven months to build the theatre. Morrison and Nye were credited as co-architects. The front elevation was indeed very close to that of the Granada Bedford and predecessors. The name sign in red neon was surrounded by horizonal green neon strips which went on and off in sequence, creating a rising and falling – or concertina – effect.

Before the Second World War, a vertical sign that hooked onto the roof with the Granada name on both sides was added on the other end of the frontage above a row of exit doors.

This was the first in another series of "standard" Granadas. For his interior scheme in the Italian Renaissance style, Komisarjevsky revised many of the details, most of the changes being applied to the five standard Granadas that followed.

The plentiful space at Cheam enabled a lofty and impressive main entrance hall with round-headed mirrors high on the side walls. The back of the foyer recalled Tooting with its side staircases and central access to the stalls. The auditorium was slightly more ornate than those of earlier standard Granadas. The three arches on each side wall had a new, more delicate pattern of pierced grillework with a vertical emphasis. The mock balustrading was redesigned and did not project over the side exit. The usual fresco depicting classical figures appeared high on each splay wall though not above the proscenium arch. The circular main ceiling decoration had a more intricate classical design in the radiating segments and was now surrounded by a line of plaster beading which curled off to enclose pateras in the corners of the ceiling. The customary chandelier was suspended from the centre. Although an ashlar effect was retained below the grilles, the side walls further back featured an octagonal pattern.

The most significant alteration to previous standard schemes was the decoration of the ceiling over the back of the circle, which had previously been left essentially plain. This now displayed richly ornamented recessed panels while further decoration enhanced the back section of the main ceiling.

A report on the opening records that details in the auditorium were picked out in vivid pinks, greens, blues and gold against a background of a pinky-brown pastel shade. The seats were in red while the carpets were of similar colour.

The balcony seating was arranged in one smooth curve, as at Bedford and without Masey's undulations. Besides the Wurlitzer organ, there was a fully equipped 12 ft. deep stage. The proscenium opening was 52 ft. Seating was said to be 2,000, although the actual figure was 1,668 – virtually identical to the Granadas at Maidstone and Bedford. However, North Cheam seemed to have been a little longer and narrower, to judge by the extra pilaster and area of plain wall inserted between the proscenium arch and the grilles, and also the double pilasters between the grilles rather than the single ones everywhere else.

North Cheam was probably the finest of all the standard Granadas with the happiest combination of exterior, foyers and auditorium.

Granada Greenwich

Eight days after North Cheam, on Thursday 30 September 1938, this Granada was opened by Gracie Fields. Piped on stage by the Dagenham Girl Pipers, she started off being "proper posh" before telling the audience in her Lancashire accent: "Well, I don't suppose you want to hear me talking, you want to hear me sing. Shove a piano on the stage, lads!" And she sang "Sing As We Go", "I Never Cried So Much In All My Life" and "Sally", encouraging the audience to join in the last of these, and then leading everybody in the National Anthem. After the news, the films *Elephant Boy* and *Midnight Taxi* were shown along with a Silly Symphony and a Wurlitzer interlude by Donald Thorne who, as at North Cheam, created an amusing novelty, here making

The Granada Greenwich. 1937 exterior view (courtesy of Mike Ostler): the clock at the top of the vertical sign (which has the words "Greenwich Time" over the top) was removed during the Fifties. Main foyer view dates from 13 July 1962 (Photo Coverage).

The Granada Greenwich. Auditorium shots were taken on 4 May 1965. The decoration on the second line of panels from the top has been painted out. Bingo is being played on some nights and two lights have been suspended from the ceiling over the front stalls to raise the level of illumination. (Photo Coverage.)

fun of the building, staff and the local Charlton Athletic Football Club, one of whose stars presented a football to the first child enrolled in the club for Saturday morning shows.

The Granada Greenwich was built on a narrow island site along Trafalgar Road, Greenwich, well out of the town centre, almost opposite one entrance to the Blackwall Tunnel. It would always suffer from the absence of the "walk in" trade associated with main shopping areas and did not have any café-restaurant.

The design was by C. Howard Crane, the prominent and prolific American architect responsible for the gigantic Fox theatres at St. Louis and Detroit (among very many others), who had set up practice in Britain during the American Depression. He had worked for Granada on what became the Gaumont Holloway and, as previously mentioned, the Bernsteins had taken over his scheme for Slough. At both Greenwich and Slough, Crane's interior decorative scheme was replaced with designs by Theodore Komisarjevsky.

The Granada Greenwich towered above the street as a dark brick mass relieved by light faience cladding at ground level. The frontage was curved at the side nearest the town centre, with tall windows set into the corner. There was no central window above the entrance (on opening night, Gracie Fields was determined to greet the thousand of fans gathered outside and sang them three songs from the roof). In place of a window was a convex wall clad in more light-coloured faience, with two wrap-over vertical columns carrying three neon strips. In between them, four lines of slotted lettering advertised the current programme. A canopy curved out over the entrance, with more announcements on its front edge.

A name sign was mounted horizontally at the top of the front elevation, as well as on a huge vertical sign to one side. This had an illuminated electric clock on both sides of the rounded top, in recognition of the cinema being at the home of Greenwich Mean Time.

Rather surprisingly, Komisarjevsky did not deliver a classical scheme of decoration. In the modernistic main foyer, a staircase on one side turned past the tall windows. There was a metallic feel to the balustrading and wall decoration.

The Greenwich auditorium closely repeated Komisarjevsky's decorative scheme for Edmonton four years earlier. This did not seem to have gone down well with Sidney Bernstein as it had not been used since. So why was it revived here? This might have been a more economical scheme for a theatre less assured of success. The relative proximity of the Woolwich Granada may have encouraged a marked change of style. However, I suspect that the key factor was the narrowness of the site. With a huge total of 1,924 seats, the auditorium was much longer than most. To properly show off the ornamental grillework of a standard

The Granada Harrow. Exterior on 21 April 1965. This auditorium view dates from May 1949. Note the phantom piano along with the organ console. (Photo Coverage.)

Granada, an auditorium needed to be wide with splay walls set a more of an angle towards the audience. Also, the usual circular ceiling decoration around a large chandelier would not have fitted comfortably whereas the actual V-shaped treatment emphasised the increasing narrowness at the screen end. However, in place of the laylight at Edmonton, Greenwich displayed a five-pointed star on the ceiling in glass and chromium which provided the main lighting, supplemented by two long pendant fittings

The three decorative panels on the ante-proscenium walls were on the same plane rather than slightly staggered as at Edmonton, and a greater height dictated a further set of horizontal bars across vertical silver flutings. The second row across of six panels between the horizontal and vertical flutings was decorated with wavy, curling lines suggestive of musical clefs.

A contemporary description (*The Ideal Kinema*, 7 October 1937) indicates that the proscenium treatment followed that of Edmonton but the 1965 view of the auditorium reproduced here (none earlier being available) shows a different design – perhaps this area was rebuilt, as it was at Edmonton? The screen was said to measure 30 ft. by 24 ft. and to be among the largest in the world.

The Greenwich theatre was equipped with a three-manual Wurlitzer costing £2,720 and full stage facilities including a fly tower. However, it did not have a car park until late 1939 when space was cleared at the rear with, it was claimed, room for 200 cars.

Granada Harrow

The Granada Harrow opened its doors at 7pm on Monday 25 October 1937. The opening ceremony was performed by the ubiquitous Jessie Matthews and Sonnie Hale. On screen, Gracie Fields starred in *The Show Goes On* while Ruby Keeler and Allen Jenkins appeared in the supporting feature, *Ready Willing and Able*. Harry Farmer played the Wurlitzer organ.

This was the second large, modern cinema to appear in the centre of Harrow, following the Dominion which had opened at the beginning of 1936. They were in sight of each other on opposite sides of the road. Neither was fully in the centre of the town – but the Granada was closer and well placed at the point where two important roads merged. It was on the corner of a side road with a slip road in front, attached to a long parade of shops with flats above.

There was a car park for over 200 vehicles behind the shops (patrons were charged sixpence per car, with a threepenny charge for motorcycles).

The architect was J. Owen Bond, not otherwise associated with Granada, suggesting that this scheme may have been acquired

The Granada Harrow. The balcony in May 1949.
Signs here read "Way Out" rather than "Exit" to conform with
Middlesex licensing requirements. (Photo Coverage.)

rather than initiated by the company. The exterior was of red brick with the auditorium set straight back, extending in width behind the adjacent parade. The dull frontage featured above the entrance a large central window split into seven vertical sections, behind which lay the café-restaurant.

Beyond the usual low entrance hall with ticket windows in the side walls lay a double height foyer which extended to the right, to approximately the width of the auditorium. The layout and decoration were similar to East Ham. Tall pilasters were decorated with cartouches, while two standard Granada chandeliers of the smaller type were suspended overhead. Doors led off to the stalls while at the far end a spacious staircase led up to the circle. At the top of the stairs was a wide promenade with entrances to the circle at each end and access to the café-restaurant (which also had a street entrance on the corner). Part of the side wall at this upper level was mirrored, matching mirrors on the other side.

It was claimed that the auditorium held 2,222, but a seating figure of around 1,900 seems more likely as it certainly had 1,822 seats in 1963. The decoration followed the Komisarjevky scheme as revised for North Cheam with some slight adjustments. Here, on the splay walls, further decorative grillework appeared above the round-headed grilles in line with the capitals of the main pilasters (this area was left blank at North Cheam). The side exits were under the grille nearest the proscenium arch. Harrow matched North Cheam with two full-height fluted pilasters close together by the proscenium arch, but lacked the gap and additional pilaster. The grilles had the same pattern as North Cheam but with single intervening pilasters. The area was more compact than at North Cheam.

This was perhaps the best of all the Granadas in which to appreciate the decorative pierced grillework from the balcony, as the exceptional width of the auditorium meant that the side walls curved in sharply towards the proscenium arch, half-facing the audience. The grillework to the right masked the organ chamber. The usual friezes depicting idealised processional scenes appeared at cornice height on each splay wall but, as at North Cheam, the space above the proscenium arch was given over to decorative grillework, probably masking ventilation openings.

The ceiling treatment followed that of North Cheam, except that the corners of the main expanse were left plain at Harrow. However, Harrow had corbels along the side walls of the balcony. The ceiling was again richly decorated in the full-width recess over the back of the balcony but here it was coffered in a repetitive scheme of moulded squares.

The Wurlitzer cost £2,720 (the same as Greenwich's). There was no fly tower although the iron safety curtain could be raised thanks to a specially designed projection in the roof. There were four dressing rooms and a band room.

Although this Granada was extensively used for live shows later, the only live element, apart from the organ, until well into the Second World War was amateur variety, introduced on Friday nights from November 1937.

The Granada was for its first twenty or more years one of the most successful cinemas on the circuit.

Granada Clapham Junction

This Granada opened two weeks after Harrow on the Monday evening of 8 November 1937 with Victor McLaglen as the guest of honour. He had returned from Hollywood to make *We're Going To Be Rich* opposite Gracie Fields. Four thousand people turned out to cheer the burly English character star as he arrived, with space provided for one thousand schoolchildren to watch safely from Plough Road. The traffic lights had to be switched off and thirty commissionaires joined the police in controlling the crowds. The Trumpeters of the Scots Guards did a "turn" in the street before playing to the packed house inside.

The films for the opening were *History Is Made At Night* and *Mr. Stringfellow Says No*, together with a live performance by Bobby Howell and His Band, while the Wurlitzer was again inaugurated by Donald Thorne.

The cinema occupied a dominating position at the top of St. John's Hill, its stage end overlooking the busy railway station and the town centre with a vast neon-lit name sign set high up on the back wall, visible for miles away (as was the large poster space just below which advertised the programmes). Granada took over the site of Battersea County School (later Battersea Grammar), enabling it to move to more pleasant surroundings at Streatham.

In fact, the cinema's location wasn't quite ideal, as it required an uphill trek from the station and the heart of Clapham Junction, while the entrance was at the far end of the site at a road junction. The Imperial and the Grand were more accessible opposite the main station entrance, but Granada had done well to find a site in this heavily built-up area that allowed a huge capacity and even a small car park.*

Certainly the Granada was the largest and finest cinema in the area. Like the Imperial, the Shakespeare and Pavilion on Lavender Hill and the Globe in Northcote Road were much smaller, old-fashioned halls, while the Grand was a former live theatre.

The architects for the Clapham Junction Granada were Leslie C. Norton and H. B. Horner and they produced a very pleasing

*Odeon did go one better with a site by the station but this had only a very narrow entrance from Falcon Road – the scheme was killed off by the War.

Granada points out its co-operation with the industry trade union, best known as the National Association of Theatrical and Kine Employees. (Bottom: BFI – Sidney Bernstein Collection.)

The Granada Clapham Junction. Exterior in 1937. Note the sign for the café lounge over the windows on the side wall. (Author's collection.)
The outer foyer on 9 October 1964 (Photo Coverage).
Main foyer view from 1937 shows stairs to the café lounge in the left hand wall and cloakroom under the stairs to the circle, with the doors

to the rear stalls out of view to the right. (Author's collection.)
View of the huge balcony (14 April 1965) brings out the rich ceiling decoration, the front side rows, the illuminated grilles on the back side walls, while the circle fascia reflects the undulation of the rows of seating. (Photo Coverage.)

The Granada Clapham Junction in 1937. (Author's collection.)

streamlined exterior, mainly in orange brick, with the corner entrance curving around to the side road, a long side wall with windows to the café-restaurant, and an arresting fly tower at the far end. The roof was concealed from view in the street outside.*

The cinema claimed 3,001 seats in "three acres of splendour", with 427 more seats being sacrificed to provide more space in the foyers and more leg room between the rows. In fact, there were 2,475 seats, making it the third largest Granada after Tooting and Walthamstow, with just a few seats more than East Ham. The seating was of a new type incorporating rubber cushioning by Dunlopillo in place of springs in the upholstery.

The Granada Clapham Junction was given special treatment by Theodore Komisarjevsky, making it far superior to the standard type of Granada. At the time, he was ill in Switzerland and it is said that he was forbidden to talk on the telephone – his instructions for the decorative treatment (or, more likely, his answer to queries) had to be relayed through his doctor to Granada's head office and then on to the architects.

This was the only cinema opened by Granada to have its entrance across the actual corner. There was an island paybox in the low outer lobby (with a further ticket window in a side wall). The long, lofty main foyer had a staircase at the far end leading up to a promenade. The extensive use of mirrors on the walls once more helped to create an impression of an even larger space. Separate stairs through a doorway in the side wall led to the "café lounge" over the entrance.

The balcony, entered from the far sides, had the seats arranged in undulating rows as in the earlier Cecil Masey theatres. The ends of the balcony front dropped forward to provide two short rows of extra seats. The side walls had a faint pattern of hexagonal shapes interrupted by three small, roundheaded double openings with backlit grilles. The ceiling over the circle was raised in the centre and richly decorated in a repetitive pattern with illumination from four suspended chandeliers of the standard Granada type.

As at Woolwich, a panel or screen was set diagonally across the wall where it narrowed on each side at the front of the balcony. Komisarjevsky broke up the main splay wall decoration into three sections as usual, but here they were separated by double engaged columns rather than pilasters. There was decorative grillework of a new repetitive design on the two outer sections and two different classical paintings of female figures in the centres. These replaced the friezes of figures found on the cornices of other Granadas. In the ceiling over the front stalls

* F. C. Mitchell later claimed to have designed the theatre and his name is certainly on plans of this period, presumably working for Norton and Horner. Mitchell later designed many cinemas in his own name, including the Ambassadors at Cosham, Hayes and Kingswood (Bristol) for London and Southern.

Stop Press! Flash!! Late News!!!

GRACIE FIELDS

TO-NIGHT
(Saturday) | Will make a Personal Appearance on the stage at the Opening Performance | GRANADA Greenford

GRANADA• BY BROADWAY
GREENFORD

NOV. 15
WEEK
FOR SIX DAYS
Daily from 2

ALICE FAYE
NED SPARKS · PATSY KELLY
BEN BERNIE AND HIS BAND
Wake Up And Live

CLAIRE TREVOR · LLOYD NOLAN
King Of Gamblers

DUDLEY BEAVEN
ACE RADIO ORGANIST
AT THE MIGHTY WURLITZER

A SPACIOUS
CAR PARK
operated by
National Car Parks Ltd
adjoins the theatre.

Service
with
a smile

PRICES: Stalls 9d 1/- 1/3. Circle 1/6. Reserved Loges 2/-. Reduced Prices for Children. Bargain Matinees before 3.30 Children's Matinee every Sat. morning at 10. Admission 3d BE SURE TO JOIN THE GRANADIERS CLUB

THE WONDER THEATRE OF 1938

The Granada Greenford. The opening advertisement invites children to join the Granadiers Club.

The Granada Greenford. Exterior dates from April 1954 when Granada ran the car park behind the theatre. Within the next five years both the vertical and horizontal name signs were changed for an italic seriffed style, the shop nearest the entrance became a Miss Candy outlet, and the shop on the corner turned into a Granadagram record shop.

The week's attraction, Snow White and the Seven Dwarfs, was a Granada circuit revival. The following week's Roman Holiday had already played at rival cinemas as an Odeon release in late October 1953 and manager Harry Mansfield has laid on this scooter stunt to support its early revival at the Granada. (Courtesy of John Young.) Inner foyer and auditorium shot date from 24 March 1965 (Photo Coverage).

was placed the standard Granada chandelier with large decorative roundel of the style introduced at North Cheam.

This theatre had full stage facilities and eighteen dressing rooms. Its extensive capacity for live shows may have been partly dictated by the presence nearby of the Grand, which combined films with variety. For several years, the Granada offered three big acts every week plus a double bill of films. As at Greenwich, the screen was said to measure 30 ft. by 24 ft., making it one of the largest in the world.

Granada Greenford

Opened on the Saturday evening of 13 November 1937, only five days after Clapham Junction, this was a Granada of the standard type, larger than most, allegedly seating 2,001. Gracie Fields became available at the last minute to carry out the opening ceremony, arriving from her day's work at Denham studios with Victor McLaglen on *We're Going To Be Rich* (which would be shown here a year later, for the week of 21 November 1938). The opening attraction was the Alice Faye musical *Wake Up And Live*, supported by *King Of Gamblers,* with Dudley Beaven at the Wurlitzer.

Charles Dixon and Henry Braddock were the architects, with Cecil Masey credited as consultant, and Komisarjevky handled the interior decorative scheme, again providing vital last-minute details from his sick bed in Switzerland via his physician. The site had previously been occupied by a Roman Catholic church and the cinema was built in seven months after demolition of the old buildings.

Like North Cheam and Harrow, this Granada was set back from the main road with its own carriageway, shared by the attached row of shops (single storey in this case) with the auditorium behind. The relatively simple brick entrance block featured a small tower onto which a vertical name sign was fitted, its shape as usual outlined in neon.

As at North Cheam, there were steps up from the back of the outer foyer (which had the usual box-office windows on the side walls). Extending off to the left, with a staircase at the far end leading to the balcony, the main foyer was close to a mirror image of Harrow except that there the columns were full height and here they are only expressed at first floor level. Also, mirrors seem to have been confined to the end wall above the stairs, where they reflected the ceiling and chandeliers.

The auditorium varied only slightly from North Cheam or Harrow. The most obvious new touch was the festoons placed between the capitals above the side grilles, an area left plain at North Cheam and used for further grilles at Harrow. The four chandeliers over the rear circle were grouped in the centre, allowing the sides to be stepped down. Coffering above the chandeliers followed the style of Harrow.

Masey's involvement with Greenford did not extend to undulations in the rows of circle seating. As at Harrow, frescos appeared at cornice level but not above the proscenium arch which had pierced grillework.

A Wurlitzer organ was installed as usual along with limited stage facilities. There was a staff of thirty-seven. A car park, initially operated by National Car Parks, adjoined the theatre. All the seats were cushioned in the new and more comfortable soft rubber of Dunlopillo, as at Clapham Junction.

Located in a rapidly expanding area of West London near Southall, this Granada was not situated at a major crossroads nor did it form part of a major shopping or leisure area. It was not quite in a solo situation as far as film bookings went, being barred from some releases by the much smaller Playhouse until that closed in 1959. Along with existing cinemas in the area, it was not allowed to open on Sundays at this time. Never an outstanding success, this would become the first of the purpose-built Granadas to close.

10 • 1938/39: Three More Granadas

The circuit expansion programme concluded with the openings of the Granada Welling and Granada Slough in 1938. A final Granada appeared at Kingston in 1939, after the outbreak of World War Two, but this was a take-over from another promoter during construction. There was one further cinema forced onto the Bernsteins which would have been built but for the War. The East Molesey and Woodford schemes were still listed on theatre notepaper being used in 1940 as "under construction" but East Molesey, as previously noted, had been put "on hold" and Woodford seems to have been in the same state.

Further sites had been tentatively considered. One at Waltham Cross, Hertfordshire, is revealed by a letter in Sidney Bernstein's papers dated June 1939 from Nicholas and Dixon-Spain, who had been appointed architects and were anxious about payment for work on this and the Mile End and Ponders End schemes. Granada responded that all three were "not likely to move". Another site at Westerham, Kent, was explored at some time in the Thirties but it has not been possible to discover when.

However, a scheme for a Century at Bedford was in active progress when war started. A drawing published in the *Bedfordshire Times and Independent* (14 April 1939) indicates that this would have been a full-scale partner to the Granada, not a modest undertaking like the first Century at Cheam Village. In July 1937, the local council sold two-thirds of what was known as the Island Site for £15,000 to the cinema promoters Cohen and Rafer who had recently opened the Regal Kettering (eventually to become part of the Granada circuit). Another well-known team of entrepreneurs, Bacal and Lee, were linked with Cohen and Rafer, and the group announced an £80,000 cinema in Bedford to seat 2,500. The architect for the Kettering cinema, George Coles, set about planning the building and placed the entrance at the corner of Dame Alice Street and Harpur Street (the site also opened on to St. Loyes). Although the proposed seating figure was most likely an exaggeration for publicity purposes, clearly this would have been a very large building and a dangerous rival to the Granada.

Hence the Bernsteins and their local partner, Ernest Blake, went into action. In April 1938, Granada (Bedford) Ltd. bought the site from Bacal, Lee and associates. Sidney Bernstein immediately sought to acquire the remaining third of the Island Site. Although the press commented that agreement with the Council over price was unlikely, it seems that Granada did reach terms for the whole site. The architects Lyons, Israel and Elsom, who had designed the Granada Wandsworth Road and other proposed theatres, were brought in. The published sketch (on newsprint too faded to reproduce here) shows a massive brick building with the auditorium extending at right angles to the entrance along Dame Alice Street. Work went ahead on clearing the site, but further progress was halted by the start of World War Two.

Granada Welling

The first cinema in Welling, Kent (now part of Southeast London), was an Odeon designed by George Coles and opened in October 1934. Two rival schemes to provide competition came along in early 1937. Lyons, Israel and Elsom designed a cinema for the corner of Westwood Lane and Bellegrove Road for undisclosed clients, probably Granada. George Coles drew up plans for a 2,000 seat cinema with café, six shops and a car park to be built in the High Street for Archibald Michaels and Montague Cohen.

Granada (Welling) Ltd. was registered in February 1937. The Granada cinema that opened on Wednesday 2 February 1938 was designed by George Coles and located on Bellegrove Road, a continuation of the High Street, so Granada seem to have switched schemes. The ever-ready Jessie Matthews and husband Sonnie Hale made a personal appearance for the opening, Robinson Cleaver performed on the Wurlitzer, and the feature attractions were *Kid Galahad* and *Easy Living*.

Externally, the Granada Welling was the dullest pre-war building to come off the Coles drawing board. The street façade is so elementary that it looks post-war.

The large expanse of brickwork above five tall recessed windows called out for a name sign but Granada opted for a fin to one side, the crest as usual curving over the parapet. A fin was well advised as the cinema was located on a very long stretch of straight road and the sign could be seen from a substantial distance away.

Handbill from BFI - Sidney Bernstein Collection.

This advertisement from the inside front cover of World Film News' *April 1938 issue represents an indirect form of financial assistance to a highbrow publication, undoubtedly approved of by Sidney Bernstein. It lists Granadas East Moseley (sic) and Woodford as "under construction".*

The Granada Welling. View from opening in February 1938 (Tony Moss collection). Foyer shot (11 March 1976) shows the generous size of the area and effectiveness of the mirrors.

Above top: the passage at the head of the staircase, with entrances to the circle at each end (31 May 1961). Auditorium view dates from 1 November 1968.

(Photo Coverage.)

The Granada Welling. Auditorium view from 1 November 1968 shows the revised ceiling and grillework designs and treatment of the rear circle ceiling. (Photo Coverage.)

Internally, the Granada Welling offered the luxury of a standard Komisarjevsky decorative scheme with some variations. Komisarjevsky received no credit at all in the official publicity for any of the Granadas covered by this chapter – his theatrical career had largely taken him to America and his past work may have been considered Granada property to be applied and adapted by others.

There seems to have been only one set of doors into the foyer and the payboxes were placed just beyond them on each side. The tall windows on the front allowed a generous amount of light to spill into the huge and spectacular main foyer which was arranged in the manner of North Cheam with stairs each side to the balcony and a passage between leading to the stalls. A small café-restaurant was provided. On the side walls at first-floor level were three arched mirrors with spiral columns between, corresponding to the three arched grilles on the splay walls of the auditorium, but these were smaller than at North Cheam and so less effective.

The auditorium, which had around 1,500 seats (400 less than claimed in opening publicity), extended straight back behind the foyer but was set off centre so that one entrance to the balcony was at the top of the stairs from the entrance hall and the other was reached down a long, wide passage to the right. Although decorated basically in the standard style, the auditorium displayed some innovations. The design of both the grille-work on the splay walls and the decoration of the ceiling above the main chandelier was changed: the latter area was no longer divided into segments from the centre but had a lavishly ornamented inner circle and more richly decorated outer rim with the space between relieved by overlapping loops of raised plasterwork. The ceiling extended to the back wall on one level except for the usual recess for the projection ports. The ceiling in the recess was richly decorated with a slightly different arrangement of panels. These and other alterations were not major – nor a dramatic improvement – and were only applied to this one theatre. Welling was still unmistakably a Granada using Komisarjevsky's standard style.

Granada Slough

As previously stated, Granada took over plans drawn up by C. Howard Crane for a new cinema at Slough, Berkshire. Crane's work was revised by Cecil Masey and the interior decoration based on work by Theodore Komisarjevsky. Built at a stated cost of £70,000, the Granada opened on Wednesday 23 March 1938 with 1,710 seats, seven weeks after Welling. It was the first new cinema in Slough since the Adelphi opened in 1930 although the London and Southern circuit had built an Ambassador at nearby Farnham Royal.

YES, SIR !

SLOUGH

will soon have its

GRANADA

wonder theatre

• please pronounce it GRA-**NAH**-DAH

The Granada Slough. Handbill from BFI – Sidney Bernstein Collection. Exterior on 24 January 1966, with the usual Miss Candy shop added and separate entrance to the café on the corner. A small vertical sign was placed on the far end wall, just round the corner. (Photo Coverage.)

The Granada Slough. The restaurant was in use when this picture was taken on 12 May 1960. The central mirror seems to have been damaged and never properly reinstated. The "running dog" frieze ornamentation was unusual but had also been seen at Shrewsbury. View of the back of the main foyer dates from 20 June 1973 when tripling was being carried out, with new poster frames on the wall for the three auditoria and an ugly concessions counter set below the three mirrors shown in the view looking forward.
The auditorium is seen in copy photographs dating from April 1949. The ceiling here had additional coffering over the balcony. (All Photo Coverage.)

Leslie Howard, who was starting *Pygmalion* at Pinewood Studios, made a personal appearance as the guest of honour, being piped through the stalls and onto the stage by the Dagenham Girl Pipers to make a speech and declare the theatre open. The films were *Artists and Models* and Howard's comedy *It's Love I'm After*.

The Granada extended lengthways along Windsor Road without space in front for an attached parade of shops. Unlike Crane's dramatic exteriors for the Granada Greenwich and Gaumont Holloway, this had a dull but respectable frontage in brick with stonework around the three rows of small windows above the canopy. The main name sign was set above the windows. No fin sign is known to have appeared here. A car park was provided.

A large café-restaurant was installed above the outer entrance hall, overlooking the main foyer. Unlike most cinema cafés, Granada's were usually open to view and easily accessible from the foyer to encourage patrons to visit them. But, like most cinema cafés, it had another entrance at street level to draw in people not seeing films.

Slough had the least graceful of Granada foyers, although it was huge and fitted out with more elaborate chandeliers, like those at Walthamstow and Tooting, rather than ones of standard type. The staircase to the balcony at the far end lacked impact, with no mirrors or other decorative effects on most of the end wall. On the promenade to the circle, there were further more elaborate chandeliers.

The auditorium followed the standard design from North Cheam onwards with the addition of a double row of coffering across the ceiling over the balcony before it was stepped up at the back for the projection ports. Here further coffering in a matching style occupied the centre of the ceiling which was stepped down at each side. Whatever Masey did to revise Crane's work, he left the balcony seating in straight curves.

Because of its proximity to the film studios at Denham and Pinewood, the Granada Slough was soon (or, possibly, from the start) specially equipped with extra projectors to enable "double-headed" projection – the showing of sound and picture on separate interlocked reels. This enabled sneak previews of films to gauge audience reaction at an early stage in editing.* Screen size was once again put at 30 ft. by 24 ft. Limited stage facilities were provided.

In November 1938, a modern independent cinema called the Commodore opened at Cippenham, a western district of Slough, in what Sidney Bernstein considered was a flagrant imitation of the Granada style.

* This information comes from a note contributed by Jim Pople to Kevin Brownlow's *David Lean A Biography* (1996). The only other commercial cinema similarly equipped was the Gaumont Camden Town.

Granada Kingston

The last cinema to open as a Granada arrived more than eighteen months behind Slough, after war had been declared. It was a take-over of a Hyams and Gale scheme at Kingston upon Thames. In February 1938, Phil Hyams contracted with the owners of the site, the Oriel Property Trust, to build there. Kingston already had several cinemas including the huge Regal (dating from 1932) and an Odeon (1933) on the edges of the town centre. The new site was in a very central location, between the small Kinema (opened in 1910) and the medium-sized Elite (dating from 1921).

As the Hyams company's regular architect, George Coles drew up plans for the cinema, to be called the State, and these were passed in March 1938. However, as war became more and more likely, Major A. J. Gale, the financial expert and partner of Phil and Sid Hyams, was worried about losing their existing cinemas in bombing raids and so they decided to reduce their commitments, selling not only their interest in Gaumont Super Cinemas' Holloway scheme but also trying to dispose of the Kingston project after building operations had begun. Sam Byre was appointed to find a purchaser and he approached Sidney Bernstein in January 1939. Bernstein's first offer of a £3,500 profit was rejected by Hyams and Gale but a sum of around £5,500 was accepted in March, with £500 to be paid at once and £5,000 to follow within five years. Granada undertook to spend at least £50,000 on completing the cinema and attached parade of shops.*

Not much work could have been done at Kingston before Granada took over as the company was able to redesign the interior to take a Komisarjevsky decorative scheme with standard fittings (Cecil Masey was named as consulting architect). Granada's new plans – which scrapped Coles' proscenium arch with a curved top as well as a restaurant over the front entrance – were approved on 1 June 1939.

Completion proved difficult once war was declared and, on 19 September, Bernstein offered a bonus to the builders if they finished within five or six weeks. This seems to have done the trick as the Granada Kingston finally opened without ceremony on the Friday afternoon of 3 November 1939.

The front elevation was a vast improvement on Coles' work at Welling. Though still simple, it had three round-headed windows with matching porthole windows above, and a corner tower. It seems that a large vertical sign was put up even though it would have had to remain unlit at night during the war.

* This was not the only cinema offered to Bernstein at this period. In June, Lou Morris tried to interest him in taking over his scheme for Quarry Hill, Grays, Essex, but was forced to complete it himself – as the Ritz, it finally opened in November 1940. Morris also made extended efforts to interest Bernstein in buying the recently opened, loss-making Majestic Bridgnorth, Shropshire. He dropped his price in April 1939 to £17,000 (from £28,000 a year earlier) but still could not persuade Bernstein to take it on.

The main entrance hall was impressively large and lofty. There would have been room to install a café on the first floor as at Slough* but its absence allowed daylight to spill through the three tall windows across the hall while three sets of double mirrors on the side walls further increased the impression of spaciousness. Despite the height of the foyer, the round window heads were cut off by the ceiling when they might have complemented the rounded mirrors on the walls. Space for a fourth window over the entrance was blocked in, leaving the three windows off centre and not completely in alignment with the ceiling beams.

There was also an awkwardness about the staircases at the other end, which were rather narrow and set unusually far apart. Three doorways were placed at the head of the stairs, a main one in the centre and two to each side – but the left-hand doorway was blocked and filled in with mirrors.

The Granada Kingston seemed to have an enormous auditorium. This was set at right angles to the entrance hall, extending to the left behind a row of shops that were part of the development. A seating figure of 2,000 was once again claimed but it was actually around 1,800, still significantly larger than most standard Granadas. The pierced grillework on the splay walls and the decorative treatment of the ceiling followed the example of North Cheam. However, the circular decoration above the main chandelier was placed inside a saucer dome, as at the Phoenix Theatre, rather than on a flat ceiling, presumably because Coles' original design had provided for a dome. The cornice friezes of small figures appeared both above the proscenium arch and along the splay walls. The proscenium opening was particularly wide.

As at Welling, the ceiling outside the dome extended to the back wall at one level except for the recess for the projection beams which had the usual coffering. Usually, the projection ports were set into the back wall, but at Kingston the operating box was built out slightly, over the back promenade and back row of seats – obviously another feature inherited from Coles' original scheme.

Full stage facilities and a Wurlitzer organ were included. Granada as usual put the screen size at 30 ft. by 24 ft., "among the largest in the world". A technical innovation was the first installation in Europe of RCA High Fidelity sound which used eighteen speakers to distribute the sound more evenly, reducing harshness and reverberation. A car park was provided in Cromwell Road, just behind the cinema.

The Granada Kingston. View above dates from 12 June 1968, with later style block letter vertical. The shop to let at the end was at one time used by Granada TV Rental.

Right top, the main foyer on 23 February 1966 still has its floor tiled rather than carpeted. Barely visible is the usual ashlar effect on the lower side walls, as in the auditorium.

Right below: the circle lounge with more mirrors and original furniture and a view of the standard auditorium (both 13 April 1965).

(All Photo Coverage.)

* Many years later, Granada considered adding a café at first floor level by building over the open-air passage down the side of the entrance block.

11 • Take-Overs And Aspects Of Circuit Operation In The Thirties

Take-Overs and Management Deals

Besides building new cinemas, Granada was able to expand its circuit by taking over existing halls either completely or in partnership with local interests. Most of the partnership arrangements eventually led to full ownership by Granada. There were, however, a few instances of deals that unravelled.

There was the case of the Regal Watford where, as previously described, the Bernsteins had brought in George Coles and Theodore Komisarjevsky to refurbish the building. Cecil Bernstein was a director of the operating company, Courtwood, along with R. Sokoloff and B. Sokoloff. The Bernsteins were none too pleased when in 1934 one (or both) of the Sokoloffs re-opened the former Borough Theatre in Stratford as the Rex cinema, creating added competition for the West Ham (Stratford) Kinema nearby which was having difficulties already in film booking, playing late runs on split weeks. This seems to have led to the partnership at Watford breaking up, with the Bernsteins pulling out. However, there had been considerable difficulty obtaining films for Watford because of the powerful competition there. This town, for example, was the only one where the Bernstein chain lost the popular United Artists release *The Bowery* to a rival theatre.

Rugby in Warwickshire became a Granada stronghold in stages. In 1932 Halford W. Reddish, who was a big name in the Rugby Cement company, headed a company which was building the new Plaza in association with the Manchester-based J. F. Emery circuit, which was to run the theatre. When Emery suddenly withdrew, the Bernsteins stepped in, sweetening their involvement with a promise of life directorships for the various local board members of the Plaza Theatre (Rugby) Ltd. The local company took over the town's Regent before the Plaza opened in January 1933, and this also came under Bernstein management. Cecil Bernstein joined the board of directors.

Besides arranging the Plaza's opening attraction, *Here Goes the Bride*, starring Jessie Matthews, Bernstein Theatres supplied the manager, Noel Hobart (who had opened the Granadas at Walthamstow and Tooting), and the organist for the Christie, Reginald Foort (who stayed two weeks). Designed by J. H. and R. B. Lyddington in association with the noted architects Leathart

and Granger, this large (1,700 seat) cinema possessed a 40 ft. wide and 28 ft. high proscenium opening, a 32 ft. deep stage that would see extensive use, four dressing rooms, car park and café. This was not an outstanding building architecturally but it became very profitable.

Plaza Theatre (Rugby) Ltd. also acquired the smaller Regal cinema around the middle of 1933. One disgruntled local director, W. Ralph Bates, declared in December 1935 that the Bernsteins were acting as if they owned the cinemas. The three cinemas were not fully acquired by Granada until September 1944.

Rebuilding on a larger scale was the motive behind the take-over of the Clock Tower cinema at Wandsworth, South London, from April 1934. As a conversion of a cadets' training headquarters, this cannot have been a very satisfactory picture house. It was replaced by the Granada Wandsworth Road in 1936, as previously described.

In August 1934, the Bernsteins took an interest in the Cinema at Loughton, Essex, in a deal with Mr. and Mrs. Conrad March, becoming responsible for its management. However, complete control did not follow until twenty years later.

In September 1934, Granada acquired the large Plaza at Mansfield, Nottinghamshire, which had opened four years earlier. This would become a key theatre, the best of the six in the town. Granada also booked the town's Hippodrome, which became a Bernstein theatre in January 1936.

In November 1934, the same month that the Bernsteins opened their Granada at Shrewsbury in Shropshire, they acquired an interest in two cinemas at nearby Oswestry: the Regal and the King's Theatre, both of which had opened the preceding year. Sidney Bernstein became a director of the Oswestry Regal Cinema Co. Ltd., with E. B. Garrett the chairman. The two cinemas were not fully taken over until 1955.

As mentioned earlier, the Bedford Empire was added at Christmas 1934 as an adjunct to the opening of the Granada there.

In the mid-1930s, Bernstein Theatres were also booking two London area cinemas, the Elite Wimbledon and Playhouse Hampstead, although the arrangements were short-lived.

An important deal that somehow collapsed dates from January 1935 when Bernstein Theatres expected to take over five cinemas

Left, top and centre, and above top: the Plaza Rugby, seen here as the Granada. Exterior seen in September 1955, foyer and auditorium on 11 May 1954.
Bottom left and above: the Regent (later Century) Rugby was also a substantial hall, as these 1953 photographs indicate.
(All Photo Coverage.)

The Cinema Loughton is seen in April 1959 as the Century with the frontage considerably modernised (Photo Coverage).

in Hertfordshire. The Bernsteins thought they had acquired the County and Castle cinemas at Hertford and the Hermitage at Hitchin, or at least the interest in them held by J. G. and R. B. Wainwright. In addition, the other two cinemas in Hitchin, the Playhouse and Picturedrome, were to be leased following the death of their owner, William N. Blake, who, with E. E. Blake, had joined forces with the Bernsteins in Bedford. All five theatres were listed as part of the circuit on company notepaper in 1936, so it seems that the Bernsteins did manage them for a brief period.

In 1936 Granada took over the one cinema it didn't already own in Shrewsbury, the Royal County. This former live theatre was the smallest and least important of the town's four picture houses.

For the rest of the decade, the Bernsteins concentrated on opening new cinemas rather than making further acquisitions.

Circuit operation
It is difficult at this distance in time, not having lived through the period and with none of the key figures surviving, to provide a comprehensive picture of the way Bernstein Theatres operated before World War Two. But some revealing details emerge, mostly drawn from the Bernstein collection at the British Film Institute. Any overall comment is complicated by the way that the industry was changing rapidly, with new circuits and new cinemas springing up everywhere, particularly by the Odeon circuit establishing itself as a national force and block-booking many of the best new pictures. Increased competition meant, for example, that many cinemas which had previously split the week between two new main releases now played one of them for a full six days.

Booking problems
In 1933, Granada had difficulty obtaining enough suitable films for its theatres at Tooting, Watford, East Ham and Stratford (West Ham). The Watford problem was solved by letting the theatre go; at Tooting the situation seemed to ease itself; but East Ham and Stratford would long remain difficult to programme.

Sidney Bernstein was often at loggerheads with the other circuits. In East Ham, his Kinema was barred from ABC first run by the Coronation Manor Park one and a half miles away and then from ABC second run by the Broadway East Ham. In October 1933 Bernstein wrote to ABC head John Maxwell, asking that the bar on the East Ham Kinema by the Broadway be lifted so that they could play films concurrently – the two cinemas being far enough apart, in his opinion, not to hurt each other. Maxwell's response was to offer the lease on the Broadway, which Bernstein declined. Maxwell soon disposed of the Broadway anyway but the bar by the Coronation remained.

The Kinema was a Denham hall half-owned by Gaumont-British. The economic sense of building a new, much larger Granada in its place is hard to fathom: because it seated sixty more than Gaumont's huge Premier Super, Bernstein may have hoped to take away the lucrative Gaumont weekly release. But this didn't happen, and Gaumont even upgraded the Premier Super with a modern façade and a new vertical sign that curved over the top of the building, imitating that of its new rival.

Like the Kinema before it, the Granada was prevented from taking the ABC release by the Coronation Manor Park. From July 1938 it also lost films to the new East Ham Odeon close by. It had to rely heavily on live variety to bolster its weak film selections, and offered shows that were great value for money in terms of their length, running as much as three and a half hours. Despite its programming difficulties, the Granada East Ham proved to be a long-term survivor.

In 1938, Bernstein began correspondence with Odeon chief Oscar Deutsch over problems that the newly opened Odeon Deptford was causing the Granada Greenwich. Bernstein alleged that the Odeon was attempting to bar the Granada from playing the same films and wrote: "... in these days when everybody is trying to restrict bars, and when we ourselves have agreed in the case of Tooting and Sutton to allow concurrency with you at Morden and Epsom, this new desire on the part of your film booking department is particularly unreasonable."

An unidentified member of Odeon's booking department informed Deutsch: "The distance from the Odeon Deptford to Greenwich is 1.7 miles, while the distance from the G.B. [Gaumont-British] New Cross [Kinema] to Greenwich is 2.1 miles. The G.B. Lewisham [Gaumont Palace] to Greenwich is 2½ miles, and both these G.B. theatres bar Greenwich. Surely we, being the nearest, are entitled to the same privilege, and I have discussed this matter with Mr. Jarratt [Gaumont-British chief], who agrees that this is a fair and reasonable bar. It is understood, however, that should we book a film for Deptford which is not a circuit film, a concurrency should be allowed with Greenwich, but that all circuit films are entitled to bar. This has been agreed by Metro [MGM] and United Artists."

In April 1939, Odeon consented to a full concurrency provided that it received reduced terms from film distributors and the Granada Greenwich ceased including stage shows. Bernstein informed Deutsch in June 1939: "... in view of our film booking position we consider variety – which we introduced before the Odeon opened – is essential." The Granada's biggest hurdle remained its poor location out of town. It was able to play the ABC circuit release concurrently with ABC cinemas at Blackheath and Lewisham. (The rival Trafalgar cinema in Greenwich, slightly better sited by being nearer the town centre, played many Gaumont releases.)

Deutsch replied that lack of good films might have compelled the Granada to run variety but that, if the cinema had access to all the Odeon circuit product, "then the only reason why you have to play variety would be removed". In fact, Odeon and General Film Distributors jointly insisted that the Granada Greenwich should not stage any variety when playing the Deanna Durbin hit *Three Smart Girls*. Bernstein replied that, under these circumstances, he didn't expect the Granada would play the film.

Around 1943, when the Trafalgar cinema was taken over by Odeon, Granada lost all access to the Odeon release but by then the theatre was able to gain the Gaumont main circuit programmes.

Grouping Granada

On 28-30 October 1933, two months after the rebuilt Empire Edmonton opened, Bernstein Theatres moved its headquarters from 197 Wardour Street to 36 Golden Square, which would remain the group's address until recent times.

In July 1934, Granada Theatres Ltd. was registered with capital of £100 in £1 shares to link together the various cinemas that were owned by separate companies. They would still be referred to as Bernstein Theatres for the rest of the decade and the individual companies remained in existence. According to the company history *Here We Were*, in 1934 the circuit's capital and reserves were £300,000 and its profits £31,500.

Sidney and Cecil Bernstein were directors of each local company, usually with Maurice King and Ernest A. Willder. H. I. Robinson was a director of Maidstone. The role of Ernest Blake at Bedford has already been mentioned and he was an additional director there. By 1939, the directors of Granada Theatres were the two Bernsteins, King, and Richard J. Willder.

Sidney Bernstein

The head of Bernstein Theatres continued to make himself conspicuous as a figure in trade affairs.

The following story, headlined "Sidney Bernstein's Tilt at Critics", appeared in *The Bioscope*, 5 February 1930:

"There is a sly touch of humour in the announcement made last evening by Sidney Bernstein, well-known London exhibitor, that he has scrapped his booked programme at the Rialto, Enfield, for the week commencing Monday, February 17th, in order to make way for a test run of the MGM all-negro subject *Hallelujah*, which left the Empire, Leicester Square, last week.

"'My object is to discover what the suburban public thinks of the lay press critic,' said Mr. Bernstein to a *Bioscope* representative. 'I saw the film privately before the press view, and I told [MGM head] Sam Eckman, Junr., that in my opinion *Hallelujah* was not an artistic production. But I predicted that the critics would regard it as an artistic picture and, as you know, they 'fell for it.'

"'Now I am going to ask the suburban public – the Rialto,

⸿ If you are interested in the development and betterment of films—— if you want to help us get the best films that can be produced for you

PLEASE
ANSWER
THESE
QUESTIONS

⸿ Kindly return this Questionnaire to the Rialto Talkie Theatre, Enfield or to 197 Wardour Street, W.1.

	Yes	No
Does the theme attract you ?		
Did the atmosphere grip you ?		
Do you like unusual themes ?		
Do you agree that it is "the most profound study of human emotions any film has yet contrived "?		
If not, which film has moved you more ?		
Is this a masterpiece ?		
If not, say which film, silent or talkie, you consider is a masterpiece :—		

	Yes	No
Do you agree that " Nina Mae McKinney has enough personality for a dozen ordinary film stars" ?		
Did you come to see this film because of what the critics have said ?		
Which critic or newspaper criticism do you regularly follow ?		
Which critic or newspaper gives you an accurate forecast of what you are going to see ?		
Did you expect more than you saw ?		
Are you often disappointed after seeing what the critics have praised ?		
Do you keep away from a film if you are told it is "artistic" ?		

REMARKS—*If we have forgotten anything on which you feel strongly please write your views here :—*

_____

_____

_____

_____

THE Critics have unanimously declared *Hallelujah* a masterpiece. Do you agree with the critics ?

⸿ Here is a special problem which we invite your co-operation.

⸿ Your opinion, willingly in the past, has helped us to programs in accord with wishes and your tastes.

⸿ An unknown artist is acclaimed as one of the greatest of actresses. "Such a tempest of personality has not been seen on the screen before" (G. A. Atkinson). An unusual theme is put forward as "the most profound study of human emotions any film has yet contrived" (A. W. Mutch). The director is praised for providing "a master of rhythmic sound, emotional sincerity and honestly told drama" (C. McManus).

⸿ The head of the B.B.C. has aroused a storm of protest by saying that the public must not be given what it wants. What is your opinion on this all important problem ?

⸿ Our questions have been chosen to put the issues at their clearest. Do not be influenced by the critics, use your own judgment, say what you think, freely without prejudice and without favour.

1.—Who are your favourite film stars ?

MALE.

1._____
2._____
3._____

FEMALE.

1._____
2._____
3._____

2.—Which film stars do you dislike most ?

MALE.

1. ☐
2. ☐
3. ☐

FEMALE.

1. ☐
2. ☐
3. ☐

2a.—Do you actually stay away from a cinema where a film is showing which features any of the stars you dislike ? *If so, put a cross in the square (above) against the name or names of those stars about whom you feel so strongly.*

3.—Which film actors or actresses you have seen in comparatively small parts would you like to see in star roles ?

MALE.

1._____
2._____
3._____

FEMALE.

1._____
2._____
3._____

4.—What kind of feature film do you prefer ?

SOCIETY DRAMA   MUSICAL COMEDY
COMEDY   LOVE-ROMANCE
HISTORICAL   WAR
THRILLER-ADVENTURE

(Place the above in order of preference)

First
Second
Third
Fourth
Fifth
Sixth
Seventh

4a.—What kind of SHORT films do you like best ?

CARTOONS   SCIENCE
TRAVEL   SPORT
INDUSTRY   MUSICAL
ANIMAL LIFE

(Place the above in order of preference)

First
Second
Third
Fourth
Fifth
Sixth
Seventh

4b.—Do you object to short advertising films ?

(Say Yes or No)

5.—Do you like coloured feature talkies ?

(Say Yes or No)

5a.—Would you rather that those you have seen had been photographed in black and white in the ordinary way ?

(Say Yes or No)

6.—Mark with a X which you prefer:

(a) Two "Big" pictures of normal length (about 1 hr. 20 mins. each) in a program ☐

or

(b) One super picture lasting *more than two hours* supported by several short films ☐

(Mark only one of these alternatives)

7.—Do you like stage shows included in cinema programs ?

(Say Yes or No)

8.—Name your favourite film director if you have one:

Which of his films did you like best ?

9.—Of the newspapers and other periodicals that you read which do you consider :

(a) Has the best film criticisms?

(b) The best film news and gossip ?

9a.—Do you listen-in to the B.B.C. film criticisms ?

(Say Yes or No)

10.—How many times a week do you usually go to the pictures ?

(If you go less than once a week put a x)

11.—Have you any ideas for the improvement of cinema entertainment generally ?

12.—What was your opinion of the films listed below ?

Please put a cross (X) in the column which indicates your opinion, as follows:
Column 1—OUTSTANDING ; Column 2—GOOD ; Column 3—FAIR ; Column 4—BAD.
For instance, if you thought a film was "Fair" then put your X in the third column opposite the film title.

	Outstanding	Good	Fair	Bad		Outstanding	Good	Fair	Bad
"Anna Karenina"					"Mr. Deeds Goes to Town"				
"The King Steps Out"					"Things to Come"				
"It's Love Again"					"East Meets West"				
"Follow the Fleet"					"Mutiny on the Bounty"				
"Jack of All Trades"					"The Country Doctor"				
"Captain January"					"Tudor Rose"				
"Under Two Flags"					"Rhodes of Africa"				
"The Ghost Goes West"					"The Trail of Lonesome Pine"				
"Captain Blood"					"David Copperfield"				
"Modern Times"					"Lives of a Bengal Lancer"				
"Klondike Annie"					"Desire"				
"A Midsummer's Night Dream"					"Magnificent Obsession"				
"The Informer"					"The Story of Louis Pasteur"				
"Wife versus Secretary"					"When Knights Were Bold"				

Name (Mr., Mrs., Miss, or Title)._____

Please put a tick in the square which indicates your age:

Under 21	21 to 40	40 to 60	over 60

Address._____

It will be very much if you care to indicate your age; the information, of course, will be kept confidential.

Published by The Bernstein Theatres Ltd., 34 Golden Square, W.1. Printed by The Jackson Press P.12

West End and Regd. Offices : 36 Golden Square, London, W.1 Telephone : Gerrard 3554 (8 lines)

PLAZA SUTTON

Proprietors, Plaza (Sutton) Ltd.

SUTTON 4440

•

CARSHALTON ROAD WEST
SUTTON, SURREY

Dear Patron,

    I have much pleasure in informing you that you have won two guest tickets at this theatre for your answers to my fifth film Questionnaire.

    In sending you the accompanying tickets I would like to take the opportunity of thanking you for the trouble you expended in filling in the Questionnaire form.

    The information thus gathered, which is unobtainable by any other means, will prove of immense value in the arrangement of film programs calculated to appeal to the majority of patrons.

Yours faithfully,

Sidney Bernstein

Sidney L. Bernstein.

Top left: the questionnaire issued at Enfield for the special showing of Hallelujah *in February 1930.*

Bottom left: the Bernstein Questionnaire 1936-7.

Note that the letter above from 1937 lists Granadas at Bow Road and Woodford under construction.

(All BFI – Sidney Bernstein Collection).

Enfield, is chosen as a representative suburban hall – what they think of the lay press critiques of this picture. The hall itself offers no outstanding attraction; I shall run *Hallelujah* with a 'topical' as the only supporting item, and each patron will be supplied with a questionnaire, upon the replies to which the result of the test will be based.'"

This is Bernstein the gadfly, out to draw attention, entitled to his opinion that *Hallelujah* was not an artistic production but flying in the face of critical opinion which rates it highly to this day. There would hardly have been anything novel in critics praising a film that average cinemagoers disliked. But perhaps it was less a case of Bernstein the gadfly than Bernstein as P.T. Barnum, for the attendant publicity apparently resulted in *Hallelujah* doing excellent business at Enfield.

Bernstein asked audiences if they agreed with the view that it was "the most profound study of emotions any film has yet contrived" but ninety per cent of patrons did not fill in his questionnaire. Many respondents were annoyed that another, inappropriate feature film was, in fact, shown – a revival of the silent *Our Dancing Daughters*. A narrow majority of those who filled in the questionnaire decided that it was indeed as good as the critics made out, but a larger majority denied it the label of "masterpiece" – although, as this group, from a list provided, defined a masterpiece as *Ben Hur, Atlantic* or *The Singing Fool*, its standards of judgment were ridiculed at the time.

Bernstein made much more of a success out of a further series of general questionnaires, the results of which attracted national publicity. Complex questions were included in July 1931 when Sidney urged cinemagoers to answer two questions in particular as fully as possible: "Do you view with concern/equanimity the dissemination throughout the country by the medium of foreign pictures of (a) alien manners (b) alien phraseology (c) alien standards of taste (personal adornment, household decorations, etc.)?"; and "Do you consider that an abundant supply of representative British pictures is essential for the propagation of (a) British ideals (b) British business ethics?" Only the better educated cinema patron would have understood the questions, let alone have a view on them, and it is only too clear what answers were expected...

In 1935, a quarter of a million questionnaires were issued between May 7 and 19. 124,837 were returned. It took until the end of September to analyse the responses. One question asked about organ solos. There was an 84.6% vote in favour with 15.4% against. Women and the under-21s were more in favour than other groups. The question was, of course, asked of audiences used to organ solos in Bernstein theatres who would have gone elsewhere if they strongly objected and not been around to fill in the questionnaire.

A 1937 questionnaire was issued in early January and posed

twelve simple questions. For the best completed responses, a £5 cash prize and 200 free seats were offered at each theatre.

This is not the place to list or comment upon the results of each poll, only to reiterate that, whether or not they had any influence on politicians and film-makers, they were given national prominence and certainly were most worthwhile for keeping both Sidney Bernstein and Bernstein Theatres in the public eye.

Bernstein remained on the board of The Film Society, which arranged club screenings of notable foreign films that were not being shown in Britain. There is no reason to suppose that he arranged further screenings of these films publicly in his cinemas – he knew full well that the films had esoteric appeal and his cinemas were far too large and usually not in a suitable location.

However, he was not above an educative gesture where shorts were concerned. "He had South London audiences of 3,000 in commercial cinemas, applauding Len Lye's abstract films when they were still new to the intelligentsia," reported Tom Driberg in a war-time profile of Bernstein.

And perhaps Bernstein is behind some of the occasional surprises to be spotted among the bookings to the big theatres. Fritz Lang's study of a child murderer, M, received a full week's run as the main feature at Walthamstow in November 1932, and also played a half-week at the Empire Edmonton. The semi-documentary Man of Aran (1934), released by Gaumont-British, was screened at some Bernstein Theatres to a poor response. At Walthamstow, the manager reported that it was "over-rated... without popular appeal here" (the week's admissions, including a different Sunday show, totalled a low 19,187). At Willesden, it was noted that the Robert Flaherty picture was "a big disappointment and we had many complaints". In January 1938, Michael Powell's offbeat The Edge of the World was released to just a handful of off-circuit cinemas, but it did play for a full week at the Granada Greenford as "The film the critics raved about!" and at East Ham as one of the two features supporting the primary attraction, the music hall programme.

Another oddity was the experimental booking into the Granada Tooting of the German film War Is Hell in August 1932, directly after its opening run at the Marble Arch Pavilion. This picture argued the case for disarmament and was apparently sponsored by the League of Nations. It had an "international cast" of little-known foreign players. Paired with a new Hollywood picture Carnival Boat, it was helped by being the farewell week of a run by popular organist Harold Ramsay.

Sidney Bernstein certainly took the credit for an odd innovation of a different sort tried out at Walthamstow. This is the text of a press release dated 6 November 1933, sent to the Daily Film Renter: "With the object of relieving the monotony from which cinema queues inevitably suffer, Sidney L. Bernstein is trying an experiment of providing Corinthian bagatelle tables for patrons to play with while awaiting admission. He has had two tables specially constructed. They have just been introduced to the queues at the Granada, Walthamstow, and have proved tremendously popular with the public. The queues for the first time are kept happy and amused during their 'vigil'. The usual penny-in-the-slot device has been eliminated from the Granada machines so that no money is necessary to bring the balls into action. You just press the knob and play on. These two machines, unlike the rather gaudy models found in public houses, have been made in polished wood to blend with the architecture of the Granada, and are mounted on rubber tyred wheels so that they may be moved along with the queues. On the end of each machine is a notice which reads: FOR YOUR AMUSEMENT WHILE WAITING. FREE – TRY YOUR SKILL – FREE. IF YOU SCORE 6,000 OR OVER SHOW THE ATTENDANT. SUCH A SCORE ENTITLES YOU TO TWO FREE CIRCLE SEATS FOR NEXT WEEK. PLAY ONLY ONCE AS YOUR NEIGHBOURS IN THE QUEUE ARE WAITING THEIR TURN."

General film booking

Granada's booking department had at least one coup when it gave Gracie Fields' first film, RKO's Sally In Our Alley (1931), a full circuit release after others fought shy. The result was a huge hit that had to be re-booked into some of the cinemas.

A record survives of Granada's experience of showing Charles Laughton's The Private Life of Henry VIII for six days at two of its biggest theatres in early 1934. At Tooting, 39,070 paid admissions were recorded and manager J. Hutchings noted of The Private Life of Henry VIII and its accompanying feature Midnight Club: "A grand combination. I think we can honestly say that everyone enjoyed both films. All week, excepting Saturday, we were very slack from 3 to 6 o'clock. [Organist] Don Baker had a good average reception..." But at Walthamstow the following week, manager E. Hall reported admissions of 30,891 for the British historical epic and commented: "Rather disappointing... I do not think Henry was Walthamstow's meat. A splendid picture enjoyed by all who came to the better seats."

One aspect of booking policy is well worth emphasising. Granada were never worried about losing face by booking a recent success played by a rival or by reviving an older picture. The 1932 Smilin' Through was returned "by special request" to Bedford during the slack mid-December period of 1935. In May 1932, Viennese Nights was repeated at the Granada Tooting "by public demand" with a new Hollywood feature and guest organist Mr. X, who turned out to be Harold Ramsay. In the following month, Tooting offered patrons a "Great Revival Week" of The

HOW COULD ? WE REFUSE ?

•

GRACIE FIELDS

England's Greatest Comedienne, in

Sally in Our Alley

•

THOUSANDS HAVE ! ASKED US TO SHOW IT !

•

Feb. 22 for 6 days

GRANĀDA

HOE ST, WALTHAMSTOW

ONE OF THE
BERNSTEIN
THEATRES

ALSO — IN EVERY PROGRAM

3

VARIETY ACTS

AND

ANN HARDING

IN

DEVOTION

GRANADA TOOTING BROADWAY

APRIL 30th

ON THE STAGE

JACK HYLTON AND HIS BAND

PAUL MUNI

THE WORLD CHANGES (A)

ZASU PITTS
THELMA TODD

ONE TRACK MINDS (U)

Far left: a hit film of 1931.

Left: note the remarkable simplicity of the advertising (a pity if you wanted to know the showing times). Sometimes at Tooting, as here in April 1934, the live booking was the major draw. The films were new but not of enormous appeal.

Below: list at left shows the temporary attachment of cinemas at Hampstead, Hereford and Hitchin to the circuit.

(All BFI – Sidney Bernstein Special Collection.)

● Associated with...

TOOTING :
 GRANADA.

WALTHAMSTOW :
 GRANADA.

EAST HAM :
 KINEMA.

EDMONTON :
 EMPIRE.

ENFIELD :
 RIALTO.

HAMPSTEAD :
 PLAYHOUSE.

LEYTONSTONE :
 RIALTO.

PLUMSTEAD :
 KINEMA.

SUTTON :
 PLAZA.

WILLESDEN :
 EMPIRE.

BEDFORD :
 EMPIRE.
 GRANADA.
 PALACE.

HERTFORD :
 CASTLE.
 COUNTY.

HITCHIN :
 HERMITAGE.
 REGAL.

LOUGHTON :
 CINEMA.

MAIDSTONE :
 GRANADA.

MANSFIELD :
 HIPPODROME.
 PLAZA.

OSWESTRY :
 REGAL.

RUGBY :
 PLAZA.
 REGENT.
 REGAL.

SHREWSBURY :
 EMPIRE.
 GRANADA.
 KINGS.

All Orders and Receipts to
be on the Company's official
forms. None other valid.

West End and Regd. Offices: 36 Golden Square, London, W.1. Telephone : Gerrard 3554 (6 lines)

WEST HAM KINEMA

Proprietors Denman (London) Cinemas Ltd

ONE OF THE
BERNSTEIN
THEATRES

MARYLAND 1208

WEST HAM LANE
STRATFORD, E.15

PERSONAL.

FOR ADULTS ONLY.   January 1936.

Dear Patrons,

    I have just returned from a pre-view showing of the film DAWN OF LIFE, and I feel it my duty to tell you all something about it.

    DAWN OF LIFE tells the story of that great army of women awaiting motherhood, of the physical and mental sufferings of the lying-in room, labour wards and waiting rooms. Science has to decide which it shall save— mother or child, while the despairing young father looks on helplessly.

    It would spoil your enjoyment to unfold the whole of this astounding drama, but I can assure you that the climax presents one of the most daring problems ever screened. DAWN OF LIFE is no ordinary propaganda film, for Loretta Young, Frank McHugh and Aline McMahon are all starred in it. Above all, there is nothing sordid about DAWN OF LIFE. On the contrary, you will find it 100 per cent. entertainment.

    Several newspapers have expressed doubt as to its suitability for public presentation. To these I would say that anything so sincerely, so tenderly, so conscientiously handled as DAWN OF LIFE, definitely renders a great and noble service to the cause of humanity, and I honestly believe that to miss seeing the film would be to miss something very precious.

    DAWN OF LIFE comes to the KINEMA, February 3, for three days.

Yours sincerely,

John C. Roberts

MANAGER.

Desert Song plus *The Millionaire*. Then in July came a week of "2 Big British Films A Day" – all revivals, many boosted by personal appearances of their stars. *The Lives of a Bengal Lancer* was given a second run at Tooting, Walthamstow and elsewhere in May 1935. In June 1938, the seven-year-old Gary Cooper gangster drama *City Streets* reappeared as the main feature at Edmonton, Sutton and elsewhere. The smash hit *The Citadel* was a "special revival" at Willesden just three weeks after its appearance at ABC cinemas in the area.

However, the showing of the 1934 *The Count of Monte Cristo* as "The Sensation of the BBC, Now the Sensation of the Screen" at Tooting and Clapham Junction in May 1938 was not an early instance of what would become a regular Granada ploy of reviving film versions of current radio serials but a general Odeon circuit revival.

After Greenford opened in November 1937 it was soon top-billing not just *City Streets* but other oldies such as *Scarface*, *All Quiet on the Western Front* (with *Captain Blood*), and *Mr. Deeds Goes to Town*, even though it had access to the weekly main Gaumont circuit release. *Scarface* was revived at the same time at North Cheam and probably elsewhere.

Perhaps the biggest double bill revival was the fire and flood pairing of *In Old Chicago* with *The Hurricane* at Tooting in November 1938 – all this plus Robinson Cleaver at the organ!

The long-established pairing of *Dracula* and *Frankenstein* was given screen time at Harrow and Sutton in the Spring of 1939. Granada seems to have spearheaded the return of Cecil B. DeMille's *The Sign of the Cross* in the summer of that year. Revivals offered the advantage of being available on more attractive terms, but they were clearly also popular with audiences as the policy continued into the Fifties, far more extensively at Granadas than at the other major circuits.

At some of the theatres it was possible to combine the main new films from two of the major circuit releases. Leytonstone, Sutton and Tooting often advertised "the *two* best releases of the week". The same policy was followed at many of the big Gaumont halls. This stopped during the War.

The Century Cheam Village opened as a cinema specialising in re-runs as "The Home Of Great Films You Intended To See" and it named the studio and director of each week's attraction in the printed monthly programme (Sunday was a separate conventional show of old films). The great films were generally the recent box-office hits like *100 Men and a Girl* or *Mutiny on the Bounty*, although they also included *The Informer* (with the misinformation that it was "directed by Phil Rosen"), but occasionally the Century ventured into the foreign film market, exclusively presenting the subtitled *La Kermesse Heroïque* after a six-month West End run as "Witty... brilliant... and ooh, la! la! so daringly

French". The Century also seems to have given *Green Pastures*, the Warner Bros. biblical fable with an all-black cast, a belated area premiere in April 1938, putting on a morning preview for local worthies to encourage good word of mouth. There was no suggestion of a "tilt at the critics" this time.

On occasion, Granada displayed a penchant for exploitation that would have delighted P. T. Barnum – or the Ripley of Believe-It-Or-Not in the case of the live appearance at the East Ham Kinema in 1934 of the "Amazing Giraffe-Necked Woman from Burma – Sensation of Bertram W. Mills' Olympia Circus". The Empire Willesden booked *Shall the Children Pay?*, an obscure item for adults only promoted with letters marked "Personal" that described it as "a serious film... It will not shock you, but it will certainly make you think." The same approach was used for a film about motherhood, *The Dawn of Life*, when it played the West Ham Kinema in January 1936 and became a standard promotional technique for stories of unwed mothers, childbearing, rape, etc. in the immediate post-war years.

More than other cinemas, Granada always made a great show of its theatres' birthdays. The favoured approach was a mystery special programme – "No Names – But a Promise! We promise the greatest show you have ever seen" – developed in the late Twenties at Willesden, Enfield and elsewhere. In the early Thirties, the anniversary week brought not only a mystery programme but a piece of cake: "No Names Only a Promise. But a big screen and stage show you'll never forget! A piece of birthday cake for every lady and child." The cakes (11 ft. 6 ins. high on a beaver-board frame with a huge candle and real icing for Tooting's first anniversary; one weighing half a ton for the third) were exhibited in the foyer. These never stretched to feeding the male patron – surely a cause of resentment?

The Granada Tooting's first birthday celebrations followed the "No Names – Only a Promise" policy whereby staff were sworn to secrecy over the titles of the films to be shown and the names of the variety acts. According to the *Daily Film Renter* (15 September 1932), the week broke every record for the theatre, with 63,018 admissions. Over 6,000 children flocked to the special Saturday morning show, the queue forming at 6.30am, ninety minutes before the doors opened. Only half could be admitted. The main feature shown that week was *Lord Babs* and the programme included a special compilation prepared by Adrian Brunel and Ivor Montagu of excerpts from newsreels and films of the past year.

An unsigned description survives of the live show. "The organ recital consisted of a special birthday medley. With appropriate slides, a special birthday stage presentation was introduced. The new 50 ft. screen – used for the first time this week – on which was projected as a background the front elevation of the

BIRTHDAY GREETINGS

Top left: first birthday celebrations on the stage of the Granada Woolwich in April 1938, being led by the lady with microphone in front of the Union Jack. The exterior decoration of the theatre can be seen on the first page of this book.

Left: leaflet for Walthamstow's sixth birthday claims over nine million admissions.

Above: this advertisement shows the Sergeant as he was first used (from early 1938) in press advertising, placed behind the name of the town.

(All BFI – Sidney Bernstein Collection.)

Granada with cloud effects, was raised displaying a huge birthday cake with a ballet dancer posed in front of it. A dance followed, the actions of which implied to the audience that the cake was in honour of the first birthday. At the close of this dance, she threw flowers, picked off the cake, to the audience, and finished by drawing the attention of the audience to the cake which slowly opened into a fountain with running water. An illuminated sign reading BIRTHDAY GREETINGS TO ALL was then lowered in the flies; also balloons were released, falling all over the stage, to the accompaniment of the organ playing 'Auld Lang Syne'. The effect was enhanced by fairy lights which surrounded the organ console, and brought the organ solo to a climax in a blaze of light."

For the second anniversary, Tooting audiences were shown *Goodnight Vienna* plus *No One Man*, and another spectacular stage act was devised. In a letter dated 12 September 1933, Granada's public relations chief Ewart Hodgson informed *The Daily Film Renter*: "It was while dickering about looking for some novel angle to celebrate this birthday week that we lighted on the idea of having eight pianos on the stage being played simultaneously by eight crack pianists, under the baton of Harold Ramsay. Some people – they shall be nameless – vouchsafed the opinion that such an act was impossible. We went on with the job, however.

"First of all, the music had to be specially orchestrated for eight pianos; that work was done by Tony Lowry who arranges the music for Jack Hylton and many of the other big dance bands. Lowry spent the best part of a month on that job but succeeded in the end in turning out a first class programme which included Gershwin's 'Rhapsody in Blue', 'I Cover the Water Front', Ravel's 'Bolero', 'Sweetheart Darling' and a pot-pourri of Russian melodies embracing Rachmaninoff's Prelude, 'Dark Eyes' and the finale of the 1812 Overture.

"That part of the job accomplished, Ramsay and the eight pianists practised and rehearsed for three weeks. The result, from the point of view of public appreciation, was a triumph. The eight pianos were played with all the precision of a duet.

"When we put up the idea of broadcasting to the BBC, they did not hesitate and a few days ago they gave the act twenty minutes on the National programme."

The act was retained for a second week at Tooting.

According to newspaper reports, birthday shows played to packed houses. Patrons at Bedford's first birthday show found themselves enjoying the Sydney Howard comedy *Where's George*, the drama *Air Hawks*, the 5 Sherry Bros. on stage, and a preview of *Whom the Gods Love*. Tooting's third birthday programme was openly advertised, as were those of Granadas opened later in the Thirties.

As part of his cinema's first birthday celebrations in March 1939, Jimmy Turton, manager of the Granada Slough, decided to create a "Pavement of the Stars", a British version of the handprints and signatures in cement displayed at Grauman's Chinese in Hollywood. He wanted impressions of hands and feet and signatures from any film star in the vicinity. Will Hay started off the pavement (which was at the stage end of the theatre) and later additions included Sabu's in August 1939.*

Granada also made a habit of labelling its September attractions "Welcome Home" programmes to help draw patrons in again after their summer holiday break.

Like other cinemas outside the biggest city centres, Granadas changed main programmes every week (some of the lesser theatres also changed mid-week). Such were the enormous crowds for *Pygmalion* with Wendy Hiller and Leslie Howard (supported by B feature *Sinners in Paradise*) at the Plaza Sutton in January 1939 that the undistinguished programme advertised for the following week (*Black Limelight* and *Gangs of New York*) was cancelled and *Pygmalion* held over ("Are you going to miss it? Not b— likely"). This was said to be the first time that any film had played two weeks at a Granada. (While Bernstein Theatres were running the Regal Watford in October 1933 the smash hit *Cavalcade* had played four times a day for a pre-arranged two weeks.)

Being general release halls, Granadas rarely had the opportunity to present a premiere. But their size sometimes counted in their favour. At Christmas 1933, Tooting shared the world premiere of Paramount's *Alice in Wonderland* with the Hollywood studio's West End flagship, the Plaza. On 30 April 1937, Sidney Bernstein loaned East Ham for the charity world premiere of a major British musical, *London Melody*, starring Anna Neagle, the show being in aid of the Tower Hill Improvement Fund and attended by the Duchess of Gloucester.

Then Clapham Junction was provided for a gala charity premiere in the presence of the Duchess of Kent. It was the first European showing of *Letter of Introduction* on Monday 31 October 1938 in aid of the Queen's Hospital for Children at Hackney. Making her first visit to a suburban cinema, the Duchess kindly went on stage to accept two toys for her children made by unemployed

* Around May 1951, John Wayne and Bob Hope both provided impressions of their hands and feet in modelling clay to be transferred to concrete later at Slough. The Granadas Clapham Junction and Tooting decided to start "Pavements of Fame" at that time. Clapham obtained the handprints and footprints of Bette Davis and Gary Merrill, and Tooting secured the footprints of the current Tarzan, Lex Barker, but there is no evidence that these were ever placed outside the theatres and no further examples have come to light. The Gaumont Birkenhead had preceded Slough with a concrete impression of Nova Pilbeam's extremities when she opened the cinema in May 1938, and this cinema added others later. If any of these "pavements" survive is not known. A new one has been started in Leicester Square in recent years.

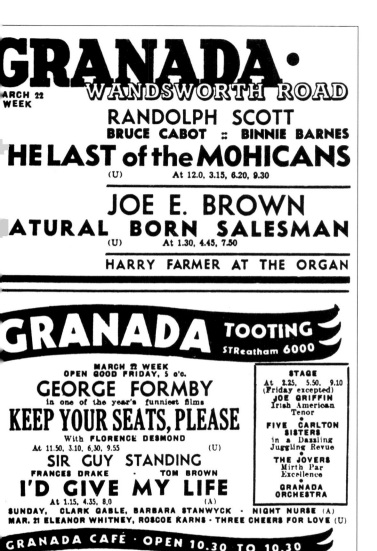

GRANADA·
WANDSWORTH ROAD
ARCH 22 WEEK

RANDOLPH SCOTT
BRUCE CABOT :: BINNIE BARNES
HE LAST of the MOHICANS
(U)　　　At 12.0, 3.15, 6.20, 9.30

JOE E. BROWN
ATURAL BORN SALESMAN
(U)　　　At 1.30, 4.45, 7.50

HARRY FARMER AT THE ORGAN

GRANADA TOOTING
STReatham 6000

MARCH 22 WEEK
OPEN GOOD FRIDAY, 5 o'c.
GEORGE FORMBY
in one of the year's funniest films
KEEP YOUR SEATS, PLEASE
With FLORENCE DESMOND
At 11.50, 3.10, 6.30, 9.55　　　(U)

SIR GUY STANDING
FRANCES DRAKE · TOM BROWN
I'D GIVE MY LIFE
At 1.15, 4.35, 8.0　　　(A)

SUNDAY, CLARK GABLE, BARBARA STANWYCK · NIGHT NURSE (A)
MAR. 21 ELEANOR WHITNEY, ROSCOE KARNS · THREE CHEERS FOR LOVE (U)

GRANADA CAFÉ · OPEN 10.30 TO 10.30

STAGE
At 2.25, 5.50, 9.10
(Friday excepted)
JOE GRIFFIN
Irish American
Tenor
•
FIVE CARLTON
SISTERS
in a Dazzling
Juggling Revue
•
THE JOVERS
Mirth Par
Excellence
•
GRANADA
ORCHESTRA

Two styles of advertising in use in March 1937. Note how eye-catching and clean the one is for Wandsworth Road.

---

ex-servicemen from Battersea. Although one press report had her occupying an ordinary one-and-six stalls seat, it is clear that she sat in the front row of the circle as a plaque was later placed there to commemorate the fact. The film started at 9.48pm and didn't finish until 11.30pm. One hopes the Duchess didn't have to get up early the next morning.

On another occasion around January 1939, Sidney Bernstein offered the free use of the Granada Greenford on a Sunday (when the cinema was normally closed) and arranged for staff to be present for a concert by the Greenford Women's Co-Operative Guild to raise food and medical aid for the Loyalist (anti-Fascist) side in the Spanish Civil War. The event was specially licensed by Middlesex County Council but the theatre was withdrawn and the show cancelled after "representations had been made to Mr. Bernstein from the higher authorities". Bernstein could not be contacted for comment as he was "in Switzerland".

Guest appearances by stars brought occasional touches of glamour. In June 1939, Gene Autry greeted the youngsters at a Saturday morning show at Clapham Junction. On a Wednesday in August 1939, Tyrone Power appeared in person on stage at 9.15pm at Tooting as part of a tour to promote his latest film, *Jesse James*. The cinema had filled to capacity by 4pm and Power talked to the overflow crowd outside from on top of the canopy.

Late night shows were not entirely unknown but were usually held for charity. Bedford staged its first charity midnight matinee on Friday 18 September 1936.

Coming to Granadas in the Fifties, it was a disappointment to this writer that, unlike almost every other cinema, they did not issue monthly programmes – perhaps because they liked to keep bookings flexible or once again wanted to be different. However, in the Thirties, weekly programmes were issued at Tooting (and probably elsewhere) with cast lists and a gossip column. And monthly programmes were issued by all the theatres in the mid- and late Thirties. These contained a column of trivia, signed "El Señor" at Granadas and "Mr. X" at the non-Hispanic halls.

Live [except organs – see Chaper 21]
After Tooting opened in September 1931, for the entire first year there were no bands, variety acts or any stage shows at all, only the organist. But variety was introduced in 1934 almost every week – major draws including Jack Hylton and His Famous Band, Max Miller, and Billy Cotton and His Band. Then from October 1938 the organ became the only added attraction in some weeks.

In late 1933 and 1934, Charles Manning ("The Svengali of Music") was to be found conducting "His Magic Baton" with an orchestra of twenty-five at Walthamstow, Leytonstone, Tooting and Edmonton, then appearing with "His Granada Band" for a week at the West Ham Kinema.

A circus with real elephants took to the stage at Tooting for the week of 15 January 1934 together with films. For Christmas 1935 and the four succeeding years, a circus was the main draw at Tooting, supported by two films, resulting in shows running nearly four hours. The same circus played a week earlier in 1938 at Clapham Junction and a week later in 1939 at East Ham.

The Granada Clapham Junction seems to have had stage shows every week from opening in 1937, perhaps to compete with the Grand Theatre a short distance away. Sometimes these were more important than the films: Arthur Askey and Richard Murdoch in a stage version of their hit radio show *The Band Waggon* were billed over two cheap screen attractions at Clapham Junction in March 1939, as was Tommy Trinder leading *Tommy Trinder's Party* in June.

Current fads were exploited. In late 1938 and early 1939, two badminton champions competed on stage at Tooting and Clapham Junction as part of every live show for a week. In August 1939 famous boxer Jack Doyle teamed up with film star Movita to put over a love song three times daily at East Ham, Tooting and Clapham Junction.

Amateur variety was widely staged. Walthamstow put on Amateur Hour Shows in March 1937 with West End comedian Freddie Forbes as compère. Amateur contests were almost the only form of live attraction other than the organists at Greenford, Harrow, North Cheam, Mansfield (Plaza) and Willesden. They were usually an added Friday night attraction. Some theatres like Bedford, Maidstone, Slough and Sutton (Plaza) seemed to have almost no live use other than the organist in some weeks. No doubt the competition and level of business dictated policy, as with the dependence on variety to boost business at Greenwich.

It may be recalled that the Granada Shrewsbury opened in 1934 with a declared policy of one live week to every three of films. But in its first year it managed only two weeks of plays including a thriller *Ten Minute Alibi* in March 1935. These plays averaged 6,393 patrons compared to 7,756 for fifty weeks of films, although the prices of admission for live shows was more than twice as high. It had proved difficult to persuade actors to abandon West End and film work for as remote a place as Shrewsbury. However, Shrewsbury Operatic Society arranged to present *The Vagabond King* in April 1936, starting a long tradition of amateur light opera at the theatre.

Granada did have one performer besides the star organists who became an invaluable asset – worth booking to every large theatre. His name was Bryan Michie. This genial giant of a man was in his early thirties, well established as a BBC radio personality, when he started with Granada, hosting discovery shows of new acts. Billed as "The incomparable compere from the BBC", he toured in mid-1938 with the *Bryan Michie Granada Discoveries of*

Two examples of 1939 advertising.
(BFI – Sidney Bernstein Collection.)

1938, visiting such theatres as Bedford, Clapham Junction, Greenford, Tooting and Wandsworth Road (always supported by two films). His *Discoveries of 1939* featured the "12 Top-Line Amateur Acts of the Year" with Jack Fields' Granada Orchestra, a one-hour show three times a day plus two films: week-long visits were made to Bedford, Greenford, Rugby (Plaza), Slough, Tooting, Walthamstow and Woolwich, perhaps elsewhere. He would continue to host talent shows for Granada in the Forties and early Fifties and does not seem to have appeared in rival cinemas.

Taking at random the district cinema listings in the London *Evening News* for Saturday 1 April 1939, Granadas that advertised film shows plus live acts were Greenwich and East Ham (both presenting Nat Gonella), Clapham Junction ("Stage MUSIC HALL with **EIGHT BIG ACTS**") and Tooting ("Big Stage Show") while Greenford and Walthamstow appended the names of organists and Willesden just added "Organ". The only other local cinemas advertising live acts with films were the Gaumonts Camden Town, Hammersmith, Holloway, Kilburn (State), Lewisham, plus other G.-B. theatres: the Shepherds Bush Pavilion, Elephant and Castle Trocadero and Stepney Troxy.

And pantomimes

Although Granada became famous for pantomimes after the Second World War, they made their first appearance in the Thirties. A "full-length, complete" *Jack and the Beanstalk* with cast of sixty headed by Violet Fields performed three times a day at Tooting in the week of 6 January 1936 supported by a feature *Ginger* and the Our Gang short *Little Papa*, the whole continuous show taking 3 hours 15 minutes. This was claimed to be the first time a full panto had been combined with a film show.

In the week of 8 August 1938, *Snow White and the Seven Dwarfs* was performed live with two films in support at Clapham Junction. The first and only pre-war pantomime to play on its own with separate performances was *Dick Whittington and His Cat* which opened at Maidstone on Boxing Day 1938 and moved to the Plaza Rugby on 2 January 1939.

Granadiers

Children's shows were not a runaway success. After they resumed at the Empire Willesden on 8 February 1930 under the auspices of the local Education Committee, the results were "disappointing".

In the Thirties, as before, when the main attraction of the week was suitable, such as *Tarzan The Ape Man* or *Daddy Long Legs* in 1932, this was given a screening on the Saturday morning of the week's run at Granadas – a far cry from the worn prints of aged B features that were the norm in the Fifties.

Bernstein Theatres did not initiate long-term children's clubs.

These were begun by the County circuit in association with United Artists, the distributor of Walt Disney's cartoons, with the first of a series of Mickey Mouse Clubs opening at the Regal Golders Green.

A Granada Children's Club was formed at Tooting in the autumn of 1933. In 1935, when Mickey Mouse clubs started up in Odeons and other cinemas, Sidney Bernstein responded with a club called Kinemates. In his history of children's shows, *All Pals Together*, Terry Staples comments: "A privilege of being a Kinemate was the right to book seats in advance, a scheme intended to reduce the crush that could build up outside a cinema long before the box office opened. The name Kinemates was short-lived, perhaps because nobody was sure how to pronounce it. It was replaced in 1937 by Granadiers clubs in Granadas and Rangers clubs in Empire cinemas. There came to be a Disney connection, but it was Donald Duck, not Mickey Mouse. On the Granadiers' badge he was in military uniform, and for Empire children he was dressed as a Ranger."

In a paper given to the November 1936 Conference on Films for Children in London, Sidney Bernstein outlined the advantage of providing a "nursery for film-goers" to create a "'picture-minded' generation", and pointed to the goodwill children's shows generated from parents and the children themselves as well as the desirability of diverting fidgety and clamorous children from adult shows where they might be occupying seats at half-price that could have been sold for the full amount.

Bernstein declared, "There is a uniform admission price of threepence, and our children's matinee admissions in the year ending in September 1936 were 650,000. I must make it clear however that whether the attendances are good or bad, in no case are the matinees financially successful. Indeed a strict balance sheet shows a loss, though so small as to be negligible. From the goodwill angle however, these performances have proved beneficial...

"Our figures show that at each theatre it is necessary to gather an audience of 700, paying threepence admission, before first costs are covered. This figure does not allow for management, rent or depreciation. (Incidentally, depreciation is quite a serious charge. The child is a destructive and untidy creature. Peanut shells, sticky sweets on expensive upholstery, even slashed arm pads and seats are common consequences of our performances.)

"Secondly, there are difficulties of supply. There is an entirely inadequate supply of films which will satisfy the child's wants..."

Managers of Granadiers' clubs were usually called "Uncle Jack" regardless of their real first name.

Sundays

Many cinemas were not allowed to open on Sundays. Granada campaigned hard to force a local vote on the issue of Sunday cinema opening and then to persuade people to turn out and vote in favour. A typical case in point was Sutton where a vote took place on Saturday 20 March 1937. There was a forty-two per cent turnout with a majority of 6,284 in favour, and the Plaza opened its doors on a Sunday for the first time on 1 August 1937. Similar time-consuming, expensive but successful campaigns were conducted at Walthamstow in 1932, Enfield in 1938 and Greenford in 1939.

Staff

The number of employees at new Granadas varied, from eighty-two at Clapham Junction to forty-two at Slough. As one would expect from Sidney Bernstein's leftwing outlook, he recognised the National Association of Theatrical and Kine Employees and negotiated agreements over wages and hours worked. In 1938, there was, however, an unexplained strike by the projection team at Harrow after an hour of amateur variety, leading to a 45-minute gap before operators arrived from the Capitol and Majestic Wembley to resume the show.

A completely new uniform for female staff was introduced around September 1936 consisting of blue trousers (same as men's uniforms), gold blouse, blue cloaks lined in gold, and a hat of the American sailor type. With a spare blouse, these uniforms cost five guineas each.

Attendance figures?

Along with a series of obviously humorous statistics, attendance figures were given in leaflets issued to commemorate birthdays and at first promised to indicate the relative success of new Granadas.

Walthamstow claimed to have attracted 9,184,815 admissions in its first five years.

At Tooting, 2,137,722 tickets were sold in the first year (up to 26 August 1932). A year later, a cumulative total of 4,456,225 (to 25 August 1933) was declared, a phenomenal increase of 2,318,503. The next two years added 2,416,275 and an extraordinary 3,039,950 admissions. But then Granada gave out a fifth anniversary total of 10,283,526. Yet the figures for the first four years almost reached that total, adding up to 9,912,450.

For Maidstone, a three-year total of 2,233,549 patrons was claimed. Sutton Plaza apparently sold 2,283,549 tickets in two years, closely followed by 2,263,584 in the same time span at Bedford.

For Woolwich, a first year total of 1,332,486 admissions was announced.

North Cheam registered 882,763 in its first year. But Granada gave out exactly the same figure at the first anniversaries of Greenwich and Harrow.

At Greenford, the number came out as 674,222 which then became the figure issued for Welling and Slough.

Perhaps, in the spirit of P. T. Barnum, all the figures are exaggerations (like Granada's seating figures), or perhaps some of the figures are accurate and the repetitions, for example, occurred because there wasn't the time or the energy to add up the real totals. However, they do seem to confirm the poor performance of Maidstone in its early years, achieving fewer admissions in three years than Bedford in two.

The circuit as a whole was said to have achieved 10,876,233 admissions during 1936.

12 • Granada At War

War had become increasingly likely in the early part of 1939. In May, during Bedford's National Service Week, the Granada programme included *The Warning*, a short depicting air raids which encouraged locals to sign up for training in how to deal with them.

When war was finally declared on the morning of Sunday 3 September 1939, the Granadas – along with all other British cinemas – were not permitted to open that evening and had to remain closed as a precautionary measure until further notice. Anticipating the shut-down, Golden Square had issued detailed instructions on what should be done to keep staff busy: spring cleaning, maintenance, filling sandbags, carrying out fire drills, and so on.

The authorities envisaged that some cinemas might eventually re-open in areas which proved to be safe from air raids. When there were no immediate attacks, exhibitors campaigned to have cinemas re-opened. They gained the support of London County Council chairman Herbert Morrison who contacted the Home Office and outer London cinemas – including the Granadas Cheam, Harrow and Sutton – were allowed to resume performances on Saturday 9 September, followed by the others in the inner London area on Friday 15 September.

No exterior lights were allowed because of the black-out regulations and patrons had difficulty finding the front doors after dark. Managers appeared on stage between every film to announce that the audience would be advised of any air raid warnings but that the show would continue. Patrons were advised that it would be much safer to remain and the police recommended that only those within five minutes' walk of home should leave. One Granada declared itself the best place to be: "COME TO THE GRANADA WHERE IT'S SAFER THAN HOUSES!" advertised Maidstone in late September 1939.

The call up began to reduce staff, as only chief operators were exempt. Women projectionists were trained and commenced work at many Granadas from January 1940 onwards.

As dozens of alerts took place without a single enemy air raid, audiences became tired of shows being interrupted for the same precautionary announcements. Eventually it became the practice to superimpose a slide on the picture. Very few patrons now left.

Organists and variety artists continued to be featured extensively during the war. Amateur nights of variety took place, usually on Fridays, at Edmonton, Greenwich, Harrow, North Cheam, Welling, Woolwich, and elsewhere. Bryan Michie continued to lead week-long contests for amateur performers.

Cecil Bernstein recalled the period in *Here We Are*: "We argued that the war-racked public would expect organ shows to be included in our programmes. We kept our organists on the payroll. Then, when cinemas were allowed to re-open soon after the out-break of war, we directed and encouraged our organists to build up community singing.

"In September, 1940, came the first big blitz on London. Audiences stayed in cinemas all night. The show carried on with reserve films and heartening community singing led by the organist who sometimes played for as long as an hour at a stretch.

"It was natural that during the war current song hits and old choruses which lent themselves to community singing should form the staple diet demanded by cinemagoers. 'Pops' accompanied by slides carrying the lyrics went down better than any other form of organ programmes."

Sidney Bernstein's war

As conflict loomed in 1939, Sidney Bernstein was determined to contribute his talents to the war effort and had prepared a paper on how film might best be used for propaganda purposes. Early in 1940, he was invited to join the Ministry of Information as an unpaid films adviser and suspended his business connections with Granada, leaving Cecil in full charge. Sidney was active in formalising arrangements for exhibitors to regularly show official short films and arranged for Granada managers to include in their reports to Golden Square comments, which were forwarded to him, on the audience reaction. He had a part in devising a scheme for cinemas in the same locality to share a single newsreel to conserve film stock. He made trips to America to gain showings for British propaganda documentaries, to encourage Hollywood executives to support Britain, and to liaise with the American

Office of War Information. One of his coups, according to Tom Driberg's 1944 profile, was to persuade Metro-Goldwyn-Mayer to forego the extra income from limited roadshow bookings of *Mrs. Miniver* and give it an immediate general release across America so that its sympathetic depiction of life on the British home front could have a more immediate impact.

Among the films Bernstein supervised was a 1940 ten-minute documentary about the Blitz, *London Can Take It*. Choosing his American journalist friend Quentin Reynolds to deliver the commentary (which helped to make it a huge success with American audiences), he started Reynolds off on a flourishing speaking career in radio.

As the war turned in the Allies' favour, Bernstein took charge of a series of documentaries to be shown to the people of liberated countries. One of these – *L'Echec d'une Stratégie (The Failure of a Strategy)* – was compiled from newsreels under the direction of David Lean with Bernstein as executive producer. In 1944, he arranged for Alfred Hitchcock to come from Hollywood and make two fiction shorts in French about the French Resistance: *Bon Voyage* and *Aventure Malgache*.

In 1945, when Bernstein was one of the first to see the German concentration camp at Belsen, he decided that a film record should be made by the Ministry of Information of Nazi atrocities there and at the other camps that would be beyond refutation. He recruited Hitchcock to come back again to assemble the mass of Allied and confiscated German film that had been gathered. Called *Memories of the Camps*, the film was almost completed when a decision was reached that it would not be helpful to show such material to the German people at that time, and the footage was shelved.

While working with Bernstein, Hitchcock expressed his resentment of the restrictions imposed by Hollywood producers and suggested that they became partners in a new film production company. Sidney took up the idea and they formed Transatlantic Pictures to make films in both England and Hollywood.

The Blitz

The "phoney war" lasted just over a year. Air-raids on London began on a massive scale on Saturday 7 September 1940 and continued for fifty-seven consecutive nights, usually after dark. The biggest risk was taken by the projectionists who kept the show running from their positions at roof level with only steel helmets for protection.

During the raids, audiences stayed but sat near the sides and under the balcony (where there was one) in case the ceiling collapsed. Cinemas were compelled to shut at 9pm and attendances slumped, with the best supported shows being the matinees. No Granada closed because of reduced patronage and some, like Woolwich and Greenwich, were very popular with soldiers stationed nearby. In 1940, the Granada Tooting opened on Christmas Day for the first and only time.

Audiences liked to stay in the cinema after closing time as their preferred form of shelter. Staff could not cope with continual all-night sessions and managers had to insist that, unless there was a particularly intense air raid in the immediate vicinity, the nearest official shelters had to be used at the end of the scheduled show.

The Kinema West Ham (Stratford) was hit by a bomb which destroyed three dressing rooms and closed the building for several weeks. Some cinemas survived direct hits as bombs failed to explode. The Granada Greenwich had to shut for eight days until a bomb embedded in the stage near the organ could be removed. A suspected bomb in the auditorium floor, along with fire damage, put Sutton out of business for a while. But the cinemas stayed open whenever possible, even after windows and doors had been blown out.

A crashed Heinkel bomber was put on display in October 1940 in the car park at Tooting for five days, the proceeds of admission going to help the local Spitfire Fund to the tune of £55.18s.11d. Visitors took pieces away as souvenirs, leaving little for scrap. Some local residents protested at the exhibition, fearing that it would provoke retaliatory attacks. This was not the only display of enemy aircraft as a fund-raising device.

Advertising everywhere was severely restricted and, when the threat of enemy parachutists loomed, cinema hanging cards and streetposters could not give the town name in case it aided an invading enemy to find its bearings. Street names were allowed and locals, of course, knew where the Granadas Powis Street, Hoe Street, Sheepcote Road and St.John's Hill were to be found. One Century gave the Germans a sporting chance of discovering their whereabouts, being at "Station Way C---m V-----e" with the full name visible through the stickers on hanging cards. Later, town and street names were often dropped altogether.

Local press advertising was also removed for more than a year, in South London at least, perhaps as an economy measure or in recognition of the fact that audiences were now restricted to the immediate area and could find out what was showing in person.

As the war progressed, local heroes were paraded on stage. Newsreels became increasingly popular as patrons looked for glimpses of their nearest and dearest in footage of the troops. Some Granadas repeated the news at the end of the programme for the benefit of late-comers.

Many of the theatres were located in the most heavily bombed areas. The Granada Woolwich was close by Woolwich Arsenal

GRANADA CLAPHAM
invites all you

X-PRISONERS of WAR
TO
ATCH UP WITH HISTORY

HERE'S YOUR OPPORTUNITY TO SEE THE SPECIAL FILM
GRAM COVERING EVENTS IN THE WAR AT HOME AND
OAD WHICH HAPPENED WHILE YOU WERE AWAY

SPECIAL FREE PERFORMANCE
HAS BEEN ARRANGED AT

RANADA, CLAPHAM JUNC.

NDAY MORNING, DEC. 16, AT 10.30 a.m.

Ex-POWs (*with one guest each*) ARE CORDIALLY
ITED TO APPLY FOR TICKETS . . . . **NOW**

a postcard, phone or call at the theatre giving your rank, name and
ess. Tickets (and how to get there instructions) will be sent to you.

ORE CONVENIENT YOU CAN GET YOUR TICKETS BY APPLYING
RANADA, TOOTING; GRANADA, CHEAM; OR CENTURY, CHEAM

*Above: in December 1945, the Granadas at Clapham Junction,
Harrow and Walthamstow invited former prisoners of war to a
free Sunday morning show to "Catch Up With History" and see
footage of the events they missed at home and abroad.
Over 300 attended at Walthamstow where the show included
the full-length semi-documentary* The True Glory.

*Two Granada take-overs. Above: a rare picture of the Plaza Plumstead
in 1951, decorated for "Festival Time" – the Festival of Britain or a
special film season? Below: the Globe Clapham Junction as it looked in
January 1949 with landscape views dating from its 1930 opening on the
side walls, and (right) after redecoration in July 1951 when it was renamed the Century (both from Photo Coverage).*

The Plaza Sevenoaks brought Granada into a town it had considered entering in the Thirties, and it would never be a major earner. The main opposition was an Odeon (the former Majestic). It is interesting to note how heavily Granada played the organ card here. Robinson Cleaver re-opened the Plaza's organ on 27 October and was quickly followed by Reginald Porter Brown, John Madin and Lloyd Thomas. This was a hot seat for any manager, being close to Sidney Bernstein's country home, Coppings, and frequently scrutinised for any deficiencies in its operation. The Carlton at Sevenoaks was put up for sale after two years and sold to independent operator Miles Byrne as a going concern.

In February 1948, the Bernsteins formed a new company, the International Seating Corporation, in association with George Coles and a furniture manufacturer, but this was said to be a long-term venture with no immediate plans. The long-established Granada subsidiary, the Kinematograph Equipment Company, remained the supplier of seating to the circuit.

In May 1948 Granada bought the three South London cinemas of the Alfred O'Connor (A.O.C.) chain: the Regal Kennington, State Thornton Heath and Broadway Deptford. The Regal and State were large, quite modern second-run cinemas playing split weeks. All three cinemas were soon dramatically relaunched.

The Broadway, built as a live theatre, was a good prospect as it could take the ABC release. It was closed for two months while a George Coles scheme of improvements was carried out. The theatrical decoration was too embedded to be removed, as the publicity acknowledged: "The 'new look' will delight you," it said, adding: "Although new, it still retains that grand old atmosphere you love so well." The name was not changed at this time.

Granada were able to transform business at the State Thornton Heath by gaining the Gaumont circuit release on first run, to the chagrin of the huge independent Davis Theatre in nearby Croydon which also played it. However, there was a sufficient distance between the two theatres for a concurrency to be fair – even if the previous owners hadn't had the power to arrange it. The State was good enough to be renamed Granada.

With its rounded corner entrance, streamlined look and fly-tower, the huge Regal Kennington had a superficial resemblance to the Granada Clapham Junction (they opened within days of each other in November 1937) and could easily be mistaken for an original Granada after the circuit had stamped its image on the building and renamed it. Granada must have had hopes of introducing the Odeon release (after all, Odeon itself had planned to build a cinema very near here on the site of the Kennington Theatre) but it remained stuck with split-week revivals and off-circuit programmes, barred by the Odeon Camberwell and Odeon's Brixton Astoria.

Early in 1949 a long gestating take-over of the Medway Cinemas circuit was concluded. This gave Granada control of exhibition at Dartford, Kent, where it gained four properties. Only the State and the Rialto were significant: the Scala Theatre was already leased out for live theatre use, and the Gem was soon closed, if not already shut. The State was quickly overhauled and renamed Granada, while the Rialto later became the Century.

The Medway take-over included a subsidiary company that brought Granada into the remote territory of Grantham, Lincolnshire. The State was the only modern cinema in the town, opened in 1937 and designed by J. Owen Bond who was also responsible for the Granada Harrow that year. It was quickly smartened up and renamed Granada. (Along with the State Grantham came a site at Ipswich which seems to have been put up for sale the following year.)

At all these take-overs, children's matinees were quickly introduced or restyled along Granada lines. Terry Staples, author of *All Pals Together*, the history of children's shows, cites how the song ran in Grantham:

> We're one for all and all for one,
> The Grantham Granadiers.
> We play the game at work or fun,
> The Grantham Granadiers.
> And if the skies are overcast
> We'll find a silver lining.
> You'll know us when we shout 'I serve'
> The Grantham Granadiers

He notes that the Granadiers' song "combined several elements: patriotism, in its tune ('The British Grenadiers'); swashbuckling, in its use of the rallying cry of the Three Musketeers; a declaration of civic probity; and promotion both of the company and of each cinema."

Three further Medway properties belonged to another subsidiary, Excelsior Super Cinemas. These were in outer Southeast London: the Rialto and Albany at Upper Norwood (Crystal Palace) and the nearby State at Sydenham. All had been designed and built between 1928 and 1931 by A. C. Matthews, whose State Thornton Heath (opened in 1932) had already passed to Granada.

George Coles was brought in to help modernise the Rialto. The old-fashioned look of the exterior promptly disappeared as it was painted a lighter colour and renamed Granada with a more prominent vertical sign hooked onto the roof and a new canopy extending the full width of the frontage. The Albany was a smaller, single-floor cinema almost adjacent to the Rialto, which had been hastily built by Matthews to keep other cinema chains out. This was extensively reconstructed and re-opened as the Century in 1950.

The State Sydenham was about a mile and a half away by main

"Haven't You Heard?

.... soon the State, Sydenham, is going to become GRANADA...a service-with-a-smile theatre ... all the best film programs and such comfort ....."

...ranada Theatres have been pleasing the ...lm-going public for the last twenty-five years, ...stifying their belief that running a cinema ...eans more than selling a seat and projecting ... film.

...'ll be saying it often so start saying it now—GRA-NAH-DAH!

"Wonderful News!

... in just two weeks the State, Sydenham, is going to be renamed GRANADA...one of the famous service-with-a-smile theatres ... an assurance of the fullest enjoyment in your leisure hours."

The vast resources of Granada Theatres ensure the newest successes from the world's studios presented in an atmosphere of relaxation and comfort.

You'll be saying it often so start saying it now—GRA-NAH-DAH!

Wait till I tell You!...

next week there's going to be a gala opening of the GRANADA which used to be the State ... there'll be a surprise for the first patron which promises fun...and the famous service-with-a-smile for everyone. The whole town will be there ... but it won't be complete without you..."

In twenty-five years Granada Theatres have entertained 520 millions of satisfied patrons... evidence of their choice of films and the use of every modern device in presenting them.

...'ll be saying it often so start saying it now—GRA-NAH-DAH!

"Come On!...

the State is now GRANADA... everyone's going to the new service-with-a-smile theatre where you'll find a difference in atmosphere... more comfort... civility ... a feeling that you personally are welcome."

It is of course the GRANADA slogan in action–"SERVICE-WITH-A-SMILE." So please forget ~~State~~...it's no harder to say

GRANADA

You'll be saying it often so start saying it now—GRA-NAH-DAH!

Start Saying Gra-NAH-dah! This is the standard set of flyers devised by Granada to promote a change of name to Granada or Century at recently acquired cinemas. At Chichester and Kingston the old name was half-retained: it may have been "no harder to say Granada" but it was definitely more of a mouthful to say "Granada Exchange" and "Century Elite". (BFI – Sidney Bernstein Collection.)

The King's Hall Leyton, seen as the Century in March 1955 – smart but still old-fashioned, with circuit-style light fittings in the ceiling of the auditorium (Photo Coverage).

road from Crystal Palace. This was the only cinema in Sydenham (others had closed during the war) but there was major circuit competition nearby at Penge and Forest Hill. It was large enough and sufficiently well-appointed to be worthy of taking the Granada name and it was able to play the Gaumont circuit release concurrently with the King's Hall (later Gaumont) Penge.*

During this period, Sidney Bernstein remained heavily involved in film production. However, in June 1949, he found time to write from Hollywood to Theodore Komisarjevksy who had become an American citizen and was living in Darien, Connecticut. Bernstein sent elevations and photographs of the entrance halls and auditoria of the cinemas at Rugby, Aylesbury, Sutton, Thornton Heath and Mansfield to Komisarjevsky who was to come to England and carry out alterations to these theatres. No other information about this assignment has come to light and it seems doubtful if Komisarjevsky did make the journey over or offer any suggestions. F. W. Mudd was the interior decorator for the improvements of this period and onwards, until 1957 at least (he is well remembered by managers for his supervision of repairs generally).

New cinemas were given a brash, modern look that was essentially superficial and applied more to the exterior and entrance halls than the auditoria. Frequently, the drum-shaped light fittings of the Thirties' Granadas would be added to foyers. In some cases (such as Thornton Heath), the subsidiary type of balcony chandelier was fitted to the ceiling of the auditorium; in other cases (including Sydenham) the existing auditorium light fittings remained.

In July 1949, Sidney Bernstein became interested in the purchase of the large RKO circuit in the United States, which had to be sold as a result of the government forcing studios to divorce themselves from their theatre chains to foster competition. Granada sought dispensation from the British government to spend a maximum of $3 million – it would be paying less than $6 million as its share of the transaction (the other parties were not identified) and only half would have to be put up in precious dollars. In fact, the RKO theatres were not sold until the early 1950s and Granada was not involved.

Two final acquisitions of the decade were the Palace Slough, closed by fire since 1945, and the King's Hall at Leyton, northeast London.

George Coles and W. F. Mudd went to work at Slough and the building was completely modernised and re-opened as the Century at the beginning of 1950. It was a large cinema – 1,400 seats – but had to take the secondary name because of the Granada already in the town.

The King's Hall was a medium-sized, old-fashioned cinema less

* The Medway deal might have included the circuit's closed Capitol Wembley, Middlesex, which was never re-opened.

than a mile from the Granada Walthamstow and slightly further away from the Rialto Leytonstone. However, it was a valuable addition as it could tap into the Odeon circuit release. Building restrictions may have been the reason why Granada did little or nothing to identify it with the circuit until late 1951 when three months of major improvements were carried out for it to re-open as the Century.

An important addition to the circuit was the return of the war-damaged Granada Wandsworth Road with a low-key re-opening on 12 September 1949 after nearly nine years of darkness.

Granada now had fifty-six cinemas compared to thirty-four a decade earlier. As Sidney Bernstein was so pre-occupied with film production, it could well be that the much of the initiative for the rapid expansion of the circuit during this period came from Cecil Bernstein and his colleagues. The additions were no doubt lucrative during the boom years but hardly any of them matched up to the pre-war group in terms of profitability.

Granada would add a few more cinemas during the Fifties and later, but its major expansion period was over.

Sixth Questionnaire

The sixth Bernstein Questionnaire was issued in 1947 after a ten year gap. Two thousand of the forms were sent to leading figures, including famous friends of Sidney Bernstein. 217,400 replies were received, compared to 159,000 ten years earlier. An Uncle Jack's Quiz for children was also put out, the response helping to refute claims that Saturday morning films had an alarming effect on their audience.

Film booking

The adherence by individual Granada cinemas to any major circuit's programming was far from strict. As in the Thirties and war years, the cinemas would often revive an old hit rather than play a lacklustre new circuit release. *Casablanca* played Tooting in October 1945 for no special reason, but a BBC radio serialisation of a book would often prompt the circuit to dust off a classic film version of the same material. *The Count Of Monte Cristo* was widely booked in January-February 1946 for this reason: it played Bedford for the third week, having been shown there in February 1935 on first release and revived at the time of an earlier BBC broadcast in May 1938. Granada's director of publicity, Ewart Hodgson, wrote on 1 February 1946 to Sidney Bernstein, on a trip abroad, praising the genius of the circuit's chief booker, Herbert C. Fontaine: "Font's idea of taking out *The Count Of Monte Cristo* from the shelves sheltering old films has proved once again what an old showman the bloke is. *Monte Cristo* has packed them in everywhere: for instance, an average of about £240 a night at East Ham."

The Granada Wandsworth Road "welcomes you again".
Exterior and stairs down to foyer on its re-opening in September 1949 after extensive war-time bomb damage had been repaired.

The Granada Wandsworth Road. The main foyer in 1949 looks arid and uninviting compared to Komisarjevsky's foyers with a similar layout. In the auditorium, the Frank Dobson decorative motifs have been restored (see page 127 for war damage) but other details such as the light fittings and the bare ceiling of foyer and auditorium may have been alterations. The organ was reinstated. (Author's collection.) Views of under balcony promenade and balcony date from 16 June 1965 (Photo Coverage).

In 1947, *Beau Geste* went into Tooting, Clapham Junction and many other theatres to take advantage of the BBC radio serial based on the book by P. C. Wren: "You've Heard the Serial on the Air... now SEE the Full Film Story of *Beau Geste*". In April 1948, it was the turn of *The Four Feathers* ("The sensational BBC serial") while a year later the new thriller *Sorry, Wrong Number* was promoted as a "Sensational BBC radio success" at Tooting.

Granada also took a fancy to RKO Radio's Tarzan pictures with Johnny Weissmuller after the Gaumont circuit stopped booking them, beginning with *Tarzan's New York Adventure* and *Tarzan Triumphs* towards the end of 1947. In fact, Golden Square regarded Johnny Weissmuller as an excellent bet, booking some of his Jungle Jim adventures from Columbia, including *Jungle Jim* and *The Lost Tribe* in 1949, after he gave up playing Tarzan. (The circuit's liking for jungle frolics extended to another distributor's Bomba series.) Granada's bookers readily embraced Weissmuller's successor as Tarzan, Lex Barker, giving wide showings to his escapades.

In late 1947 and the first half of 1948, all the major circuits were forced to book a large number of reissues because the Hollywood companies refused to bring in new productions in protest at the *ad valorem* tax suddenly imposed by the Labour government. The backlog of American films already in the country was eked out, but attendances suffered. Cinemas with stage facilities booked more live shows to draw in audiences.

It's New and Exclusive!
When the import tax was withdrawn with effect from 3 May 1948, a flood of Hollywood films became available for showing, far more than could be fitted onto the three major circuits. Granada gave many of the surplus pictures its own circuit release, following the same sequence as the majors' programmes, playing first in the North and West London area, then in the North and East London area, and then in South London, before spreading out to the regions. These films were usually advertised as "Exclusive to Granada" or "It's New and Exclusive!". Although exclusive in each area, they were available to independent cinemas elsewhere. In cinemas which normally played a major circuit release, these bookings would replace it. As more Granadas were linked to the Gaumont programme than the Odeon or ABC ones, it was that release which suffered the biggest loss of revenue. Naturally, Granada slotted its exclusives into weeks when the Gaumont selection was weak and unappealing. Other films were spot-booked, playing the circuit in a more haphazard fashion, as opportunities arose.

RKO Radio supplied some major titles, including the John Wayne romantic drama *Tycoon* (in Technicolor) and the Robert Mitchum western *Blood on the Moon*.

Granada took several MGM films, including *The Unfinished Dance*, *If Winter Comes*, *Killer McCoy* and *The Birds And The Bees*, although this distributor rarely provided exclusives in later years. The previously mentioned thriller *Sorry, Wrong Number* was an exclusive from Paramount which also supplied another major picture, *The Emperor Waltz* with Bing Crosby. Undoubtedly, both would have been booked to Odeon or Gaumont had not there been such a pile-up of product. Some of Paramount's advertising for the latter film recognised the more limited spread of venues by stating in advertisements "It may not be at your local cinema... but it *will* be in your district". Paramount would remain an occasional source of exclusives.

20th Century-Fox also had surplus problems in 1948 and unloaded its highly acceptable Victor Mature pictures *Fury at Furnace Creek* and *Cry of the City* onto the Granada chain in separate weeks. However, the biggest Fox tie-up of this period came with an exclusive deal by which Granada premiered the documentary-style thriller *The Street With No Name* early in 1949. Fox could not find a slot in the West End and decided to supply it direct to Granada. "An Event!! Harrow's First Film Premiere" trumpeted the Granada there when it gave the film its first public showings in this country, concurrently with its sister theatres at East Ham, Enfield, Hounslow and Willesden on the first leg of London release. However, the Fox connection largely faded for the time being.

Granada, of course, had the same quota obligations as any other exhibitor but this did not mean that every British film on circuit release was automatically taken, especially where supporting features were concerned.

The booking department was often sympathetic towards British films that were refused by the major circuits. Of eleven rejected for first feature showing at Odeons and Gaumonts as potentially huge loss-makers, several were taken up by Granada as co-features, including *Bless 'Em All* and *Skimpy In The Navy*, both Adelphi releases starring Hal Monty (who played several live engagements at Granada), *High Jinks in Society* (also Adelphi), *The Gorbals Story* (Eros) and *Over The Garden Wall* (Mancunian). As these films had been so heavily stigmatised, one suspects that they were booked on very favourable terms.

Live shows
Granada continued to draw on the pulling power of Bryan Michie with talent spotting contests in 1946 and to lift some of its programmes with star organists.

As previously mentioned, the number of live shows was stepped up as a result of the film drought in the second half of 1947. Clapham Junction brought on the clowns with a circus in October 1947. For Christmas, it was decided to stage various pantomimes

A Granada exclusive in 1949. "The Service-With-A-Smile Theatre" slogan had been introduced at the foot of all press advertising in August 1943 and lasted, along with the Sergeant, until May 1953. (BFI – Sidney Bernstein Collection.)

This supplementary September 1949 advertisement looks forward to the cleaner advertising style of the late Fifties. Note the circuit spelling of "program". (BFI - Sidney Bernstein Collection.)

for the first time since before the War. *Babes In The Wood*, which featured over seventy artists, four lorryloads of scenery, and a stage crew of twelve, started at Tooting on Boxing Day for two weeks, moved to Sutton and then Woolwich for a week, ending up at Clapham Junction for a final six days at the end of the month. A version of *Cinderella* played at Shrewsbury for two weeks, then went to Rugby for a similar period. *Aladdin* was staged at Maidstone.

At Greenwich an hour of "high-speed" variety accompanied a double-feature programme in an attempt to perk up business in weeks of February and July 1948. "All-star" variety appeared some weeks with films at Harrow, Tooting, Walthamstow and Woolwich besides continuing as part of the regular policy at East Ham.

In early 1948, Eileen Joyce, often accompanied by the Royal Philharmonic Orchestra, gave piano concerts on Sunday afternoons at Tooting, Sutton, Woolwich, Harrow and Kingston after which the cinemas re-opened for their Sunday film programmes. Joyce made many return visits and other classical performers were engaged: Pouishnoff gave a piano recital at Sutton, while the violinist Campoli performed with the backing of the Pinner Orchestra at Harrow.

International Ballet replaced films in consecutive weeks at Sutton, Woolwich and Clapham Junction in February and July 1948. There seems to have been a note of caution at Clapham Junction as the dancers were given only three days there. But the shows were so well received that the company returned to all three theatres in January-February 1949 and played at the Granada Tooting as well. Also in July 1948, the Carl Rosa Opera went to Woolwich and Sutton. It played Clapham Junction in December of that year.

During 1948 the Granada Tooting went over to weeks of live musicals: *Goodnight Vienna* with Bruce Trent and Sara Gregory in March and *The Dancing Years* with Barry Sinclair in October. Sutton also went completely live with Phyllis Calvert in *Peter Pan* in March. Maidstone presented a week's run of both the hit drama *The Winslow Boy* (with Anton Rodgers and Roger Delgado) and the hit farce *Worm's Eye View*. Later, in June 1950, Woolwich, Clapham Junction and Sutton had the musical *Annie Get Your Gun* live in consecutive weeks.

Tooting hosted a series of one-night stands on Sundays (two shows) by singers who were appearing at the London Palladium (closed for the day), although there were restrictions on the use of stage sets and costumes. These seem to have started with Lena Horne on 23 November 1947 and continued in 1948 with Danny Kaye (29 February), Martha Raye (25 April), Carmen Miranda (23 May), the Andrews Sisters (22 August) and Betty Hutton (3 October). On a Sunday in September 1949, however, it was Walthamstow that welcomed the Ink Spots.

Billy Cotton and His Band appeared twice daily to liven up a film show at the Granada Slough in September 1948. At Shrewsbury that same month, a week of George Formby with Beryl replaced films.

Star-maker Bryan Michie was on hand again in 1948, offering "one hour of joy" in a show called *Talent With Speed*. He also spread his own talents to the stage of the newly-acquired theatre at Kettering and played Leytonstone, which was not usually on the live show circuit.

Other cinemas that remained on films still used their stages during intervals for beauty contests and other local events. The Granada North Cheam, for example, made a big splash with Surrey's Bathing Beauty Queen in August 1948.

Although 1948 was the peak year for live use of the Granadas, the film crisis created by the *ad valorem* tax set in motion the practice of staging concerts, pantomimes and occasional live weeks for the years that followed. The wider use of the cinemas was admirable, but the film distribution side lost valuable revenue.

Films, incidentally, were not the only items sometimes in short supply. Sweets were rationed and there were continual problems in obtaining adequate quantities of confectionery and cigarettes. John Roberts, manager of the Granada Tooting, became a legend among confrères by obtaining his own supply of sweets – powerful jellies from Ireland, some of which are believed stuck to the auditorium floor to this day. Roberts was later promoted to sales and restaurant executive.

Lights On

After putting their outside lighting back on to celebrate the end of the war, the Granada cinemas, like all others, were compelled to switch off their neon signs and other illumination by post-war restrictions to save energy. The ban was finally lifted on 2 April 1949 and most cinemas made a big occasion of lighting up again. At Tooting, four thousand people cheered as local resident and Labour minister Emanuel Shinwell touched a switch on the stage which floodlit the façade.

Another glamorous moment was responsible for "Bright lights, flags and the biggest crowd seen in the Wandsworth Road for more than ten years" (*South Western Star*, 30 September 1949). The occasion was a personal appearance by Jean Kent during the week's run of her musical *Trottie True* shortly after the re-opening of the Granada. She went on stage to recall her experiences of making the film but declined to sing because she had no music. "Wandsworth Road being Wandsworth Road, wanted to know why a little thing like absence of music should prevent Jean Kent singing," reported the *Star*. "'Sing anything,' they called. 'What about 'Knees up Mother Brown'? suggested a powerful male voice from the back of the stalls. Miss Kent compromised

with 'White Wings,' followed by 'When Irish Eyes Are Smiling,' and everyone was happy – including the owners of the scores of autograph books which keep Miss Kent busy in the office of Manager Hewitt."

A rare but fitting opportunity to host a gala event came the way of the Granada Shrewsbury on 15 October 1950 when it staged the charity provincial premiere of Michael Powell and Emeric Pressburger's period drama *Gone To Earth*, based on the Mary Webb novel and partly filmed in the area.

Newsreels

In April 1949 Sidney Bernstein caused a storm by cancelling the showing of newsreels at Granadas. He declared in a press release that this was a fight for better newsreels as in his view they were boring – with the sole exception of Pathe News. He accused the producers of becoming complacent because the special war-time contracts under the Film Control Order of 1943 were still in force. Cinemas had been allocated specific newsreels which, in most situations, they still had to share with the opposition in order to save on film stock, and so there was no competition. Bernstein reported that for the past year he had experimentally dropped the newsreel (British Movietone) at one theatre (Aylesbury) with no noticeable effect on audiences. Granada, through its subsidiary London and District Cinemas, was sued over breach of this particular contract and finally lost the case on appeal to the House of Lords. But Sidney Bernstein did not give up: he was prepared to fight the case all over again for each and every one of his cinemas.

As it happened, the Film Control Order was almost immediately revoked – in October 1950. In the following month, Granada was only showing newsreels at six cinemas in monopoly or solo situations. Then the newsreel companies wanted to increase their prices and in protest Granada started its own newsreel, *International Review*, a British edition of the Hearst *Telenews*, which was also taken up by some independent cinemas. It was viewed with some embarrassment by managers. This was eventually dropped and Granada started taking British newsreels again from 1 March 1952. Newsreels would be entirely abandoned early in 1957.

Circuit affiliations

Ignoring the interruptions of the circuit's own exclusives, here is a broad indication of how the individual cinemas seem to have stood with regard to the three major circuit releases around the end of the decade:

Acton: the Granada played the ABC release concurrently with ABC's Savoy East Acton some distance away. Town's Odeon and Gaumont took their respective releases.

Aylesbury: the Granada played ABC releases – and some Gaumont programmes, split with town's Odeon.

Bedford: the Granada played the pick of the three circuit releases in the absence of any major circuit. Circuit's Empire took best of remainder with independent Plaza (bigger than Empire) and Picturedrome seemingly also rans.

Cheam: the Granada had a spell of cheaper split-week revival programming around 1947 but usually played the ABC release, often concurrent with the independent Sutton Picture Theatre (later Curzon); the Century played off-circuit, with many foreign films (including several French Film Festivals), revivals, and some of the Granada exclusives.

Chichester: the Granada played ABC releases as the town had an Odeon and Gaumont.

Clapham Junction: the Granada played primarily the Odeon release, with occasional strong Gaumont releases and rare ABC programmes; the Century and Essoldo took left-overs, with the Century emphasising ABC programmes; the Imperial screened the crumbs.

Dartford: the Granada took the best of the batch, with the Rialto (later Century) playing the rest. No opposition.

Deptford: Broadway (later Century) took the ABC release, as the local Odeon and nearby New Cross Gaumont took the other two main releases.

East Ham: the Granada was off-circuit, barred by the local Odeon and Premier Super (Gaumont) as well as by ABC's Coronation Manor Park and (when it later re-opened) Carlton Upton Park.

Edmonton: the Empire/Granada played ABC or Odeon release with Gaumont's Regal taking the Gaumont release.

Enfield: the Rialto took the Gaumont release, competing with ABC's Savoy and the independent Florida (which took Odeon programmes).

Epsom: the Granada played Gaumont releases, fitting in with the Odeon Epsom and ABC's nearby Rembrandt Ewell.

Grantham: the Granada took the pick of the product; opposed by three small independent halls.

Greenford: the Granada played Gaumont releases, with a minor circuit's small Playhouse taking the Odeon line-up.

Greenwich: the Granada played the Gaumont output against the local Odeon and nearby ABC Roxy Blackheath.

Harrow: the Granada took the Gaumont release concurrent with the outlying Gaumont Rayners Lane, competing with ABC's Dominion Harrow and several outlying Odeons.

Hounslow: the Alcazar/Granada was off-circuit, barred by ABC's Regal, Gaumont's Dominion and the Odeon Hounslow West.

Kennington: the Granada was off-circuit, barred by ABC's Elephant and Castle Theatre, Gaumont's Elephant and Castle Trocadero, and the Odeon Camberwell/Odeon Astoria Brixton.

Kettering: the Granada played ABC releases against the Odeon and Gaumont's Pavilion.

Kingston: the Granada took the Gaumont split against ABC's Regal and the Odeon; the Century Elite competed for off-circuit product with the Kingston Kinema.

Leyton: the King's (later Century) played Odeon releases against the local Gaumont and ABC's Ritz.

Leytonstone: the Rialto screened the Gaumont line-up while ABC's Rex took its release and the independent Academy (later acquired by Granada) picked up Odeon.

Loughton: the Century played split-week or occasional full week Odeon and Gaumont first runs.

Maidstone: the Granada played primarily Gaumont releases against three ABC halls and one independent.

Mansfield: the Granada took the Odeon programmes against ABC's Grand and Gaumont's Empire; the Hippodrome was off-circuit.

Oswestry: the Regal (later Granada) took its choice of circuit releases, the best of the remainder going to circuit's King's (later Century).

Plumstead: the Cinema (later Century) played first-run Gaumont and other releases, often on split weeks. Some Gaumont releases passed to circuit's smaller Plaza instead.

Rugby: the Granada took the pick of circuit releases, the rest going into the chain's Regent and Regal.

Sevenoaks: the Granada took the ABC line-up and competed with the town's Odeon for a share of Gaumont and off-circuit releases (both played many split weeks).

Shrewsbury: the Granada had the pick of new films, with the circuit's Empire following and its King's taking dregs on split weeks.

Slough: the Granada took the Odeon or Gaumont release but was denied ABC programmes by ABC's Adelphi (when Granada took this over, it continued to play the ABC release); Century chose from the left-overs.

Stratford (West Ham): the Kinema (later Century) obtained many split-week and full week Odeon releases despite the proximity of the Odeon Forest Gate, but was also often off-circuit; barred by ABC's Rex and the Gaumont from their releases.

Sutton: the Granada most often played the Odeon release, competing with the Gaumont and the small Sutton Picture Theatre (which often played ABC concurrently with Granada Cheam).

Sydenham: the Granada played Gaumont releases, with Upper Norwood Granada and Century covering the other main releases.

Thornton Heath: the Granada played the Gaumont release, usually concurrent with the huge independent Davis Croydon. Barred by ABC's Savoy Croydon and Rex Norbury from ABC shows and by the Odeon Croydon from Odeon programmes.

Tooting: the Granada played the Gaumont release or some top Odeon programmes (from RKO, Columbia) (but few Odeon titles in the 1950s when Odeon product was usually taken by Southan Morris/Essoldo's Astoria); barred from ABC release by ABC's Mayfair.

Upper Norwood: the Granada and Century usually shared ABC and Odeon releases, with the top film in any week going to the larger Granada, which also showed a bias towards ABC programmes.

Walthamstow: the Granada played the Gaumont release against ABC's Dominion with the independent Carlton taking the Odeon shows.

Wandsworth Road: the Granada was unopposed – usually played ABC or Gaumont programme but also took some of the strongest Odeon releases.

Welling: the Granada played the Gaumont release against the local Odeon and ABC's Regal Bexleyheath.

Willesden: the Granada played the Gaumont release, being up against the Odeon Harlesden and ABC's Ritz Neasden.

Woolwich: the Granada played the ABC or Gaumont release against the Odeon opposite with the independent Cinema (taken over by Granada in 1952) usually presenting left-overs. (The ABC release was lost to ABC's new Regal from 1955.)

It will be seen that Granada was far more often in a position to take the Gaumont circuit release than the ABC or Odeon selection. And the Granadas that relied on the Gaumont line-up included many of the biggest and best – Tooting, Walthamstow, Harrow, Kingston – as well as strong second-league theatres at Greenford, Greenwich, Epsom, Welling, Willesden, etc.

So rigid was the circuit arrangement that Granada was unable to play either *Rope* or *Under Capricorn* very widely as both were released by Warner Bros. through its normal outlet, the ABC circuit, opening it up only to Granadas attached to the ABC release. Granada did attempt to compensate by combining both as a second-run double bill in October 1951 at Maidstone but this cannot have paid off as further bookings have not been spotted.

Rope is promoted in the box at bottom right in this advertisement from December 1948. Granada supported the West End runs of Sidney Bernstein's productions of Rope *and* Under Capricorn *in all its local press advertisements but not their bookings at rival local cinemas. (BFI – Sidney Bernstein Collection.)*
Victory in a poll at Loughton resulted in films being shown at the Century on Sundays from 26 December 1948 (BFI – Sidney Bernstein Collection).

14 • *Into The Fifties*

In the early Fifties, besides introducing the Granada name at Upper Norwood and the Century name both there and at Slough, Granada stamped its identity more clearly on a number of other cinemas.

At the very beginning of the decade, the Granada Exchange Chichester finally became just the Granada in advertising. At the end of 1951, the Empire Edmonton and Alcazar Hounslow were promoted to Granadas by name. Some insiders still feel that Hounslow was not worthy of the honour and should have received the secondary appellation of Century as happened to the King's Leyton, the modernised Globe Clapham Junction and the Rialto Dartford at this time; but, of course, at Clapham Junction and Dartford the Granada name was already taken whereas at Hounslow the circuit only had the one cinema.

At Kingston, the Elite became, rather awkwardly, the Century Elite with the word Elite larger than Century. And in 1952 the Plumstead Kinema became a Century. The re-branding of this period may have been encouraged by a similar exercise on the part of Rank in spreading the Gaumont name (and, to a lesser extent, that of Odeon).

News of cinemas for sale, supplied by specialist estate agents, continued to arouse the curiosity of the Bernsteins. In 1950-51 they had a report made on the cinema situation in Bedminster, a district of Bristol, when the war-damaged Hippodrome was up for sale, and George Coles was dispatched to survey the building. Granada compiled a preparatory list of all the Manchester area cinemas seating 1,200 and over, excluding the three major circuits and the local Moorhouse chain, with details of approximate takings and circuit opposition. A member of staff visited the County Reddish and Longford Stretford when these became available but Granada was wary of entering the unfamiliar ground of Manchester suburban second-run and the Longford did not seem to be doing well (Essoldo took them both over in August 1950). Inspections were made of some Rank properties that were up for disposal, including the Hoxton Cinema and Trocette Bermondsey in the London area, but the reports were not favourable (hardly surprising – if they'd been any good, Rank would have still wanted them).

In *Persona Granada*, Denis Forman suggests that Sidney and Cecil Bernstein "enjoyed property-spotting for its own sake just as train-spotters enjoy spotting trains" and that very few of the cinema (and non-cinema buildings) they looked at could have been of serious interest.

Even into the CinemaScope era, Granada toyed with expansion. John Roberts, of Irish jellies fame, made a thorough on-the-spot survey of Kidderminster's independent cinemas in late 1953/early 1954 which concludes: "I think Kidderminster must be crying out for at least one other super cinema [besides ABC's Central], although I should imagine there is room for two in addition to the ABC providing the capacity is below 1,000. The Futurist could obviously be operated at a good profit but the Grand requires a considerable amount of money to be spent on it to bring it up to reasonable standard. (There is also another 'fleapit' in the town, the Empire Cinema.) ... I suggest we should ask the agents for a detailed plan of these properties, so that we can check the possibility of rebuilding on one or both of these sites."

The odd acquisition was made. And odd it does seem that the company should have taken over the 900-seat Woolwich Cinema to supplement its Granada, especially with ABC likely to reappear in the town at some stage (its rebuilding of the Hippodrome had been interrupted by the War). The Cinema was well placed near the Arsenal with a busy walk-in trade and could for the time being take the weaker ABC and Gaumont releases not wanted by the Granada, plus reissues. There was one advantage of size: the booking department immediately renegotiated more favourable terms for the line-up inherited from the previous independent owner. And Granada had the money to smarten up the Cinema to become a Century.

Then there was the more substantial acquisition of the Adelphi at Slough, which Granada took over from the ABC circuit at the end of March 1953. The Bernsteins already had a Granada and Century there. With 2,014 seats, the Adelphi was the largest cinema in the area and fully equipped for theatrical use. It had a huge ballroom as well. However, it was a drab-looking building, sited well away from the town centre and without much passing trade.

The Adelphi Slough. Exterior, 29 September 1961. Note the prominence given the ballroom, also the poster for a forthcoming stage show. Foyer on 26 March 1965, with poster near far wall on easel advertising forthcoming wrestling evening, while poster to right promotes an amateur stage musical. Light fittings have not been changed to the circuit style. The huge auditorium, undated but circa 1953 to judge by the set-back screen and tabs. (All Photo Coverage.)

The Century Woolwich, seen here on 13 March 1957, was distinctly inferior to the Granada. The confectionery counter can be seen at the right of the entrance, placed to attract custom from passers by. The box office can just be made out set further back, on the left behind a category board. "Laughter at sea" is provided by a revival of Abbott and Costello Meet Captain Kidd. *The auditorium has non-standard light fittings for the circuit. There is no carpeting along the rows of seats. (Photo Coverage.)*

ABC had been losing money heavily, despite extensive live show use. Granada could expect to obtain more favourable booking terms now that it ran all the cinemas in the town itself, although Rank with its outlying Ambassador at Farnham Royal claimed exclusive first run of the Odeon circuit release. Granada asked Rank in vain to allow the Adelphi to play Odeon releases concurrently. Sidney Bernstein wrote to ABC chief Jack Goodlatte expressing dismay at the run-down state of the Adelphi, declaring that Granada had assumed an ABC house would have been maintained in better condition and suggesting compensation for having been misled; but Goodlatte not surprisingly refused, pointing out that Granada had been able to inspect the property before taking it over. The seats, carpeting and plant were all apparently in a very bad state, and Granada spent £17,000 on improvements. In later years, the company liked to refer to the Adelphi as having been "practically derelict" when it arrived.

Granada concentrated all live shows in Slough at the Adelphi, beginning with the Billy Cotton show *Wakey! Wakey!* in the week commencing 25 May. However, the Adelphi's Saturday morning children's shows were switched to the Granada. Live show takings improved under Granada but were still only "moderate" and the Adelphi continued to lose money at an increasing rate. The manager complained directly to Sidney Bernstein that he was almost entirely confined to the ABC release while the Granada picked from Gaumont, Odeon and Fox programmes and the Century took any choice leftovers. However, Bernstein refused to make any changes, clearly not wanting to affect the profitability of the Granada.

Granada also managed the Regent King's Cross when it became a cinema in 1952, but this forms part of a later story concerning the owning company, Variety Theatres Consolidated.

Rugby became the scene of Granada's very first postwar closure when the least of its three cinemas there, the Regal, went on 5 January 1953.

Two other halls did not survive in the CinemaScope era. The Plaza Plumstead was dropped in December 1954 but had never been highly regarded. But the Century Elite Kingston was of some significance – an old-fashioned, medium-sized hall, it was immediately adjacent to the Granada on a more conspicuous site known as Elite Corner. It seems that C&A Modes made an irresistible offer in order to build a new store in its place. As previously mentioned, the Century Elite had programming problems, fighting with the Kinema for off-circuit leftovers, although it possessed a large and successful café (in which one of the first Gaggia espresso machines had been recently installed).

It seems likely that the Century Elite was still mildly profitable. At any rate, it was given a plum attraction for its last week which took it into the very first day of 1955: trainee John Young remembers huge audiences for the revival of Chaplin's *Modern Times*.*

Other cinemas were too large, at least during term-time matinees. In July 1954, Granada wanted to close the balconies at North Cheam and Epsom on weekday afternoons, but staff still had to remain on duty to release the shutters blocking off the projection ports in case of fire.

Thought was given to closing some cinemas for two weeks in the summer of 1954, particularly in towns where the company had two outlets, but this was in order to relieve staff shortages. It had become easier to recruit part-timers. Manager Brian Gauntlett remembers that at Harrow the floor staff were re-organised into three shifts of part-timers – afternoon, evening and weekend – the major drawback being that three sets of uniforms were needed.

Cafés were in decline. Between 1949 and 1954, the ones at Epsom, Upper Norwood (Rialto/Granada), Tooting, Welling, North Cheam and Woolwich were closed (the space at Cheam was leased out to a dance school from 1 June 1954). That at Rugby was set to close on 2 February 1953 unless an outside operator could be found.

In February 1954, the café side as a whole was losing money. At the start of April, Granada cafés were operating only at Grantham, Harrow, Kettering, Kingston (in the doomed Century Elite), Maidstone, Mansfield, Sevenoaks, Slough, Sutton and Walthamstow. Those at Bedford and Shrewsbury (at both Granada and Empire) were leased out (but would return to the fold). Later in the year it was reported that the cafés at Maidstone, Kingston and Kettering were operating profitably but those at Grantham, Harrow, Mansfield, Sevenoaks, Slough, Sutton and Walthamstow were not, although the Slough café had only gone into the red for the first time in the current year. Most of the losers would soon close but the right manageress and menu could make a huge difference and Grantham later became hugely profitable again. Some of the cafés, like Grantham's, were linked to the RAC and also served local Rotary Clubs.

A new concept of snack bars in shopping units attached to many of the theatres was introduced at Maidstone in August 1953. These were called Havasnack (Sidney Bernstein wanted to call them Havasnak without the 'c' but was, for once, overruled). Further Havasnacks quickly appeared at Mansfield and Kingston Century Elite in addition to the existing cafés, and all made a profitable start. Others were added in later years.

The loss of the popular Century Elite café prompted a look at the lack of catering facilities at the Granada in Kingston. This

* C&A was taking a close interest in cinemas: in 1955, it stopped Gaumont rebuilding the bombed Super at Ilford by taking over the site, similar in triangular shape to that of the Elite, for another new store.

THE LEADING CIRCUITS IN JANUARY 1951

	Cinemas	Seats '000	Average no. of seats
Rank (Odeon + Gaumont)	546	820.2	1,502
ABC	404	595.8	1,475
Essoldo	92	100.3	1,090
Sir A.B. King	89	98.1	1,102
S.M. Associated	64	59.1	923
Granada	54	80.1	1,483

This table clearly indicates that although Granada had only a fraction of the number of cinemas run by Rank and ABC, they were of comparable average size whereas the other medium-sized circuits tended to have lower average seating figures indicative of lesser properties. (S.M. Associated was taken over by Essoldo in August 1954. Sir Alexander King's cinemas were all in Scotland and include Caledonian which he booked. Among other circuits, Star had 51 cinemas and Shipman & King had 40 cinemas at this time.)

Source: book, The British Film Industry, p148/9.

The Century Elite Kingston, circa 1953. Note the three parallel strips of neon running along the curve, just above the entrance. The café entrance was halfway along the side wall with a small vertical sign above, the lettering not visible in the dark shadow. Signs to the right on the lower wall point to a "Havasnack Bar". (Photo Coverage.)

Another BIG Cine-Variety Show at *GRANADA*
☞ **ON THE STAGE** ☜
The Famous Jimmy Wheeler Show

Radio and TV's Popular Comedian
JIMMY WHEELER
Ay' Ay' that's yer lot!

TheSensational **SKYLONS** AERIAL THRILLS	Wizard of the Brush **LORRAINE** CHALK AND CHATTER	**FRANCOIS & ZANDRA** NOVEL DANCERS

Radio's Comedy Girl | **AUDREY JEANS** | BOB HOPE'S Stooge

☞ *Plus 2 Mighty Films in Colour* ☜

James Stewart Rock Hudson **WHERE THE RIVER BENDS** Colour ⓤ	Jeff Chandler **YANKEE BUCCANEER** Colour ⓤ

June 20 week **GRANADA** East Ham

All this in one great show!

★ SCREEN & STAGE ★

★ CHARLTON HESTON
★ RHONDA FLEMING
★ FORREST TUCKER
★ JAN STERLING

PONY EXPRESS ⓤ
Racing across 1500 miles of danger-filled wilderness.

Gilbert Harding
SPEAKING OF MURDER ⓐ
KAY WALSH · BETTY ANN DAVIES
HOWARD MARION CRAWFORD

3.30   7.50
MUSIC HALL
70 MINUTES OF NON-STOP VARIETY

JO, JAC & JONI
Direct from this year's Royal Variety Performance

THE FIVE ULMS
Sensational Equilibristic Presentation

VICKY FITZPATRICK
Ireland's Golden-Voice Soprano

RAVIC & BABS
Sensational Tower Skaters

MUNDY & EARLE
Fooling For You

MISS LILLY
Europe's Greatest Acrobatic Contortionist

PEGGY O'FARRELL'S TWENTY TINY TAPPAS

GRANADA TOOTING Nov **23** week

Granadagrams

Every week to give you pleasure,
You'll find them here in rhythmic measure,
They will amuse you for a while,
Another SERVICE-WITH-A-SMILE.

PATRONS ARE INVITED TO SUBMIT VERSES ON *GRANADA*
10/6 WILL BE PAID FOR ANY VERSE USED

Granadagram Number 37
Tennis players, looking grim,
Serve their 'cannon balls' with vim,
They should learn GRANADA style
Delivering Service-With-A-Smile.

Submitted by : Mr. C. KOHN, 18 New Park Court, S.W.2

GRANADAGRAM NUMBER 123

GRANADA has a slogan
    that is very hard to beat,

It's practised in our theatres,
    our cafes, and the street,

From doorman to the usherette
    who shines you down the aisle

The motto's universal,
    it's "Service-With-A-Smile"

Left: typical live show with two old films at East Ham, occasional live show at Tooting with off-circuit new films.

Above: Granadagrams started in 1950 and continued for many years, being displayed in foyers and contributed by staff and patrons.

(All from BFI – Sidney Bernstein Collection.)

Right: menu at Granada Rugby for 27 November 1952 (courtesy of David Eve).

LUNCHEON MEN[U]

GRANADA RESTAURANT RUGBY. 27/11/5[2]
SPECIAL 2/9 LUNCHEONS
CREME OF KIDNEY SOUP
CHOICE OF :-
FRIED FILLET OF COD & CHIPS
BRAISED OX HEART
BEEF RISSOLES & ONION SAUCE
CABBAGE WITH CREAMED OR CHIPPED
                        POTATOES
CHOICE OF SWEET
ROLL   COFFEE

CREME OF KIDNEY SOUP.................
FRIED FILLET OF PLAICE & CHIPPED
                        POTATOES....

ROAST VEAL & STUFFING................
STEAK PUDDING........................
GRILLED HAM & GRILLED TOMATOES.......
GRILLED BACON & BAKED BEANS..........

CABBAGE.........6   CREAMED SWEDES...
CREAMED OR CHIPPED POTATOES..........

STEAMED SULTANA PUDDING & CUSTARD....
JAM TART & CUSTARD...................
SAGO PUDDING WITH JAM................

VELCREAM (PER PORTION)...............

VANILLA ICES.....................6 &
STRAWBERRY ICES..................6 &
COFFEE ICES......................6 &

ROLLS 1½   COFFEE .

was the time when George Coles was asked to draw up plans for extending the circle foyer over the side passage to add a café or coffee bar. He thought it unlikely that planning permission would be granted. Granada seems not to have considered inserting an upstairs floor across part of the lofty entrance hall. In the event, no catering was ever introduced at the Granada Kingston.

Further Hitches

Sidney Bernstein continued with plans for new Transatlantic productions. In 1951, he purchased the David Dodge novel *To Catch A Thief* as a further Alfred Hitchcock subject, as well as the novel *The Bramble Bush* by David Duncan.

In 1951, he spent some time in Canada on pre-production work with Hitchcock for *I Confess*. However, the project was taken over by Warner Bros., along with the rights to *The Bramble Bush*.

At the end of 1953, Bernstein went on a tour of the Far East, ostensibly scouting locations for an unidentified Hitchcock project likened to a John Buchan story. *To Catch a Thief* was sold to Paramount for $125,000 in December 1953 with Hitchcock attached and became a hit film in 1955, starring Cary Grant. The Henry Cecil novel *No Bail For The Judge* was optioned for £2,000 as a potential Hitchcock thriller but its featuring of prostitution raised potential censorship problems. Thought was given to transferring the setting from London to Chicago but the book was dropped in November 1954. Bernstein discussed with Hitchcock an original story about capital punishment, *Dark Duty*, submitted by a prison governor's wife. It was later offered to David Lean. Hitchcock expressed a desire to remake his 1934 hit *The Man Who Knew Too Much* and in December 1954 Bernstein informed him that the rights had been obtained from Rank. But this project was also taken over by Paramount and resulted in a hit film by Hitchcock with James Stewart and Doris Day.

There were other film proposals which did not involve Hitchcock. In April 1954, Sidney Bernstein optioned Kingsley Amis' best-seller *Lucky Jim* for £200 in association with producer-director John Boulting. The option lapsed and was taken up by Michael Balcon before being retrieved by Boulting who made a hit comedy out of it with his brother Roy. In 1954, Bernstein was also involved in plans for a Crazy Gang comedy which may have evolved into the 1958 flop *Life Is A Circus*, made by a company called Vale for British Lion.

Programming

Bryan Michie made his last appearances in 1950, still looking for new talent at Walthamstow in June and later that year providing an *Hour Of Happiness* at Willesden, Maidstone, Mansfield (helping draw a huge audience of nearly 20,000 in a week) and Grantham.

RKO Radio became a key supplier of exclusive product in the early Fifties. Besides more Tarzans and a number of routine releases, two films in particular stand out.

Firstly, RKO released *Stromboli*, the volcanic drama that starred Ingrid Bergman whose extra-marital affair with the film's director, Roberto Rossellini, and birth of a child out of wedlock, provoked an almighty scandal, especially in the United States. The film was dire but the affair had created curiosity. RKO decided not to show it to the critics or give it a West End run but to rush it out, signing up Granada to premiere the film in all the forty towns where it had cinemas on the same day. Reputedly, 160 other halls also screened the film simultaneously, but Granada spearheaded the release. This was a very unusual and expensive step as it required a huge number of prints, not many of which would be needed for long afterwards. Although Granada could be accused of bad taste in taking the film and might possibly have upset some patrons, Sidney Bernstein would not have hesitated: not only was there the exploitation potential in the best P. T. Barnum tradition but there was also his friendship with Ingrid Bergman dating from *Under Capricorn*.

And, secondly, in 1952 Granada took RKO Radio's X certificate *The Thing From Another World*, which did excellent business. (RKO released fewer pictures after 1952 and its relationship with Granada dried up.) Unlike the Odeon and Gaumont circuits but like ABC, Granada did not hesitate to book films with the X certificate, introduced around 1950, which banned under 16s. X films could clearly draw big audiences but were felt by Rank to damage the family viewing habit. The Granada Bedford, for example, played *Detective Story, A Streetcar Named Desire* and *Women Of Twilight*, when they might have been deflected to the smaller Empire instead. Paramount's Technicolored *The War Of The Worlds* was refused showing time on Odeon or Gaumont but widely booked by Granada in 1952 (usually accompanied by a British film, *Laxdale Hall*). Only at Greenwich did Granada have a disastrous time with X films. The location of the cinema away from a shopping centre made it heavily dependent on family audiences.

Columbia was a source of numerous films as it had far too many releases to fit onto the Odeon or Gaumont circuits. Granada made a rare mistake in taking its biopic *Valentino*, starring Anthony Dexter as the silent screen idol, and it had to be replaced by *Lost Stage Valley* and *Fury Of The Congo* at later bookings in less sophisticated areas. In 1952, Paramount's *The Greatest Show On Earth* was certain to be a smash hit on Odeon release and Granada played it wherever it could; for its other cinemas, the circuit booked Columbia's new foreign legion adventure *Ten Tall Men*, starring Burt Lancaster, rather than take the weak Gaumont or ABC selection pitted against Cecil B. DeMille's

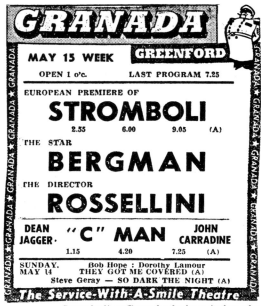

Stromboli *at Greenford where it shared a European premiere with the rest of the circuit. Notice the equal billing given to the film's director.*

The Empire Bedford, seen here in 1953, was extensively modernised the following year but retained its name. (Photo Coverage.)

circus epic. *Ten Tall Men* enabled Granada to achieve very good figures. The company was also more receptive than Odeon and Gaumont to Columbia's early Frankie Laine musicals, and both *Rainbow Round My Shoulder* and *Cruisin' Down The River* lit up many Granada screens.

United Artist also had an excess of product, some of which found its way onto the Granada circuit. Granada's fondness for Chaplin (commercially sound, but also influenced by Sidney Bernstein's friendship with the star) was demonstrated in a special revival of *City Lights* in 1951 (as well as by frequent bookings of Chaplin shorts from other distributors).

When an off-circuit UA film – a thick-ear melodrama called *99 River Street* – was booked at one Granada, it annoyed the staff no end. Granadas had various prize drives for better business between groups of theatres over set periods and, more than forty years later, North Cheam projectionist Barry Haigh can still recall: "We were in competition with all the other Granadas and they used to send a league table each week. We were winning quite comfortably, we were quite ahead, and then instead of getting the ABC release one week we got a terrible thing called *99 River Street*. And it was the last week of the competition and we lost our position. We came third, and all the usherettes and everybody was upset about it." (In fairness to Granada's booking department, it should be pointed out that *99 River Street* replaced a weak ABC release – *Beat the Devil* – which might not have done any better.)

Granada also found screen time for some productions from a lesser American studio, Republic, both when its output was released in this country by British Lion and when it set up its own distribution organisation in 1951. Exclusive presentations were made of the John Wayne western *Rio Grande* as well as of *The Red Pony,* while Granada arranged the London premiere of *The Bullfighter and the Lady* at Kingston in September 1951 (although it seems to have been a flop, as it was not booked widely after that). Granada's bookers were particularly partial to Republic's Roy Rogers westerns as B features. A few were taken by Odeon and Gaumont but Granada gave them far more playing time.

Many minor distributors found a haven for their pictures in the Granada chain, although it seems likely that they accepted reduced terms reflecting a weak bargaining position. International provided the critically acclaimed *Four in a Jeep* plus *Mr. Universe* in Spring 1952. Monarch gained screen time for its Marx Bros. comedy *Love Happy* (dumped by United Artists because of controversy over the participation of the anti-British writer Ben Hecht). Lux's dubbed Italian drama *Bitter Rice* had a South London premiere at the Granada Tooting and was spot booked around the circuit, so successfully at the Plumstead Kinema that it returned for a further three days at the smaller

Plaza. Eros delivered *Prehistoric Women* in 1951 and, the following year, a re-issue of Universal's *Phantom Of The Opera* with Claude Rains, double-billed with its British production *13 East Street*.

Granada even helped out the Rank distribution company, General Film Distributors, which normally supplied all its output to Rank's Odeons and Gaumonts. Because of Rank's opposition to playing X films at this time, GFD's double-bill of *Life After Dark* and *Abbott And Costello Meet Dr. Jekyll and Mr. Hyde* went into Granadas and independents instead.

Many British films did not obtain a major circuit release, and some of these received a welcome from Granada. *Laxdale Hall* and *13 East Street* have already been mentioned, but a record survives of the deal made with the minor British distributor, Adelphi, over the farce *My Wife's Lodger,* featuring Diana Dors. This was booked to the entire circuit for a flat figure of £1,500. For the most part, it replaced one half of a Gaumont double-bill that Granada regarded as having dubious appeal – a thriller from United Artists starring Ray Milland and called *The Thief*, which had the gimmick of lacking any speech. This went out on the Gaumont circuit double-billed with the GFD release *Yankee Buccaneer* starring Jeff Chandler in December 1952. Granada retained the Technicolor swashbuckler to play with the British comedy. The circuit's booking department calculated what the renter's share of takings would have been under a normal deal and found that it had gained approximately £600 by paying the flat sum.

Granada also exercised muscle in improving terms for some of the major circuit releases it played. Records survive to show that when Granada contracted to play a weak Gaumont programme – *Fair Wind to Java* plus *While The City Sleeps* – it agreed to pay the distributor, Republic, twenty-five per cent of the receipts for most of its theatres but gained a reduction to twenty per cent for Tooting and Walthamstow, two of its biggest halls, and as a sweetener was given a free Sunday revival double-bill from the distributor for every theatre.

Organists were still used on occasion, as an added attraction in weeks when poor business was anticipated. (Sidney Bernstein was peeved to notice that they had been performing at Willesden and Enfield when both had a strong draw, *On The Waterfront*, in 1954.)

Children's matinees

A rare professional insight into the world of Saturday morning pictures is provided by a report dated 23 October 1952 from S. Hyman who had attended three children's matinees on successive Saturdays at halls with varying levels of business: the Granada Kennington had a fillings average of .87 in 1951 against Harrow's .61 and Hounslow's .44.

Seemingly prompted by the availability of the first picture made by the Children's Film Foundation and addressed to company secretary Joe Warton rather than to Cecil or Sidney Bernstein, the report reads:

GRANADA KENNINGTON: 4 October 1952.
Almost capacity attendance. Before the program started, the organist played popular songs with slides. The children sang some of them very heartily. There was a good deal of noise, but no hooliganism.

Stage show: (1) all birthday children were lined up on the stage and each was given an ice-cream. The audience sang "Happy Birthday"; (2) several children came onto the stage and sang popular songs – fairly well received. (3) a competition had been arranged for impersonations of Charlie Chaplin and several children came on in various disguises. Each was given an ice-cream, and the winner was given ice-cream, chocolate, and nuts! (4) The Granadiers' Song – all enjoyed this; (5) "God Save the Queen" – impressive because of the silence Mr. [George] Mullins [the manager] obtained without any fuss.

Cartoon. *Mighty Mouse.* A sort of Mickey Mouse-Superman character is the star. He flies off magically to rescue three friends trapped by cannibals on a desert island. Great deal of violence and a number of frightening characters.

Short. *Cats.* A sort of documentary about lions, tigers, leopards and cats. Little more than a dull series of photographs with a silly commentary. Generally uninformative, and the children were not very impressed.

Feature. *Fraternally Yours*, with Laurel and Hardy. L&H scheme to deceive their wives in order to go to the annual convention of an American friendly society. This was an old film and too verbose for children, although they appeared to follow most of it. They certainly enjoyed the slapstick episodes. On the whole, this film was unsuitable for children – it was too long, it presented a very odd view of marriage, and it was too American in content – the opening scenes of a meeting of the Order of the Sons of the Desert must have been almost meaningless to most of the audience.

Serial. *Superman.* The usual sort of mixture of magic and muscle. The serial is generally thought to be the most popular item with children, but familiarity appears to dampen interest. There was a great deal of talking whilst it was showing, and the children were only occasionally interested. However, they may have been tired at the end of a long program.

Comments. Mr. Mullins appears to be unusually interested in the matinees and to have given them a great deal of thought.

He tries to keep the children happy and reduces obvious discipline to a minimum – he encourages them to give a really good yell at the end of the stage show before the films started. He was pleasant and friendly with all who wanted to talk to him, and clearly was well known to all the children. All the staff seemed similarly keen and on their toes all the time. They did not interfere with the children's activities more than was absolutely necessary.

GRANADA HARROW: 11 October 1952.
About two-thirds capacity. I arrived at 9.30 but the program had already started.
Comedy. Laurel and Hardy. Good slapstick which the children enjoyed very much.
Stage. The organist played some popular songs with slides. Mr. [George] Bond [the manager] stood by the organist and conducted the singing. Then he asked the "birthday" children to the front, o.p. side, to be given an ice-cream (they were not visible to the audience). Finally, he talked to them about the need to be careful on crossing the road when leaving.
Feature. *Old Mother Riley – Detective*. Apparently a war-time film about Old Mother Riley helping the police break up a black market in food. Rather naive, with several long conversational episodes which the children loathed. But there was also some good slapstick and several good chases.
Serial. *Sky Raiders*. Well produced and well acted 'serious' serial about foreign agents trying to steal new inventions for aircraft being built for the American government. Quite well received.
Comments. Mr. Bond said that all classes of children came. But there seemed to be more lower-middle and working class children than others. He thought that (1) non-capacity business was general locally; (2) that children watching television the night before would not come to matinees; and (3) the children preferred coming with their parents to ordinary programs.

GRANADA HOUNSLOW: 18 October 1952.
About half full. Mr. [Len] Bullen [manager] went up on the stage before the show started, and told the children off for complaints that had been made about some of them behaving badly after leaving the theatre. He also announced that programs consisting only of shorts would be started soon.
Cartoon. Two were shown, featuring the Talking Magpies. They were both rather vicious and irresponsible, possibly frightening, and not very amusing.
Short. About training race horses. Good, interesting, and well received despite the commentator's strong American accent.

Feature. *Dick Barton Strikes Back*. A good film about secret agents planning to wipe out the population of cities by means of a mysterious high frequency broadcasting unit, ending up with chases and fights all over Blackpool Tower. Despite the violence, it did not seem to frighten the children.
Serial. *Sky Raiders*. As at Harrow.
Comments. Mr. Bullen said he had tried everything to improve attendances but the opposition was too strong. This is probably an insuperable difficulty – there are four other cinemas within a mile of the Granada. And there are few middle class residents to be attracted. Furthermore, the stage is too small to be used much, and there is no organ or piano. Mr. Bullen has even found it impossible to get a suitable record to accompany the Granadier's Song, and suggested that a trailer film might be made. At present, the Song is not sung.

General comments. (a) Both Harrow and Hounslow seemed to use rather crude ways of keeping the children in order. It seems important that the matinees should not be like school in any obvious way, and the children should be treated with as much respect as any other patrons. They should not be given lectures on behaviour, nor have torches flashed at them to see whether they are sitting properly, nor should a whistle be blown in the middle of the performance because the manager thinks there is too much noise. It might be a good idea to get the children to help in keeping order by appointing suitable children to help supervise the audience. (b) The problem of booking suitable films is apparently very great. On the whole, the films I have seen are unlikely to have done any harm to the children. They might have done more to stimulate the children's imagination and intelligence. It is difficult to make any positive proposals without a thorough knowledge of the problem. But it may be worth pointing out that "obvious" films for children – such as Laurel and Hardy, and cartoons – are not always suitable.

Gift tickets
One policy, believed to have been introduced in the early 1950s, seems to have been unique to the circuit. Granada managers would track down the addresses of people moving into their district and send them a "Welcome neighbour" complimentary pass for two to introduce them to the theatre. Brian Gauntlett recalls that the two big piles of postcards that you could be sure to find in any manager's cupboard were the welcome neighbour cards and the Granadiers birthday cards which gave them free admission on their birthday.

Not unique, short-lived, and now barely remembered by managers was Granada's promotion of Gift Tokens in competition with those of the major circuits. These went on sale, for use at any Granada cinema, from 7 December 1953, costing four shillings and sixpence, nine shillings or thirteen shillings and sixpence. A cheaper version of Granadiers tokens was also tried.

All change

> 3-D, or not 3-D – that is the question –
> Whether 'tis wiser at this moment to instal
> A plastic screen in glitt'ring silver sprayed,
> Or bide awhile and let things take their course
> Standardisation-wards? To pause, to wait –
> No more; to look around, before I leap
> Into a new dimension. To pause – to wait –
> Perchance to miss the boat: ay, there's the rub.
> Methinks the opposition even now
> Doth calculate his aspect ratio.
> Yet who can say what ratio may come
> When we have shuffled through these hectic days?
> Shall my own screen be one point seven five
> In width, to one in height? Or less? Or more?
> What curvature compared to length of throw,
> That my dear Patrons may with vision clear
> Enraptured gaze upon the films to come?
> 'Tis said that Hollywood hath pinned its faith
> In farflung CinemaScope, whose awesome sweep
> Would utterly engulf my little Hall
> And occupy the car park. Then again,
> The cost must yet be counted, at whose sum
> I'm sicklied o'er with the pale cast of dread...

– from "An Exhibitor's Soliloquy",
opening text for a Pathe Equipment advertisement*

After the improved standards of home life in America, including television, started eating away at attendances in cinemas over there and then elsewhere, Hollywood responded in several ways. More films were made in colour since television could only offer black-and-white. Cinema screens became larger and wider to differentiate them from the television picture which had essentially the same ratio as the traditional picture house image.

Panoramic screens with a ratio of approximately 1.8:1 were widely introduced, even though they cut off the top and bottom of films which had not been shot with these proportions in mind. But, when wide screens were installed at Slough and Walthamstow at the end of May 1953, they had to wait a while for new aperture

* The full typewritten text was found in Granada files relating to 1954. It has not been ascertained whether this was merely a draft or actually used in advertising.

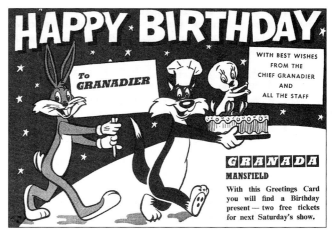

A Granadiers birthday card from the early Sixties.

John Wayne poses with usherettes and commissionaires at the foot of the stairs in the foyer of the Granada Tooting on Wednesday 28 February 1951. The usherettes are seen in the standard winter uniform which consisted of an orange cape with a chain at the neck, a silk blouse very full in the arm, a pillbox hat, and blue slacks, with which they had to wear dark shoes. (The summer outfit was a lighter pair of slacks, a short-sleeve blouse and no cape.) Wayne also visited the Granada Acton and possibly others on the circuit which was giving his latest western Rio Grande *an "exclusive" booking. (BFI – Sidney Bernstein Collection.)*

remember theatres waiting to open for the first showing of CinemaScope and he was literally putting the last few screws into the motorbike drive chain."

A "Miss Stereophonic Sound" went around the circuit explaining the system to the local press and gaining acres of publicity, usually posing with local dignitaries in projection boxes. For this role, Sidney Bernstein personally approved the choice of a 21-year-old blonde science graduate, Tessa Fenton, as combining the requisite beauty and brains. (Bernstein had an eye for glamour and once lamented the impression a particular Granada gave with too many middle-aged and unprepossessing females on the staff.)

Granada had an advantage in that most of its big cinemas possessed proscenium arches wide enough to fit a CinemaScope screen without expensive structural alterations. This was because they were designed to take live shows. The old screens were usually set well back on the stage but the CinemaScope screens had to be brought forward so that the full width of the image would be visible from side seats. At Harrow, for example, the old screen of 25 ft. width by 18 ft. was set 15 ft. behind the proscenium opening. The new 'scope screen was still 18 ft. high but had a width of 45 ft. 6 ins., and was set up only 2 ft. behind the opening. At the Granada Bedford, the new wide screen was 50 ft. wide but still fitted comfortably within the existing proscenium arch.

The screen and the three speakers behind were initially put in a fixed position which ruled out live shows. Annual beauty contests held on stage at Walthamstow and Woolwich were switched to Edmonton and Greenwich instead. However, ways were devised for using the stage at the key theatres. The speakers were put on trolleys that could be wheeled away. At Tooting the screen could be flown but at Harrow, where there was no fly tower, it was rolled up into a long box and shifted to the back of the stage.

However, many of the cinemas taken over by Granada did present problems. At Thornton Heath, Sydenham and elsewhere, the old side-opening curtains were replaced with festoon drop curtains to enable a wider screen to be installed. However, side opening curtains were retained at Epsom despite a narrow proscenium arch.

A record of sound installation costs for certain halls shows as many as twenty-eight speakers being dotted around the auditorium at Walthamstow at a cost of £4,074, while Epsom, Hounslow and Kettering each received only fourteen auditorium speakers at a cost ranging from £2,290 to £2,955. The cheapest of fourteen listed installations was at Upper Norwood where eighteen auditorium speakers cost £2,290. The much larger Woolwich and Clapham Junction Granadas managed with eighteen and sixteen speakers respectively, but at a much higher cost (£3,733 and £3,686), presumably because they required more extensive wiring or were of better quality. Tooting was another expensive installation at £3,933.

The speakers were provided by Westrex and RCA. Bernstein spotted the company emblems on speakers at two of the cinemas and ordered them to be removed, later requesting that the speakers and wiring be painted to match the surrounding decoration.

New screens cost between £378 at Walthamstow and £480 at Tooting. The two anamorphic lenses fitted on the projectors usually cost £550 each. New normal high-definition lenses for showing non-'scope films cost £92 in all.

Not all the important Granadas were fitted out with stereophonic sound. At Aylesbury, Edmonton, Enfield (Rialto), Leytonstone (Rialto), North Cheam, Sevenoaks, Willesden and the Slough Adelphi, Granada played CinemaScope features with only optical sound. These were cinemas that did not regularly play the Fox releases. Many were attached to the ABC release, and it seems that Granada were less willing to replace the ABC release with a Fox booking than they were to drop a Gaumont release: this may have been because the ABC programmes tended to be stronger or the distributors tied to ABC made more of a fuss. In the case of North Cheam, not only was it an ABC outlet but the better placed, more successful Granada Sutton was nearby and Fox pictures primarily played there.

Stereophonic sound was advertised along with CinemaScope but, where it hadn't been installed, the wording alongside the 'scope logo simply referred to a "New Wonder Screen Presentation", the same tag line also being employed on occasions when Granadas with a full installation could not obtain a stereo print. This occurred at Dartford, for instance, when it played many ABC CinemaScope releases like A Star Is Born.

CinemaScope also resulted in an amendment to standard presentation procedures. Barry Haigh, chief projectionist at North Cheam, recalls: "We had a directive when CinemaScope came in that we were not to show the certificate on the tabs but we had to open them before it came on the screen, which was a bit awful because you'd hear the motor opening the tabs."

The seating capacities of the Granadas seem to have been little reduced, if at all, even though other cinemas often took out the front rows of stalls seating because they were too close to the 'scope screen. When Kingston showed its first 'scope picture, there was five times the usual number of "transfers", people paying upgrades to better seats – presumably to distance themselves from the screen. (I am reminded of a cartoon in Picturegoer of a husband and wife seated right up against a 'scope screen, each watching a different end and relating to the other what was happening.)

Essoldo moved much faster than Granada on CinemaScope and

GRANADA Rugby with . . . CinemaScope

4-TRACK MAGNETIC ★ STEREOPHONIC SOUND ★

WHAT IS CINEMASCOPE?

Q Is it just another wide screen?
A You can forget any wide screens you've ever seen. They bear no relationship to CinemaScope which, with 4-track Magnetic Stereophonic Sound is the most forward step in film presentation since motion pictures were invented.

Q Does it add realism to a picture?
A CinemaScope has been scientifically designed to give you the same wide angle of vision that you have in real life—which is nearly 3 times greater than you get in any other type of presentation.

Q How will this affect me when watching the film?
A It will give you the amazing feeling that you are actually there in the picture, taking part in the action.

Q What difference does 4-track Magnetic Stereophonic Sound make?
A It completes the feeling of realism. When a character is speaking the voice comes from whichever part of the screen he happens to be, and as he moves across the screen the sound of his voice travels with him exactly as it does in real life.

Q Is CinemaScope like the 3-D films we have seen?
A No. For one thing you don't need special glasses. But the combination of specially treated screen, 4-track Magnetic Stereophonic Sound and an amazing device known as an anamorphic lens produces a remarkably life-like sense of depth.

CINEMASCOPE PUTS YOU RIGHT IN THE PICTURE

CINEMASCOPE WITH 4-TRACK MAGNETIC STEREOPHONIC SOUND AND BREATH-TAKING COLOUR BRINGS TO VIVID LIFE...

King of the Khyber Rifles

TYRONE POWER
TERRY MOORE • MICHAEL RENNIE

AUGUST 30 WEEK

Left: everything you wanted to know about CinemaScope. (BFI – Sidney Bernstein Collection.)

Below left: CinemaScope at the Granada Woolwich, which retained side-opening curtains. (Photo Coverage.)

Below right: the CinemaScope screen at Harrow really fills the width of the proscenium arch and is angled slightly to face the projectors and provide a better view for circle patrons. (Photo Coverage.)

Overleaf: Granada emphasises the added significance of stereophonic sound. (BFI – Sidney Bernstein Collection.)

stereophonic sound. It laid out £250,000 on thirty installations and had 'scope up and running at Portsmouth in February 1954 and at Stockport and Brighton from 1 March. Granada's firsts were at Harrow and Kingston on 7 June in time for the initial CinemaScope attraction that played the London suburbs. This was the Fox Movietone Royal Tour documentary *Flight Of The White Heron* and the first local cinema to show it was the Essoldo Penge where it opened on Sunday 6 June for a seven day run. On the following day, the Granadas Harrow and Kingston commenced their showings at the same time as seven other Essoldo halls.

Granada aimed to have further CinemaScope and stereo sound installations in place by Greenford, Slough and Woolwich by 28 June but admitted it would be difficult to bring off. In fact, only Harrow made it with *The Robe* opening for a two-week run. The following week *The Robe* appeared at the Granadas Kingston and Slough (for two weeks) and at Greenford, Welling and Woolwich (for one week). Granada experimented in advertising: at Slough and Harrow, *The Robe* was advertised as playing for two weeks from the start, but at Kingston it was announced for one week and then "retained by public demand", although booked in advance for a fortnight.

CinemaScope spread through the Granadas at a leisurely rate. It opened in Rugby on Monday 30 August, Mansfield on 6 September, but did not reach Bedford until Monday 25 October. Willesden waited until May 1955, just before the circuit's secondary cinemas were fitted out. All had to install CinemaScope in the end as it became widely adopted by the film industry and alternative non-'scope versions were no longer available.

For Granada, the Fox arrangement had many benefits. There was enormous initial public interest in CinemaScope and Fox's early productions in the process were generally superior attractions. Although the installation costs were heavy, Granada undoubt-edly recovered its investment, helped by a special allowance from Fox (there are references to this in Granada papers, but the details are obscure and it seems to have been highly confidential).

Some indication of the impact of CinemaScope comes from the attendance figures at the Granada Tooting. In 1954, these reached 1,014,951, the first seven-figure total since 1950 and ten per cent higher than 1953. In 1955, admissions rose even further to 1,034,185. Nationally, cinema attendances fell in both years, slightly in 1954 and dramatically in 1955. In 1956, when the effect of 'scope had worn off, the Granada Tooting figure plummeted to 760,774 and continued falling, as did the national totals. The benefit is clear from figures relating to the circuit as a whole (see table).

The Fox CinemaScope pictures raised the standing of the Granada circuit as its theatres were usually the first ones in their areas to have them. Most of the competing cinemas on the major circuits – Odeon, Gaumont, and to a lesser extent ABC – were slow to install CinemaScope and must have looked behind the times.

Another great advantage for Granada was that it enabled three off-circuit theatres to move into top-grade first-run presentations. The Granada East Ham dropped its regular variety shows when playing the Fox films and booking chief H. C. Fontaine specifically referred to the "terrific impact of CinemaScope" here, although Sidney Bernstein was irritated that the stage hands still had to be paid for doing little or nothing. The Granada Hounslow became the circuit's most enthusiastic outlet for Fox pictures, showing virtually all the early CinemaScope attractions for two weeks. And the Granada Kennington finally escaped from its split-week bookings of revivals and off-circuit releases.

A comparison of the groupings of theatres in the winter business drive of 1955 compared to two years earlier (see page 154) reflects the changes. The top earners all remained in place but were joined by Kennington and Maidstone from the middle group. Hounslow, Leyton and Sydenham moved into the middle group from the lowest one. The bottom bunch were augmented by the recently acquired Grantham Picture House and Century Pitsea as well as by the two Oswestry theatres, now fully owned.

Granada did not commit its entire circuit to Fox. As in the case of the earlier "exclusives", it was primarily those theatres tied to the Gaumont release that now gave priority to showing the CinemaScope output – which, of course, included virtually all the biggest Granadas. The circuit had the best of both worlds as cinemas played the Fox release for as many as twenty weeks a year and interweaved them with the top attractions from the major circuit to which they were affiliated. At several sites, newly unveiled CinemaScope screens shrunk for a week to accommodate *On The Waterfront*, which showed that hit films could still be made in black-and-white on the ordinary wide screen.

Losing the Fox pictures was a serious blow to Rank. With the reduction in the number of new American films being made, it became harder for Rank to find enough circuit programmes of adequate or better appeal, and the Gaumont release in particular began to show signs of strain. However, for Fox the new release pattern was never satisfactory. The distribution of Granadas, Essoldos and other participating cinemas was very patchy and many outlets were not as large or as attractive or as well located as the rival Odeon or Gaumont cinemas. Fox did not earn as much money from the new circuit as it would have done had it stayed with the Rank chains.

The first wave of Fox CinemaScope pictures consisted of *The Robe, King Of The Khyber Rifles, How To Marry A Millionaire, Beneath The 12 Mile Reef, Prince Valiant, 3 Coins In The Fountain, River Of No Return, Hell And High Water* and *Night People*. Some

GRANADA THEATRES RESULTS 1952-55

	seats	takings	admissions	adm. per seat	UK adm. (millions)
1952	62,386	£1,296,179	22,011,931	353	1312
1953	63,250	£1,332,646	21,006,398	332	1285
1954	65,547	£1,441,383	23,166,687	353	1276
1955	69,640	£1,636,182	23,824,993	342	1182

What these figures, partly disguised by an increased number of seats from Granada taking over new cinemas, reveal is that the circuit bucked the downward trend in cinema admissions by its showing of CinemaScope pictures, achieving the same number of admissions per seat in 1954 as in 1952 even though UK total attendances had shown a drop of 36 million. And, far more spectacularly, Granada largely resisted the big slide nationally in 1955, remaining well ahead of 1953 in the key figure of admissions per seat.

Source: BFI – Sidney Bernstein Collection.

COSTS 1955

Film hire 28.5%   Wages 24.2%
Advertising 2.9%   Repairs 6.2%
Other expenses 28.3%

Source: BFI – Sidney Bernstein Collection.

The Century Shrewsbury displays its special CinemaScope sign above the entrance in March 1957. (Photo Coverage.)

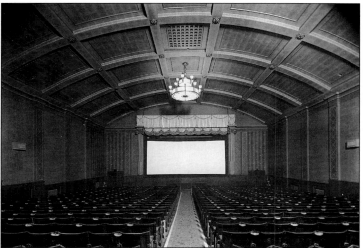

The Granada Hounslow spruced up in 1954 for its new lease of life playing 20th Century-Fox CinemaScope releases. The auditorium boasts a small chandelier of the standard circuit type and a new festoon curtain (raised for this photograph) to allow the maximum width of screen. (Photo Coverage.)

Granadas, from their continuing access to major circuit releases, also ran the first CinemaScope pictures from other studios, especially those able to tap into the ABC release like Dartford, Deptford, North Cheam, Upper Norwood and Wandsworth Road. From August 1954, the Granada Rugby played stereo prints of the first Gaumont release in CinemaScope, Universal's *The Black Shield Of Falworth* (released by Rank's GFD), and the ABC release *The High And The Mighty* (from Warner Bros.) before its first Fox picture, *King Of The Khyber Rifles.*

The Granadas that were most fully committed to the Fox circuit and CinemaScope pictures were: Bedford, Chichester, Clapham Junction, Dartford, East Ham, Epsom, Grantham, Greenwich, Harrow, Hounslow, Kennington, Kettering, Kingston, Loughton, Maidstone, Mansfield, Rugby, Shrewsbury, Sutton, Sydenham, Thornton Heath, Tooting, Upper Norwood, Walthamstow, Welling, Willesden and Woolwich.

At Grantham, where films normally played only half the week, the early Fox productions played a full six days. While the Clapham Junction Granada screened most Fox pictures, it was often out of sync with other South London Granadas as it fitted them in around strong Odeon programmes. There was flexibility at Sutton, as some Fox releases played at nearby North Cheam instead (a few, like *Island In The Sun*, played both). Wandsworth Road with access to all three major circuit's releases was one of the theatres least involved with Fox releases, but even here occasional programmes would appear. In Leyton there was both an Essoldo and Century and the smaller Essoldo seems to have taken the line-up as the Century had the Odeon release (although frequently replaced by non-Fox off-circuit bookings).

The one film after the initial batch that seemed to play the absolute maximum of Granadas was the musical *There's No Business Like Show Business* and it was also among a number of films that were booked for a full seven day run starting on a Sunday: these were either very popular draws or films of particular appeal to the regular Sunday audience. *There's No Business Like Show Business* opened on Sunday because of the drawing power among teenagers of one of its stars: the singer Johnnie Ray (who had performed live at the Granada Tooting).*

Besides some larger cinemas previously listed, the Centurys

* Ivan Cluley vividly remembers arriving at around 3pm to take charge of the Granada Acton on the opening Sunday of *There's No Business Like Show Business*, noticing huge queues of Teddy Boys and their girls as far as the eye could see. To his horror, the chief projectionist told him the print hadn't turned up. He alerted his managing director, Victor Chapman, and the booking controller, John Gregory, then changed the running order to start with the supporting film, which had been scheduled for showing only once between two showings of the big film. To his relief, Chapman (still dressed in his gardening clothes) turned up with a copy in his car while Gregory arrived with another copy by taxi ...

and other older, secondary cinemas which were equipped with CinemaScope at a later date also lacked stereophonic sound. The Empire Bedford was the earliest second-rank cinema to be fitted out, presenting CinemaScope less than two months after the Granada, from 20 December 1954.

In some cases, drastic structural alterations were necessary. At the Century Leyton, extensive stage alterations took place to fit a new 30 ft. wide screen, more than twice the width of the old one, with a vertically rising curtain in gold satin in front.

The company frequently carried out an overall refurbishment of lesser sites while adding CinemaScope and re-opened them with a flourish, upgraded to the Century name. This happened to the Regent at King's Cross, and to the Regent Rugby, which had a particularly awkward curving proscenium arch and did not receive CinemaScope until July 1955, almost always playing split weeks. At Oswestry, the two theatres were equipped in an odd order: the Kings received CinemaScope first and re-opened as the Century in December 1955 with three day runs of Cinema-Scope pictures. The Regal did not gain 'scope until the summer of 1956, at which time it became the Granada. Further re-namings of this period resulted in the Broadway Deptford and Shrewsbury Kings each becoming a Century.

Although Fox's pictures were usually widely played, its British-located costume drama *That Lady* (Olivia de Havilland with eye patch), was hardly shown at all in Spring 1955 after a disastrous press and presumably weak run at Walthamstow where it was gamely promoted as having been banned by the fascist dictator of Spain, Franco: "You CANNOT see it in Granada Spain but you CAN see it at Granada Walthamstow". Fox's Christmas release *The Virgin Queen*, with Bette Davis as Queen Elizabeth I, fared little better. In 1956, *Secret Interlude* (a renaming of *The View From Pompey's Head*), *Hilda Crane*, and (surprisingly, given its British setting) the thriller *23 Paces To Baker Street* all received very limited exposure on the Granada circuit. Some Fox pictures needed stronger support than the shorts and B features normally booked, and the Marilyn Monroe musical *Gentlemen Prefer Blondes* was dusted off to accompany *On The Threshold Of Space*.

By the beginning of November 1955, Granada recognised that the "CinemaScope honeymoon" was over. Audiences were now taking the wide screen for granted, and the 20th Century-Fox output included many poor pictures. Where CinemaScope had once dominated local press advertising, it was now reduced in type size and prominence. A special sign showing the Cinema-Scope trademark which had been suspended from many canopies when 'scope films were showing was withdrawn in March 1956. In July 1957 managers were advised that Cinema-Scope need no longer be mentioned in advertising.

Above: the Granada Kennington with a Fox CinemaScope attraction, Man in the Grey Flannel Suit, *on 21 September 1956. The large poster on the side wall for* The King and I *advertises the film as playing at the Carlton Haymarket now and the Granada soon. Below, the foyer of the Granada Kennington with circuit light fitting. Note intricate decorative panel of plants at top right. (Both Photo Coverage.) No auditorium view from Granada cinema days has been located.*

SEE **Yul Brynner** with **Deborah Kerr** in RODGERS & HAMMERSTEIN'S **The King and I** U

A 20th CENTURY FOX **55 CINEMASCOPE** PICTURE

NOW SHOWING AND AGAIN ALL NEXT WEEK AT THESE THEATRES!

ACTON GRANADA	**ILFORD** ESSOLDO
CALEDONIAN RD. ESSOLDO	**KENNINGTON** GRANADA
CHELSEA ESSOLDO	**KILBURN** ESSOLDO
CLAPHAM JUNC. GRANADA	**KINGS CROSS** CENTURY
EAST HAM GRANADA	**KINGSTON** GRANADA
ENFIELD RIALTO	**PALMERS GRN.** QUEEN'S
GOLDERS GRN. IONIC	**SUTTON** GRANADA
HACKNEY ESSOLDO	**TOOTING** GRANADA
HARRINGAY REGAL	**WALTHAMSTOW** GRANADA
HARROW GRANADA	**WATFORD** ESSOLDO
HAYES ESSOLDO	**WILLESDEN** GRANADA
HOUNSLOW GRANADA	**WOOLWICH** GRANADA

FROM SUNDAY OCT.14 – CROYDON DAVIS

STILL AT THE **CARLTON** HAYMARKET AND **RIALTO** COVENTRY ST. W.1.

Pre-releases

Although Fox's dispute with Rank had partly concerned extended runs for its films, only *The Robe* among the earlier Cinema-Scope titles seems to have been widely shown in Granadas for two weeks rather than one.

Then, in October 1956, Fox devised a special release for *The King And I*, its hit musical, in collaboration with its usual outlets. The film opened while still playing in the West End for two-week "pre-release" runs at a number of cinemas in London and elsewhere at slightly increased prices of admission. Several (including four Essoldos) began the run on Sunday 7 October while Granada started on the following day (this was not a good film for the Sunday crowd), in the London area at Acton, Clapham Junction, East Ham, Enfield, Harrow, Hounslow, Kennington, Kings Cross, Kingston, Sutton, Tooting, Walthamstow, Willesden and Woolwich. Harrow benefited from the elaborate display transferred from the front of the Carlton Haymarket with the title in sequinned lettering. At Hounslow, *The King And I* ran for five weeks, a record for the town. At Bedford, it stayed for three weeks. Many theatres, like Woolwich, had the film back for a third week after a short gap. At Upper Norwood, it played for four weeks during 1956, though not continuously. At the Century Loughton, once the home of split weeks, it ran for two straight weeks in November.

Anastasia was the next special Fox attraction to play a fortnight at many Granadas in Spring 1957. An attempt to hold *Island In The Sun* in the autumn of that year for two weeks was not universally successful. At Woolwich, the second week was cancelled and a revival double bill of *There's No Business Like Show Business* and *The Girl Can't Help It* substituted, the latter title to fit a personal appearance by its star Jayne Mansfield on the Monday evening. The widespread two-week run of *A Farewell To Arms* in Spring 1958, starting five days after the Royal Gala Premiere, did not work at North Cheam where a set of Fox reissues was substituted for the second week. However, a few weeks later *The Young Lions* seems to have played at North Cheam and elsewhere for a full fortnight.

Pre-announced two-week suburban runs were not confined to the Fox circuit. When *Doctor At Large*, the latest in the hugely successful series starring Dirk Bogarde, had its circuit release in 1957, it played an extra week in advance in the London suburbs at selected Gaumonts as well as at the Granadas Greenford and Tooting. And when the smash hit *Bridge On The River Kwai* went out in February 1958, it also opened a week early for a two week run at several suburban Odeons as well as at such Granadas as Clapham Junction and Tooting.

In addition, special presentations of major films began taking place in the late Fifties, with separate performances for two or three weeks at increased prices. These included *Around the World In 80 Days* and *The Ten Commandments* and cut across normal distributor/circuit affiliations. Thus the Granada Sevenoaks, primarily an ABC release outlet, played both these, despite their distributors' normal ties to the town's Odeon, as well as *Gigi* (for three weeks) and *The Nun's Story*, both from distributors normally supplying ABC. Similarly, the Granada Kennington was able to book *Gigi* to supplement its Fox first runs. (Usually, these engagements did not include Sundays when the standard double bills of old films would be presented.) Such presentations went in waves of theatres, beginning with the strongest outlets: weaker sites like Edmonton and Greenford would only participate late in the day with films like *Oklahoma!* or *The Ten Commandments*.

Projectomatic

First introduced to Granada at North Cheam in April 1957, this automatic projection system, invented by Essoldo around 1953 and originally known as Essoldomatic, used pulses (marks on the side of the film just outside the sprocket holes) that were linked to pegs in a drum which were placed in different positions to activate various basic functions. The drum rotated and each peg completed an electrical circuit.

Projectomatic could change over the reels, open the curtains, alter the screen ratio, start and stop the gramophone for the interval music, and raise and lower the footlights. It was quite an important development and Barry Haigh, who was chief projectionist at North Cheam, recalls Sidney Bernstein coming along to spend twenty minutes in the box, being shown how it worked – or was supposed to work.

As Haigh recalls: "The first week we had Projectomatic, we were showing the ABC release, a film called *Kismet* – quite a lavish MGM musical with Howard Keel and Ann Blyth and Vic Damone – and Granada wanted to show local dignitaries what it could do. And on the last performance on the Friday night of the first week they had virtually an invited audience with people like Harry Secombe and Roy Castle, the Mayor of Sutton, and one or two of the hierarchy of Granada. Everything went well with it until we got going on *Kismet*. The projector started, and the next pulse put the footlights down and opened the tabs, and the censor's certificate came on and once that happened you got another pulse which reverted the system back to doing ordinary change-overs.

"And this thing picked up a loose pulse just after *Kismet* started and it closed the tabs, brought the footlights up, brought the houselights up, and played 'God Save the Queen' before we could do anything about it. It picked up a stray pulse somehow.

"They supplied a little jar of silver paint and you marked the edge. And some of this paint used to come off and, when you rewound, it could stick on another bit of film. After a while they got a tape which was much better."

Despite these teething problems, Projectomatic had been widely installed across the circuit a year later. Although it could start the gramophone record rotating for interval music, it still needed human assistance to place the pick-up arm in the groove. Cinema Theatre Association members had the system explained by the chief on a visit to the Granada Tooting some years later.

End of the Fox circuit

In January 1958, the Rank Organisation patched up its quarrel with 20th Century-Fox and began booking the studio's releases again, including its blockbuster *Peyton Place*. However, Fox agreed to allocate only half its product to Rank's Odeon and Gaumont circuits, retaining the other half for its established outlets, including all its British productions to help these cinemas meet their quota obligations. Fox also promised an even split between the two sides. *The Young Lions* and *The Fly* were two strong attractions that went the way of the Fox or fourth circuit. However, this arrangement was superseded by Rank's decision, announced in October 1958, to combine its Odeons and Gaumonts into two new circuits from early 1959. This brought about the end of the fourth circuit. The last Fox release it played was a strong draw, the British western spoof starring Kenneth More, *The Sheriff Of Fractured Jaw*, which opened at Granadas on Boxing Day for a ten-day run, with the first half of the week before Christmas Day being given over to Fox Cinema-Scope revivals.

16 • Besides CinemaScope

Special bookings

When the Fox arrangement stárted in mid-1954 it supplanted almost all other special bookings for the circuit. In any case, there would have been few other exclusives available, as a prime supplier, RKO Radio, had substantially reduced its output and the shortage of product generally meant that most worthwhile releases found ready berths on the three major circuits.

However, Granada still found opportunities to express its individuality, especially where shorts were concerned. C. A. Lejeune, the film critic of *The Observer*, declared in 1957: "There is no film of quality, long or short, that Granada won't play, no matter how cold the shoulder turned on it by bigger circuits. So we had through Granada the first real introduction to Eartha Kitt in the film *New Faces*. We had Ed Murrow's *African Conflict*, made for American Television. We had a chance to look again at *Thursday's Children*, a touching documentary about the training of deaf-and-dumb children, which seemed to have disappeared without trace after its first West-end showing. We had *Time Out Of War*, a wonderful little film about a human interlude on a hot summer's afternoon during the Scarlett O'Hara war, which was awarded one of the most coveted prestige prizes at the Edinburgh Festival. We saw all these things because the people behind the Granada Group have a fixed notion that audiences are a lot more grown-up than they are generally supposed to be."

New Faces, a film version of a Broadway revue released by British Lion, had the appeal of being an early CinemaScope production, but it was not shown that widely by Granada and did have a prior West End run.

Undoubtedly, Sidney Bernstein was the inspiration behind the showing of offbeat shorts. He directly initiated the idea of picking up and showing *African Conflict* in the cinemas after hearing about this study of South African apartheid from Ed Murrow, an old friend from the war years. Granada was the actual distributor of this 45-minute documentary report which had been made for Murrow's American TV series *See It Now*, and gained a U certificate from the British Board of Film Censors. It was originally announced that Granada would show a series of *See It Now* programmes and also make them available to schools and churches. Granada arranged a showing of *African Conflict* for the press and screened it at eighteen of its London cinemas over three weeks, using six prints. No other programmes in the series seem to have followed.

The circuit release that Granada alone gave *Thursday's Children*, the short by Lindsay Anderson and Guy Brenton which won an Academy Award, certainly provided challenging viewing material for audiences drawn by Fox's South African 'western', *Untamed*, with which it was mostly coupled. There was a further total contrast in type when another Anderson documentary, *We Are The Lambeth Boys*, was later booked to support *The King And I*. (Granada's efforts were appreciated: I know of one budding film critic of the time who stills remembers suffering through *The King And I* in order to see *We Are The Lambeth Boys* again.)

The Oscar-winning dramatic short *A Time Out Of War* was played with a top attraction, *Anastasia*, at many Granadas, and with its tricky construction certainly made demands on the audience.

Granada also got behind a British Lion production, *Child's Play*, a 59-minute featurette which supported various Fox CinemaScope pictures and received unusually emphatic treatment in press advertising with all the wording reversed out of a black block.

Remarkable as it is that educative and experimental shorts should have been screened so widely in large mainstream cinemas, they were very much the exception and also fitted Granada's need for shorts to accompany long Fox 'scope films. But Granada had no hesitation in other weeks about booking Fox's deplorable 'Pocket Edition' remakes of past classics such as *Laura*, which were primarily a series for television showing, or showing B westerns.

Unlike many cinemas, the circuit did not duck the Marlon Brando version of *Julius Caesar*, and when it played at the Granada Bedford in May 1954 patrons were assured that it was "Exciting as any gangster film" (rather as *Citizen Kane* had been sold to Harrow patrons back in 1942 as "Stark uncensored story of a millionaire...and a blonde").

Besides the occasional film booking, there are further instances of Granada in a didactic frame of mind. A free art exhibition called

Pictures You Can Live With, consisting of twenty-five reproductions of works by Van Gogh, Renoir, Degas, Matisse and others, was inaugurated with a twelve-day run at Tooting before being displayed for six days at eighteen other sites in turn. Drawings by the late film critic and caricaturist Richard Winnington were exhibited in mid-1955 at several London Granadas including Sutton and Tooting. While many other cinemas held exhibitions of photographs and paintings, these were usually arranged by individual managers to display the amateur work of local societies as a good will gesture, gaining newspaper coverage and attracting visitors who might then come back as cinemagoers. The Granada touring exhibitions of outstanding works of art seem to have been unique. There is no record of the level of interest they aroused.

Granadas also offered more information about their films than most cinemas. Managers were required to type out a cast list and the name of the film's director for display on the noticeboard in the foyer. Sidney Bernstein insisted this had to be neatly typed in a block in the centre of the space, and more than one manager recalls a great deal of fingerwork with the tab and space bar to obtain the required effect.

Early in 1956, Sidney Bernstein issued his fifth and last Questionnaire, the first in ten years. "Granada listens to the voice of the Patron" read the reply-paid card (to be sent, as usual, to Bernstein personally at Granada headquarters). He invited a response to just a handful of questions: "Which film did you enjoy most in 1955. Which film did you enjoy least in 1955? Who (male and female) do you consider gave the most outstanding performance? Which newcomer (male and female) impressed you most? Which newspaper film reviews guide you?" The most popular film was *The Dam Busters,* an ABC release shown first run at comparatively few Granadas and the smash hit of the year at British cinemas. The results of the Questionnaire no longer gained much press attention.

Two by Chaplin

In the midst of Granada's run of Fox 'scope and stereo attractions, it seemed an anachronism when the circuit arranged its own exclusive re-issue of Charles Chaplin's speechless *Modern Times* (1936), supported by the Harlem Globetrotters feature *Go! Man! Go!*, starting in December 1954. Chaplin's old films still retained considerable drawing power but this exclusive deal seems to have resulted from Sidney Bernstein's long-standing friendship with the comedian. Granada arranged a press show of *Modern Times* at the London Pavilion. It played twenty-six Granadas in a staggered run – mostly the top halls, but, as previously mentioned, at Kingston it became the last ever programme at the Century Elite rather than playing the Granada.

FROM THE **GRANADA** Group

THE GRANADA THEATRES LIMITED
Telephone: GERrard 3554   36 GOLDEN SQUARE, LONDON, W.1

"GRANADA BOOKS CHAPLIN EXCLUSIVELY"

Charlie Chaplin's "MODERN TIMES" has been booked exclusively to Granada Theatres and will be shown from December 13.

First Playdates:

December 13	Granada, HARROW
	Rialto, ENFIELD
December 20	Granada, GREENFORD
	Granada, HOUNSLOW
	Granada, WALTHAMSTOW
	Century, LOUGHTON
	Century, STRATFORD
December 27	Granada, CLAPHAM JUNCTION
	Granada, EPSOM
	Granada, GREENWICH
	Granada, SLOUGH
	Granada, SYDENHAM
	Granada, THORNTON HEATH
	Granada, WELLING
	Century, CHEAM
	Century, KINGSTON
	Century, PLUMSTEAD
	Century, WOOLWICH
January 3	Granada, EAST HAM
	Granada, KENNINGTON
	Granada, WILLESDEN
	Century, DARTFORD
January 10	Granada, RUGBY
	Granada, SEVENOAKS
January 31	Granada, KETTERING
February 14	Granada, CHICHESTER

With the compliments of Anthony S. Gruner.

150/ASG/BC/GG   8.12.54.

Press release for a Granada exclusive.
(BFI – Sidney Bernstein Collection.)

Granada goes to bat for Chaplin.
Below: the heavy dot border to advertising was introduced in April 1955 as an eye-catching device. Sidney Bernstein had spotted it in The Guardian in February 1954 and suggested its adoption. To some, it is reminiscent of chaser lights. (Both from BFI – Sidney Bernstein Collection.)

More of a test was Chaplin's new British-made *A King In New York* which was refused by the major British circuits, partly because its attack on McCarthyism was deemed of limited appeal and partly because it did not have a big distributor behind it to demand a release. Jympson Harman, the respected film critic of the London *Evening News*, went further, insisting that the film was being cold-shouldered for fear of upsetting Hollywood and prejudicing the acceptance of British films in America. Granada played the film widely when it was released in October – November 1957, stoking up the controversy for its publicity value. Its theatres were joined by many Essoldos and independent cinemas plus a few ABC halls.

Other special bookings
At the other end of the scale from award-winning shorts, Granada became the first prestigious circuit to book a nudist film in a big way. *Garden Of Eden* was turned down by the British Board of Film Censors but given a local certificate by many local authorities. When Granada arranged a special screening at Dartford for council members, such was their devotion to duty that twenty-four of them turned up to view it. In many areas, including London, Essex and Shropshire, *Garden Of Eden* received a U certificate, allowing all ages to attend. Granada coupled the film with various Technicolored Hollywood action pictures from Universal-International (distributed by Rank) and played down the sensational aspects. The film was booked by many other independent cinemas but the Granada circuit was particularly receptive because its distributor, Orb, was a small outfit set up by former chief booker Nat Miller. Over the years, Miller could count on Granada, unlike the three major chains, for widespread bookings of his product.

During 1956, Granada started pairing the two Rank comedy hits *Genevieve* and *Doctor In The House*: this combination, known as "The Doc and the Crock", would be repeatedly booked over the years. There was also a large number of spot bookings for the subtitled X-certificate Brigitte Bardot feature *The Light Across The Street*, released by Miracle Films, although in Tooting it was seized by the rival Essoldo hall, the Astoria.

The booking department was placing many foreign films at the Century Cheam Village, both in special weeks or seasons and for months on end in one-day Sunday bookings. Most performed badly but, after a booking of the Jacques Tati comedy *Mr. Hulot's Holiday* took an outstanding £469, the film was shown selectively elsewhere. When the Odeon circuit took the French suspense drama *The Wages Of Fear* in 1954, Granada played it wherever possible, doing excellent business at Clapham Junction. In Bedford, it was booked for a week at the Granada rather than one of the lesser cinemas. Some foreign films were

GRANADA SUTTON
VIG 4440

open 1.20 Oct 26 week last show 7.30

the Funniest Funny Man in Films . . .

JACQUES MONSIEUR HULOT **TATI**
MY UNCLE

colour 2.30 5.30 8.30 u

plus DISNEY'S **MEN AGAINST THE ARCTIC**
colour 1.45 4.45 7.45 u

sun Oct 25 | Tony Curtis **PURPLE MASK** | all u colour show | Van Heflin **TANGANYIKA**

cafe available for private hire ● phone VIG 5653 for details

NORTH CHEAM FAI 8818

monday OCT 26 WEEK thursday
open 1.45 last show 7.5 open 1.55 last show 7.5
Howard Keel Jane Powell Kenneth More Kay Kendall

Seven Brides for Seven Brothers **GENEVIEVE**
2.15 5.40 9 o'c u
1.50 5.20 8.50 u Dirk Bogarde Kenneth More
IT'S A DOG'S LIFE **DOCTOR IN THE HOUSE**
3.45 7.15 u
3.45 7.10 u

sun Oct 25 | Jack Palance **ATTACK !** a
Keith Larsen **DIAL RED O** a

Two of Granada's favourite standby programmes in the same week at North Cheam, replacing a weak ABC release. Seven Brides For Seven Brothers *was always being revived at Granadas. It was shown, for example, at least six times for three days or more with various other films at the Century Pitsea ("Seen it before? But you'll see it again!" ran the advertisement on the fifth occasion), and at least five times between 1956 and 1964 at Sutton, in the same district as North Cheam. When it was given a full Rank circuit re-release in 1969, double-billed with* The Sheepman, *it was once again widely booked on the Granada circuit.*

Doctor in the House *and* Genevieve, *known as "The Doc and the Crock" and often advertised as "Twice As Funny Together", played most Granadas in a revival double-bill in the summer of 1956 and again in the summer and autumn of 1959. Perhaps the last time they were tried was in March 1968 at the product-starved Granada East Ham.*

The style of advertising above, with the title reversed out in blocks and no dot border, started in late April 1958. It also became the style used on the vertical signs outside of theatres.
(BFI – Sidney Bernstein Collection.)

also played at the Century Elite Kingston in its last years and tried at the Empire Shrewsbury and Century Woolwich. In July 1956, an experiment of booking *Nana* with Martine Carol into the huge Sutton cinema proved disastrous, even with a British comedy revival, *The Captain's Paradise*, tacked on. *Nana* was in its fourth month in the West End and this was its first showing anywhere else in the London area. It didn't help that the Curzon in Sutton was showing a less sophisticated foreign film that same week, *Unmarried Mothers. Nana* was taken off after Wednesday and replaced by a standard stand-by: *Seven Brides For Seven Brothers.*

VTC and Other Theatres
Sidney Bernstein's involvement with his brother Cecil in Variety Theatres Consolidated Ltd. might seem puzzling until his past interest in live theatre is recalled. In the autumn of 1951, the Bernsteins acquired one tenth of the company's capital, seemingly from the estate of the late Walter Payne, and wanted to become directors. The company's chairman was a veteran of early film exhibition, Reginald C. Bromhead, while Gerald A. W. Heath was managing director. The Bernsteins were initially offered one directorship only but demanded two and both joined the board in June 1952.

The company operated a number of music halls – the Regent King's Cross (which was leased out to a theatre group involving former Odeon executive W. G. Elcock); the Empress Brixton; the Chelsea Palace; the East Ham Palace; and the Palace Walthamstow – and it was about to buy the Metropolitan Edgware Road. VTC also owned the site of the South London Palace at the Elephant and Castle, which had been destroyed by bombing in 1941. In July 1952, the company regained possession of the Regent King's Cross after the theatre venture failed, and a management agreement with Granada was immediately announced. A subsidiary, Granada (Management) Ltd., re-opened it as a cinema, being paid a percentage of the profits.

VTC was doing so badly by January 1953 that both Sidney and Cecil Bernstein returned their directors' fees. In the spring of 1954, VTC's architect, Leonard Allen, was asked to look into the possibility of running the Chelsea Palace as a cinema and installing CinemaScope. Then, in the summer of 1955, Cecil Masey produced plans for replacing part of the stalls area with shops. However, the Palace remained in live use. The 978-seat Palace Walthamstow closed in February 1954 and in the following autumn was surveyed for possible cinema use. The East Ham Palace had also closed but re-opened on 6 September 1954, only to close again after failing with nude shows. In 1955 Sidney Bernstein replaced Reginald C. Bromhead as chairman of VTC and from then on the fate of the company became, in the

The huge bulk of the Century King's Cross (8 June 1965) with the fly tower at the back and a very large Miss Candy shop built into the corner. View of tilted CinemaScope screen dates from 27 February 1967. (Photo Coverage.)

public mind if not in terms of actual ownership, the responsibility of Granada.

In fact, Sidney Bernstein was keen for Granada to acquire VTC because some of the properties could be put to profitable use: in particular, there was an opportunity in Brixton for the Empress to become a Granada cinema and play the Gaumont and Fox circuit product. In July 1955, architect David E. Nye was commissioned to draw up plans for the conversion. The estimates were much higher than anticipated and the work was postponed until mid-November 1956 when Nye received instructions to proceed immediately.

Max Miller was the last big music hall performer there. Work was scheduled to start on Monday 17 December while the building was closed for pantomime rehearsals. The pantomime, *Aladdin* (with Alma Cogan as "guest star"), ran for two weeks, followed by a final week of variety. Then new portholes were cut through a back wall and projectors installed from the just closed Century Slough. Sound equipment came from the similarly defunct Century Cheam (an ancient sound system already at the Empress, surviving from Sunday film shows, was discarded). A new rear stalls entrance was created – the old one just beyond the main entrance doors was filled with a paybox and patrons were dispatched to the left to reach their seats. The rows of front stalls seats were moved six inches closer, to 2 ft. 6 ins. apart, as they became the cheapest rather than the most expensive seats in the house.

Re-opening as the Granada Brixton took place a week later than scheduled, on Tuesday 5 February 1957 with that week's Gaumont circuit release, *Three Violent People*. One of the lesser stars of the western, Forrest Tucker, was on hand to lead the celebrations with the curvaceous Sabrina. In time-honoured tradition, the opening was filmed newsreel-style in black-and-white and I remember the footage being shown at the Granada Thornton Heath.

The seat backs in the steep balcony at Brixton were extremely hard and painfully shaped, probably retained from live theatre days (I can still recall the discomfort from watching the whole of *Gone With The Wind*). The Granada was bad news for the Clifton out on Brixton Hill, towards Streatham. This had lost the Gaumont release when the Gaumont Streatham re-opened and responded by installing CinemaScope to bring Fox's films to Brixton for the first time. The Granada took these away and the Clifton struggled along on split-week revivals and left-over new releases for a few months, then closed. The Granada was far enough away from Streatham, in the centre of Brixton, that it could take the Gaumont release as well as the Fox output.

By 1958, VTC's financial situation was causing great concern: the Metropolitan Edgware Road was losing £150 a week as a live venue in the year ending February 1959. Brixton was barely

The Granada Brixton. Rather ugly externally, this theatre was located down a side road, the entrance corner being just visible from the main shopping street. The fly tower was at the far right. (This 10 March 1965 photograph shows live attractions – the London Festival Ballet and Saturday wrestling – competing with an exploitation film.)

Above: the auditorium in November 1962. Below right: The upper circle remained but was rarely used (10 March 1965 photograph). Below left: the main paybox apparently occupied a former entrance to the auditorium (November 1962). (All Photo Coverage.)

Top across: the former Broadway Pitsea on 14 February 1955, about to re-open as the Century. The old canopy survives. The shop spaces have yet to be converted into a snack bar and Miss Candy shop. Workmen are seen put finishing touches to the foyer, which boasts a standard circuit chandelier. The auditorium is ready for occupancy. (All Photo Coverage.)

Bottom across: the former Academy Leytonstone seen on 22 November 1955, reborn as the Century after seven weeks of alterations including patching of the auditorium roof and installation of a Miss Candy shop. Auditorium views show before (with the old Academy-ratio screen set back on the stage) and after. (All Photo Coverage.)

profitable although King's Cross was doing better. A temporary solution to the Met's problem was to turn it into a Granada Television studio for seven weeks in the summer of 1958.

Apart from VTC, there was the strange case of the Embassy Swiss Cottage. Granada had been interested in Spring 1954 in building a new cinema within a London County Council development at Swiss Cottage. Granada, or Sidney Bernstein himself, took over the medium-sized closed Embassy, a live theatre, in the middle of 1955 and it remained in hibernation for the next year, during which period George Coles drew up plans to convert it into a cinema, removing the stage to gain a further 116 seats. Bernstein then tried to sell it, declaring (in a letter dated 7 June 1956) that he had bought the Embassy "because of my desire to be again actively associated with the 'live' theatre, but TV [the new Granada ITV company] has taken more of my time than I anticipated". He disposed of it to the Central School of Speech in the autumn of 1956, writing to Tyrone Guthrie (24 October 1956) that selling the building was "quite a heartwrench for me... I so wanted to run the Embassy as an experimental theatre... but we have all agreed the need of the Central School is more important."

There was a further instance of Sidney Bernstein's fits of enthusiasm for live theatre when, according to *The Daily Telegraph* (2 March 1955), he approached Prince Littler offering to buy both the Stoll Theatre Kingsway and the St. James' Theatre after architects submitted plans for replacing them with offices and showrooms. Bernstein wanted them to continue as theatres but was told the St. James' was not for sale. Both were demolished in 1957.

Other additions

In June 1954, Granada acquired the 600-seat Broadway at Pitsea, Essex. This was really a means of reaching the substantial population of the nearby new town in Basildon at a time when building restrictions prevented the erection of a cinema there. Granada spent £30,000 on renovation, installing a 35 ft. wide curved screen for CinemaScope but no stereophonic sound. Reopened as the Century, it incorporated a restaurant, snack bar and sweet shop. Programmes were mostly shown for three days with a mid-week change and drew heavily on the Fox Cinema-Scope releases.

In December 1954, Granada took over the ancient, now run-down Academy at Leytonstone from a hard-pressed independent owner. It seated just over 1,000 in stadium style, with a barrier across to segregate the more expensive rear seats. Of course, Granada already had the larger Rialto in this north London suburb but the Academy was a good buy because it took the lucrative Odeon release. George Coles was put to work on a thorough renovation and it was relaunched after nearly two months as a Century.

The bombed remains of the Rivoli Whitechapel. The original entrance was behind the arches on the near block and the auditorium is presumably the block in the background. (Photo Coverage.) The photocopies below show one proposed design for the new frontage. (Courtesy of D. W. C. Sparke.)

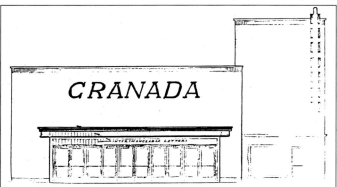

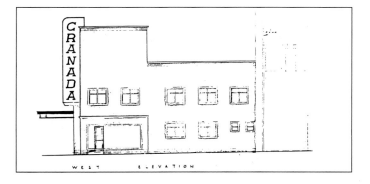

Granada also bought up the opposition in Grantham, Lincolnshire. Two closed cinemas and the active Picture House seem to have been involved. Like the Granada, which was almost next door, the Picture House had a café. The Picture House was closed after eighteen months, leaving only the Granada.

Granada's most daring move, if accurately reported, came in 1956 after a group headed by Serge Semenenko bought control of Warner Bros. Granada was said to have bid $5.6 million for the thirty-seven-and-half per cent stake that Warners held in the Associated British Picture Corporation, which owned the ABC cinema circuit. Semenenko decided not to sell the shares, so Granada were denied a share in one of the three big circuits.

An odd episode of thwarted expansion concerned the closed Rivoli Whitechapel, East London. This large cinema had been under Rank control as part of the United Picture Theatres circuit when it suffered serious bomb damage in 1940. By 1955 Sidney Bernstein had acquired a controlling interest, and he had plans draw up by George Coles (one of its original architects). These provided for a reinstatement of the building at an estimated cost of £99,725 (excluding outfitting). There would be 1,272 stalls seats and 252 in the circle (the cinema originally had 2,268 seats). Bernstein had doubts about proceeding because of the opposition in the area, and was willing to sell the property for £50,000 in October 1955 even while Coles was drawing up his plans. Bernstein wrote to Kenneth Winckles, head of Rank's cinema operations: "I, personally, control the [Rivoli] which, as you know, was damaged during the war. The main walls, roof and circle are intact and plans have been prepared and approved for the re-modelling of the cinema to include a large foyer, shop and kiosk. Its seating capacity will be 1,524. As the building is structurally sound, the cost of the proposed development will not be excessive. Are you interested? I have not offered it elsewhere." Within days, Winckles replied that Rank was not interested.

In February 1956, Bernstein decided to turn it into a Granada and discussed various designs for a fin sign on the exterior. He informed Winckles of his intentions and sought confirmation that the cinema would be able to play the weekly first-run Gaumont release.

Winckles was not encouraging: "The present booking position in this district is somewhat different to that existing before the war, in as much as the Troxy, Commercial Road now takes the Gaumont release programme. The population in this area has diminished and the present seating in theatres is more than adequate. For this reason I would ask you to seriously reconsider your decision to reinstate the Rivoli, Whitechapel Road as we consider this would be economic suicide for all concerned. If you should decide to proceed, we should be forced to fight the position through the normal barring channels."

Bernstein replied that he believed the Troxy had played the Gaumont programme concurrently with the Rivoli before the war. The real problem was that Rank had since acquired cinemas at Stepney and Bethnal Green (both by now Odeons, playing the Odeon release) which had led to the Bethnal Green Foresters being switched from the Odeon release to the Gaumont. Rank's argument about a declining population was undoubtedly true and the opening of the Granada would have been bad news for its cinemas in the area. Initially, Bernstein was not to be dissuaded. By October 1956, a provisional licence had been obtained from the London County Council for the rebuilding and re-opening of the former Rivoli and the work was to be carried out "as soon as possible". But it never happened and the site was used for other purposes.

A puzzling letter from Sidney Bernstein dated 25 April 1955 survives in the files of the architect David Nye: "We have recently acquired a cinema at Wembley and desire to make some alterations to the entrance hall and elevation. Naturally, we are in a hurry. Could you kindly undertake this work for us?" The property that changed hands at this time was the Wembley Hall Cinema, an independent cinema which was taken over by Rank. Perhaps Granada had it first and decided to pass it on to Rank, but this must have happened very rapidly as the refurbished cinema opened on 23 May 1955 as the Gaumont. Or perhaps Bernstein is referring to the long-closed Capitol Wembley and dropped his plans when Rank made its take-over.

Slimming down

Even CinemaScope could not save all the theatres. In 1955 Sidney Bernstein described the Century Cheam Village as "a serious 'blot' on our Group" and appealed to all executives for ideas to deal with the situation. The Granada Greenwich, too, was showing an increased loss but it was hoped that a change of manager would result in an improvement.

Any ideas for Cheam Village proved useless and the Century went in December 1956, but of course the nearby Granada North Cheam continued. Other lesser properties were culled. The Century Slough went in January 1957, but the circuit had two larger cinemas in the town. Some were closed "for the summer" or for "a rest period", never to re-open, an approach which had the advantage of defusing any protests. This technique was used to close the Grantham Picture House (July 1956) and the Century Upper Norwood (May 1958), but again the circuit retained a larger, more important cinema in each town that could now be expected to do better business, although local cinemagoers' choice was seriously reduced.

Cinemas were also used in the battle to reduce or abolish

Entertainments Tax, a "temporary" tax introduced in World War One. According to Granada (as quoted in the *Sutton Advertiser*, 29 August 1957), the Century Cheam Village, closed eight months earlier, would definitely re-open if there was a substantial reduction in tax, but the spokesperson did admit that there was a company interested in building maisonettes on the site. An anti-tax trailer which I saw with *The Spanish Gardener* in February 1957 showed some closed Rank cinemas as well as a glimpse of the still operating Century Upper Norwood in its argument that "These lights must not go out".

As an instance of how closing cinemas did improve business at the nearest survivors, at least in the short term, there is the case of the manager of the Granada North Cheam who parked a publicity van outside the Odeon Worcester Park on its very last day in September 1956, wooing children leaving the Saturday morning show into becoming Granadiers with such success that his attendance figure the following Saturday were the highest for four years.

Some locations showed signs of strain by going on "restricted opening": cutting out most or all weekday matinees outside of children's holiday periods. The Century Rugby opened for a single evening show at 7pm on weekdays from October 1957. More strikingly, the Granada Kettering dropped afternoon shows during this year. The town of Kettering was notorious in the trade for its apathy towards cinema. (Rank sold its Gaumont for redevelopment in 1959, then despairingly closed its Odeon in 1960 to stand empty until bingo came along. This left an independent competing with the Granada, which resumed matinees at some point.)

By 1958, Granada recognised that several of its bigger cinemas, which had never been very successful, needed to cut their operating costs or be closed. These were identified as the Granadas at Cheam, Epsom, Sevenoaks and Sydenham. Other loss-making cinemas were the Century Deptford and the Adelphi Slough.

Granada's days of cinema expansion were over. There would not be another addition to the circuit for seven years, partly because Granada had a "new toy" to play with.*

* Rather daringly, a small chain called Southern Cinemas renamed its Gem at Southall, West London, the Century in March 1955, put up a Granada-style vertical sign and used the circuit type of lettering on the sign and in press advertising – but not with quite the same flair. It even played Fox Cinema-Scope product like a Granada. It had certainly fooled this writer into mistaking it for a Granada property until more detailed research for this book proved otherwise. Arthur Hawkins, who was manager at the time the Gem became the Century, recalls that Granada were furious and even went to court in an unsuccessful attempt to force a name change. The cinema closed on 17 August 1957 but the Century sign lingered during years of use as an Asian cinema.

"The new toy": Granada Television

Television had come a long way since a working Baird set was exhibited as a novelty for several weeks in the foyer of the Granada Tooting between 11.30am and noon in the spring of 1932. Like the other major groups in exhibition, Granada had sought a licence in November 1948 to erect a television station which would have been used to transmit programmes by closed circuit onto screens at cinemas. In this way, it was hoped to harness the appeal of television for the benefit of exhibitors. Some cinemas did in fact use large-screen television to show the BBC coverage of the Coronation but they did not include any Granadas.

In March 1954, Granada applied to the Postmaster-General for a licence to run a commercial television station in the Manchester area. Why there? Apparently, it had nothing to do with avoiding direct competition with the cinema chain. "I looked at two maps," Sidney Bernstein has been quoted as saying. "One showed population density. The other showed rainfall."

The Independent Television Authority gave Granada one of the first three licences, to operate from Monday to Fridays with another company gaining the weekend. Bernstein told shareholders in the annual report issued in March 1955: "This region, for which we applied expressly, will eventually serve a population of over ten million. There is little doubt that this region comprises the most closely knit section of the industrial population and that it has traditions in entertainment and culture which are unique in Britain." Shrewd as this choice of location would prove to be, it took Granada a long way from its existing roots. The company acquired a site for a studio in April 1955. (The resulting building was no architectural marvel.)

Sidney Bernstein soon had a private plane for hopping up to Manchester. His attention became focussed on the television launch and his post-Hitchcock plans for film production were dropped.

Granada Television started on 3 May 1956. "They were like kids with a new toy," says Brian Gauntlett of Sidney and his brother Cecil. "There aren't many of us who get a second chance at fifty-five," Sidney later recalled, "particularly when it involved all the things we were trained for the first time round." Sidney originally planned to run the television side and leave Cecil in London in charge of the cinemas. But there was so much work that he needed Cecil as well and it was Victor Chapman who ran the circuit. Managers addressed their weekly reports to Cecil but it was Chapman who responded to points made. Chapman succeeded Cecil as managing director of Granada Theatres around 1961.

The television station cost far more than predicted and stretched the financial resources of the group, especially when advertisers were initially reluctant to take air time. According to

Denis Forman's *Persona Granada*, the cinemas were pledged to raise capital for the television operation which only survived through a secret financial arrangement with Associated Rediffusion's London station.

Many theatre staff were recruited to work in television. Sales and restaurant executive John Roberts was appointed the first sales director of Granada Television. John Hamp, a discovery of Bryan Michie (he did a mime impression of Johnnie Ray) who had become the publicity and variety booking executive, went on to the position of light entertainment director at Granada TV.

Commercial television made some use of the theatres. In the autumn of 1955, before Granada Television started, ABC TV's *People Are Funny*, fronted by Derek Roy, went out live on alternate weeks from Woolwich, Tooting and Walthamstow. Part of the quiz show *Double Your Money* with star-host Hughie Green was televised live from the stage of the Granada Tooting on a Wednesday in January 1956. In February 1957, VTC's Chelsea Palace became the studio for the half-hour *Chelsea Revue* which was transmitted to all the three ITV regions of the time. Then the building was modified internally to suit regular television use and renamed Studio 10 Granada, the home of *Chelsea At Nine*, Granada's answer to *Saturday Night At The London Palladium*, which went out each week from the autumn of 1957. The Palace would remain exclusively in television use for several years before being closed and demolished.

Television was the enemy of cinemas. The hit series *Wagon Train* took away so many patrons that it became difficult to use Monday nights as a barometer for gauging the week's attendances (and arranging a change of programme midweek if necessary).

Granada's annual report in April 1956 hardly mentioned the cinema circuit but was full of the new television side. At the annual general meeting in May 1957 Granada Theatres Ltd. was reduced to part of a new Granada Group Ltd., reflecting the wider range of activities.

Ancillary attractions

Granada began taking over some of the shops alongside its theatres. The name "Miss Candy", applied to the girls who carried the ice-cream trays, was used for a series of confectionery outlets. Wherever possible, these were in the shop immediately adjacent to the cinema entrance so that they could serve the public through the front door but also provide patrons with sweets, cigarettes and soft drinks via a counter cut in the side wall of the cinema foyer. Thirteen had been opened by July 1956. At Thornton Heath, Miss Candy blocked an exit staircase which had to be extended onto the side of the building.

"Photo Me" self-portrait booths were also tried out, the first being installed at Harrow in the summer of 1959. Manager Brian

Gauntlett called it "Mr. Flash" in an attempt to match "Miss Candy" until Sidney Bernstein spotted the name in a weekly report and brought up the risk of encouraging indecent behaviour.

On 14 November 1957, Granada had Petula Clark open its first Granadagram shop selling records at Greenford. After this, she launched one at Wandsworth Road the following May. Although they were not a great success, a third and final shop appeared in Sutton in 1964.

The company also ran for a while at least one petrol station, attached to the car park at Sutton.

Operating procedures

For many years Granada had a distinctive policy of keeping cinemagoers in the dark.

"Why did they bother with architects?" wonders projectionist Barry Haigh. "You never had an interval at Granada. You never had the house lights up. You'd just go straight through. When Miss Candy, as they called her, sold the ice-cream, you'd put a slide on and the spotlight on her down in the front stalls, but you didn't put the house lights on."

Les Bull, long-time editor of the *CTA Bulletin*, recalls many years of visiting the Granada Maidstone. "In the late Forties through to the early Sixties, they would show films continuously. This doesn't mean just the usual continuous performance that all cinemas ran – but that they showed films from opening time to closing time without putting up the house lights at all! There were never any intervals, which meant that even ice cream sales from the trays were done in the dark.

"If you arrived for the last complete performance and entered the auditorium as the previous showing of the main feature finished, you found your seat in the dark because trailers for the Sunday one-day-only programme were put on the screen immediately. Then it was straight into the supporting feature, followed by the advertisements, Gaumont British News, next week's trailers, and so to the main feature. No break at all! This was often the cause of considerable frustration to patrons as there was never time for people to come and go at the end of the show without disturbing others.

"Another peculiarity of the Granada was its method of showing trailers. There was never any introductory or forthcoming attraction titles. The trailer was just shown with a line along the bottom of the screen telling when the film would be on. And the trailers were shown in reverse order, i.e. the supporting film trailer was shown first, followed by the trailer for the main feature.

"Maidstone Granada was such an impressive cinema that it was a source of disappointment to me that I so seldom saw the auditorium with the lights up. As a schoolboy my visits were invariably to the middle shows during term time so I came and

left in the dark. It was only at holiday times or Saturday morning matinees that, if I got there as soon as the doors opened, I could get a good look at the surroundings before the lights went down.

"The stage was fitted with several sets of drapes, those nearest the audience being dark red velvet with gold tassels at the bottom. These opened at the start of the day's shows and remained open until closing time. At the end of each film just the intermediate curtains were used."

CTA president Tony Moss comments: "It was usually as Les Bull says: straight through with no interval or house lights – certainly true in the late Forties and Fifties at theatres I visited, i.e. Tooting, Clapham Junction and Wandsworth Road. I can remember an interval at the Granada Thornton Heath a while after take-over with – wonder of wonders – the rather nice house tabs closing! Generally, Granada-built theatres only had winched house tabs; certainly true at Walthamstow. Apart from that one instance at Thornton Heath, I cannot ever remember house tabs being used at a Granada, apart from Tooting in order to set the stage for an organ show by John Madin. Intermediate tabs were winched together at Wandsworth Road for the re-opening of the Wurlitzer, in order to set the phantom grand piano on the stage. Sutton had a nice gold in front of black set of drapes that were flown just before the show started."

It seems that, because so many Granadas were equipped for live use, the main tabs were set up to be winched open by hand from the stage, and it was impractical to do this very frequently when the stage was not in regular use. During the CinemaScope era, I do recall the new reefer curtain regularly descending and rising at a fast clip at Thornton Heath but as I tended to arrive just in time for the main feature I am hazy about intervals. Usherettes, of course, would point out empty seats with their torches and ensure that patrons were safely seated in the dark. I suspect that Granada again liked to be different and put its shows through at a rapid pace. Intervals at other cinemas could certainly be tedious.

Proper intervals with the house lights up had been the policy before World War Two, but then there would have been stage hands or extra staff to work the house tabs.

Another feature of post-war policy was the removal of any indication of certificate and company trademark from the front of the trailers. While the trailer was running, a slide announcement was intermittently superimposed on the bottom edge of the picture giving the censor's certificate along with the period of showing. When the feature films themselves were screened, many studio and distributor trademarks were removed from the start of the films as part of Sidney Bernstein's campaign against manufacturers taking unnecessary credit. It is said that at one time Granada cut off all company trademarks but were forced by Metro-Goldwyn-Mayer and then by the other major studios to retain them. This in-house memo from Cecil G. Bernstein clarifies the situation as it stood in 1955:

Granada was particularly anxious to remove any sign of its British rivals, Associated British and the Rank Organisation (Sidney Bernstein was known to refer to J. Arthur Rank as "The Miller"). Among the big American distributors, United Artists was the only company affected by the ban in 1955 and its silent, static, chevron-like trademark would not have been greatly missed. Of course, the projectionists had a lot more work taking off the trademarks and then re-attaching before returning the prints. It is not clear when this practice finally ceased.

Sidney Bernstein also disliked distributors' posters. All Granada front of house publicity had long been designed at two poster shops set up at Walthamstow and Kingston. The shop at Kingston was called Posterprint and run by John Barnett, who was widely admired by managers for his skills as a designer and artist. Although Granada used distributors' quad posters for local outdoor advertising, many for Fox and other exclusives were specially designed and printed in house. The printing of flyers (then called throwaways) was entrusted to an outside supplier, the Jackson Press, headed by Connie Jackson who was familiar with Sidney's strict requirements as regard typefaces, layout, spelling of "program", etc.

A manager's view
Brian Gauntlett recalls: "Granada managers were much envied by their counterparts on the major circuits, as the weekly and daily returns were kept to a bare minimum, the emphasis of management being focussed on showmanship, public relations

image, customer care, and ensuring the highest standards of comfort and maintenance. However, a manager of a Granada Denman house would have all the CMA (Rank's management company) returns to complete as well as the weekly letter to Sidney Bernstein together with Granada's weekly business comparison sheet.

"With few exceptions, Granada maintained a policy of regularly transferring their managers from one theatre to another. Periods spent at a particular theatre could vary from six months to three or four years. This system gave the opportunity of injecting individual managers' expertise and skill into more than one situation. Promotion also played a big part in the manager's ambition to get to the bigger and busier theatres. At all their provincial theatres, Granada provided up-market company houses for managers and their families at a nominal rent of £2 per week. Assistant managers were transferred even more frequently in their quest for full managerial status.

"Granada managers' promotional activity was well recognised within the industry. Managers were constantly encouraged to think up original ideas to capture the public's attention and spotlight both future product and the theatre. The stunts were reported via the weekly letter to Sidney Bernstein and recorded the following week in the company newsletter. Not only were promotionally active managers rewarded with a two guinea publicity prize, wives would also receive a two guinea cheque – nothing like encouragement from the missus.

"Managers, however, were discouraged from sending details of their publicity campaigns to the *Kine Weekly* or joining the 'Kine Company of Showmen'. Granada jealously guarded managers' promotional activity and kept it 'in house' by recording the information in a cross index file. The stunts could then be copied, revised or updated by brother managers.

"Managers were expected to be in evening dress and standing on the front of house by 5.30pm, ready to greet their evening patrons. The only exception to wearing evening dress was Sunday as it was felt that it would create an element of snobbery with the teenage customers. Managers and assistant managers drew twelve shillings and sixpence from petty cash to cover the laundry of dress shirts. In those days you could also claim tax allowance on the replacement cost of a dress suit.

"Prior to the close of house, all free-standing publicity frames were reversed – a final reminder to patrons of forthcoming attractions. The manager would also be on the front (still dressed in his dinner jacket) to receive patrons' comments and to wish them good night and a safe journey home. Sometimes there would be a distribution by the staff of leaflets and giveaways plugging next week's film.

"There was a standard procedure at the end of the show. The

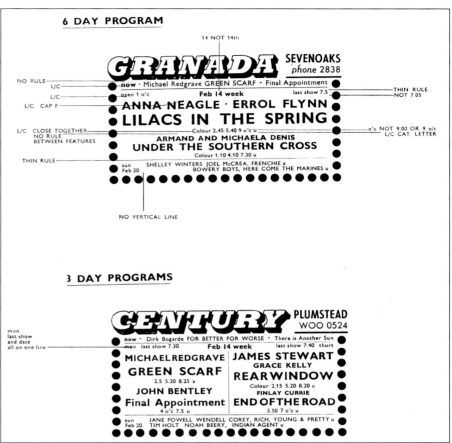

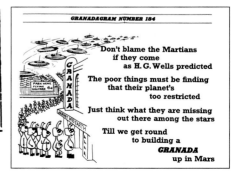

One of the better Fifties Granadagrams. (BFI – Sidney Bernstein Collection.)

manager would position himself in front of the stage and request call backs from duty staff on the individual clearance of toilets to ensure that no-one was locked in overnight. All ashtrays at the backs of seats were emptied into tins which were then topped with sand.

"Rigid procedure on a Monday morning was the screen presentation rehearsal of the adverts, filmlets, trailers (Sunday and week), the 'open' and 'close' reels of the main feature and support. During the matinee show the manager would watch the entire program from his cue seat in the circle. This had a buzzer under the seat and one buzz meant sound up one point, two buzzes drop sound one point, and three buzzes a picture problem, e.g. out of focus, half or quarter picture rack. (There were other cue buzzers at both the rear of the circle and stalls.) While the manager carried out this important duty, he was not to be disturbed (other than in an emergency) by staff or even by head office."

Live shows

After CinemaScope started, there was a drop in the number of live shows. The pantomimes were suffering from the changing times and an attempt was made to refresh them with skiffle being added to *Robin Hood* at Christmas 1957 when it played the regular sequence of Tooting, Sutton and Woolwich. This proved to be the last panto at Tooting. At Christmas 1958, Granada staged none anywhere, substituting an operetta at Sutton, but pantomime did return to Shrewsbury and Woolwich a year later, toplined by pop group The Mudlarks.

The theatre most active with full weeks of live shows during the rest of the year was the Granada Shrewsbury, followed by the Adelphi Slough. The Carl Rosa Opera made its last appearance on the circuit for several years at both these theatres and at Sutton. Maidstone and Rugby also continued to have occasional six-day live shows.

The Granada Tooting presented a week of music hall acts about twice a year along with a double bill of films, often a weak circuit release. In 1955, the British drama *The Ship That Died Of Shame* was boosted by a 45-minute stage show twice daily which, with a B feature, made a 4 hour 10 minute show – all this at normal prices! Perhaps Tooting's biggest added attraction of these years, which played for two weeks in March 1956, was *Dancing Waters,* the terpsichorean show with fountains of water, as seen at the Radio City Music Hall, which also involved John Madin on the organ.

Woolwich also added at least one stage show, to an off-circuit booking of a Randolph Scott western *Rage At Dawn* and the Bowery Boys comedy *Hold That Line* in March 1956. East Ham remained the most frequent purveyor of live entertainment with four-hour shows of variety and two films (poor new films or more substantial reissues) in the weeks between Fox CinemaScope exclusives.

The last Sunday afternoon piano concert by Eileen Joyce took place at Maidstone in February 1954. It was now principally the era of the pop stars.* As before, the Granadas were booked as part of a tour by promoters, so that artistes like Johnnie Ray were also seen in other circuits' cinemas. Sunday night live concerts were frequently staged at Tooting and Woolwich with David Whitfield, Max Bygraves and Dickie Valentine among the star performers. (Shrewsbury booked performers like Whitfield and Valentine for a whole week.)

The big American entertainers continued to appear. In 1957, Johnnie Ray made his third Good Friday appearance at Tooting and in August was seen at Clapham Junction, Walthamstow, East Ham, Sutton and Woolwich. This was the first live show of this type at Sutton – and the only one staged at Clapham Junction, presumably because it normally made more sense to book entertainers in the nearby larger Tooting theatre but in this case Ray had already played there just a few months before. (Clapham Junction had withdrawn from the pantomime circuit after its January 1953 *Robinson Crusoe*, so this one live show stood out all the more.) Nat King Cole was live at Woolwich on a Sunday in April 1954. Guy Mitchell played Tooting and Woolwich on Sundays in May 1954. Eddie Fisher was a Good Friday attraction at Tooting in 1955 and Pat Boone did a Boxing Day special there in 1956.

In the spring of 1957, the removal of entertainments tax from live shows encouraged their proliferation. Woolwich staged a six-day variety show headed by Dickie Valentine and featuring Ivan Dolin's Granada Orchestra. One-night concerts began moving from Sundays and Good Fridays to weekday evenings at the expense of new films. Friday night bookings of Slim Whitman at Woolwich in May 1957 and of Johnnie Ray at Sutton two months later could not have pleased the distributors of the week's film programmes who lost one of the best nights – but they had to submit as cinema attendances continued their remorseless decline and other ways of increasing income could not be denied.

Films stars made some guest appearances. Jayne Mansfield went on stage at Tooting and Walthamstow in September 1957. At Slough in November 1957, Bob Hope performed for fifteen minutes at a sneak preview of his latest film comedy, *Paris Holiday*. At Loughton, Jeffrey Hunter appeared live on 16 August 1957.

* John Young recalls one nostalgic act: "Marie Lloyd's daughter did a stage tour at several theatres in the mid-Fifties but by this time impersonations of her mother's act were not in vogue and the tour was not very successful." Marie Lloyd had, as mentioned previously, been taken fatally ill while appearing at Edmonton.

The Hippodrome Mansfield became the Century in 1955 with repainted exterior. Interior view seems to be of older vintage with an Academy-ratio screen. (Photo Coverage.)

Granadiers also received some celebrity visitors: Epsom welcomed Forrest Tucker and Vera Lynn in 1957.

The circuit's organs were still used, primarily in an attempt to boost weaker attractions, until 1956. After 1956, the consoles would only normally be raised for special concerts, broadcasts and occasional preludes to road show films.

Even partially live evenings attracted tax relief, and Granada took up the idea of presenting the film *The Bolshoi Ballet* at advanced prices preceded by a live piano recital at Harrow, Woolwich, Shrewsbury and Maidstone in 1958. Davis' Theatre Croydon had initiated this idea for the premiere run of the film (which had been shot there).

Granada were competing with the other major chains and some independents in putting on live shows. In Bedford, the rival Plaza was first off the mark bringing in the Ted Heath Band Show and others. Granada retaliated with its first live show for many years on Wednesday 12 February 1958, headlined by Tony Brent. This was a big success and other one-night shows followed at monthly intervals.

Rugby, Kettering, Aylesbury and (briefly) Kennington were added to the live show circuit in 1958, and during the first half of the following year Dartford, Grantham and Mansfield followed. Kingston belatedly joined in from September 1959. Some shows now took place on Saturdays, depriving film distributors of their best night, and it does seem that initially only lesser film programmes could be obtained for the rest of the week.

Granada certainly made a far higher proportion of its circuit available for live shows than any of the other large chains, specially adapting some of its medium-sized cinemas to enable pop concerts to take place. New dressing rooms were provided at Dartford and Aylesbury and work was carried out at Mansfield while at Sutton in early 1958 the orchestra pit was enlarged and some seats taken out to improve its facilities for full stage shows soon after its successful first one-night pop stand of Johnnie Ray on Friday 23 August 1957. And Brian Gauntlett recalls that, at Harrow, "In the autumn of 1958, the largest 'roller high-definition' screen in the world was installed. It weighed over half a ton and was 48 ft. wide and 25 ft. high. It took twenty men nearly fifteen minutes to lift the screen from a special transport lorry on to the stage. It was designed so that it needed no central support and could be rolled up and locked mechanically in under eight minutes. The manufacturers claimed: 'It supersedes the silver screen and has the same type of finish as artificial pearls. It throws back twice as much light as an ordinary white screen.' The screen cost £1,500 and was specially constructed for Granada Theatres in order to gain extra room on stage for live perform-ances. The additional stage space was soon put to use when four thousand local schoolchildren attended the Granada Harrow during three chilly mornings in February 1959. The occasion – a concert by the London Symphony Orchestra conducted by Muir Matheson."

Walthamstow presented a problem as, like Harrow, it lacked a flytower. But here the screen was taken to the back of the stage to clear space. An apron was also constructed over the pit to extend the stage, putting the organ console on the lift out of action.

Sutton continued to weave up-market live attractions between pop shows and it was now the only Granada and the only London-area venue to feature live weeks by the Carl Rosa Opera, although it visited many other non-Granada cinemas in the provinces. Along with Shrewsbury and the Adelphi Slough, it hosted a week of Gilbert and Sullivan from the D'Oyly Carte company and it continued to present musical revivals like *The Student Prince* with John Hanson in the summer of 1959 (a show which also played a week at Woolwich).

Bedford attempted to interest the town's Italian-speaking element by booking the Marino Marini Quartetto (of "Volare" fame) with a leaflet promoting it in Italian. The group also played Shrewsbury but with Joan Regan sharing the bill.

Besides the ever popular crownings of Dairy and Carnival Queens and other beauty contest winners, there were gimmick attractions like the Cycle Roller Contest of March-May 1960 that played nightly for a week at a time, going from Harrow to Edmonton, Woolwich, Slough (Adelphi), East Ham, Sutton and Kennington before the finals were held at Tooting.

Television created stars who could draw crowds into the theatres with live shows. There were stars of pop shows like Cliff Richards and comedy performers like Bernard Bresslaw, who scored as Popeye in Granada TV's hit sit-com *The Army Game* and headed one-night shows at Maidstone, Aylesbury, Grantham, Rugby and Mansfield late in 1959. (Bresslaw also starred in a feature film spin-off of the series, *I Only Arsked!*, made by Hammer and released by Columbia through the ABC circuit in early 1959.)

In a variation on the old Bryan Michie amateur talent shows, Carroll Levis took over the Shrewsbury stage for a week in September 1957 with his "Sensational TV Star Search" which offered the winner a chance to perform on the box. This show also guaranteed a professional level of comedy through "guest star" Terry-Thomas.

In 1959 Hughie Green presented his TV quiz show *Double Your Money* with cash prizes for contestants from the audience at Maidstone, Bedford and Grantham. With singer Alma Cogan and others in support, it played for one night of two shows at each theatre. Other television stars who became stage headliners at Granadas included singers Marty Wilde, Cliff Richard, Tommy Steele, Adam Faith and Lonnie Donnegan, who all did extensive

The Regal Oswestry was fully acquired in 1955, improved and renamed Granada the following year. These are June 1959 photographs. (Photo Coverage.)

tours. Major American artists like Jerry Lee Lewis also continued to appear at the larger theatres.

An especially lively time was experienced with *Let's Move It!*, a one night stage show that played several Granadas. The *Harrow Post* headlined "ROCK 'N' ROLL RIOT" after the show on Thursday 12 March 1959. "Amazing scenes at the Granada Harrow led to a near riot during the Cliff Richard rock 'n' roll show... Over 400 people surged to the front of the house and thronged the gang-ways..." Ted Bigney, Granada's touring stage manager, was reported as saying: "We thought the Granada East Ham show was rowdy, but tonight beats anything we have ever seen on the circuit."

And Wrestling

The first use of wrestling – "Professional Free-Style Wrestling" – in a Granada theatre took place at Woolwich on Wednesday 29 April 1959 with the main bout being George Kidd versus Ken Joyce. The show was arranged by Paul Lincoln, a wrestler himself under the name of Doctor Death. This seems to have been a success as, on 22 June 1959, Paul Lincoln presented a Monday evening of wrestling with the same main contestants at Waltham-stow, and provided different stellar attractions and supporting contests for a second evening at Woolwich (Tuesday 30 June) and initial evenings at Kettering (Monday 29 June) and the Adelphi Slough (Monday 20 July). All these bouts were staged on traditionally poor evenings, so the loss of revenue to film distributors was minimised.

In October, wrestling was tried out at Rugby and East Ham. It was soon a once-a-month attraction at many more theatres, including Edmonton. At Greenford, over one thousand were turned away at the first Tuesday session in March 1960. However, an attempt to launch wrestling at Dartford the same month seemingly failed. It returned with more success in the mid-Sixties, reaching a peak of six evenings during 1966.

Professional wrestling brought live entertainment back to the Granada, former Empress, Brixton from Wednesday 22 February 1961. It would continue there, eventually becoming a regular Saturday night feature.

Wrestling took much longer to be tried out at Tooting because the theatre's hugh capacity made it more risky. Here the shows were promoted as a "Wrestling Spectacular" and four star names were presented rather than two. Wrestling also became a mainstay of the Metropolitan Edgware Road, being held on Saturdays for its last three years.

Teddy Boys

As stated earlier, cinemas had occasionally shown new films on Sundays but traditionally, because of the obligation to pay a levy on takings on charity, this was a day when old films were booked at flat rates. Ivan Cluley started working at head office booking Sunday films and recalls that Tooting's show was very expensive at £10 a programme while Dartford paid only £4 for the main feature and £3 for the supporting one. The start of the programme was usually restricted to 4.30pm. The films were mostly dramas with plenty of action and violence.

Opening time on Sundays around 4pm would attract a crowd of teenagers who could be restless and noisy, especially waiting for the programme to start and during intervals. (The first surviving report of problems relates, surprisingly, to the Century Cheam Village.)

At Walthamstow in early 1954 Granada experimented with a disc jockey playing records in the twenty minutes before the Sunday show started. This spread to many other locations over the following months. By 1957, besides record requests, most of the Granadas were regularly featuring local talent shows between the Sunday films. These often took the form of contests for skiffle groups, with several heats and a final with a cash prize.

According to John Young, "There were tough areas where your audience was very much on the yob side and that would cause headaches. What has now transferred onto the football terraces was in the late Fifties very much prevalent in the cinemas."

Alex Bernstein, the son of Cecil, remembers being manager of the Century Clapham Junction. "It was in the days of the Teddy Boys. Sunday night was the bad night. They went drinking on Friday night, dancing on Saturday night, and beating up the cinemas on Sunday night. They used to come with their flick knives and cut up the seats and throw things at the screen. You had to throw them out."

"Basically, we got the boyos," says Ivan Cluley. "They didn't come to see the film. They came to walk around, they were just there to chat up the birds..."

At one head office conference, it was suggested that all Teddy Boys be refused admittance but Sidney Bernstein refused to allow this: he did not want to judge people by their clothes. Managers learned to recognise troublemakers and bar them. John Young: "On a Sunday afternoon, one would go round the queue and, based on previous knowledge, one would say who came in and who didn't." Young points out that the problem was aggravated by the policy of segregation by seat prices with all the rowdy element gathered together in the cheapest seats at the front. When in later years the stalls seats became all one price and the audience spread out, the problem largely disappeared.

Youths who were turned away would go from cinema to cinema until they got in and some managers, like Brian Gauntlett at the Granada Harrow, would observe which way they were headed and alert the first opposition hall they would encounter.

There were other solutions to keeping audiences in order. Willesden was a very tough house that required constant vigilance – although Brian Gauntlett notes that the theatre was also patronised by more sophisticated customers from Dollis Hill. "To combat the youthful rowdy-of-the-day, increased ceiling lighting was installed over the entire front stalls area – and was most effective," recalls Gauntlett. This "hooliganism lighting" was widely fitted, but it had the adverse effect of removing the privacy and comfort of darkness. Ian Johnson, a Loughton regular, recalls the strong downlights there gave an uncomfortable feeling of sitting in broad daylight.

Despite the damage that was caused, attendances were good and Sunday shows normally highly profitable, given the low flat rates paid to the distributors. Gradually, a once weekly change of programme became the norm for ABC, Odeon and Gaumont, but Granada remained flexible for much longer.

Certain films could attract trouble during the week. In the autumn of 1956, many Granadas played *Rock Around The Clock* as the week's Gaumont release. In South London, the film was not shown anywhere on the Sunday to fend off trouble. This simply switched the bother to the following night. Fifty youths were refused admission at Woolwich on the Monday. The audience inside booed, whistled and hissed at the supporting programme, and there was dancing in the aisles during the film, which had to be stopped for three minutes to restore order. After the show, two thousand youths marched along Powis Street bringing traffic to a halt while some "rhythm-crazy" people went so far as to beat out a rock 'n' roll rhythm on the sides of buses! This "mob" lingered in Beresford Square for an hour, and six arrests were made. At Tooting, three security men refused admission to scores of known troublemakers and fifty plainclothes policemen sat amidst the near capacity audience which behaved itself. A crowd of youngsters which gathered outside the cinema after the show was dispersed by police reinforcements with a number being arrested. A much rowdier time was had at the nearby Gaumont Balham which seems to have been less prepared.

The Century King's Cross regularly had some of the unruliest audiences on the circuit. The assistant manager of another theatre recalls hearing at secondhand that its grand re-opening as the Century was marred by youths in the upper balcony turning on the main fire hose and drenching the invited audience, and at least one of the Bernsteins, in the stalls. One manager there was reputedly dangled by his legs from the front of the balcony by a bunch of yobs: he was moved to Wandsworth Road, although this hardly represented greener pastures.

Plans but no action
In the late 1950s Granada contemplated making fuller, mixed use of some of its largest cinemas and engaged architect David Nye to come up with ideas and provide pencil sketches of what might be possible. In each case, it was intended to retain some cinema use.

At Walthamstow, Granada wanted to explore the idea of replacing the foyer with a store while retaining the auditorium behind. On Tuesday 17 February 1959, Nye met Granada's in-house architect C. W. Sully at Walthamstow to look over the building. Nye responded on 9 March with a rough sketch plan (which is not attached to the surviving correspondence) for replacing the front with a three-storey building for a store, or a store with offices on the top floor. A new entrance foyer would be provided. Exits from the cinema would be altered to discharge patrons onto a new service road on the lefthand side of the building and onto the existing mews to the right. As only two exits would be possible from the balcony, seating needed to be reduced to 500 and Nye suggested either removing alternate rows of seating and levelling off the floor between or putting a new wall halfway across (which left dead space behind). The Granada board discussed this on 21 April and called for a cheaper scheme more in line with the potential increase in income that might result. Nye responded with a smaller cinema with shops and dance school (further details unknown), very approximately costed at £45,000. Then in July the architect considered more drastic alterations, retaining the stalls floor and using the balcony for either a dance hall or bowling alley, or both (one above the other), but concluded that the cost of removing the existing balcony and providing a new floor or floors extending to the stage would not be justified by the likely income. In addition, there were problems of sound insulation between the various elements. Sully informed Nye on 31 December that Granada had decided to drop the conversion idea.

For the Granada Tooting, Nye submitted a draft scheme for a smaller cinema and dance hall, which the London County Council had approved in principal. In a letter dated 30 September 1959, he reported: "The theatre divides quite easily and reasonably economically and I am proposing that the balcony shall become a stadium type cinema to sit approximately 1,300 people with a new suspended floor at balcony front level and with a new lightly constructed stage and proscenium to contain a screen to give a 50 ft. wide picture. The whole of the stalls floor would be given over to the dance hall to accommodate 1,000 dancers with sit-out space at the sides and on some of the back tiers."

At Clapham Junction, Granada were contemplating a complete redevelopment of the site as offices with smaller cinemas to take advantage of new restrictions on offices that were expected to come into force in central London.

17 • The Sixties

The Rank and National Release

After Rank decided to provide its best Odeons and Gaumonts with a new "Rank release" and the others with a "National release", the radical new pattern took effect in late January 1959.

Although the National grouping could in theory match the number of outlets for Rank and ABC programmes, it was allocated the dregs of the new releases with only the occasional plum and its strength was undermined from the start by Rank revealing that half of its participating cinemas were going to be sold as soon as a suitable price could be obtained for them.

It is not known whether Rank discussed the new release scheme in detail with Granada before announcing it. Sidney Bernstein acknowledged that it made sense but noted that it would hit Granada badly. It certainly altered the position of most of his cinemas – for better or for worse.

In the London area, the Granadas at Greenford, Greenwich, Harrow, Thornton Heath, Tooting and Walthamstow gained by replacing the Gaumont/Fox release with the Rank release. At Clapham Junction, the Granada automatically progressed to the Rank release.

At Sutton and Kingston, Rank conceded the best new release to the Granadas, putting its own clearly inferior cinemas into the National grouping. But elsewhere Odeons seized the Rank release in less clear-cut situations.

The Granada Woolwich was adversely affected as the Rank release was allocated to the Odeon opposite. With its greater capacity, the Granada should have taken it but the Odeon was certainly a large and attractive cinema in its own right and Rank had the upper hand.

The Granadas at Epsom and Welling lost the Rank release to rival Odeons. At Epsom, the Odeon was clearly the superior theatre but at Welling the Granada should have been chosen over the smaller, older, less well-sited Odeon. At Brixton, the Granada inevitably lost out to Rank's huge Odeon Astoria. At Leyton, the Century exchanged its hold on Odeon programmes for the National line-up as the larger Gaumont improved its position with the Rank release.

At Enfield, the Rialto found itself sharing the Rank release with the independent Florida, playing every other programme. At Leytonstone, the Rialto replaced the Odeon release with the Rank release while the Century took the National.

At East Ham, the Odeon took the Rank release but the Granada finally gained part of a circuit release: it played many National programmes, seemingly in a split with the local Gaumont.

The Granada Willesden had no chance of winning the Rank release over the superior Odeon at Harlesden and had to accept the National line-up.

The changes did nothing to solve a problem of over-capacity in some towns. Granada reached a deal with Rank by which each circuit shut two or three cinemas in certain towns where they were in bruising competition. On 15 October 1960, Granada closed Epsom while Rank reciprocated at Chichester. A week later, Granada pulled out of Sevenoaks while Rank obliged at Welling. This left Granada in a solo situation at Chichester and playing the Rank release at Welling. The closed buildings were offered for sale with a covenant restricting further use as a cinema as this would have defeated the object of shutting them down. On 29 October, the Granada Hounslow and Odeon Kettering closed their doors – possibly a coincidence or possibly the third and final round of adjustment. The Granada Kettering gained the Rank release.

In Granada's case, the arrangement simply brought forward the inevitable closure of the long-standing problem theatres at Epsom and Sevenoaks, while Hounslow had a bleak future since the end of the fourth circuit deprived it of any important product.

The Robert Cromie-designed Epsom cinema is remembered by projectionist Barry Haigh as "a bit of a warren" with a nondescript route to the circle via staircases that contrasted poorly with the resplendent reception areas at purpose-built Granadas. It also had, unusually, DC electrical supply and the high pitched whine of the generator in the basement could be heard in the auditorium. While managing there, Brian Gauntlett recalls this Granada attracting a snobbish audience: if they paid for cheaper tickets, they let it be known "it wasn't worth paying more" for that particular film and would be careful to sit under the balcony where they couldn't be seen from upstairs. The cinema could rely on a full house from racetrack visitors in Derby Week – when

The Granada Epsom. Exterior view from 29 April 1958.
The café closed before the cinema did. Auditorium views (above and top right) date from 29 April 1955. The proscenium arch looks rather narrow for a good CinemaScope picture. (Photo Coverage.)

Above: exterior of the Granada Sevenoaks on a wet day in October 1960, the month when it closed its doors forever. (Photo Coverage.)

pubs and restaurants in the town would remove their fittings and carpets as a precaution against damage.

Epsom's film supply in its last year was so poor that two of its best weeks came with ABC shows relinquished by the nearby Rembrandt Ewell during a roadshow engagement. These were *The Angry Silence* (its star, Richard Attenborough, helped with a personal appearance on the first night, explaining his reasons for making the controversial trade union drama) and *Inn For Trouble*. "But the Granada Epsom's top business weeks of 1960," recalls Gauntlett, "were with repertory programmes, which consisted of a split week of *Julius Caesar* and *Henry V* and another split week of *Great Expectations* and *Oliver Twist*. These off-circuit re-runs were aided by excellent promotional campaigns and were well supported by schools in the area."

At Sevenoaks, the Granada still had a restaurant and organ when it closed and looked in reasonable health, having played *Gigi* for three weeks in its final year, along with two week runs of *The Nun's Story* and other special attractions between bookings of the regular ABC release. But some weeks were split with duff product when matinees took place only on Mondays and Saturdays. Sevenoaks developed a reputation, like Kettering, of pronounced apathy towards cinema. The Granada had one final attraction which drew huge crowds for two days at the beginning of November: the sale of just about all its contents (the organ was removed separately to a private residence). With so many cinemas closing everywhere, there was no demand for its fixtures and fittings. The screen went for £2, seats for around six shillings each, carpets for approximately £1 a yard...

A similar sale of contents on 8 and 9 November 1960 followed the closure of the Century Dartford after a lucrative offer was accepted from a supermarket chain. This left the town with only the Granada. The Century Plumstead also shut down around this time.

The closure of opposition cinemas, independent of any special arrangement, occasionally helped a Granada improve its access to product. With the demise of the Gaumont Acton in April 1959, the Granada could sometimes duck a poor ABC release for a better National programme. And ABC's decision to convert its Rex Leytonstone into a bowling alley in Spring 1961 enabled the Century to take over the ABC release as well as revert occasionally to the National one (but it still did not last much longer).

The National release collapsed by October 1961, although selected films still played surviving Rank cinemas in the same release pattern.

Final week at the Century Dartford (its name mounted on the end of the canopy in October 1960). Next week's show is the one at the Granada and the poster board at right advertises the sale of fixtures and fittings. The interior view dates from March 1957 with the curtains opened to reveal the large CinemaScope screen. (Photo Coverage.)

Diversification

After making a success of television, Granada began widening its interests dramatically. Bingo started slowly but would grow in size to overtake the cinema side, sometimes at its expense.

There was the television rental chain. This began in 1960 as Red Arrow (using the arrow symbol of the television company) and grew steadily, becoming known as Granada TV Rental (in a P.T. Barnum touch, sets were delivered with a little Red Indian perched on top, about nine inches high and made of rubber, solely to create a talking point). In 1968, Granada absorbed the rival chain of Robinson Rentals.

The theatres were obliged to give foyer space over to promoting the local rental branch, which was often in the parade of shops next door. On at least one occasion, sets on display were stolen from the foyer. Managers now had television sets in their offices, and it is not true they could only receive ITV.

Moves into other rental businesses – office furniture (Black Arrow) and "Rentaflower" (Green Arrow) – were less successful.

In 1961, Granada started in book publishing, reflecting Sidney Bernstein's taste for the arts. The group expanded rapidly in this area, first buying up MacGibbon and Kee, then a half-interest in Jonathan Cape, the whole of Rupert Hart-Davis and the paperback imprint, Panther Books. All these would eventually be amalgamated under the Granada name. In 1970, the Novello music publishing company was added. A large building next to the Granada Tooting, said to have been an old tram terminus, was used for storing books and the keys were held by the cinema manager.

Like Rank and ABC, Granada also went into bowling alleys as a seemingly surefire move. But Granada did not convert cinemas: it built new bowling centres in the north of England, beginning with the Granada Bowl at Belle Vue, Manchester, and acquired others, including the small Fairlanes group in the Midlands (later renamed Granada Bowls). Almost all these failed and some would be converted to bingo.

Granada extended its motoring interests beyond the solitary petrol station at Sutton by pioneering motorway service areas. In 1964, the first opened near Toddington, Bedfordshire, on the M1, sixteen miles from Bedford. Its launch was orchestrated like a theatre opening and Granada Bedford manager Ivan Morgan was sent to take charge. (Granada always regarded managers as transferable between various parts of the company: cinema men went into bingo and television as well as motorway service areas.) On the wall of the manager's office at Toddington was the usual engraving of P.T. Barnum. Toddington was soon followed by others near Frankley (M5) and Heston (M6). A very large crystal ball would have been needed to consider building cinemas alongside them.

Miss Candy shops were now spreading far from cinemas. There was one in Chiswick High Street, West London, by 1965, another at Clapham Road, Stockwell, South London, by 1967, and one in North End, West Croydon.

In 1970, the company replaced its Posterprint works in Cromwell Road, Kingston, with Britain's first fully automatic car wash, intended to be the start of a nationwide chain. This took the catchy name of Supawash and cinema manager Brian Gauntlett was seconded to publicise the launch, arranging for television stars Bernard Yovens (of Granada TV's *Coronation Street*) and the Topper Girls to provide a starry send-off. Its connection with Granada was not advertised. As no more Supawashes followed, it cannot have cleaned up financially.

These new areas of enterprise serve to reflect the waning significance of the theatres within the Granada group and the emphasis on expansion elsewhere. This is understandable as cinema attendances nationally during the Sixties more than halved – from 500 million in 1960 to 215 million in 1969. It was difficult to be optimistic.

Film booking

Although Granadas playing the new Rank release had a much improved product flow, their adherence to it was not total. By the autumn of 1960, Hollywood main features of dubious appeal like *Inherit The Wind* and *The Fugitive Kind* were largely replaced by reissues such as *Shane* and the old favourite, *Seven Brides For Seven Brothers*. Some British films, such as *Two And Two Makes Six* in 1962, were also widely replaced. Tooting was more apt to drop British pictures than others in the London area: *The Amorous Prawn* was replaced by a split week of Elvis Presley revivals in late 1962. Often, as a compromise with distributors, lesser cinemas such as the Century Clapham Junction would play films dropped by the large Granadas.

The circuit continued its practice of booking different second features, often replacing a nondescript British B feature with a past hit such as *Lucky Jim* (in support of *The Young Savages* at Harrow in July 1961) or *Hobson's Choice* (in support of *In The Doghouse* at Tooting in January 1962).

Granada also extended its policy of booking acclaimed documentaries. *Terminus*, John Schlesinger's 30-minute study of Waterloo Station, played in support of *Sergeants 3* at Harrow and Tooting in Spring 1962, although not at Walthamstow. *Volcano* played at Harrow, Tooting and Walthamstow in support of *The Inspector*. The Academy Award winner *Giuseppina* supported *The Miracle Worker* at Harrow and Tooting (and was later booked by some up-market Odeons).

A Granada experiment in late 1962 replaced supporting features with "cartoon classics" at several cinemas, particularly in the Christmas holiday period.

Even for Granadas with the Rank or ABC release, attendances became increasingly polarised between the big hits and routine films of negligible appeal. The major attractions would be booked for two weeks or more, even in towns like Grantham with only

Saturday morning queue, not all teenagers, at 10.08am in freezing February 1963 weather for Cliff Richard's Summer Holiday *at Aylesbury, waiting for the first screening immediately after the children's show. A policeman stood by the whole time. The front-of-house lighting was kept on all day. The hanging board under the canopy and poster above it advertise the next live show.*
(Courtesy of Brian Gauntlett.)
Auditorium at Aylesbury in June 1963 (Photo Coverage).

one cinema. Hits would be brought back again and again, often in double bills. The Bond films were endlessly revived in different combinations. *The Great Escape* kept coming back...

One of the box-office highlights of the Sixties was *Summer Holiday*, which broke records at fourteen out of the seventeen Granadas that played the film on its first release, i.e. all those with access to the ABC release. The Cliff Richard musical scored at Leytonstone Rialto, Edmonton, Grantham, Shrewsbury, Aylesbury, Acton, Slough Adelphi, Clapham Junction (the highest take in 1963), Greenford (despite one day lost to wrestling), Oswestry, Wandsworth Road (despite two days of bingo), North Cheam, Crystal Palace (Upper Norwood) and Dartford. Brian Gauntlett recalls: "In February 1963, Aylesbury showed *Summer Holiday* – which produced full houses every night. On the Saturday of playweek three thousand people queued to see the film. There were queues outside the cinema from 9.45am to 9.15pm – two extra shows were added that day, which ended at 11.35pm. The movie created a new box-office and sales record. The admissions record was still held by *The Dam Busters* in 1955." The number of admissions would have been difficult to beat as the seating had been re-spaced to give more leg room. *Summer Holiday* would be another film frequently re-booked.

Even the weaker cinemas on the circuit sometimes had their day. In 1961, the Tony Hancock comedy *The Rebel* did particularly well at Welling and Crystal Palace, and was held for a second week at North Cheam where audiences flocked to support the famous resident of "23 Railway Cuttings, East Cheam". (At some point, Sidney Bernstein declared that "North Cheam" made the Granada sound as though it was at the North Pole and it became the Granada Cheam.)

The Norman Wisdom comedy *A Stitch In Time* did wonders in early 1964, providing Tooting with the highest take ever at any Granada with a normal film programme.

Granadas occasionally hosted gala film evenings. Aylesbury premiered the Paul Newman drama *Hud* on Monday 17 June 1963 in aid of a children's charity. "All tickets were sold two weeks prior to the event," recalls Brian Gauntlett. "There was a Hollywood atmosphere as the celebrities arrived. Besides Patricia Neal, one of the stars of the film, they included Roald Dahl (the then husband of Patricia Neal), Ludovic Kennedy, Moira Shearer, Wendy Hiller, the Bishop of Buckingham, Peter Sellers (then Britain's major film star, who arrived in a pink American Buick with the registration 'PS1'), and ex-prime minister Earl Atlee."

The European charity premiere of the Jack Lemmon comedy *Good Neighbor Sam* also took place at Aylesbury, on 30 October 1964.

In 1968, there was only one place to hold the world premiere of *Up The Junction*, despite its unflattering depiction of South

London life. To the music of a barrel organ, Pearly Kings and Queens lined the red carpet to greet stars and other celebrities as they arrived at the Granada Clapham Junction on Wednesday 24 January. However, Bob Morgan, who was about to join the circuit as booking executive, remembers feeling embarrassed by the standard of presentation and wondering whether he had made the right career decision.

Granadas were also popular with producers and distributors for sneak previews. On a Sunday evening in 1963 a preview of Columbia's *The Victors* was held at Grantham with an anxious producer-director Carl Foreman splitting his time between watching the audience in the auditorium and fine-tuning the presentation from the projection box.

The booking department still continued to favour a few films refused a major circuit release. In 1965, Granada widely showed Roman Polanski's acclaimed British production *Repulsion*. But a star-less double-bill booked into Thornton Heath in the summer of 1963 – *The Quick And The Dead* and *The 5th Battalion* – had to be pulled mid-week with an old standby – *Seven Brides For Seven Brothers* or *High Society* – substituted for the last three days.

The company was so prone to last minute changes that Ivan Cluley recalls: "The renters used to keep somebody back on Fridays because Friday evening was when they would get calls from Granada wanting to change all their programmes. It was a legend in the trade that Granada would always change at the last minute." This meant that the wrong programme would be advertised in the local paper, requiring managers to issue leaflets and devise stunts to draw attention to the new and hopefully more attractive booking.

While managing Harrow, Brian Gauntlett recalls that the Granada sometimes changed programme to play a hit film a week or so after an opposition hall, as happened with *Room At The Top* after it had run at the Dominion up the road and *The Inn Of The Sixth Happiness* after it had played the Odeons at South Harrow and Wealdstone. Even if such a booking was pre-planned, it could not be advertised while the film was playing at the other cinemas. Again "stop press" handbills to be distributed, usually headed "By Demand – It's Here!" or "Here – At Your Request!"

The same strategy was also used to relieve the suffering of a National release house such as the Granada Willesden which played *The Magnificent Seven* close on the heels of the Odeon Harlesden and *Hercules Unchained* in the wake of the Ritz Neasden, both in 1960.

Granada brought on one last-minute change by having second thoughts about a notorious exploitation film. *Mondo Cane* was advertised for a week at the Century Leyton in May 1963 but patrons turned up to find that an old horror film *Them!* had been substituted. Head office stated that the lurid documentary had been withdrawn as "a matter of policy" without further elaboration except to add that it might be shown at a later date. To the best of my knowledge, it was never shown at any Granada: someone must have decided it was beyond the pale. However, the publicity at Leyton improved business at the less fastidious Cameo Walthamstow which played it the same week.

Another picture of the *Mondo Cane* variety was shown. At Christmas 1966, the Granada Bedford offered a less than festive double bill of *Devils Of Darkness* plus *This Shocking World*. So shocked at the first showing of the latter film were ten men and one woman that they fainted and the Red Cross had to attend for the rest of the week (or is this merely recycling a good publicity story?) Thank goodness there was Norman Wisdom in *The Early Bird* and Walt Disney's *Peter Pan* for the rest of the holidays.

In 1967 Nat Miller linked his Orb Films with Granada for a very successful circuit release of the subtitled Japanese sex-and-horror film, *Onibaba* (*The Hole*), which was refused a censor's certificate. As in the case of *Garden of Eden*, local certificates were sought and usually obtained. The nudist cycle was still going, and *Onibaba* usually played with Orb's *Nudist Paradise*.

In the same year, the film *Ulysses*, based on the James Joyce classic, was also turned down by the British Board of Film Censors because of its language but granted a local X (London) rating to play with huge success at the Academy art house in Oxford Street. Granada booked it widely where local certificates could be obtained as a special attraction at increased prices. At Mansfield, in January 1968, it was retained for a second week.

At all the big theatres, new films were still the backbone of the operation. But one day film specials, pop concerts, wrestling and nights of bingo became increasingly important. More than ever, the Granadas became host to a variety of entertainment for all levels of taste.

Road shows

Granada joined in the spreading practice of mounting "roadshows" at its top theatres, with advanced booking at increased prices (often excepting Sundays, when standard revivals would play).

Such engagements were now dominated by cinemas of the major chain – Rank or ABC – with which the distributor was usually allied. Late in 1961, Columbia's *The Guns Of Navarone* had its first London suburban runs of four weeks at six Rank cinemas plus the Granada Harrow. Clapham Junction and Slough then shared it with six Rank halls at the end of the year. The Granada Sutton joined four more London-area Rank cinemas with a four-week booking in February 1962. At Kingston, the film played the Odeon in the first wave, although later Columbia pre-releases went into the Granada.

GRANADA RUGBY 2255

THIS WEEK AND NEXT

Matchless in Magnitude—
Unsurpassed as Entertainment!

SPARTACUS (A)

TECHNICOLOR®

KIRK DOUGLAS · LAURENCE OLIVIER · JEAN SIMMONS · CHARLES LAUGHTON
PETER USTINOV · JOHN GAVIN

and TONY CURTIS AS ANTONINUS

Music composed and conducted by ALEX NORTH
Directed by STANLEY KUBRICK
Screenplay by DALTON TRUMBO
Based on a novel by HOWARD FAST · Produced by EDWARD LEWIS
Executive Producer KIRK DOUGLAS · A Bryna Production
Released by Universal-International through Rank Film Distributors Ltd.

TWO SEPARATE PERFORMANCES DAILY 1.45, 6.45
Matinee doors open 1.30; evening 6.30.
(Sat. only open 1.15 and 6.15)
SEATS: CIRCLE 6/6, 5/- (bookable evenings only);
STALLS 5/-, 3/6 (children 2/6, 3/6)

SUNDAY FEB 18 - OPEN 4.15 - LAST SHOW 6.45
JOHN GAVIN
A TIME TO LOVE AND A TIME TO DIE
CINEMASCOPE COLOUR a
PLUS STAGE 6.50 IN PERSON
DANNY STORM
Direct from Saturday's 'Thank Your Lucky Stars' TV Appearance
Singing his latest recording "HONEST I DO"
Also GLEN DALE · ROBBY JAMES & the STROLLERS

WRESTLING · THURS MAR 1 · 7.45
First time here—Fabulous FRENCH WRESTLING TEAM
LES BLOUSONS NOIRS
THE FRENCH TEDDY BOYS
v.
BRILLIANT ANGLO-SPANISH TEAM
CORTEZ BROTHERS

	AMERICAN-STYLE TAG TEAM MATCH— ONE HOUR NO ROUNDS
Bobby Hill v. Brian Chamberlain	International Heavyweight Bout 'Georgeous' TERRY GAVIN v. (Boston, U.S.A.) DON 'Gorilla' MENDOZA (Halifax)

STAGE - ONE DAY ONLY - SUN MAR 18

# BILLY FURY	# JOHN LEYTON
SHANE FENTON and the FENTONES	JOE BROWN and the BRUVVERS
JACKIE LYNTON	RICKY STEVENS	TONY MELODY

PETER JAY AND THE JAYWALKERS
MARTY WILDE
ADVANCE BOX OFFICE OPEN NOW: 3 6 5 6 7 6

CENTURY
£50 BINGO £50
JACKPOT CLUB JACKPOT
EVERY FRIDAY 8 o'c. Doors open 7.30
SMOKING · PROFESSIONAL CALLER · COMFORTABLE SEATS
NEW "DOUBLE GAME PER CARD" SYSTEM
YOU MUST HOLD MEMBERSHIP 24 HOURS. ENROL NOW

GRANADA WALTHAMSTOW COP 7092
open 1.40 April 20 week

DWARFING THE MIGHTIEST!
TOWERING OVER THE GREATEST!

JOSEPH E. LEVINE PRESENTS

ZULU 'U'

A STANLEY BAKER · CY ENDFIELD PRODUCTION

starring
STANLEY BAKER · JACK HAWKINS · ULLA JACOBSSON · JAMES BOOTH · MICHAEL CAINE

Original Screenplay by JOHN PREBBLE and CY ENDFIELD
Suggested by an Article Written by JOHN PREBBLE · Directed by CY ENDFIELD
TECHNICOLOR® · TECHNIRAMA® · A DIAMOND FILMS LTD. Production
A PARAMOUNT RELEASE · Narration Spoken by RICHARD BURTON

2.30 5.25 8.25
SEE THIS GREAT EPIC IN THE ELECTRIFYING ATMOSPHERE
WHICH ONLY THIS THEATRE IN EAST LONDON CAN GIVE
WITH ITS FABULOUS MODERN SOUND EQUIPMENT
Special Supporting Prog. includes 4 CARTOONS
Plus SPECIAL PRESENTATION ON STAGE
EVERY NIGHT (except Friday) AT 7.45 OF
ROGER LAVERN
(EX-TORNADO OF 'TELSTAR' FAME)
AND HIS ELECTRONIC ORGAN

ON STAGE FRIDAY NIGHT ONLY AT 7.45
CARNIVAL QUEEN FINALS
The Winner Being Crowned By East London's Own
JOE BROWN

ON STAGE sunday Apr 19 6 o'c & 8.30
ROY ORBISON FREDDIE AND THE DREAMERS
TONY SHERIDAN EZZ RECO CHRIS SANDFORD
WAYNE FONTANA and THE MINDBENDERS GLEN MASON
THE FEDERALS
Book Now 10/6, 7/6, 5/-. Write, Call or Phone COP 3550

ON STAGE sunday May 10 6 o'c & 3.30
DAVE CLARK FIVE
THE HOLLIES Special Guest Star MARK WYNTER
THE MOJOS THE KINKS TREBLETONES FRANK BERRY
Book Early To Avoid Disappointment 10/6, 7/6, 5/-

A variety of attractions at Granadas in the Sixties. And bingo at the Century Rugby. (BFI – Sidney Bernstein Collection.)

GRANADA EDMONTON EDM 5200
open 2.5 MON APL 6 for 5 days last film 8.45
(THURS—WRESTLING)

'BROAD, BREEZY and BAWDY'
A PETER ROGERS PRODUCTION

CARRY ON JACK A

Starring KENNETH WILLIAMS · BERNARD CRIBBINS
JULIET MILLS · CHARLES HAWTREY
DONALD HOUSTON and CECIL PARKER

Produced by PETER ROGERS EASTMAN COLOUR
AN ANGLO AMALGAMATED PRESENTATION THROUGH WARNER PATHE

4.20 6.5 8.45

THE VERDICT
2.20 5 o'c 7.45 u

SUNDAY, 5th APRIL ONE DAY
ANNE HEYWOOD CARTHAGE IN FLAMES
5.40 8.20 u
STEVE McQUEEN GREAT ST. LOUIS BANK ROBBERY
4.30 7.35 a

STAGE
SUNDAY APRIL 26 6. o'c & 8.30

ADAM FAITH & THE ROULETTES
BRIAN POOLE & THE TREMELOES

THE UNDERTAKERS	DAVE BERRY & THE CRUISERS
EDEN KANE	

BOOK NOW 5/- 7/6 10/6

WRESTLING
THIS THURSDAY APRIL 9 7.45

'JUDO' AL HAYES & 'REBEL' RAY HUNTER	v	WILD MAN OF BORNEO SOCIETY BOY
HAYSTACKS v BOB KIRKWOOD		DENNIS DEAN v EDDY WILLIAMS

BOOK EARLY 3/6 5/6 7/6 10/6

Above, a typical Granada entrance hall at Bedford in 1961 (photographed 14 March) – but with one side wall opened up as a confectionery and cigarettes counter from the Miss Candy shop next door, which also drew customers through a street entrance.

Below, same hall modernised four years later (12 April 1965) with inner doors removed, new light fittings and paybox, and altered ceiling. Note the advance booking office at the rear, for the many roadshows and live attractions, also the boards advertising the restaurant and the programme at the town's Empire.

(Photo Coverage.)

Harrow was the only Granada among seven cinemas (the others all Rank) that took *South Pacific* for four weeks directly after its mammoth run at the Dominion, although Clapham Junction featured in a second wave of three-week bookings two months later. One major Granada that seems to have been excluded from roadshows was Tooting – the Streatham Odeon (ex-Astoria) took them instead.

The Granada Kingston participated in the "Premiere Showcase Theatres" grouping of London suburban cinemas which opened United Artists' James Bond picture *Goldfinger* just three days after its West End world premiere in September 1964. Seven Rank cinemas made up the core of the group, with the single Granada and a single Shipman & King cinema (Astoria Purley) as a sop to these two circuits. Kingston did huge business with *Goldfinger* over three weeks and later played *What's New Pussycat?* (three weeks) and *Thunderball* (four or five weeks). Some of these runs included very successful midnight shows on Saturdays.

On regular release, *Goldfinger* went on to break records for takings at seventeen Granada theatres: Walthamstow (in both first and second weeks), Harrow, Slough, Welling, Sydenham, Leytonstone, Enfield, Greenwich, Dartford, Greenford, Sutton, Mansfield, Oswestry, Kettering and Slough again (Adelphi).

Harrow and Kingston regularly featured in special runs, including pre-releases of *A Man For All Seasons* and *The Taming Of The Shrew*. Not all the roadshow films measured up: the pseudo-Bond *Casino Royale* was widely booked for a fortnight in May 1967 but at Kingston and Dartford (and probably elsewhere) it had to be taken off after the first week.

One day specials

Another way of improving business, adopted by all the circuits, was to revive up-market specialised films for one day bookings. These would help business on a weak night (most often Tuesday) of a poor week generally, but required extensive publicity. They would sometimes gain the support of schools which would arrange group visits or recommend the films.

In the case of Granada, these special bookings seem to have started with *Der Rosenkavalier* in early 1965. Soon every available film of opera and ballet was dusted off (*Aida, The Bolshoi Ballet, The Royal Ballet, An Evening With The Royal Ballet, Madame Butterfly, The Tales Of Hoffman*, etc. etc.) and, as the supply ran down, even marginal items like *The Story Of Gilbert And Sullivan* were tried. Soon being interweaved with these was every Shakespearean film still in circulation: after the three Olivier classics (*Henry V, Hamlet, Richard III*) came Marlon Brando's *Julius Caesar*, Orson Welles' *Chimes At Midnight* and *Macbeth*, and a Maurice Evans *Macbeth*. There was non-Shakespearean

Olivier too, in *The Beggar's Opera*. The search for suitable titles spread to literary adaptations like *Jane Eyre*, starring Welles, and Disney's *Fantasia*. By 1970 films like Olivier's *Richard III* were being repeated.

Live shows

A typical live show tour in the early Sixties by a popular performer like Roy Orbison would include more than twenty venues. Legitimate theatres and city halls would be visited, but the majority of sites were cinemas, being booked on any day of the week for two evening shows. The Granadas at East Ham, Harrow, Kingston, Tooting, Walthamstow and the Adelphi Slough participated in two Orbison tours in September-October 1963 and April-May 1964, representing virtually all the London area dates, being supplemented outside London by the Granada Bedford, various Rank cinemas, and other places.

As previously noted, smaller cinemas took up live shows, but they were limited in the performers they could attract. Brian Gauntlett recalls: "Sadly, the Beatles, Cliff Richard and the Rolling Stones never played Aylesbury – as it just did not have the money-taking seat capacity [1,200 seats] to attract the figures demanded by the agents. But most of the *Top of the Pops* stars played Aylesbury during the hey-day of rock 'n' roll. They included Helen Shapiro (a record breaker), Adam Faith (another record – with £500 in advance bookings three weeks before show night), Brian Hyland/Little Eva (this only produced two-thirds capacity), Little Richard, Craig Douglas, heart-throb John Leyton (who played the Granada the same week as the Odeon Aylesbury was showing him on screen in *The Great Escape* and they broke their box-office record) – and Billy Fury (the top money-maker in the early Sixties at Aylesbury). But my personal favourite was Jimmy Jewel and Ben Warriss, true gentlemen of the boards, a joy to have in the theatre – and they never needed a rehearsal."

At Tooting, the Beatles appeared live, supported by Roy Orbison, on 1 June 1963 at 6.45pm and 9pm. All seats were sold more than a week beforehand and there were huge queues for the limited standing available on the night. Walthamstow was another theatre large enough to land the Beatles. Here the advance booking office for the October 1964 concert was set to open on a Sunday at 7am in an attempt to minimise congestion in the high street. An enormous queue formed on the preceding Friday night but everyone was sent home by the police. Another queue on Saturday morning was dispersed. The queue was finally allowed to form at 11pm after the end of the evening show. A stall selling teas and pies did a roaring trade from the theatre exit-way. Three dozen police were on duty all night but the behaviour of the waiting fans was described as perfect. Over 4,000 tickets were sold the next day, mostly to locals, before the box-office closed

at 9pm. The remaining two thousand were sold over the next couple of days.

At Bedford and Shrewsbury, a pop star could perform for a full week. At both these theatres Tommy Steele headed *The Tommy Steele Show* twice nightly for a week in Spring 1961. They also continued the music hall tradition, especially Shrewsbury with full weeks of variety headed by Frankie Howerd, Tony Hancock, Tommy Trinder, Jimmy Edwards, Billy Cotton and others. Pop headliners The Shadows and Gene Vincent played one night only in Shrewsbury. Bedford also had weeks of variety headed by Jewel and Warriss and Max Bygraves, but Frankie Vaughn, who did a week at Shrewsbury, played only a day there.

Some pop stars exceeded their welcome. Gene Vincent's fourth visit to Bedford on Wednesday 29 November 1961 was one too many and he faced a sea of empty seats. Stage shows here stopped after a "fiasco" with Small Faces in April 1966 and, apart from three concerts in early 1967, were not revived until April 1968. In March 1960, Rugby had tried a three day run of a variety show headed by Jimmy Clitheroe and Ronny Hilton, but audiences were poor and the cinema reverted to one night stands by pop stars.

Over the circuit generally, amateur shows on Sundays continued to boost the one-day revival double-bills, as it had during the Fifties. "Managers were encouraged to present budding rock groups as an added attraction to the Sunday program," recalls Brian Gauntlett. "These amateur groups (and there was no shortage of them) would audition on a Sunday morning for a possible booking three or four weeks later. The groups were billed in the local press ad and on a quad poster in the foyer. Payment was usually £5 while the manager could submit a 'special pay claim' for a guinea. If there was a particularly popular group, then they would be re-booked and found further bookings at other Granada theatres. Considering the cost of these groups coupled with a flat-rate booking, Sundays were usually quite profitable."

The Granada Bedford recruited fifty-two bands to compete in a fifteen-week Sunday night contest. The Granada East Ham not only had Sunday band shows but also Monday night talent contests in the early Sixties.

Pantomimes continued at a few theatres for the first half of the decade, except for Christmas 1961 when none were staged. The Granada Shrewsbury played them the most, followed by Sutton, while Maidstone, Brixton and East Ham also hosted one during this period. (Despite its film booking problems, East Ham had never been a regular theatre on the panto circuit.) Shrewsbury then replaced pantos with family variety shows at Christmas. This theatre was still regularly used for whole weeks at a time for amateur musicals and operas, visits from the Royal Ballet and D'Oyly Carte, variety shows, and (for the first time since 1948) the occasional straight play before or after the West End (Anna Neagle in *Person Unknown* in 1965, Cicely Courtneidge and Jack Hulbert in *The Amorous Prawn* in 1966, Margaret Lockwood and Tony Britton in *Lady Frederick* in 1970). However, films got the upper hand at Christmas 1969 when *Oliver!* broke the long run of festive live shows.

Sutton branched out spectacularly with a live week of the musical *Fings Ain't Wot They Used To Be* starring the West End cast in October 1962. It also benefited from the closure of the Streatham Hill Theatre: the D'Oyly Carte had been performing there regularly but now returned to Sutton in July 1963 for a week.

Over on the ABC circuit, the very first Granada at Dover, now renamed the ABC, was also putting on occasional live shows, beginning with "Disc Stars of 1961" on 26 October 1961.

Closed circuit television was available to provide another form of live special event. At Tooting in August 1966, it was used to relay the Mohammed Ali versus Brian London fight from Earls Court. At East Ham, manager George Mullins remembers a match from America shown live at 3am that only lasted a few minutes – but there was no trouble from the audience.

Café-Restaurants
Café-restaurants were down in number to eleven at the beginning of 1965 but some were still thriving. In 1964 Grantham's had gained an extension for private functions called the Newton Room (Sir Isaac Newton was born and educated in the town). Under the highly professional eye of manageress Mrs. Musson, who had come from the Picture House when that had been closed, this was one of the biggest profit-makers on the circuit, breaking the record for takings four times during 1964/65. Others were still operating at Harrow, Kettering, Maidstone, Mansfield, Pitsea, Slough, Walthamstow – and Shrewsbury.

The Shrewsbury restaurant was one of the biggest in the town but closed in early October 1967. Its core customers had been farmers attending the livestock market nearby and their movements had been restricted during a foot and mouth epidemic, after which business never recovered. Slough's restaurant closed during this period and Kettering's went in 1969.

Some of the theatres in the late Sixties replaced restaurants with ground-floor Fiesta Bars serving snacks (the successor to Havasnacks), often established in one of the adjacent shops (as at Maidstone).

... And bingo
Major circuit cinemas began to be used for bingo from May 1961, especially in less sophisticated "working class" areas where film attendances had dropped most severely.

The Century Mansfield had struggled on into the Sixties without access to any of the circuit releases. Although Rank closed its Empire in January 1961, allowing the Century to inherit the National release, it shut down four months later to become the first of Granada's cinemas to offer bingo, initially on Wednesdays and Fridays only. It was many months before even an extra day – Sunday – was added.

When in June the circuit re-opened the Century at Shrewsbury for two nights of bingo a week, this was an inexpensive experiment in making use of an already closed cinema. The same procedure was followed at Woolwich from August with the defunct Century. However, the Century Rugby seems to have been deliberately closed as a cinema for re-launching as a part-week bingo club.

The large Granada Kennington had struggled on with the National release and other scratch programmes. The last outstanding film presentation was its two-week run of *Gigi* from 10 April 1961 with separate performances. How well that fared in one of the toughest areas served by the circuit is not known. Judo was tried as a Saturday night attraction later the same month. The Granada then closed abruptly on 15 July "for the summer" with a suggestion that it would return at the end of September. But it re-opened before that as a bingo club, using the Granada name, on Sundays, Tuesdays and Thursdays, initially preceded by "request time" at the organ. Bingo soon spread to Fridays while wrestling was for a while a regular feature on Saturday nights.

Alex Bernstein, a director of the Granada Group at the time, recalls: "There were people [on the board] who were incredibly stuffy and against the idea of going into bingo. Sidney was very much in favour of bingo because it was very profitable. It was quite a battle but Sidney was a great propagandist and he called them bingo social clubs to get over that. Ironically, when we sold a few bingo halls to property developers from time to time much later on, we were accused of selling a valuable social asset."

Bingo was also introduced on three nights a week at the Metropolitan Edgware Road. Together with the wrestling on Saturday nights, it enabled the Met to operate at a profit for the first time in many years. Unfortunately, the building was in the way of massive road "improvements" (the new flyover) and was compulsorily acquired by the London County Council for £150,000, closing in June 1963.*

* The road scheme had threatened the Met since 1959 and Sidney Bernstein had long harboured dreams of building a new theatre on what was left of the site plus adjacent property, together with offices, shops and flats. George Coles drew up plans dated 11 January 1963 for a theatre to seat 1,350 (816 stalls and 534 circle) with fly tower and rehearsal room. However, the LCC gave first priority to providing a new police station on the site as the old one was being lost. The same road alterations claimed the Gaumont Edgware Road. No theatre was built.

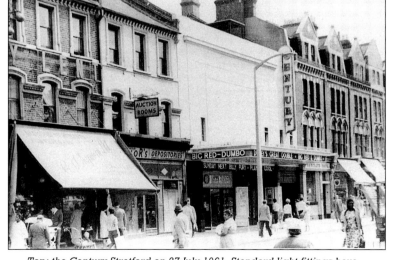

The end of three Centurys. Above: exterior and interior of the
Century Oswestry seen on 23 March 1966 in its final days of film
use. Extra lighting has been installed in the auditorium for the
days of the week when bingo was already being played.
(Both Photo Coverage.)

Top: the Century Stratford on 27 July 1961. Standard light fittings have
been added to the single-floor auditorium. Later bingo alterations
removed almost all the decorative detail. (Photo Coverage.)
Below: the Century Clapham Junction, seen here in 1966, became a
supermarket. (Courtesy of Keith Skone.)

At some of the less successful cinemas, bingo was introduced, initially on one night of the week. It then spread to a further day or days after it had caught on, with films still being shown at other times. In every case, bingo eventually took over entirely.

At Stratford and Leytonstone, the Centurys introduced a night of bingo towards the end of 1962 and both went over to full-time bingo early the following year. Exceptionally, the Willesden Granada seems to have gone straight from full-time cinema to bingo in 1962.

Other sites settled down to a combination of cinema and bingo that lasted for several years. The Woolwich Granada was the first of the original Granadas to introduce bingo, initially on Tuesdays from 5 December 1961. It spread to two days in December 1962, retreated to one day in 1964 and was withdrawn entirely in April 1965 to make way for a four-week roadshow engagement of *Mary Poppins*. However, such plums did not come very often and from June 1966 bingo was reinstated on three days, cutting cinema use back to just four days of the week. This made booking films very difficult and within a few months bingo took over full-time. Considering its general lack of access to prime releases, a cinema the size of the Granada Woolwich had done well to hang on that long.

At two other ailing Granadas – Greenwich and Wandsworth Road – bingo was introduced on one night and then two in the early Sixties. Four or five years later, it replaced films entirely. At the Century Oswestry, bingo spread to several days a week before ousting films entirely at the start of 1966 – but in this town there was still the Granada to play them.

It was from 1966/67 that bingo began really taking hold with the end of any films at Woolwich, Wandsworth Road and Brixton. In 1967, it was decided that the Granadas at King's Cross, Crystal Palace (Upper Norwood), Edmonton and Greenwich would be better off as bingo halls, leading to a switchover the following year (see next chapter).

Brixton had long been starved of good film product. Bingo was announced for Wednesdays in 1963 but the idea was dropped, presumably because of a poor response to advance promotion. The Granada had occasionally returned to its live theatre origins, reviving pantomime after a seven year gap with *Aladdin* (starring Joe Brown) in January 1964 and *Puss in Boots* with Richard Hearne the following Christmas. In March 1964, a bill of different old-time music hall acts played two consecutive weeks. A one-night James Brown Show in Spring 1966 was a rare pop event. Wrestling was tried and proved popular, becoming a Saturday fixture. Full-time bingo arrived in February 1967, partly with a view to Brixton replacing Kennington which was under threat of compulsory purchase for a redevelopment scheme that never happened.

Other closures

Cinemas could still close without becoming bingo halls. The Century Loughton was sold to be replaced by shops (Ivan Cluley suggests that had it stayed open it would have become a "little goldmine" after the Co-Op built a new superstore opposite).

Other cinemas closed for conversion to supermarkets – the Centurys at Leyton and Clapham Junction in 1963 and 1964, followed by the Granada Greenford in 1966. Greenford was the first of the original Granadas to be completely lost to leisure use. In one respect, it fared better than many: although the interior suffered destruction, the exterior was retained and is little altered more than thirty years later (1998) with the fin tower sporting a vertical Tesco sign in place of the old Granada one.

The declining number of Granadas was reversed in name at least when, in the middle of 1967, the Rialtos at Leytonstone and Enfield became the last cinemas where people had to start saying Gra-nah-dah.

An addition

Granada acquired the ailing Regent at Bishop's Stortford, Hertfordshire, from Percy and Eric Smith in August 1965. Because of the Quaker beliefs of the Smiths, the Regent had never opened on Sundays (except for charity shows during the war years) and never screened X certificate films. It had given up afternoon shows except on Saturdays. It also lacked a children's club.

Mary Poppins broke the cinema's takings record just after Granada took over: a good omen. But the long-serving staff did not adapt readily to Granada's methods, especially as one of the Smiths lived in a flat opposite and kept dropping in to stir them up. Granada had to change managers twice in the first year to sort out the Regent and turn it into "one of the Granada theatres". Matinees were resumed; a Granadiers club began on 16 October 1965; Sunday revival double-bills commenced on 26 July 1966; sex and horror films with X certificates became frequent, along with the usual one-day bookings of ballet, opera and Shakespeare films.

After the first year, Granada set about upgrading the building. George Coles and Partners drew up a renovation scheme that filled in the old-fashioned arched entrance with new doors and a Granadashop (the successor to Miss Candy with a wider range of goods, including tights, prints of pictures, newspapers and magazines), took out two rows of seats and spruced up the building. None of the circuit's classic light fittings was introduced. All the work was done without closing – only ten matinee performances were lost – and, in the hands of manager Brian Gauntlett, the cinema officially became the Granada on Monday 30 January 1967 with the gala opening of *My Fair Lady*, attended by a cluster of show-biz personalities and the heads of many film

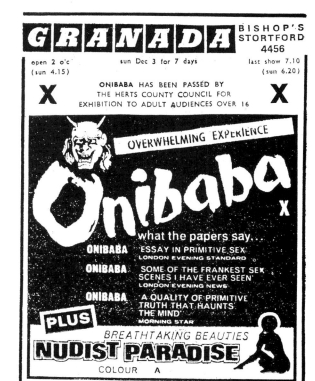

The Granada Bishop's Stortford. Exterior after modernisation has removed all sign of the original wide arched entrance and introduced a shop serving both passers by and patrons. Auditorium views before and after modernisation. (All Photo Coverage.)

Right: local certificate for Onibaba. (Courtesy of Brian Gauntlett.)

distribution companies. This was the last acquired cinema to take the Granada name.

Later in the year, the Granada played *Onibaba*. Gauntlett comments: "By November 1967, only eighteen city and county councils had granted permission for *Onibaba* to be screened in their licensing areas. This figure included Hertfordshire County Council, which covered the Granada Bishop's Stortford, but excluded Essex County Council. This meant the film could not be screened at the Odeon Harlow, only seven miles away. I quickly seized on the opportunity to capture adult Harlow cinemagoers away from their local cinema. Such was the relationship between Granada and Orb that Nat Miller agreed with me to equally share all costs of advertising expenditure without any further detail or limit. A giant publicity and press campaign was organised, which attracted patrons from as far away as Southend and Bedford. The cinema broke its Sunday box-office record and the film produced capacity evening business throughout the week. Being an ex-Granada man, Nat Miller sent a thank you telegram to the staff."

Granada continued to be interested in cinemas for sale but its appraisals did not always envisage keeping them open on films. In July 1967, estate agents Goddard and Smith wrote to the company listing forty-seven Odeon and Gaumont cinemas that were on the market at an asking price of £1.75m. Granada demanded and received the takings for the last two years in order to assess the cinema potential of each building but the bingo and re-development possibilities were also explored. Granada then expressed an interest in thirty-eight sites, declining five in Scotland plus the Odeons at Park Royal, Deal and Skipton and (because of a very short lease) the Gaumont Hendon. By this time, however, an offer from Classic for the entire batch had been accepted.

The organ

The organs lay mostly idle, but occasional examples of use have surfaced. Welling's instrument returned to life in the hands of a local resident, Peggy Pritchard, on the evening of Monday 9 March 1964 and was played on successive Mondays for a month to gauge the audience reaction. It was the first time this organ had been played publicly since 1956. The experiment was not extended.

On 7 March 1968 there was a live organ broadcast from Tooting at 1.30pm before the first showing of that week's film, *Here We Go Round The Mulberry Bush*.

The Granada Acton, seen in June 1964. The poster space on the side wall which once displayed the films being shown has been commandeered to promote the television station. Earlier it carried advertising for Granada TV Rental. (Photo Coverage.)

18 • The New Guard

Around 1968, Granada set about changing its approach to running the various companies in the group, including the theatres. As one former manager puts it, "The emphasis moved from elitism and showmanship to profitability and accountability." Tight budgetary controls were introduced at management level. There were numerous changes in the executive ranks below Sidney and Cecil Bernstein. The Bernsteins themselves were becoming old. (Sidney was appointed a baron, taking the title Lord Bernstein of Leigh.)

The old policy of promoting from within was severely dented. A new booking controller was headhunted and Bob Morgan joined on 4 March 1968 from Classic; a new publicity and marketing director, a recent university graduate, arrived with a set of fresh ideas, some quite unsuited to show business; another young executive was brought in to boost kiosk and shop sales, but apparently lacked any feeling for film exhibition (in particular, dealing with a product that varied in appeal from week to week).

However, a younger managing director of theatres and bingo came from within. Victor Chapman, a veteran who had worked his way up through the ranks from being an office boy, retired in 1969 to be succeeded by Charles Stringer who had arrived as a management trainee in 1954, transferred to the equipment company and become head of the building and engineering department.

Whereas managers had previously reported directly to the managing director (a continuation of the weekly letters to Sidney), the cinemas were now grouped with bingo halls in zones or sections and area managers created to oversee them. Granada was in danger of becoming like any other company.

"They were getting into the realms of [proper] budgeting, which had not been done previously. In effect, what was happening was they were modernising the management of the company," recalls Bob Morgan. "There was a vast change: many people left for one reason or another. Stringer came in – very pro-bingo – and I watched theatres disappear from my ken. But bear in mind from the late Sixties, when I joined, cinema had a bad time anyway. Unless you booked the right film you didn't make money... There was a lack of investment in the cinemas. The salary for bingo managers was much better than for cinema managers."

Jeff Curtis, a manager of the period, remembers area meetings where bingo managers vastly outnumbered cinema managers and, after a few minutes of discussion on general housekeeping, the two or three cinema managers would be dismissed so that the rest could discuss bingo promotions. "Granada was so bingo-oriented that if it wasn't for Bob Morgan there would have been nobody with any enthusiasm for cinema there. Bob Morgan was the face of cinema for Granada Theatres," concludes Curtis.

As theatres closed, the only option for many managers was to switch to bingo. Several long-standing managers decided it was time to move on, including Brian Gauntlett and John Young who found executive berths at two cinema circuits that were expanding.

Investment in cinemas (1)
Not all was gloom and doom. Granada was still investing in some of the cinemas.

The Granada Bedford closed, for the first time ever, on 20 July 1968 to re-open on Sunday 28 July with the second largest screen in the country, beaten only by that of the Odeon Marble Arch. What had the cinema done to deserve this? It had shown particular strength in the road show era: *The Longest Day* and *Thunderball* played three weeks, *The Sound Of Music* ran eight weeks from October 1967.

"By using the most modern 70mm equipment we are able to present a breathtaking picture 1450 sq. ft. in size," trumpeted Granada, describing the result as "the ultimate in visual entertainment".

In order to fit the new screen, the orchestra pit had to be dismantled and the stage brought forward by 20 ft. A new screen curtain and pelmet were erected, obscuring the innermost of the three side-wall grilles and the frieze over the proscenium arch. The organ console had to be moved behind the new screen, which was 12 ft. in front of the original proscenium, and six rows of seating were taken out, reducing capacity to 1,476. The result was aesthetically displeasing, diminishing the original decorative scheme, but now all attention was directed towards the huge screen, almost four times as large as the one it had on opening in 1934. The new projectors could play both 35mm and 70mm prints, and six-track stereophonic sound was installed. Live

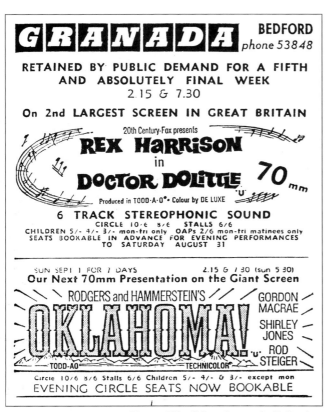

GRANADA BEDFORD
phone 53848

RETAINED BY PUBLIC DEMAND FOR A FIFTH
AND ABSOLUTELY FINAL WEEK
2.15 & 7.30

On 2nd LARGEST SCREEN IN GREAT BRITAIN

20th Century-Fox presents
REX HARRISON
in
DOCTOR DOLITTLE 70mm

Produced in TODD-A-O • Colour by DE LUXE 'U'

6 TRACK STEREOPHONIC SOUND
CIRCLE 10/6 8/6   STALLS 6/6
CHILDREN 5/- 4/- 3/- mon-fri only   OAPs 2/6 mon-fri matinees only
SEATS BOOKABLE IN ADVANCE FOR EVENING PERFORMANCES
TO SATURDAY AUGUST 31

SUN SEP 1 FOR 7 DAYS   2.15 & 7.30 (sun 5.30)
Our Next 70mm Presentation on the Giant Screen

RODGERS and HAMMERSTEIN'S   GORDON
                                  MACRAE
OKLAHOMA!   SHIRLEY
                                  JONES
                                  ROD
TODD-AO   TECHNICOLOR 'U' STEIGER

Circle 10/6 8/6 Stalls 6/6 Children 5/- 4/- & 3/- except mon
EVENING CIRCLE SEATS NOW BOOKABLE

Above: BFI – Sidney Bernstein Collection.
The giant screen at the Granada Bedford in 1968 (Photo Coverage).

shows were ruled out as the screen could no longer be moved. Children's Saturday morning shows also ceased, probably from fears that the screen would be pelted and marked.

The first film shown on the giant screen was *Doctor Dolittle*, which ran five weeks. Then came a week's revival of *Oklahoma!* (The first standard offering, *Villa Rides*, was enterprisingly advertised as being "In 35mm!"!) 70mm continued to be used where possible for new films and revivals. One day specials were soon back as well.

70mm had previously been installed at Shrewsbury without so much fuss where it was used for roadshow presentations of *Far From The Madding Crowd* and others. The only other Granada to receive the Bedford style of revamping was Slough where a new, larger screen was installed but without 70mm.

Granada further demonstrated its faith in Bedford as a cinema-going centre by taking over the town's Plaza from its independent operator, J. B. Chetham, in February 1969. This was smartened up and renamed the Century, giving Granada three cinemas in the town. Children's shows were resumed here. Live shows – wrestling, late night charity shows, a week of a stage *Sound Of Music* with the Marianettes – were now featured at the Century, along with amateur talent as an added attraction on Monday nights during 1971. Indian and Italian films were also shown for the benefit of local ethnic groups.

Film booking
When Bob Morgan joined Granada as booking controller, he recalls being told by Sidney Bernstein that he had *carte blanche* and would not be subjected to interference – although he would of course be held responsible for his mistakes afterwards. (Morgan remembers "that lovely phrase in Granada: 'With hindsight what would you have done?'")

On joining, he went on a tour of all the theatres after deciding against taking a big Warner Bros. picture, *Reflections In A Golden Eye*, starring Marlon Brando. "I came back and found Victor Chapman had reinstated it. I said, 'If you dare do that again, I'll tell Sidney exactly what you've done.' He never did it again."

In Morgan's first months, there was more red ink than black on the takings sheets and, he recalls, "I was very, very despondent. And Cecil said to me, 'Come and have lunch.' He sat me down. 'Cheer up.' And I said, 'Have you seen the figures?' He said, 'You know, I *did* do your job. There are only so many films you can play. Are you booking the best of what is available for the Granada circuit – in your opinion?' 'Yes.' 'Come and talk to me when you're showing Mr. Disney in August.' He always called him Mr. Disney." Cecil was right. It only took a Disney film or a new James Bond to turn the figures around.

Morgan inherited a special agreement with the distributors

over "break figures". "Granada had a unique sliding scale that went in one per cent steps, whereas everybody else went in five or two-and-a-half per cent steps. I credit Joe Warton for that." Such terms were under pressure from the distributors where major attractions were concerned and eventually had to be abandoned. Morgan remembers refusing to take MGM's *Doctor Zhivago* when it was first available in 1969 because the terms were so steep but doing a special deal the second time it came around. Of course, distributors were anxious to reach an agreement with Granada because in many towns – like Dartford, Grantham and Rugby – there was only the Granada where their films could play.

Morgan tried a few tricks he had learned at Classic about reviving older pictures. When the BBC had its hit TV series *The Forsyte Saga* in 1969, he brought back the Technicolored MGM film version of 1949 with Greer Garson and Errol Flynn, coupled with *High Society*. This fitted in very well with Granada's own past practice of linking up with radio serials but Morgan ruefully declares, "I remember only too well I lost my shirt." An attempt to bring back *Gigi* at Leytonstone also failed: "It did so badly I had to take it off in the middle of the week. We only had two people in in the afternoon. The other thing we did was a Garbo season – it just didn't work."

One musical had plenty of power left. Despite its exclusive London-area run of three and a quarter years at the Dominion Tottenham Court Road, *The Sound Of Music* had not exhausted its appeal to Londoners, many of whom saw it again and again. It chalked up some phenomenal runs at Granadas when it finally became available in the summer of 1968: eight weeks at Kingston, five weeks at East Ham and Welling... This was just the initial run, as it invariably came back for additional weeks.

Despite the limited number of major films being released, there were still occasional opportunities for special bookings. When Warner Bros. had a dispute over terms with its normal outlet, the ABC circuit, in late 1970, Granada snapped up *Woodstock, There Was A Crooked Man* and *Performance*. All provided welcome relief for product-starved East Ham but *Woodstock* also played "Exclusive Showcase Presentations" of two weeks at top flight halls like Kingston as well as solo situations like Grantham (although Bishop's Stortford rated only a week's run).

Perhaps the last completely exclusive Granada booking was a French animated version of *Aladdin And His Magic Lamp* which had been dubbed into English. Released by a minor distributor, Target International, it was specially shown to the critics and opened on Boxing Day 1971 at nine theatres: Aylesbury, Dartford, East Ham, Kingston, Leytonstone, Sutton, Thornton Heath, Tooting, and Welling. Bob Morgan recalls that it did very well.

When it came to Ken Russell's film *The Devils* (1971), Morgan was troubled. "I sat through *The Devils*, which was a watershed

From May 1969, the style in press advertising for the Granada name – of italicised letters reversed out of separate boxes (as seen on the page opposite) – was supplanted by a modern upright, strongly seriffed typeface, Egizio, used by the group as a whole. The distinctive use of lower case initial letters for dates and times had been discontinued. Here, in March 1971, East Ham clings on with a rare special film attraction and live events. (BFI – Sidney Bernstein Collection.)

in censorship, and I had a crisis of conscience. I went to the board and I said, 'I don't know what to do, to book it or not. It would take a lot of money. Morally, I'd be doing the wrong thing.' Sidney said, 'Mr. Morgan, according to the terms of your contract, you can book any film which has a British Board of Film Censors certificate. Has this film got a British Board of Film Censors certificate?' 'Yes, it has an X certificate.' 'In that case, the decision is entirely yours.' And that was the end of that. I booked it."

A more serious problem arose in May 1973 when the head of EMI, Bernard Delfont, overruled his managing director by banning the MGM-EMI release *Hitler: The Last Ten Days* from the ABC circuit because he felt that it made a hero out of the Fuehrer (portrayed by Alec Guinness). There was intense press interest in whether Sidney Bernstein would also ban the film. Bob Morgan recalls that he had already booked it and stood firm when Cecil (not Sidney) Bernstein made it clear he didn't want it shown. Morgan credits Michael Havas, the head of MGM-EMI, with persuading Cecil not to give him the same humiliating treatment as his counterpart at EMI. It turned out there was a stronger case for refusing *Hitler* on commercial grounds, as it performed badly. Rank's Odeon circuit also gave it a full release.

"One of the dreaded phrases" of life at Granada, recalls Bob Morgan, " was 'homework for the weekend'. One left on Friday and had to reappear on Monday with the answers to the questions that had been posed. With me, it happened when Charles Stringer came in and said, 'Bob, I want you to give thought to taking over the live department as well as being booking manager... and I'd like your answer by 9.30 Monday morning.' I knew nothing about live shows." With the help of friends at ABC on the other side of Golden Square and the advice of his daughters (if they would want tickets to see a pop group, it was booked), Morgan took a crash course in learning the ropes.

To help East Ham, Morgan contracted with producer Bill Kenwright to revive the Granada pantomime at Christmas 1973 after a gap of nine years. *Cinderella* top-lined disc jockey Tony Blackburn, TV star Anna Karen and Valentine Dyall. There were problems throughout the four-week run. "It didn't make that much and was known forever after as Morgan's Folly," recalls Bob Morgan ruefully.

East Ham had gained some film booking concessions. At Christmas 1967 it was allowed to play Mr. Disney's new *Jungle Book* concurrently with the Odeon, and held it for two weeks compared to the Odeon's one. It offered weird contrasts in film programming: *The Virgins* plus *Seduced In Sodom* one week, a Disney revival the next. By the early Seventies sexploitation was increasingly prevalent there: *Sex Is Not For Virgins, She Lost Her You Know What, Bedroom Mazurka...* Bob Morgan attempted to improve the booking position at East Ham by seeking an allocation

of the new releases from the industry's product tribunal. At the meeting, chaired by Lord Archibald, Morgan was opposed by two heavyweights: George Pinches, Rank's booking executive, and ABC's chief Bob Webster, seeking to protect the position of their competing cinemas. The Granada was awarded an allocation of, it seems, one week in five of the new releases. "It didn't do us much good. I never did get Bond or anything worthwhile," Morgan remembers, although the popular *The Three Musketeers* played there in August 1974.

In 1969, *The Killing Of Sister George* gained an X certificate with three minutes of cuts but was subject to local scrutiny and local certificates in many areas because of its explicit lesbian scenes: at the Granada Shrewsbury, it was played rather late in the day as an X (Salop) attraction.

Granada also fought a local ban imposed on *Last Tango In Paris* by Northamptonshire County Council. A private viewing for the Kettering health committee at the Granada there on 14 August 1973 resulted in its being passed with a town X certificate. Thanks to the publicity this attracted, the film opened to excellent attendances from all over the county and was retained for a second week.*

In 1975, Granada showed its old rebellious streak by booking *Hennessy*, a thriller shunned by the major circuits (and most independents) which starred Rod Steiger as an Irish terrorist attempting to bomb the Royal opening of Parliament. Surviving records show that audiences shunned it, too, and it was a heavy loser for Granada at Harrow, Maidstone, Walthamstow and the recently acquired Florida Enfield.

Undoubtedly the circuit as a whole was in an increasingly perilous state as attendances nationally continued their decline. It was as important to duck the worst losers (when they could be predicted and when there was a choice of something better) as it was to book the obvious moneymakers.** A surviving report

---

* This Granada had earlier come under attack from an anonymous member of staff over a film that had been passed by the censor. Writing as "Disgusted Worker and Viewer of Kettering" in the local *Evening Telegraph* (9 March 1972), he or she declared: "At this moment of time I am ashamed that I am a member of the Granada staff... Ashamed because I have just looked at a film that was both filthy and degrading... this film made me feel sick." It was apparently *Naughty!*, clearly advertised with the words "Warning: A film report on Pornography and Erotica Past and Present". Except that it appeared after the film's run was over, too late to affect business one way or the other, the letter has more than a whiff of P. T. Barnum about it.

** One less than scintillating offering of the early Seventies was a coarse British comedy called *All the Way Up* starring Warren Mitchell in a variation on his television bigot Alf Garnett. This was an isolated venture into production by Granada through a specially formed film division. It had a disastrous afternoon sneak preview at Slough attended by Sidney and Cecil Bernstein and Bob Morgan, and went out on general release through the ABC circuit in Summer 1970.

The Granada Kettering in its later cinema days: exterior on 18 December 1968, foyer and auditorium on 10 March 1966. Note customers in first-floor café - restaurant. Standard light fittings clash with the modern interior. (Photo Coverage.)
Above: this 1973 advertisement shows the style of the period with much reduced space and simplified heading. (BFI – Sidney Bernstein Collection.)

SLB / CGB JW AB CS CGS WRC

THEATRES WEEKLY PROFIT AND LOSS   W/E: 50.8.69   No: 48   ISSUED: 2/9/69

THEATRE	PROGRAMME	TAKINGS	% PROG COST	THEATRE PROFIT
Acton	BAMBI	655	25	54
Aylesbury	ZULU	887	34	177
Bedford E	GUNS OF THE MAGNIFICENT SEVEN	645	35	70
Bedford G	THE LOVE BUG	1928	45	585
Bedford P	NEVADA SMITH	609	25	115
Bishops Stortford	JUNGLE BOOK	959	48	173
Cheam	EVES: 3 IN THE ATTIC MATS: TARZAN AND THE VALLEY OF GOLD	771	25	175
Chichester	JUNGLE BOOK	1416	50	420
Clapham	RING OF BRIGHT WATER	840	25	3
Dartford	CHITTY CHITTY BANG BANG	2974	50	1020
East Ham	THE LOVE BUG	1362	33	416
Enfield	THE LONGEST DAY	1326	50	297
Grantham	RUN WILD RUN FREE	484	25	(43)
Harrow	THE LONGEST DAY	1779	42	513
Kettering	CARRY ON CAMPING L N S CASTLE OF BLOOD	2208 115	50 25	571 48
Kingston	RING OF BRIGHT WATER L N S CHAMBER OF HORRORS	1139 111	52 25	219 44
Leytonstone G	WIZARD OF OZ	792	26	73
Maidstone	CHITTY CHITTY BANG BANG - WK 2	1799	44	401
Mansfield G	" " " " L N S NAKED & THE DEAD	1941 78	50 20	453 24
Oswestry G	JUNGLE BOOK	606	35	(10)
Pitsea	DR DOOLITTLE	582	44	110
Rugby G	CHITTY CHITTY BANG BANG	1843	50	395
Shrewsbury E	DR DOOLITTLE	400	25	(7)
Shrewsbury G	THE LOVE BUG	1559	39	360
Slough A	SON OF GODZILLA	839	25	(35)
Slough G	ONE HUNDRED & ONE DALMATIONS	1641	40	422
Sutton	RING OF BRIGHT WATER L N S PHANTOM OF THE OPERA	1897 129	48 25	483 42
Sydenham	RING OF BRIGHT WATER	547	25	26
Thornton Heath	" " " "	839	25	184
Tooting	" " " " L N S THEATRE OF DEATH	797 111	20 25	(13) 35
Walthamstow	THE LONGEST DAY	1539	29	528
Welling	RING OF BRIGHT WATER	1088	36	184

JG/KB/19 2 1969   TOTAL   39275   8514

CONTRIBUTION ✓   W/E 24 1 76   NO: 17

	PROGRAMME	RENTER	%PROG COST	NET FILM TAKE	FILM CONT.	OTHER INCOME	WEEKLY SITE CONT.
...D G1	TOMMY ① WEEK 2	HEMDALE	25	1096	(319)		
...ORD G2	THE GROOVE TUBE	G T O	35	972	143	510	334
BISH STORT	THE EXORCIST ②	COL/WAR	25	591	(226)	102	(124)
CHICHESTER	ROLLERBALL	U A	50	2225	337	203	540
CLAPHAM 1	GONE WITH THE WIND	C I C	25	806	(27)		
CLAPHAM 2	SHAMPOO	COL/WAR	25	643	8		
CLAPHAM 3	THE UPS AND DOWNS OF A HANDYMAN	TARGET	25	620	(9)	334	306
ENFIELD	THE STREETFIGHTER	COL/WAR	42	1417	163	146	309
HARROW 1	TOMMY WEEK 2	HEMDALE	32	1586	416		
HARROW 2	THE STREETFIGHTER	COL/WAR	45	1356	250		
HARROW 3	THE UPS AND DOWNS OF A HANDYMAN	TARGET	25	802	106	492	1264
KINGSTON 1	TOMMY WEEK 2	HEMDALE	45	2003	527		
KINGSTON 2	CARRY ON BEHIND	F/RANK	34	900	164		
KINGSTON 3	CELESTINE - MAID AT YOUR SERVICE	CINECENTA	26	722	104	473	1268
M/STONE 1	THE EXORCIST	COL/WAR	29	1199	227		
M/STONE 2	LOVE IN A WOMENS PRISON	EAGLE	35	729	161		
M/STONE 3	TOMMY ③ WEEK 2	HEMDALE	25	821	(8)	304	684
RUGBY G	THE HAPPY HOOKER ④	S BARBER	25	721	(341)	123	(218)
SHREWSBURY	ROYAL FLASH	F/RANK	25	986	(162)	134	(28)
SLOUGH 1	TOMMY WEEK 2	HEMDALE	31	1396	309		
SLOUGH 2	ROYAL FLASH	F/RANK	26	742	58		
SLOUGH 3	THE VIOLATOR	FOCUS	36	987	141	492	1000
WALTH 1	THE STREETFIGHTER	COL/WAR	46	2036	444		
WALTH 2	MOTEL OF FEAR ⑤	TIGON	25	399	(192)		
WALTH 3	THE UPS AND DOWNS OF A HANDYMAN	TARGET	25	742	65	539	856
WELLING 1	CARRY ON BEHIND	F/RANK	25	921	(17)		
WELLING 2	LEGEND OF MACHINE GUN KELLY	FOCUS	25	405	(51)		
WELLING 3	THE UPS AND DOWNS OF A HANDYMAN	TARGET	28	826	240	321	493
	TOTALS			28649	2511	4173	6684

NOTE: OTHER INCOME includes profit from Sales Takings, Screen Advertising and Theatre Hire.

Distribution: SLB CGB AB CS JW AA Butters Morgan Robinson

Issue Date: 30 1 76

Profit and loss report for the week ending 30 August 1969, with crosses and a question mark added by Sidney Bernstein over points to be queried. Note the strong results from Late Night Shows, especially at Tooting where they were dropped after several months because of trouble with teenage gangs, a head office decision opposed by manager Brian Gauntlett who was happy to deal with the problem. (BFI – Sidney Bernstein Collection.)

A rare surviving example of the Theatre Weekly Contribution (Profit or Loss) report, or "weekly agony sheet" as it was known to booking controller Bob Morgan, dating from January 1976. Figures in brackets indicate a loss. Seen at right is Morgan's response to questions posed by Sidney Bernstein, with a copy to managing director Charles Stringer. A handwritten annotation indicates that it has been seen by Cecil Bernstein. (BFI – Sidney Bernstein Collection.)

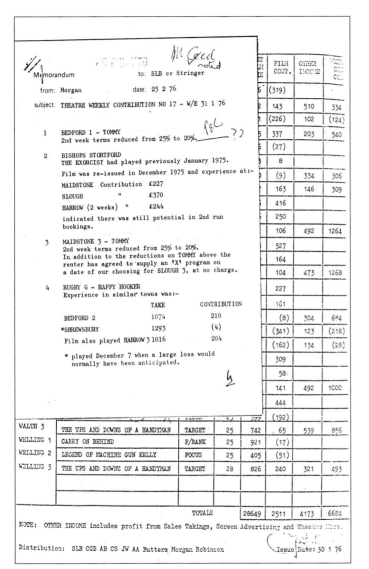

for the week ending 17 February 1973 (when all except Maidstone were single screens) shows the circuit registering small profits and considerable deficits for individual bookings with an overall loss of £1,373. A British film called *Innocent Bystanders* was the worst offender, booked on only 15% terms but still losing as much as £426 at Bedford Granada, £391 at Shrewsbury Granada and £171 at Maidstone Granada 1. Another loser was the American drama *Precinct 45 – Los Angeles Police*, booked at 25% terms and plunging Tooting, Welling, Sutton and Kingston into the red by £241, £211, £176 and £148 respectively. The box-office champ of the week was *Naughty Knickers* at Clapham Junction, making a profit of £354. However, sex films were not a total panacea: *Swedish Fly Girls* at East Ham produced a loss of £26.

The report for the week ending 10 March 1973, three weeks later, shows a much better situation: an overall profit of £3,164. *The Poseidon Adventure* led the winners with £726 profit at Walthamstow, £644 at Harrow and £248 at Leytonstone, even though terms were 49%, 50% and 36% respectively. *A Clockwork Orange* contributed £455 at Bedford in its first week (on 57% terms), although it lost £122 in its second week at Rugby (on 25%). Mr. Disney's *Pinocchio* shone with £386 at 34% at Kettering. However, Tooting and Welling were losing heavily with *The Salzburg Connection*, like Sutton which replaced it midweek with a revival of *The Vanishing Point* to no avail. The now-subdivided Maidstone was showing a loss with both the Charles Bronson starrer *The Mechanic* in the old circle and *Butterflies Are Free* in the mini-auditorium. Live shows of Syd Lawrence at Sutton and Slim Whitman at Kingston resulted in profits of £200 and £282 respectively. Shrewsbury Granada showed a surplus of £222 on the second week of *Young Winston* while the town's Empire was close behind with £181 for *The Love Pill*. Another sex film, *Au Pair Girls*, kept Clapham Junction just above water but plunged East Ham into the red by £115.

The week ending 19 May 1973 was another bad one, showing a loss of £2,173. Here some differences between areas can be noted: on South London release, the relatively sophisticated Woody Allen comedy *Everything You Always Wanted To Know About Sex* showed a profit at Kingston (£181) and Sutton (£51) but registered a loss at Welling (£85) and Tooting (£318). Whereas Clapham Junction in inner London made £139 on the black Hollywood urban thriller *Superfly*, Dartford in Kent lost £71.

General matters

In 1968, new opening times were widely and unilaterally introduced by Granada. Doors opened every weekday at 2pm and 7pm for shows starting at 2.30pm and 7.30pm with continuous performances as before on Saturdays, Sundays and school holidays. This enabled economies, reducing the hours many staff

Separate performances were introduced across the circuit in 1968 while "one level" made the best of balcony only use at Walthamstow that year. (BFI – Sidney Bernstein Collection.)

were needed, but it also created many obvious problems. As the evening show had a fixed starting time, it would necessarily end at varying times and some revival double bills ran four hours. Audiences were confused by the different arrangements at weekends and holidays and didn't know whether they could buy a ticket and come in late for just the main feature. "This was forced on me by our brilliant marketing department," recalls Bob Morgan, who sums up the idea as "disastrous".

The huge Granada Walthamstow set about creating a more inviting atmosphere by using the circle only for films from Sunday 14 July 1968 – retaining the stalls for live shows and the Saturday morning Granadiers club. The balcony provided nearly 1,000 seats and the new policy, which followed general redecoration of the site, was promoted as "Granada Top Level Comfort and Entertainment". Stalls seats had been four shillings and sixpence and displaced patrons now had to pay a shilling more for the rear circle and two shillings more for the front circle. The policy does not seem to have spread elsewhere (although Maidstone became a circle-only operation from September of that year after the River Len overflowed and more than 800,000 gallons of water had to be pumped out of the stalls).

The Granadiers' Saturday morning shows were running out of steam. A change of policy saw the introduction of a show entirely made up of cartoons alternating every other week with the traditional type of programme. The shows were no longer profitable but continued into the early Seventies. "We stopped them simply because at Grantham we had put in a new screen which cost £576 and on the first Saturday morning some little swine threw eggs at it. Forget the profits for the next twenty years!" recalls Bob Morgan, adding: "You've got to remember, also, television was taking over Saturday mornings."

An attempt was made to re-launch occasional Saturday morning shows called the Junior Readers Club at Kettering as a tie-in with the local newspaper. These started on 17 February 1973 and over 800 attended the first free show. The third show took place in August. How long they continued is not clear.

Café-restaurants were diminishing – Kettering's went in 1969, although a snack bar remained; Maidstone's become the Court School of Dancing. But Bedford's was still heavily promoted in press advertising that same year and as late as 1974 the Grantham café was noted as doing "excellent business".

Granada went into a joint venture with Charringtons to drastically re-style two restaurant spaces into bars. At Walthamstow, the pub was named the Victoria in a nod to the first cinema on the site. At Harrow, it was called the Greenhill after the name given that part of the town.

Looking back on his years with Granada, Bob Morgan declares, "Probably the most nightmarish period was the power cuts" –

caused by the national miners' dispute of early 1972. "You didn't know where they were coming, when they were coming. You had the lights out at two, they came on at three." This made it impossible to stick to advertised showing times. Eventually days were classified in advance as low, medium or high risk. On low and medium days, Granadas showed the full programme as advertised, but on high risk days only the main feature was played, at the normal price of admission. This worked if the main feature was of average length, but an epic like *Lawrence of Arabia* had to be postponed at Dartford because a power cut from 6pm to 9pm made it too late to start afterwards.

In the summer of 1974, Granada introduced cutbacks at several of the surviving single-screen cinemas. Only the circle was normally used at East Ham, Rugby and Welling with the stalls kept in reserve for overflow, holidays and any live shows. The same policy applied at Sutton in the afternoons. At East Ham, a further economy saved an estimated £5,000 per year: closing on Mondays and Tuesdays, the worst nights of the week. At Bishop's Stortford, opening time in the week was put back to between 3.30pm and 4.30pm. At Chichester, matinees were held on Wednesdays only. Oswestry opened between 6.30 and 7pm for a single show. Similar economies were to be found elsewhere.

Perhaps the most dangerous economy of all, which applied to all the Granada cinemas and was practised by the other circuits, was to reduce the size of local press advertising. Double-column advertising was cut back to a miserly single column around 1974, saving an estimated £2,500 per year. It is this writer's belief that these tiny advertisements put off potential patrons (that's if they could find them in the first place), suggesting that cinemagoing was *passé*, and that they cost far more in lost admissions than they saved. Newspapers were also less inclined to run supporting copy. Rates had shot up but big stores and other businesses still took large ads.

Some of the surviving organs were not totally silent. In March 1968, the Wurlitzer at Mansfield was heard on several Friday nights as part of the evening programme. At Kingston in 1971, David Hamilton played in the evenings before a one-day special presentation of *Richard III* and during a one-week run of *Lawrence Of Arabia*. And at Welling, manager Leo Eales was also an organist and he performed from time to time, as did Doug Sharp during the run there of *Camelot* in September 1970.

Investment in cinemas (2): twins and triples

At the start of the Seventies, the cinema circuit had slimmed down to thirty-three theatres. There were the Granadas at Acton, Aylesbury, Bedford, Bishop's Stortford, Chichester, Clapham Junction, Dartford, East Ham, Edmonton, Enfield, Grantham, Greenwich, Harrow, Kettering, Kingston, Leytonstone, Maidstone,

Mansfield, Oswestry, Rugby, Shrewsbury, Slough, Sutton, Sydenham, Thornton Heath, Tooting, Walthamstow and Welling. And there was the Century Pitsea, the new Century and the Empire at Bedford, the Adelphi Slough, and the Empire Shrewsbury.

Plans abounded for replacing them with offices. In 1971 the architects Michael Lyell Associates were asked to look at converting the flytower at Kennington (now bingo) into offices, replacing the Adelphi Slough with a new cinema and the maximum amount of office space, and preparing a scheme to rebuild Harrow as a seven or eight storey office block with shops on the main frontage and two new cinemas seating 1,000 in the basement or at ground level with the entrance relegated to the side road.

Rank and ABC had begun subdividing their large cinemas into smaller auditoria, sometimes including bingo.* Granada took a special interest in Rank's conversion of a former restaurant area into a 105-seat second cinema at the Odeon Preston in 1970, dispatching a member of staff to compile an on-the-spot report, after which George Coles' practice drew up plans to convert the ballroom at Sutton into a 204-seat cinema (Coles himself had died in 1963).

The following year Granada decided to act at Maidstone, where something needed to be done as the stalls had not been used since the flood.

The stalls area was turned over to bingo with seating for 870, reached through the main entrance, and the balcony and the former restaurant (leased out to a dance school) were converted into two cinemas with their own separate entrance on the side through what had most recently been a snack bar. George Coles and Partners handled the structural aspects while Granada's own Building Design Unit took care of the interior design. All the original

*ABC also pursued a policy of converting stalls to "luxury lounges" and keeping single screens. This is what happened to the first Granada in Dover, renamed the ABC since 1960. In 1970 it closed for a month to allow a radical overhaul. Externally, the original canopy was removed in favour of a readograph in seven sections above the entrance on which red lettering was mounted. The cinema re-opened using the stalls only, with 610 new seats in more widely spaced rows in what was now called the "lounge". In the foyer, which was painted a dark blue, the elaborate glass chandelier installed in 1930 still provided the main illumination, but the staircase to the circle and the promenade around were curtained off (the mirror at the head of the stairs remained, out of sight, with a line of lockers later placed directly in front of it). All the seating was removed from the circle and the side walls were painted black. The entire ceiling was now dark blue with strong downlighters replacing the prevous light fittings. Laylights in the balcony soffit still illuminated the rear stalls. The splay walls and side walls were painted a dark blue with a black dado, largely blotting out Komisarjevky's decoration. The front of the circle was painted an orange colour extended in a band along the side walls above the dark blue. The upper side walls were blacked out. The inner step of the proscenium arch was covered in green. It was all rather lurid and vulgar, but kept the cinema going for another twelve years.

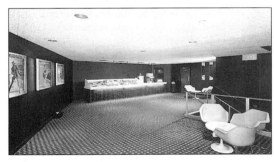

*The new look at Maidstone in January 1972
with a side entrance replacing the line of shops,
new upstairs foyer, and cinemas in the old
balcony and in the former café-restaurant space
(where the screen was normally curtained).
Some ceiling decoration remains on view.
Behind the drapes at right in the small cinema
lie the windows overlooking the street.
(Photo Coverage.)*

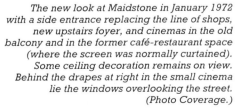

Komisarjevksy decoration below balcony level was removed by July. A new floor was built forward from the old front edge of the circle and any surviving side wall decoration was covered by orange drapes. The main chandelier was taken away and a plain false ceiling covered the original decoration. The rear walls and ceiling were painted chocolate brown. Only some ventilation grilles remained visible from 1934. 560 modern seats with orange-coloured upholstery replaced the 650 old ones. Thirty-two of the seats were of the luxury Pullman armchair type, making up the fifth row.

The treatment of the former restaurant space was along the same lines. The side walls were curtained over, hiding the line of windows on the right hand side, and ninety detached Pullman armchairs were installed in stepped rows of eight with a central aisle. Only in the ceiling with its elaborately decorated cross beams could some of the old gilded richness still be detected, although it was now painted over in more chocolate brown.

Externally, a huge sign reading BINGO finally occupied that empty space above the pediment over the main entrance. A large sign in boxed letters reading GRANADA 1&2 appeared above the line of windows on the side extension but did not overcome the impression that the cinemas were of secondary significance.

The work took eight months and cost £250,000. Granada 1&2 opened on Boxing Day 1971. The big Granada ran continuous performances, charging 45p for the ordinary seats and 60p for the row of special ones. The small Granada had only luxury seats, priced at 60p, and ran separate performances, normally fifteen shows a week, tending towards more specialised films.

Attendances in the large cinema were disappointing: average weekly admissions of 3,460 were slightly below the 3,500 per week before conversion. But the small cinema started off more successfully, averaging nine capacities per week.

This overall result discouraged further conversions along the same lines. Then in 1972 Rank began converting many of its Odeons and Gaumonts into three-screen "film centres" by a much cheaper method of "drop wall" conversions with the space underneath the balcony being blocked off and divided down the centre to create two small cinemas served by a common projection box built at the back. This left the balcony and original screen to be used for the largest cinema. From the rear of the balcony, the cinema looked the same as it had always done; further forward, the stalls area was visibly empty even if seats were sometimes left and exit signs illuminated. In the spring of 1973, Granada decided to follow Rank's example.

The company planned more luxurious conversions for Harrow and Slough at a cost of £90,000 and more economical ones (£60,000) for Walthamstow, Clapham Junction and Welling, the last three based on the cost of Rank's conversion of the Odeon Wimbledon.

Kingston was then added to the list. (At most of these locations, bingo was not a viable alternative to film use as other cinemas had already taken it up.)

Five conversions were carried out during 1973: the sixth, planned for Welling, was postponed.

The Granada Slough came first. The circuit's other cinema in the town, the huge Adelphi, closed in January 1973 with *Sex Is A Pleasure* and *Blood Demon* after Granada gained planning permission to convert the main auditorium to bingo and the ballroom to a cinema which would probably show specialised films. An earlier application for bingo alone had been rejected. There was considerable uproar locally when the Adelphi re-opened for bingo in May but no work had been done on the cinema. The Council threatened to take out an injunction forcing the building to close unless the cinema was added within six months. The chairman of the planning committee was quoted in *The Slough Observer* as saying: "We are not going to be double-crossed over this. If I had my way I would close the place in a bloody month. I have had my suspicions all along that Granada never intended to put a cinema in the Adelphi unless forced to. If they don't we will serve them with an injunction forcing them to close the place."

Golden Square responded that it fully intended to provide a cinema at the Adelphi but it was waiting to see how the Granada fared when it became a triple cinema and that a fourth screen in Slough would, at the moment, be "commercially unviable". Company secretary Joe Warton wrote to the chairman of the planning committee asking him if he had been correctly quoted in the local press and warning him that words like "double cross" could result in legal action. The Adelphi ballroom never did become a cinema, although the George Coles practice was asked to draw up plans for the conversion. In January 1974, the company considered putting a fourth cinema in disused restaurant space at the Granada, but this also never happened.

When the Granada Slough closed for conversion, the town was left without a cinema for several weeks until it re-opened in mid-June 1973. It seems a little inconsiderate to the town's picturegoers not to have delayed the Adelphi's switch to bingo until the work at the Granada had been completed.

Rank's drop wall subdivisions usually left the cinema open in the evenings during the conversion period, or closed for just the final week. But at Slough, the adaptation was quite elaborate, costing around £95,000. The two smaller cinemas jutted out from under the balcony and seated 239 and 197, much larger than the usual "minis" at Odeons and Gaumonts. The old screen, serving the largest auditorium, had to be raised to provide a clear view past the downstairs cinemas.

The Granada Clapham Junction opened as a triple a few days

The Granada Harrow as a triple cinema. Exterior dates from 21 July 1975. The front of the canopy is no longer used for advertising the shows. The "3 Cinemas" lettering was a standard addition to the faça of triples. Main foyer view (18 July 1975) shows a modern concession counter at the far end and, above it, the unsympathetic enclosing of t former café area for pub use. Note also the modern doors to the mini cinemas under the balcony. The pub here was called the Greenhill, entered from the street and from the balcony promenade. The view of one of the mini-cinemas dates from 7 January 1974. The photograp from the circle (13 February 1974) shows the glorious sight that still faced patrons using the main cinema. The two minis can be seen protruding slightly from the front edge of the circle with paterae added to each corner (the flat roofs became targets for litter). (Photo Coverage.)

after Slough, being converted at a lower cost of around £60,000 without closing. Only a year before, Granada had been discussing with Wandsworth Council the replacement of the cinema by an office block. Wandsworth had asked for a small cinema and some residential content in any new building. Granada's efforts to enlarge the site by purchasing adjacent London Transport land had been frustrated. Now the scheme was considered to be far enough into the future for a modest investment in a drop wall conversion to earn its costs back. The two small cinemas seated 191 and 187 – money was saved by not extending beyond the balcony front to make them bigger. No refurbishment of the main auditorium seemed to have been carried out and, when one sat in the former circle, the building gave a distinctly run-down impression. Either the sound system needed renewal or the conversion created acoustical problems as dialogue seemed muffled and often indistinct from the seats this writer occupied on occasional visits.

The Granadas at Walthamstow, Harrow and Kingston were all converted to triples in the last quarter of 1973. The mini cinemas in each had larger seating capacities than those at average Rank sites. In the Walthamstow conversion, the minis were tucked away completely out of view from the balcony and had slightly fewer seats (172 in each). At Walthamstow and Kingston, the front stalls seats were left in place for use if needed (they were taken out in later years).

The Kingston site had been threatened with demolition for a new road but the plans had been revised and the danger had receded by 1970. Sidney Bernstein paid a visit a few days before the mini cinemas opened here and ordered the centre paybox in the foyer to be removed, leaving only a corner one. A new projection box took over part of the circle lounge as the image was sent into the mini-cinemas from there downwards via a hole in the floor and angled mirrors, leaving more space for seats below. Even so, the roof of the minis jutted out ahead of the curved circle front to allow seating of around 200 in each.

Harrow was a more expensive conversion, put by advance estimates in the £95,000 range of Slough. Again, the two minis (seating 205 each) extended slightly forward of the balcony frae, and here the projecting flat roofs were decorated with paterae. The stalls seating was cleared and floodlights set up to pick out the decorative grillework on the splay walls during intervals. The main chandelier was not used, to avoid illuminating the desolate area below.

The total investment in these five triplings was put at around £400,000. During 1973, consideration was given to splitting Rugby into two cinemas in the balcony and a bingo hall in the stalls area, then to creating three cinemas upstairs (with 350, 220 and 110 seats) by extending the circle area forward over the stalls. East Ham was also viewed as a candidate for three or four screens. Neither scheme took place.

During 1974 the large circle at Maidstone was split down the middle and it became a three-screen operation with the existing small cinema. During this same year, the disused restaurant space at the Granada Bedford was converted into a second cinema seating 209, replacing the Plaza which was closed. Granada retained the Empire for the time being. This closed in 1975, re-opened the following year as Granada 3 but closed again a little over a year later.

It was probably during this period that the inner sets of entrance doors were removed from most of the theatres, opening up the foyer and making it more friendly. This also enabled tickets to be sold from the inner hall, although in most cases the old box-office windows in the outer hall continued to be used.

In 1975 it was decided to proceed with tripling Welling via a drop wall conversion. Here a T-shaped ground-floor projection room with a passage between the minis served all three screens directly, although the short throw to the main screen was not ideal. Around this time the entrance hall and inner passages were splendidly redecorated along with the new minis but the main auditorium was left sorely in need of similar attention.

Tripling ended the use of cinemas for live shows, except for occasional organ concerts where the instruments still survived. John Young recalls from managing Kingston: "Wurlitzers at Harrow and Kingston survived well into the Seventies. Occasional interludes of a nostalgic nature were given during film performances and Sunday morning concerts were held for cinema organ societies. At Kingston, local organ builder Dennis Coffin, at his own cost, restored the instrument, including the phantom piano, to its original condition. Through the BBC presenter of *The Organist Entertains*, Robin Richmond, I arranged regular recordings of guest organists which featured in the radio programme almost every week. Naturally, the theatre was always given a good plug. Jimmy Saville's TV programme *Jim'll Fix It* transmitted a segment I suggested to fix a 14-year-old schoolboy's ambition to play the organ during a public film performance. It was filmed at the Granada and viewed by a television audience of eight million.

"Probably the last major concert given on the Kingston organ was as late as 1978. I arranged a 'farewell' concert for Reg ('Mr. Blackpool') Dixon to a packed house. Reg had played at the opening night at Kingston in 1939."

The triple cinemas raised a booking problem, particularly where competing cinemas were taking a share of the best product, as at Clapham Junction (with the Ruby, ex-Imperial), Harrow (an ABC) and Kingston (the Studio 7). This was a shortage of new films. The gap was filled with soft porn pictures with lurid titles, usually in one of the small screens. These developed a following and were profitable. "Basically, we couldn't have existed without them," declares Ivan Cluley, then in the circuit's booking department. "There just wasn't the amount of product available."

At some locations, though, it was possible to use the small screens for occasional offbeat quality pictures and, as late as 1979, Bob Morgan remembers being pleasantly surprised when he shared a lift at Golden Square with Sidney Bernstein who wanted to know how well the Australian *The Chant Of Jimmy Blacksmith* was doing that week at Kingston.

End of the single screens

Most of the cinemas not converted to twins or triples had gone over to full-time bingo by the mid-Seventies.

As mentioned in the last chapter, the Granadas at King's Cross, Crystal Palace (Upper Norwood), Edmonton and Greenwich made the switch in 1968. Greenwich was already on bingo two nights a week and successful change of use applications from the previous year resulted in the other three dropping films. At Greenwich, because of its poor location and the proximity of the bigger Woolwich club, bingo was not a huge success and the unneeded balcony was stripped of seats and carpet. The clubs at Crystal Palace and Edmonton, along with Wandsworth Road (converted in 1967), were failures.

Edmonton had done extremely well on bingo on two nights a week before going full-time. It had been under planning blight for some years. In the last half of 1961, a draft development plan for the area had shown the theatre being replaced by a municipal car park but the scheme was not then likely to start until 1964. It was put back to 1965, then 1968, and Granada finally handed the building over to the local authority in the summer of 1969, probably without regret as it had no obvious future. King's Cross suffered a similar fate after a short time on bingo, being demolished for an extension to the adjacent Town Hall, and whether it was profitable as a bingo hall is not clear.

Upper Norwood closed after a year on bingo, then was re-opened by an independent operator. Granada regained the building and tried its own brand of bingo again, this time so successfully that it remains open in 1998 under a successor company, Gala.

Wandsworth Road soldiered on, even though it was taking attendances from the clubs at Kennington and Brixton, perhaps because there seemed to be no alternative use for the building.

Granada wondered if East Ham could compete on bingo against the Top Rank Club in the former Gaumont. A visit was made to the Rank site and the report commented unfavourably on the way it was run while conceding it was well attended. By this time, the Rank (Denman) interest in the East Ham Granada had been bought out for £133,000. While in 1969 the cinema was still making an estimated profit of £13,500, this was on the decline and something would have to be done. It was decided to explore redevelopment of this site and North Cheam as stores or supermarkets.

In fact, North Cheam went quickly, becoming the second of the original Granadas to be demolished. When it closed in the autumn of 1969 to be replaced by a supermarket and offices, it was one of the least altered of the cinemas. (It also seems to have been the only Granada with pre-war red and green neon reinstated, with the horizontal green bands lighting up from the centre outwards and then going off before starting over again.)

As at North Cheam, poor attendances had been causing worry at Sydenham for some years. The Granada was uncomfort-ably close to the Odeon Penge which usually showed the same programmes. A modest profit in 1964/65 had shrunk to £2,645 in the year ending September 1968 without including depreciation of equipment, fixtures and fittings. Supermarkets were showing a keen interest in the site and outline planning consent was given in the middle of 1968 for a redevelopment to put a new first-floor cinema over a supermarket and shops. However, Sidney Bernstein decided there was no future in a cinema here and it was sold. The developers were so keen to get going that they had scaffolding in place to pull it down before it had even closed in the spring of 1971.

In 1970, nearly a year before ABC opened its new twin cinemas in nearby Basildon, the Century Pitsea went over to bingo. The Granada Enfield followed in 1971, but the town still had a single screen ABC and Florida.

The march to bingo quickened with the Granadas at Acton, Thornton Heath and Aylesbury all changing over in 1972. (Acton and Aylesbury retained Odeons while Thornton Heath patrons now had to travel to a cinema.)

In 1973 bingo claimed the Adelphi Slough (as previously discussed) and the Granadas at Shrewsbury and Grantham.

In Shrewsbury, figures for 1971/2 showed that the Granada had achieved 198,853 admissions, resulting in a profit of £26,292, and the smaller Empire had sold 100,088 tickets, making a profit of £9,575. The Century, with 180,279 bingo admissions, made a profit of £33,824. Clearly, the big money was in bingo, and more could be made by transferring it to the larger Granada.

Variety shows were still playing the Granada, but now twice on a Friday or Saturday rather than for a full week: in January 1972 there was *The Ken Dodd Laughter Show*, which also featured Pearl Carr and Teddy Johnson, and in April came *The Frankie Howerd Show* with guest star Vince Hill. In February, the Shrewsbury Amateur Operatic Society (SAOS) continued a tradition dating back to 1936 by presenting its annual show – *Orpheus In The Underworld* – for a week. Films seemed to be doing well: *Ryan's Daughter,*

Above, the Granada Sydenham. The exterior of the auditorium (seen on 17 October 1968) had become an eyesore although the tiled entrance area was better. Note the block letter sign on the corner, installed in 1967. Auditorium photograph dates from 4 April 1955, showing the rising festoon curtain which enabled the maximum width for CinemaScope.

The right hand half of the former Granada 1 at Maidstone after division down the middle (shot taken 7 April 1976). Note how the seats no longer face the screen properly and how Cecil Masey's surviving undulations make matters worse.

6 June 1973 view of the modernised screen end of the Empire Shrewsbury after the Granada closed. Compare with view on page 17.

(All Photo Coverage.)

booked for two weeks in 70mm with six-track stereophonic sound, was retained for three. Other big films like *Kelly's Heroes* and *Love Story* played two weeks at the Granada. The circuit's secondary cinema, the 764-seat Empire, played many sex programmes, such as *Naughty!* plus *Bread*, plus move-overs from the bigger theatre including *Diamonds Are Forever* and *Steptoe And Son*.

In March 1972, head office revealed that it would be applying for a bingo licence for the Granada Shrewsbury. (At this period, applications could only be submitted once a year, in April.) Reassuring noises were made: "In the event of us pursuing any plan to convert the Granada to a bingo club it would certainly be our intention to retain at least two cinemas in the town." Faced with uproar over the loss of the stage facilities, Granada maintained that live shows were no longer viable and that it had made a loss on a number of them in the past year, but the president of the SAOS stated, "We always get full houses when we hold our shows at the Granada once a year." Granada refused to let the theatre for further stage shows, causing a crisis for the SAOS which had planned to celebrate its golden jubilee in 1973 with two productions there, *Kismet* in February and *The Gondoliers* in November.

Some films continued to draw crowds: in July, Disney's *Bedknobs And Broomsticks* was booked for two weeks and held over for a third. Musicals were prominent: revivals of *The Sound Of Music* and (in 70mm) *The King And I* jostled with a two-week run of the screen version of *Fiddler On The Roof*. Attendances in the 1,488-seat cinema were said to have ranged from 3,421 to 4,285 per week between March and October, suggesting an improvement over an average attendance of 3,161 quoted in June.

In the bid to introduce bingo, round one went against Granada. The magistrates turned down the bingo application because it had not been shown that existing facilities were inadequate. Granada immediately filed an appeal against the refusal and members of the Century Bingo Club signed a petition in support of the move. The Century had 626 seats, 8,430 members, and averaged 4,000 admissions a week. In October, a bingo licence for the Granada was granted by Shrewsbury Crown Court, mainly because the judge agreed that facilities at the Century were inadequate, leading to occasions when it was overcrowded and uncomfortable.

A Granada spokesman reiterated that the company intended to keep at least two cinemas operating ("smaller luxury cinemas") while managing director Charles Stringer even dangled the prospect of three: "The Empire could be turned into two small cinemas and the Century could be altered to provide another."

In the present day opinion of the company's film bookers, Bob Morgan and Ivan Cluley, the Granada Shrewsbury should have remained on films. Stringer declared at a press conference in February 1973 that both the Granada and Empire were making money but that the decision to convert the Granada to bingo was "governed by demand". He added: "Our intention is to put a cinema into the Century, but we have not decided whether this will be a short term or long term proposition. We are going to have a detailed survey of the building because the fabric is a little suspect."

It was also admitted that the Granada was too large for bingo and that the company would be looking at including other leisure uses at the rear, such as squash courts, saunas or a discotheque. Matinees were cancelled in January to allow 900 stalls seats to be removed. The following month, the SAOS presented *The Gondoliers* in the town's 500-seat Music Hall, cancelling plans for *Kismet* as the new venue was not big enough for it.

The Granada was launched as a bingo hall on Tuesday 17 April 1973 by Dick Emery, star of the film comedy *Ooh...You Are Awful* which had been shown there in February. It was hoped to feature cabaret regularly for the benefit of bingo club members. The large back section of the balcony was walled off, and this and the former restaurant area over the entrance were left unused (and have not been put to any use since). The standard Komisarjevsky chandelier suspended over the front of the auditorium was removed and his standard light fittings in the foyer were replaced with tacky modern ones. However, the original light fittings at later bingo clubs (East Ham, Clapham Junction) were left in place.

Granada's section manager stated in May that plans were being drawn up to re-open the Century as a 400-seat cinema. During that month, the Empire closed for five days for a £50,000 facelift in which a new box-letter name sign replaced the very old-fashioned existing vertical, the foyer was enlarged, a bigger screen put up, a new projection box built in the rear stalls, and the 70mm projectors and sound equipment from the Granada installed. As at Slough, intentions to provide further cinema facilities came to nothing. But while Slough had three screens at the Granada, Shrewsbury was left with only one. If the Century failed its structural inspection, this does not seem to have been publicised, and it remains standing to this day.

The year 1973 also saw the closure of the Granada Mansfield for demolition and replacement by a Littlewood's store. Here again Granada wanted better bingo facilities than could be provided at the smaller Century and, just before the Granada went, successfully applied for a licence to build a new bingo club on a site immediately adjacent to the Century. It was stated that the Century would be re-opened as a cinema to replace the Granada and provide competition for the town's single-screen ABC. The new Granadaclub in Midworth Street with 1,000 seats was said to be the first purpose-built bingo hall when it eventually opened on Thursday 5 August 1976, with the George Coles

The Granada Grantham before bingo. Main exterior view dates from circa 1965. The narrow width of the entrance prompted a canopy with two lines of lettering on the front edge. (Courtesy of Brian Gauntlett.) This cinema had an exceptionally large foyer (seen here in March 1959) with side doors from the car park and was often used as a short cut by the public. Auditorium shot dates from May 1963. The decorative grilles on the side walls should be lit up by small shielded bulbs in front (as at the Embassy Esher). (Both from Photo Coverage.)

Partnership as the architects. This was a low brick building of paralysing dullness. The Century did not become a cinema but was later gutted and fitted out to become an extension of the successful new club. It was entered through a doorway in the new club with a Century sign overhead. This was perhaps the last use of the Century name as other Centurys converted to bingo had been renamed Granada by this time.

When the Granada Grantham went over to bingo, it left the area as one of the most conspicuous in the country to lack a cinema.

But the most dramatic turn in theatre operations in 1973 took place at the former flagship in Tooting.

Decline of the flagship

"Gothic arches are all around the auditorium, dimly lit by reflections from the screen. When the lights go up there is Aladdin's Cave; if you walk to the front for a choc ice or orange squash and turn suddenly, the view may literally make you gasp. Pinnacle after gilded pinnacle, to the back of the gallery: one of the sights of London. Miss the Tower of London if you have to, but don't miss this."

– Ian Nairn, *London*, 1966

On 11 January 1972, Sidney Bernstein's in-tray included two contrasting communications on the same subject. One (addressed to "Dear Sidney" and signed "John B") was from John Betjeman. It read: "You would have been a proud and happy man last night had you been at the lecture given by a splendid young man on the staff of the GLC Historic Buildings Department on the rise of the super cinema in London. It was fully illustrated with slides. Your managing director was there, and he will have told you what an interesting lecture it was, and I can tell you how ably he defended the position of Granada films with regard to Tooting. David Atwell, the lecturer... thought that the two cinemas which ought to be preserved as architecture, even though their uses may have ceased to be that for which they were originally intended, were the Tooting Granada and the New Victoria. Having seen the other heroes he mentioned and made films of them – Wandsworth [?] and Finsbury Park – I agreed with him. Dear Sidney, it may well be that the Tooting Granada is your lasting monument to all you have done for entertainment and your interest in the arts, for which thank God. I can see that it is a dead loss. Is it worth it? In my opinion yes. No one will build super cinemas again, none are left in America. The State, Sydney, which I filmed in colour is about to be destroyed. Yours is the only one left in the world that I know of."

In stark contrast was the second communication, a memo from Granada's managing director, Charles Stringer: "I think I should

alert you to a move that is going on to get the Granada Tooting listed as a protected building. I went to a lecture last night at the Institute of British Architects given by a member of the GLC Historic Buildings Department on 'The Rise of the Super Cinema in London' and he was firmly making a case for the preservation of the New Victoria and Granada Tooting as buildings of architectural merit. In the case of Tooting he is referring more particularly to the interior. I have discussed this with Cecil Elsom who alerted me to the meeting and he confirms my view that this is a matter that should be considered seriously even to the extent of an early demolition of the site before the movement to preserve it becomes too strong."

Bernstein replied to Betjeman: "Dear John: I'm not sure that I would have been proud or even happy if I had gone to the Lecture at the RIBA! I really do not know what is happening at Tooting because I have been backing away from Granada Theatres these last few years. I hope Granada Tooting is not my only lasting monument – there is, of course, also the Granada Woolwich, done by Komisarjevski [sic], similar to Tooting and 'done' in one of our lighter moments! Anyhow, thanks pal for your compliments and kind thought."

Undoubtedly, the Granada Tooting had fallen on hard times. In 1965, when the circle was usually closed for matinees, it had seen 342,300 admissions, the equivalent of 2.2 capacities a week. Just five years later, in 1970, this figure had almost halved, to 174,700, equal to 1.1 capacities per week. This was slightly worse than the national decline in admissions, from 326 million to 193 million. The Granada's position was aggravated by continuing competition from the ABC (former Mayfair) in Tooting, which had just been extensively modernised, and the tiny Classic a little further away at Tooting Bec. The ABC, of course, prevented the Granada from taking any ABC circuit releases. For new films, the Granada was limited to the Rank release and the little off-circuit product available: mostly sexy foreign items like *The Oldest Profession*, shown in 1968. The best alternative to an undesirable release was a revival of a past hit (or two of them double-billed). The Rank release also played at the nearby Odeon Streatham, as well as at the Odeons in Balham and Wimbledon, and this further cut into attendances at Tooting when they were all playing the same film.

In August 1967, John Betjeman featured the cinema in one of his television programmes and Granada had undertaken some refurbishment. It is thought that Theodore Komisarjevky made a visit around this time but did not involve himself in the redecoration.

The number of live concerts had declined and there seem to have been few if any after the Bee Gees on Sunday 28 April 1968. Wrestling continued but only around four times a year.

Stars still made personal appearances. Roger Moore arrived

to promote his film *Crossplot* in December 1969 and was one of the last to sign the theatre's "All the World's a Stage" visitors' board, kept in the manager's office, which featured the signature of Frank Sinatra among dozens of other celebrities.

Going to the Granada Tooting had become a depressing experience, at least in poor weeks. I attended a routine Rank release, the western *Rough Night In Jericho*, there on a Saturday evening in 1967 or early 1968 and the whole stalls audience seemed to be bunched in one or two rows two-thirds of the way back as though seeking protection from the surrounding emptiness. The atmosphere was entirely bereft of glamour and excitement.

Some juggling of films was undertaken. In 1970, the overly sophisticated Fox British comedy *Decline and Fall... Of A Birdwatcher!* was pulled out at the last minute, too late for the local press advertisement, and replaced by a revival of a past Fox hit, *Von Ryan's Express*. Manager Brian Gauntlett put the best possible spin on it, announcing to the press: "We have had such a successful week with *The Detective* in which Frank Sinatra starred that we have decided to immediately put on another Sinatra film."

Undoubtedly there were some good weeks and as a live-wire manager Brian Gauntlett kept the theatre in the news, most spectacularly in August 1970 when he gained national press coverage with a special screening of Walt Disney's *Jungle Book* for a ten-year-old girl because she had to return home to Glasgow the day before it opened. That she could still have seen it in Scotland and that she was the niece of one of the theatre's projectionists were left unmentioned. This was showmanship in the P. T. Barnum spirit, rewarded by a letter of commendation from Sidney Bernstein himself (see *Picture House*, no. 22, Summer 1997).

The mighty Wurlitzer was still regularly used by the BBC for radio broadcasts in 1969/70. Brian Gauntlett also arranged for a local organist, Ted Beckerley, to provide a half-hour recital at 7pm nightly in support of *Funny Girl* in February 1970. The week before, patrons were invited to send in their requests for the night they would be attending. Concerts for organ clubs also took place on Sundays outside of operating hours.

Bingo was not at this time considered an option for Tooting. I have been told (though not by anyone in Granada) that an attempt by Mecca to run bingo at the small Vogue cinema in Tooting had failed and that the area was not suitable because of a large Asian population. The programme of tripling theatres had yet to start, but Tooting would not have been considered as its size made such a conversion expensive and only successful theatres were thought to justify the investment.

It is not clear what plans were being developed for Tooting when the threat of listing was raised by David Atwell's talk in January 1972. Granada were sufficiently worried to seek advice on the implications of listing. By the beginning of the following month, there were stories in the local press of a scheme to replace the cinema with an office block.

On 21 February 1972, Wandsworth Borough Council served a Building Preservation Notice on the Granada Tooting. This had the effect of temporarily listing the building for a maximum of six months while it was considered for proper listing by the Minister at the Department of the Environment. The move, without prior notification and before Granada had submitted any plans, seems to have incensed Sidney Bernstein. It is sad to report that, far from seeking to preserve what John Betjeman had called his "lasting monument", he completely opposed the conservationists. At a meeting with a firm of solicitors to discuss the Building Preservation Notice, he declared that he had had indications from the Ministry, the body that would confirm or overturn the listing, that it would meet him privately to discuss the situation. He also informed the solicitors that as an example of cinema decor the New Victoria was infinitely superior to the Granada Tooting (his disdain for the decor of the New Victoria when it opened had, of course, referred to its unsuitability for audiences).

Pressure was building up. The *Evening Standard* included the Granada in a list of nine seriously threatened buildings "whose loss would be London's disgrace". BBC TV's *London This Week* show wanted to feature the building and Granada decided that no representative should appear and seems to have refused access.

At least the cinema remained open. The firm of C.H. Elsom, Pack and Roberts produced a redevelopment scheme for a 17-storey building consisting of twelve floors of offices above 20,000 square feet of exhibition hall at ground level, occupying the equivalent of three floors, with galleries around. A basement cinema was included which would be reached by a staircase from a new forecourt leading to foyers under the exhibition area through to the 800-seat auditorium at the rear. The cinema would include the Wurlitzer from the old auditorium, placed on a lift, and the new organ pit would be the deepest part of the entire scheme. To the rear of the exhibition hall, and partly over the cinema, would be a five-level car park.

Sidney Bernstein proposed to use the exhibition space for a history of cinema, including plasterwork and other decorative features salvaged from the Granada auditorium. The inclusion of the organ in the new cinema was considered an important advantage in fighting the listing. The fibrous plaster specialists Clark and Fenn were asked to quote for making a scale model, approximately 16 ft. by 12 ft., of the Granada for display in the exhibition and reported that it would cost around £20,000 and take two years. The solicitors began seeking an expert to write a report opposing the listing of the building. Sidney Bernstein sought a meeting with a government minister to discuss the whole affair.

In a letter to the Minister for the Environment dated 2 May 1972,

Bernstein declared the current level of attendances "clearly shows that the property is no longer of interest to the cinema-going public and that, if there is any interest whatsoever in the fibrous plaster of the interior, this interest is extremely limited as is shown by the fact that fewer and fewer people are visiting the cinema. The design of this cinema was undertaken in the early 1930's to create something different to attract the cinema-going public and does not represent seriously an example of any period of architecture. It cannot be looked upon as a national monument nor as a museum – at best it can only be of interest to people who visit it as a cinema to view films. The exterior is below our usual standard, a matter of great regret to us. Needless to say, the property as it at present stands, is no longer viable and unless some form of redevelopment is possible the company will have to give serious consideration to its closure and in that event the 'listing' will be of benefit to no-one and the cinema will merely be an 'edifice' in the centre of Tooting slowly decaying through lack of use. Because of our interest in cinemas we would like to provide facilities to the film-going public, and it would be our intention that upon a redevelopment of the site a modern cinema tailored to a size to meet the present-day requirements of the area would be included. We would also be prepared to try and include an area in our plans, either in the new cinema or in an exhibition area on the site, for showing objects of interest from the present cinema. I would ask you to give this letter your consideration and hope you will agree that this building should not be put upon the statutory list."

The following month, the Department of the Environment responded by listing the Granada Tooting – not just Grade II but the much rarer Grade II* – and noted that it was "considered, for its interior, probably the finest example in England of a super cinema".

In August 1972, Bernstein visited the Granada Tooting and provided his customary list of points needing attention. "The lights in the Hall of Mirrors varied in colour", he noted, still instinctively concerned with keeping the place in tiptop shape.

In October 1972, Bernstein and others visited Wandsworth officials including the Town Clerk and the Chairman of the Planning Committee. Attention focussed on the idea of redeveloping part of the site to compensate Granada for the financial loss in retaining the auditorium. At a further meeting with officials of the Council in February 1973, Elsom, Pack and Roberts presented drawings for a twelve-floor office block on the site of the entrance foyer, leaving the main auditorium and car park intact. Parts of the foyer nearest the auditorium could also be retained in an adapted form. Wandsworth's Director of Technical Services had "no criticism in principle" of the scheme.

* The New Victoria was also listed Grade II*.

Despite the threat to the building, attendances did not improve. It was open full time, with "Junior Cinema" on Saturday mornings at 9.30. On Sunday 17 June 1973 Harold Ramsay returned to the Wurlitzer, being introduced by Robin Richmond, for a separate concert before the regular film programme.

In October 1973 Granada began looking into the implications of closing a listed building. As it happened, the timber and concrete in the canopy had become dangerous. This was removed but not replaced, leaving the steel framework exposed and giving the impression that demolition had started.

The crucial day was Wednesday 7 November, when Sidney Bernstein and company secretary Joe Warton met the chief executive and town clerk of Wandsworth, N. B. White, together with other members and officers of the Council, at 5.45pm. Forty-five minutes before that, two head office officials informed the manager of the Granada, Roger Howell, and three other senior staff in strict confidence that the cinema would be closing shortly. A head office memo indicates that it was proposed to close the Granada on the following Saturday.

And, indeed, on that Saturday, 10 November 1973, four days after the meeting with Wandsworth Borough Council, the Granada was closed without notice. Its last attraction was the Rank circuit release *The Man Called Noon* plus a re-run of *Perfect Friday*. A revival of *The Good, The Bad And The Ugly* had been advertised in the local press as showing from the following day (with a special Wednesday afternoon programme of Walt Disney films and cartoons after a Royal Wedding). The double bill of *White Lightning* and *Harry In Your Pocket* was then advertised in the papers for Sunday 18 November and week. But patrons arrived to find displays reading "Due to lack of public support this cinema is now closed". While perfectly true, this was in sharp contrast to the expressions of regret and thanks for past patronage that was customary on these occasions, at least from other circuits.

The projectors were promptly removed, although the seats and organ were left. A security firm was employed to check the building regularly at a cost of £55 per week.

In January 1974, Granada learned that listed building consent would not be given for any redevelopment of the foyer space as offices.

Fierce criticism of the closure was voiced in the local press as it reported the views of action groups and others who often directed their attacks at Sidney Bernstein rather than Granada. One campaign led by Action for the Community in Tooting (ACT) wanted the building to become a cultural and community centre. Bernstein was so irked by the attacks on himself that he sought the professional advice of the eminent lawyer Lord Goodman over whether he should complain to the Press Council.

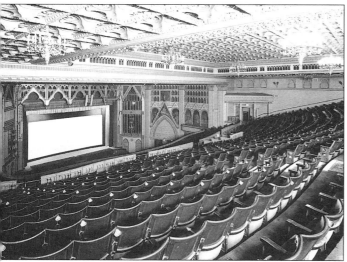

The Granada Tooting still looked good in its final years as a cinema. Exterior dates from 13 April 1969. Auditorium view, if correctly dated (24 January 1974), was taken after closure. (Photo Coverage.) An unusual notice was displayed outside in November 1973. (Photograph by Allen Eyles.)

Lord Goodman considered that Bernstein was being libelled but advised against taking action.

In June 1974, the GLC insisted, on behalf of the Historic Buildings Board, that the canopy be reinstated. Granada did not agree that the canopy was a permanent part of the building, any more than it was prepared to accept that the organ was an integral feature.

Time passed with matters seeming at a stalemate until at some point Granada began to consider bingo, perhaps after a proposal by Ladbroke's to convert the ABC Tooting was dropped. Granada submitted a planning application for bingo to Wandsworth Council on 22 August 1975.

Listed building consent for the plans was given on 21 April 1976. Granada was allowed to place a temporary flat floor over the stalls and orchestra pit and put the stalls seats in storage along with redundant metal standards and handrails which had to be carefully numbered.

Granada spent £400,000 before the re-opening of the Tooting building as a bingo hall on Thursday 14 October 1976, extolling its unique atmosphere, which had suddenly become an asset again. As a bingo club, the building had a capacity of 2,600 (compared to 2,877 seats in its final days as a cinema). Nearly 20,000 members enrolled for bingo before the first day. The *Evening Standard* welcomed the building back in its editorial column. By the end of the decade, membership exceeded 100,000 and annual admissions were 750,000.

The Granada became the most successful bingo club in the country, in 1993 achieving admissions of 10-11,000 per week and as many as 2,300 on a single evening – a happy ending that few could have predicted when it closed down as a cinema.

And Woolwich too

Granada had a further shock in January 1974 when, without prior warning, the Woolwich theatre became a listed building like its big sister at Tooting. Granada's company secretary wrote to the Department of the Environment seeking to appeal against the listing and wondering whether its change of use from cinema to bingo and subsequent alterations had been noticed. A complaint was sent to the local planning committee in the London Borough of Greenwich.

Granada had no joy at all. The DoE replied that "there is no provision in the legislation for a right of appeal against listing as such because the listing of a building in no way implies that any decision has been made about its future", pointing out that, if permission for any future development proposals were denied, a right of appeal did exist and could include the argument that the building was not of special architectural or historic interest and should cease to be listed. Greenwich's planning committee

informed Granada that the listing of a building was a distinction and very seldom indeed were objections received, while it was the standard of design and not the use of the property which counted.

But the Woolwich Granada was well established as a bingo hall and the listing had no serious repercussions.

Yet more bingo

A surviving record for the fifty-one weeks up to 21 September 1974 gives an indication of the relative performance of the twenty-two Granada bingo clubs, which as a whole were doing markedly better than the previous year. Kennington drew the most admissions (368,763) for the second year running, followed in order by Wakefield (not a former cinema), Stratford, Slough (Adelphi), Maidstone, Mansfield, Enfield, Woolwich, Aylesbury, Shrewsbury, Brixton, Willesden, Greenwich, Barnsley (not a former cinema and not open the full year), Rugby, Thornton Heath, Grantham, Acton, Pitsea, Oswestry, Leytonstone and, last for the second year in succession, Wandsworth Road (with 95,483 admissions).

Films were abandoned at the Granada East Ham in November 1974. It had struggled on, closed on Mondays and Tuesdays in its last few months, still with one-night stage shows about once a month. Granada had decided to convert to bingo in 1973, despite the competition of the Top Rank Club, but both a gaming licence and change of use application had been refused. The gaming licence came through later in the year, but permission for change of use took longer. After films ceased, it continued on occasional live shows and Sunday Indian cinema for more than a year before bingo could finally be introduced in January 1976.

1974 also saw the demise of the Granada Leytonstone and the Granada-built Gaumont Manchester. Leytonstone simply closed and was later demolished. At Manchester, Rank had twinned the Odeon and also owned the small New Oxford, both close by. Its Gaumont became superfluous and was sold off, with the stalls eventually becoming a nightclub.

In 1975, bingo took over at Kettering. The Granada had received a modest £5,500 worth of modernisation in January 1973 with new projectors, a transistorised sound system and a new 42 ft. wide screen which was installed overnight. When head office sought a bingo licence the very next month, it was stated to be merely a "protective move" and Star, owners of the town's existing bingo club (in the stalls area of the former Savoy cinema), managed to have the application turned down on a technicality.

In May 1974, the gambling licensing committee refused a further bingo application on the grounds that the existing facilities were sufficient. Managing director Charles Stringer declared that the company would appeal against the refusal and

The Granada Dartford, long before bingo. The tilework seen here on the exterior (taken 14 October 1954) was later replaced with the vertical neon tubes removed. Auditorium view (from November 1962) shows standard circuit light fittings as well as the organ console. (Photo Coverage.)

that the Granada would close anyway as it was no longer profitable. He cited attendances in a four-week period as now being around 9,000 and falling, compared to an average of 23,000 in 1964/65. The town had two other small cinemas, Studio 1 & 2, in the circle of the old Savoy but this was nowhere near as centrally located as the Granada.

The Kettering Granada closed as promised, on 8 June 1974. It had still presented live shows approximately once a month – the last was Alvin Stardust on Saturday 11 May. Eight months later it was able to re-open for bingo.

Granada had been attempting to turn Dartford over to bingo and appealed successfully against refusal of permission aimed at keeping the building open on films. In 1975, Dartford became another place without any cinema at all.

The Granada Oswestry clung on until June 1975. The company had already installed bingo at the Century, which was slightly larger than the Granada in capacity, so there was no reason to shift it. The cinema sat disused for several months after closure, until – uniquely for a Granada property – it was re-opened for films by an independent who restored the original Regal name and eventually converted it to two- and then three-screen operation. (As the Regal, it ran for another eighteen years, finally closing in 1994.)

Sutton had remained a single screen partly because the rival Star circuit had nipped in and subdivided the small Curzon into three screens, renamed Studio 1, 2 and 3. At one time this Granada had been threatened with a compulsory purchase order for a road development scheme but it had been re-arranged, sparing the theatre. From 1968, Granada had entertained ambitions to carry out a huge development scheme covering the cinema site and Council land, including a new 500-seat cinema with a possible second cinema underneath, but the local authority never seemed particularly keen.

In 1974, Granada decided to pursue a conversion to bingo and appealed after being refused permission in June. (The large Top Rank Club at nearby Rose Hill had opposed the change of use.) At the same time, Granada also considered turning the stage into offices and a showroom and investigated the cost of converting the auditorium to a triple screen operation.

Matters drifted until August 1975 when the cinema was closed by a fire which caused much damage to the stage and sound system. Company legend has it that someone phoned Sidney Bernstein to tell him, "We've sent for the fire brigade", and Sidney is supposed to have responded: "Why?"

Granada maintained that the Sutton theatre had been operating at less than one per cent of capacity, with an average attendance of 173. Company secretary Joe Warton was advised by the Borough of Sutton that there was no chance of bingo being approved nor of office development being allowed. Granada tried to win the

Council over by offering to enlarge the car park and convert the restaurant into a cinema as per the plans drawn up in 1971 by George Coles.

Permission was eventually granted for bingo on a fourth application in December 1976 but in the end the entire building was demolished and replaced by an office block, despite the town's need for a theatre which the Granada would have fulfilled admirably, as demonstrated by its history as a live venue. (In fact, the Granada had hosted a midnight charity show on Friday 5 March 1971 for the Sutton Theatre Appeal for general equipment, which was attended by over 2,000 people and ended at 3.45am. At this time, it was proposed to build a Sutton Civic Theatre in Nicholas Road as part of a new complex. In the end, a church was converted into the thoroughly inadequate Secombe Centre.)

In 1976, it was the Granada Rugby's turn to succumb to bingo. The last subdivision scheme that had been considered, in March 1974, would have turned the building into a bingo hall with a smaller cinema at a cost of approximately £120,000. At the end of 1975, films had sunk to only 100 admissions on average per performance and Granada decided to seek a bingo licence for the entire building. When this was granted, members transferred from the existing club in the smaller Century (which was then sold off to become a supermarket).

East Ham, Rugby and Sutton were the last theatres equipped for live use. Bingo now became the only live show at Granadas – a poor substitute for decades of concerts, variety, live theatre, opera and pantomimes. Proper live shows could not be allowed to interrupt the bingo sessions, although the clubs would occasionally host free cabaret appearances by well-known artistes as a promotional device.

The last theatre targeted for bingo conversion in this period was the Granada Bishop's Stortford. As elsewhere, there had been a long-running battle to overcome local objections to the loss of the town's only cinema but it closed in 1977 for a new life on bingo that lasted five years before the site was sold to Marks and Spencer for a new store.

Granada were looking at other company's cinemas for its bingo chain. In October 1977, it made an offer of £250,000 for the closed ABC Wembley subject to bingo being allowed and had prepared a provisional conversion scheme before applying for a licence in August 1978. This was refused and the cinema was re-opened (briefly) on Indian films.

Bingo expansion did bring several former cinemas from outside the circuit into the net, some previously operated by the three major circuits. These included the Odeon at Bournemouth and the Savoy/Gaumont/Classic at Leyton, both from late 1979, and the ABC Bedminster, Bristol, around the same time.

The Grand Wellington had an old-fashioned exterior but a streamlined, single floor Thirties auditorium. Bingo conversion destroyed all the ante-proscenium decoration.
Both photographs date from 30 April 1975, a few weeks after the Granada take-over. (Photo Coverage.)

Against the Tide

In December 1973, Granada made two unlikely additions to its cinema circuit. It acquired the Florida Enfield and Rex East Finchley from J. W. Davies' British Cinematograph Theatres for £185,000. The Florida cost £120,000 and the Rex £64,000, with £1,000 paid for fixtures and fittings.

Bob Morgan has a likely explanation for why Granada were interested in these small single-screen buildings. "J. W. [Davies] was a friend of Cecil's. They both played the organ. When he was going on holiday for a month, he asked me to look after them. I said, 'I can't do that because of the terms of my contract with Granada. You'll have to have a word with your friend Cecil.' And Cecil called me: 'Of course you can. What are you thinking of?'

"At East Finchley, I had to fight to get the policy I wanted in there. Sidney, Cecil, Joe Warton – the old guard – they wanted to play the Rank release. I said, 'It's not that kind of area.' There was a violent argument. It turned quite nasty at times. Then Cecil said go ahead and we never did really play the Rank release."

There is a hint that the Florida might have been going over to bingo, which would have been unwelcome competition for the Granada club at Enfield.

The two buildings continued to be operated as cinemas, and Sidney Bernstein wondered in February 1974 whether the Rex should be renamed Granada. In 1975 they were described as not reaching "Granada standard" but both operated profitably, Enfield contributing £8,978 and Finchley £3,000 in 1974/75. The Rex was sold as a going concern in November 1975 (and has survived as an independent semi-art house called the Phoenix) while the Florida was closed in June 1976 and has since been heavily converted for banqueting and other uses.

Granada also took over the Grand cinema at Wellington, Shropshire, apparently as a going concern. However, this shortly passed over to the eyes-down brigade.

In June 1979, Granada acquired H.C. Orr's Orr Enterprises, primarily for its bingo halls, rejecting the Theatre One cinema complex at Coventry because it had no regular circuit release. This group included an entertainment complex at Morecambe, Lancashire. A closed bowling alley and nightclub were rapidly re-opened as a Granada bingo club. Part of the package included Morecambe's four-screen Empire cinema and the single-screen Arcadian (with 70mm facilities). They remained open but were not viewed with great enthusiasm. In December, an internal memo regarding the Empire noted: "We have so far kept the four cinemas operating, but this is subject to regular review."

A lost opportunity

In 1978, Milton Keynes Development Corporation had earmarked a site in the new town for leisure and was seeking a developer. On 5 January 1979 Granada submitted a bid to build an entertainment complex. Granada's priority was clear: "You will note that the largest single space allocation is for the bingo club, without which the overall scheme would not be viable." The proposed club would occupy 2,000 square metres and seat 1,200-1,400 people. There was to be a three-screen cinema occupying half the space of the bingo hall, seating 250 in two auditoria and 100 in the third. A nightclub, discotheque, squash club, public house, restaurant and fast food area, fun palace, and leisure retail area were also included.

In November 1979, Milton Keynes pressed Granada for firm development proposals. An executive was dispatched from Golden Square to the United States to look at a new "tensile arch" form of construction that might be used at the site. It might be regarded as a pity that the same executive didn't examine the success that multiplexes were having in the United States by then.

When Bass Leisure won the contract to provide the leisure facilities, it knew exactly what was needed on the cinema front but couldn't find any British company that shared its vision. So Bass went to the pioneers of the American multiplex, American Multi-Cinema, who delivered Britain's first multiplex, giving the modern American chains their first toehold in British exhibition.

19 • The Eighties

At the end of September 1979, Sidney Bernstein finally relinquished power. He retired as chairman, accepting the honorary position of president of the Granada Group. He was succeeded by Alex, the son of Cecil Bernstein. Cecil died on 18 June 1981 and Sidney was never the same after that: he sometimes attended Group board meetings but he was no longer needed, his opinions no longer counted (he objected in vain to the 1982 sale of Granada Publishing).

Granada entered the Eighties with just ten cinemas still functioning, plus the recent, unsought and shortlived additions of the Empire and Arcadian at Morecambe.

There were still occasional sparks of the old Barnum spirit. Late in 1981, John Platford remembers playing the organ for a preview of *An American Werewolf In London* at the Granada Kingston wearing a gorilla mask (since a werewolf one couldn't be found). "After playing in the midnight matinee audience, I turned around to them in my monster mask. Having witnessed the reaction, I took the organ down. A sepulchral figure came onto the stage and blessed the audience that they would not be terror-struck. This event was engineered by Jeff Curtis, the manager."

For the year ending 29 September 1979, Bedford and then Slough were by far the most lucrative theatres. Next came (in order of profitability) Kingston, Walthamstow, Maidstone, Welling, Harrow, Clapham Junction, Shrewsbury (Empire) and Chichester.

The company then operated thirty-three bingo sites, all making money. The most profitable was Tooting, very closely followed by East Ham (before deducting the cost of major repairs, East Ham was £643 ahead of Tooting). Then came Wakefield and Barnsley (neither ex-cinemas), followed by Maidstone (the stalls area of the Granada), Dartford, Morecambe (the 1978 acquisition), Enfield, Slough (Adelphi), Kennington, Kettering, Acton, Woolwich, Stratford, Aylesbury, Rugby, Villa Park (not an ex-cinema), Greenwich, Mansfield, Shrewsbury and Pitsea. Weak performers were Thornton Heath, Brixton, Bishop's Stortford, Crystal Palace (Upper Norwood) and Welling-ton (former Grand). Willesden and Leytonstone (Century) were the worst. (The year's profits of some sites including Grantham, Leytonstone and Willesden were badly dented by major repairs. Recent additions at Bournemouth, Leyton, Leamington Spa and Morecambe are excluded.)

There would be further additions of former cinemas. The purchase of Lion Leisure in 1985 resulted in the return of the Granada name at Hove: the building here had, of course, never been a "real" Granada but now, belatedly, it was. The same deal also brought in the Plaza Worthing. In 1985, Granada acquired the very first Odeon at Perry Barr, Birmingham; the former Gaumont Wednesbury; and the former Plaza/Gaumont Southsea. All three had been renamed Granada clubs by November of that year. Also in 1985, Granada took over the closed ABC Ilford (but bingo here was shortlived) and the large Moderne at Winton, Bournemouth.

Among the cinemas, the Granada Chichester and Empire Shrewsbury were still both single-screen operations. The Granada Chichester had been the only cinema in the West Sussex town since 1960, playing the pick of the new releases. It seated 820 in a building that was listed for its historic significance as the former Corn Exchange. Both the listing and the shape of the building militated against subdivision into smaller cinemas. By February 1978, Granada had set its mind on conversion to bingo, proposing to spend £120,000 and pointing out that film shows had an average audience of only 123.

When planning permission was refused, Granada appealed and a public inquiry was held in 1979. In November, the Secretary of State for the Environment dismissed the appeal, noting that the Inspector had commented on "the remarkable volume of public protest... mainly voiced through a petition organised and heavily supported by young people", the lack of other public entertainment including alternative cinemas, and suggested that it was "very desirable to retain the existing use for social reasons". This was the only occasion that Granada was unable to overturn a planning decision aimed at retaining cinema use. A councillor and former mayor prominent in the campaign hailed the verdict as a triumph for democracy. Granada had threatened to stop films whatever the outcome, but shows continued for many months. Attendances (with three shows a day) averaged 300-400 per

The Granada Chichester, seen on 18 November 1961.
The cinema was once the Corn Exchange. (Photo Coverage.)

The Granada Clapham Junction, shown on 11 August 1964.
A full view of one of the best Granada exteriors. Note the
Miss Candy shop next to the entrance and the round-headed
vertical sign on the far end of the building. (Photo Coverage.)

day, indicating that most of those petitioners had failed to rally round the cinema.

The final attraction was a four-week engagement of *The Empire Strikes Back*, part of the *Star Wars* trilogy. The long runs and high terms demanded by distributors for hit pictures made life difficult for single-screen cinemas. Most patrons had already seen the film by the end of its run on Saturday 9 August 1980: there were only 300 customers on the last day, 100 at the last performance, although on the preceding Monday (with the help of rain) 1,160 had turned up.

The building remained empty and unused for more than six years and has now been transformed into a McDonalds. A Cinema 100 plaque on the side wall recalls its place in local history as the home of the town's first film shows.

Shrewsbury was more than twice the size of Chichester and the Empire did accordingly better. There was no incentive to turn it over to bingo as the Granada had already been converted for the purpose.

The Granada Clapham Junction was the worst performing triple cinema. Tripling had improved attendances for a couple of years but by 1976 they had dropped to the level of pre-conversion. When figures improved nationally, this Granada also benefited – but only by a four per cent increase in attendances when the average was around twenty-six per cent. Between October 1976 and the end of 1978, attendances in the 935-seat main auditorium had ranged from a high of 7,578 for *Sinbad And The Eye of the Tiger* (40.5% capacity) to a low of 559 for *The Comeback* (3% capacity). Granada maintained that, when headquarters administration costs were taken into account, Clapham had been losing money since 1975/76, putting the 1977/78 deficit at £15,315.

Takings had been affected by the survival of the small independent Ruby cinema which took many hit films that would otherwise have helped the Granada. Once again Granada decided to switch to bingo, even though it would take an estimated 800-1,000 admissions away from Tooting each week. The company was granted a bingo licence in June 1978 but Wandsworth Council refused an application for change of use. An inquiry was held and planning permission granted.

The Granada closed in July 1980 and was converted back to a single auditorium so skilfully that no sign remained of the recent partitioning under the balcony. £200,000 had been allocated for conversion and redecoration. While granting that Clapham Junction was no longer an ideal cinemagoing area, one could still wonder if the cinema might have done better had it been fully refurbished when tripling took place.

Clapham Junction had a substantial amount of former catering space. The café-restaurant had closed in 1940 and the following year the company's tailoring and uniform department had moved in. (Dressing rooms were used as offices by the sales and catering departments from 1945 onwards.) The former café space had been disused since 1960. Sidney Bernstein suggested converting this space to two mini cinemas when bingo was introduced but the idea does not seem to have been taken further.

The Welling Granada had always been a marginal candidate for tripling and it had not worked out as well as hoped. The company did a splendid job of redecorating the entrance hall, which could be enticingly viewed through the tall windows from the street, but the main auditorium was left dirty and uninviting. Welling was restricted to the Rank release by the nearby, better located ABC Bexleyheath which was split up three years after the Granada into four screens and proved very successful, somewhat to the detriment of the Granada. Attendances were also hurt by cable television in the area. At least one application for bingo had been refused and any conversion was complicated by the well established Top Rank Club in the former Odeon round the corner. The Granada Welling closed in July 1983, the site having been sold for demolition.*

In 1982, Granada applied for a bingo licence for the Granada Bedford, intending to close both the cinemas in the building, the only two left in the town. Following the predictable outcry, the company agreed to retain the small cinema and a gaming licence was issued. However, in this instance, no action was taken beyond renewing the licence annually.

The disappearance and alteration of more and more British cinemas had led to many listings. In January 1987 the Cinema Theatre Association successfully urged the spot listing of the tripled Granada Kingston in response to proposed drastic internal alterations. Granada was understandably furious at this last-minute setback to its plans and a compromise was worked out with the listing body which still resulted in the ruination of the main auditorium space. Although too large for audiences of that time, the space was important to preserve as, from the circle, it still gave the full impression of sitting in a vast "standard" Granada auditorium. This upstairs area was turned into a night club with a new floor extending forwards from the balcony and, incredibly, permission was granted for the main chandelier to be relocated in another part of the redevelopment entirely. Although the two mini-cinemas under the balcony were retained and enlarged, the parade of shops alongside the cinema was replaced by a two-floor café-bar with the huge main chandelier suspended from the ceiling and a third small cinema on top.

* Examples of standard light fittings, including a small chandelier from over the balcony, were removed for preservation by the Museum of London at the instigation of this writer with the full co-operation of Granada.

Only the mirrored entrance hall remained in its full glory, after which the three cinemas, called Options, were a distinct anticlimax.

In February 1987, the month following the listing of Kingston, the Granada Walthamstow was listed for its elaborate decoration in Moorish style and for being Komisarjevsky's first London cinema interior. In August 1988, the Granada Harrow was added to the list – in effect replacing Kingston as the "standard" Granada interior to be preserved.

Attack of the Multiplex

Granada was the first of the major British companies to face the direct heat of a multiplex. At Slough, a failed civic leisure centre became the core of an independent ten-screen multiplex right in the town centre which opened to the public under the name Maybox on 6 November 1987. An application to demolish the Granada for an office block was attached to the doors the week the Maybox opened. The manager remained insistent that head office were going to fight on and see which building cinemagoers preferred. The Granada and the Maybox started playing top attractions at the same time, putting the latest instalment of *Nightmare On Elm Street* on their largest screens. The Granada's forthcoming programmes, advertised in the foyer, extended to a Christmas revival of *Snow White And The Seven Dwarfs*. Yet, very abruptly, with programmes booked and advertised for the week (including *Creepshow 2*, also at the Maybox) and before the novelty of the new cinema had had a chance to wear off, the Granada was shut after the last performance on Thursday 19 November. Someone at head office seems to have pulled the plug on the spur of the moment.

Did the Granada have any future with the Maybox in town? Probably not, although the Maybox was a rather unsatisfactory and off-putting conversion. Granada could have afforded more time to find out.

The same problem arose at Bedford. A site had been earmarked near the town centre for a multiplex. The Granada was sold to a development company, then leased back until the site was actually needed.

Head office did toy with the idea of opening multiplexes. "I knew of the Bedford site when I was there, and there was talk of Granada being involved," recalls Bob Morgan, who left the company in 1988 at the time a new managing director took over. "There was a lot of debate as to whether Granada should go into the multiplex [era] but, from memory, nobody was particularly keen."

"They went through the motions that we were going to go into multiplexes", concurs Ivan Cluley, Morgan's successor in film booking. "I spent time looking at sites, a lot of which have actually come to fruition. I remember going to Preston and places

At Kingston, Granada replaced the row of shops with a two-storey café-bar that housed the old auditorium chandelier and renamed the building Options. The C&A store seen at right replaced the old Century Elite. (23 October 1988 photograph by Allen Eyles.)

The Granada Bedford becomes a Cannon cinema for its last months of operation. (Photograph by David Trevor-Jones.)

like that. But they weren't interested in cinemas. We were just an afterthought.".

The booking department at head office was closed. "I just worked from home on my own", Ivan Cluley recalls, "and it was pretty obvious that it was only a matter of time before they finally unloaded the remaining cinemas."

"We cannibalised the cinema circuit in two ways", reflects Alex Bernstein today. "One was to open the bingo clubs and the other was to sell them to property developers or develop them ourselves. We were left with half a dozen cinemas and it was ridiculous, so it was a pure commercial decision to sell."

A recent and voracious arrival on the British exhibition scene, Cannon, had taken over the Classic and ABC circuits and now made an extravagant offer of £3.3 million for the Granada cinemas, pipping another contender (said to have been Odeon) at the post. In January 1989 Cannon acquired the Granadas at Maidstone, Walthamstow and Harrow, the Options part of the Kingston conversion, and the Empire Shrewsbury, also taking over the Granada Bedford for what was left of its life. The Granada name was replaced with that of Cannon – a major indignity for the distinguished buildings at Walthamstow, Harrow and Bedford. (At Maidstone, the Granada name survived in the side road, Granada Street, and at the office building on the opposite corner, called Granada House.)

Cannon also purchased the multiplex scheme in Bedford (along with others) from Gallery, the short-lived British subsidiary of the Canadian Cineplex Odeon company. The former Granada Bedford closed in December 1990 before the Cannon multiplex had opened.

The Granada Walthamstow. Auditorium view dates from 29 January 1982. September 1996 views show the redecorated foyer and the entrance to the balcony with a new false wall at left which narrows the rear section. (All taken by Allen Eyles.)

20 • Life After Granada

A little over two years after the remaining cinemas had left the fold, the bingo clubs were also sold – but in rather different circumstances.

"We had financial problems at the time and a tremendous amount of money tied up in satellite broadcasting before it became good, and we simply wanted to get cash", recalls Alex Bernstein. "We didn't have any sentiment about bingo. We talked for a long time with Bass about forming a joint company because they had a bingo chain. In the end we felt a joint company wasn't right and they made a very good offer, so that's how we got out of the business." The Granada clubs were sold for £147 million in May 1991 to Bass, which added them to its Gala chain and renamed them.

On 5 February 1993, Sidney Bernstein, Lord Bernstein of Leigh, passed away. His final years were blighted by senility. "Sidney had gone long before he died," Denis Forman declares in *Persona Granada*.

Granada continues as a major company in 1998 but its commercial director Graham Parrott confirms, "We no longer have any freehold or leasehold interests in any of the sites formerly comprising the cinema or bingo business of Granada."

Only in one small respect does the present Granada company retain a visible link to its cinema past. The baronial entrance hall at Tooting has been broadly reproduced within the Granada Studio Tour at Manchester as a waiting area for visitors, with panels recalling the circuit's history and the work of Theodore Komisarjevsky and with the cinema organ from the former Granada/Gaumont Manchester to entertain the crowds.

Granada makes films from time to time, mostly through a television subsidiary, Granada Films, in partnership with other producers and backers.* These have usually been of the low-budget kind more seen on television than in the cinema. The

company's interest in film production has accelerated recently: in 1997, it was financially involved in the making of *Captain Jack, Girls' Night, Heart, The Misadventures of Margaret* and *Rogue Trader*. In 1998, it is talking about making bigger budget films.

In the hands of new owners, the estate of Granada bingo halls and cinemas has been whittled down as a response to market conditions.

Profits at the Gala chain of bingo clubs fell from £31 million in the 1995-96 year to £24 million in 1996-97. Bingo was hurt by the success of the National Lottery and then by the arrival of lottery scratch cards. In addition, purpose-built clubs and conversions of failed retail warehouses began replacing converted cinemas: they were cheaper to run, usually being on a single flat floor with improved scope for restaurant and bar facilities. Outside, they could often offer better and safer parking facilities, attracting younger players.

By 1994, the former Century Stratford had given way to a new and far more appealing Gala club, better located near the station. The old building has now been demolished for housing. The club at the former Granada Kennington, once among the most successful of bingo halls, had survived a threat of compulsory purchase by the Council for a comprehensive redevelopment scheme of the area some years before, but it closed very abruptly in 1997, apparently to clear the way for a new bingo hall at the Elephant and Castle. (Like Stratford, it had been heavily altered over the years and lost all its cinema atmosphere.) Since closure, the Council have apparently decided they would rather like to keep the building as part of a conservation area. Enfield also closed in 1997.

More recently, Bass sold the Gala bingo division of 130 clubs to a management buy-out led by John Kelly for £279 million in cash. Kelly was a former Granada cinema manager at Maidstone before going over to the bingo side. The change-over took place

* Granada Film Productions made an Irish drama *Joyriders* and thriller *Tree of Hands* in 1988. Granada Film Finance Corporation made *The Fruit Machine* (1988), produced by Steve Morrison. Granada Films, headed by Morrison, backed another Irish drama, *The Field* (1990), starring Richard Harris; the David Hare film *Strapless* (1990); the Richard E. Grant comedy *Jack & Sarah* (1995); and *August* (1996), a version of *Uncle Vanya* starring Anthony Hopkins (who also directed).

on Monday 15 December 1997, but one club was left out of the deal – the former Granada at Clapham Junction. This was closed "due to unforeseen circumstances" on the night before, with the staff only being notified prior to the evening session and club members being informed after the final game. According to a press report, the club had been "at a low ebb" a year earlier but attendances had apparently recovered, although staff were poised for a possible shut-down in January 1998.

Although the building was made secure, it was broken into and used for a rave at Christmas, during which time some foyer mirrors and one of the smaller chandeliers are reported to have been damaged.

Conservationists immediately initiated moves to save the building in case redevelopment of the site was behind its closure. The building was eventually listed in May 1998.

At the time of writing, Gala clubs are still operating in the former original Granadas at Tooting, Woolwich, East Ham and Shrewsbury; and in later Granadas at Acton, Aylesbury, Dartford, Kettering, Thornton Heath and Upper Norwood, as well as in the former Adelphi Slough and Century Pitsea.

● ● ● ●

The Cannon chain with its handful of former Granada cinemas became Metro-Goldwyn-Mayer or MGM Cinemas. The Maidstone cinemas took the MGM name, but the others were left as Cannons, normally indicating second-rank status. However, at Walthamstow, some £200,000 was spent to reduce the size of the balcony, installing 592 new seats in place of 900 old ones. As this was a listed building, the work was done with some care and is reversible. A new concessions counter also of more sympathetic design was introduced in the foyer. Despite all this effort, attendances remained about the same.

After Virgin acquired the MGM chain in July 1995, it decided to concentrate on the multiplexes and a few of the traditional cinemas. The remainder were taken over by the new ABC Cinemas in May 1996. The former Granadas at Harrow and Walthamstow, the cinema sections of the former Granadas at Kingston and Maidstone, and the former Empire Shrewsbury all became ABCs.

At Harrow, the arrival of a new Warner multiplex within the town centre shopping mall quickly resulted in the closure of the ABC, which had attempted to compete with the same films. On the final evening of 7 November 1996 the organ was played before and after the final performance of *Brassed Off* in the main auditorium. The car park was sold off and a Halfords store has been erected on part of the site, with the rest as parking space for its customers. Permission to turn the building into a Chicago Rock Café has been refused. Harrow has identified a need in the future for two theatres, one seating 300 and another of larger size: it could have had a flexible size theatre in the former Granada as it stands, using the front stalls with the balcony for overflow or larger events, and running the existing mini-auditoria under the balcony as specialised cinemas, which are lacking in the area (although the rake would have to be improved). Excuses were trotted out: no money, no flytower, no car park, huge upkeep. Admittedly, the loss of the car park is a major setback to its continued use. But somehow, in equivalent American towns, buildings like this have been held in such affection that the will has been there to convert them into multi-purpose community centres.

At Shrewsbury, the ABC closed on 22 January 1998, leaving the town with only a 100-seat cinema in an arts complex until a new multiplex under construction finally opens. To the surprise of many, the Empire had not been badly affected by the opening of the UCI multiplex at Telford some years earlier, but the economics of operating a single screen are difficult. A new purpose-built bingo club is also opening in Shrewsbury shortly. There is hope that this might release the listed ex-Granada from its twenty-five years of bingo servitude to become a live theatre (with, one hopes, restoration of its original light fittings and facilities to present the occasional special film show).

The Granadas at Kingston and Maidstone still have ABC cinemas within their butchered interiors and Kingston at least has its Komisarjevsky-decorated entrance hall, chandelier in the café, and close-up views of the cornice friezes in the nightclub (light levels permitting). But an Odeon multiplex opens this year in Maidstone, half a mile away from the former Granada, and Kingston is expected to receive a purpose-built multiplex within a few years.

Only the ABC Walthamstow remains open at the time of writing as a largely unaltered Granada still showing films, its largest auditorium in the balcony displaying original 1930 Komisarjevsky decoration. In the words of ABC executive Alan McCann in April 1998, "It is performing quite well. It does have its own audience which remains loyal. We have no plans to dispose of Walthamstow unless somebody builds a multiplex within half a mile."

The Granada Tooting, still a palace of splendour in March 1983....

....after its re-opening as a bingo hall. (Both by Allen Eyles.)

21 • A Little Live Music – The Granada Organs

By Tony Moss

There is no doubt that Sidney Bernstein was very much influenced in the matter of cinema presentation by his two visits to the USA, in particular the one in 1927 when he met Samuel Rothafel ("Roxy") and witnessed performances at Roxy's super cinema – the Roxy, New York.

He was not so impressed with the film fare and said to a reporter on his return: "Never have I seen such rubbish presented in such ornate surroundings. It isn't the picture which draws the public but the cinema..."

He did not fail to notice and be impressed by the Roxy orchestra of 110 musicians, its stage show of dancing girls and – perhaps most impressive of all – the Kimball theatre organ with three organ consoles played by organists in green velvet smoking jackets.

That year – 1927 – was when Sidney Bernsten set out rebuilding or refurbishing five cinemas. The Rialto Leytonstone re-opened on 6 January with a theatre pipe organ built by Compton, the only organ of that manufacture ever ordered by Bernstein/Granada (although others were inherited in theatres acquired by the circuit). It is possible that the organ was being evaluated against other British makes but it must be significant that no other Comptons were ordered.

At first the Leytonstone organ was only a two-manual instrument but it was rebuilt in 1931 with eight ranks of pipes and a three-keyboard French-style console. Alex Taylor from the Granada Tooting made guest appearances from 1931 to 1932 and Harold Ramsay made similar guest appearances from 1933 to 1934. Resident in 1939 were Ronald Hanmer, who later specialised in composition and arrangement (especially musical comedies), and Cyril Gell. The organ was removed from the Rialto/Granada in 1973 and reinstalled at St. Mary's R. C. Church, Hornchurch.

When the Empire Edmonton began its new lease of life as a cinema on Easter Monday 1927, the organ chosen was a two-manual Christie from the firm of Hill, Norman & Beard. William Hill & Son had merged with Norman & Beard in 1916 and ten years later opened a factory to build theatre organs under the name of their chairman, John Christie of Glyndebourne, the driving force behind their decision to enter the British market.

As at Leytonstone, the organ was opened by Bruce Wendell James, who later appeared at the Leicester Square Theatre and Princes Shaftesbury Avenue. The Christie at Edmonton did not last long as when the theatre was reconstructed in 1933 it was replaced by a Wurlitzer of ten ranks and a "phantom" piano, opened by a well-known visiting organist from the USA, Don Baker. (The phantom piano is a grand piano connected to and playable from the organ console, with the keys apparently played by an invisible performer.) The Wurlitzer was removed in 1969 and has now a new lease of life at the St. Albans Organ Museum.

Sidney was obviously pleased with the Christie at Edmonton as the publicity leaflet for the re-opening of the Rialto Enfield after rebuilding announced a "new wonder organ, built by Messrs. Norman & Beard, Organ Builders to the King, to contain 2,800 pipes and 35 miles of wire. The distance from Enfield to Southend."

The organ at Enfield was a two-manual one with seven ranks of pipes, replacing a "straight" church-type instrument by Jones of London. In 1935, the Christie was rebuilt to three manuals and nine ranks with a much more impressive "French style" console, and re-opened by Harold Ramsay, who had joined Granada at Tooting in 1932 from Paramount in the USA.

After reconstruction, the Empire Willesden re-opened on 27 October 1927 with, again, a 2/7 Christie organ. This was the third and last organ opened for Sidney Bernstein by Bruce Wendell James. In 1934, the organ was rebuilt to three manuals and nine ranks with a large French-style console, similar in treatment to that at Enfield. Again, the re-opening was by Harold Ramsay.

Towards the end of 1928, the Empire East Ham was refurbished, and in 1929 a 5-rank Christie was opened by George Francis Somes, who had performed the same function at the Rialto Enfield and had come from Harry Yapp's Putney Palace. The East Ham Christie had divided pipework on both sides of the proscenium and the console differed from the previous ones in that it had a dummy third keyboard. It had a short life, as it was removed after seven years when the cinema was rebuilt and was probably broken down and re-used by the organ builders.

In 1934, an accomplished dance pianist, Donald Thorne, joined Granada following appearances at the Savoy, Berkeley and Claridge's and work as an arranger to Jack Hylton, Jack Payne, Henry Hall, Roy Fox, Debroy Somers, Carroll Gibbons and the Starita brothers. Such an outstanding musician could not fail to be a shining light on the circuit and he was soon broadcasting from Granada theatres and recording at both Willesden and Clapham Junction.

In the last reconstruction in 1927, the Empire West Ham reopened as the Kinema on 14 November. The Christie organ was similar to that at Enfield and Willesden and, like those, was rebuilt to a 3/9 with a large French-style console in 1935.

When, fortified by his second visit to New York, Bernstein started building luxury cinemas, a Christie organ was chosen for the first at Dover – apparently Sidney was well satisfied with that make. Again the Christie was a 2/7 instrument, but this time the console looked more impressive with an apparent extra keyboard which on close inspection proved to be a dummy. The console was richly decorated in Japanese lacquer. In addition to Hedley Morton at the organ, the opening programme on 8 January 1930 included Leonardi & His Band with four variety acts. Sidney Amos reigned at the organ from 1932 until 1937, two years after ABC took over. In the early Fifties the ABC touring team of organists occasionally visited, e.g. Hubert Selby, but the organ was removed in the later Fifties and broken down.

For the next Granada at Walthamstow, the organ was again a Christie but a superb one of twelve ranks of pipes (above the stage) and with two attractive identical consoles, one on a lift and the other on a mobile dolly on stage. Such a good instrument required a good player, and a pioneer Wurlitzer organist with experience at the New Gallery Regent Street, and at principal cinemas in Glasgow, Leicester and Birmingham, was selected to preside at the opening – Charles Willis. José Bradley joined him, at the stage console, and they were together billed on the canopy of the incomplete frontage as "Mr. and Miss Smith".

Another well-known organist followed in 1931 – Frank Matthew from the Regent Bristol – and from the mid-Thirties until 1956 the Granada was regularly visited by the touring team. After some years of little use, the organ was restored by the Cinema Organ Society and is now regularly used for concerts – the last Christie in an operating cinema. Only the stage console can be featured as the pit has been covered by an apron stage since the Sixties. In September 1990, the organ was featured for the theatre's 60th anniversary with the International Organist of the Year, Mark Aston, at the console.

One might imagine that for the Bernstein showpiece, the

Granada Tooting, a special organ would be ordered. And one would be right! The Bernsteins splashed out with a second-hand Wurlitzer from Sacramento, California, originally an organ of ten ranks, rebuilt and enlarged to fourteen ranks and with a French-style four-manual console. The pipework was contained in under-stage chambers and there was a phantom grand piano on stage. The result was a magnificent Wurlitzer, the like of which had never been heard in the UK and it remains as perhaps the finest quality instrument we have had, certainly on the Granada circuit.

Alex Taylor came to open the Wurlitzer from Davis' Theatre Croydon, but he left to open the Elephant and Castle cinema in 1932. His replacement was first billed around Tooting as "MrX", an inspired piece of publicity (of a kind the circuit had always been good at). Mr. X proved to be one Harold Ramsay, an Englishman who had emigrated at an early age to the USA and who began his career at the Rivoli New York and had toured USA for Paramount since 1926.

Ramsay had earlier appeared as Mr. X at Walthamstow and, arriving at Tooting in December 1932, his incredible showmanship and style (in every sense) ensured his great popularity. Ramsay remained with Granada until 1936, when he moved to Union Cinemas as musical director, later controller of entertainment. His influence on the organ policy of Granada and (even more) Union did wonders for the theatre organ in the UK and lovers of the instrument owe him a great debt.

In 1933 he toured the circuit with his "Eight Piano Symphony" and, in 1934, with the "Rhythm Symphony Orchestra" which included some Gaumont-British theatres and Davis' Theatre Croydon. On his advice, a second tibbia and a gamba (strong string) were added to the original twelve ranks at Tooting in 1933. In 1935 he appeared at Radiolympia playing the first Compton electronic organ and in 1936 took part in the opening of the new BBC Theatre Organ at Langham Place. He was a prolific broadcaster and recording artist, called upon to open new organs throughout the UK.

In July 1973, Tooting suffered a cloudburst and the organ was badly damaged by flooding. However, it has been fully restored by the London Chapter of the American Theatre Organ Society and is in 100% playing condition. However, at the time of writing, both organ and console are buried beneath the bingo tables and the organ cannot be properly heard.

On 30 January 1933, the Plaza Rugby, in which the Bernsteins had some involvement, opened. Its Christie of eight ranks was opened by the famous Reginald Foort, who had made his name from broadcasts and recordings at the New Gallery and Regal Marble Arch, and Frank Newman, another fine broadcaster from Lozell's Birmingham. In fact, Newman made his first broadcast from Rugby on 18 January 1933, a fortnight before the theatre

The Phoenix Theatre, where Theodore Komisarjevsky developed many aspects of the standard Granada style, including the auditorium chandelier. (August 1982 and April 1997 views by Allen Eyles.)

The standard Granada, as seen at Harrow where the side wall grillework was specially illuminated after tripling. The main chandelier was not put on at this time but it did light up in later years. (April 1982 and July 1989 views by Allen Eyles.)

opened! The Plaza closed in favour of bingo as the Granada in 1976, at which time the organ was removed to a house somewhere in deepest Lincolnshire.

I have already noted that a Wurlitzer was installed at the Edmonton Empire in 1933 but the new Granada which opened at Maidstone on 10 January 1934 had a Christie, the last for the circuit, opened by Alex Taylor. It was an eight-rank instrument with the large three-manual French-style console, similar to the rebuilds at Enfield, Willesden and West Ham. After the theatre was badly flooded in 1968 and prior to its break-up into a complex, the organ was removed in 1970 and emigrated to Australia!

The only Granada to be built without an organ opened at Shrewsbury in 1934 while the last to open that year, at Bedford on 15 December, had the first of the standard Granada Wurlitzers - first batch. Shipped from the Wurlitzer factory in Tonawanda, it was described as a "190 Granada Special", the pipework coming from broken-down instruments reclaimed from American theatres and the console being built by S. J. Wright & Son, the British Wurlitzer agents. Consisting of diapason, tibia, clarinet, violin, violin celeste, concert flute, vox humana and trumpet, it was a most effective instrument, and five further organs to the same specification were ordered. There was a grand piano attachment and the console was the first to Granada's own design, with straight side pillars surmounted by flat mouldings.

When the stage at Bedford was altered to take 70mm presentations in 1969, the organ was removed and installed at the Pier Ballroom at Redcar, only to be taken three years later to the James Finegan Hall at Eston, Cleveland, where monthly concerts are presented throughout the year.

A very special Wurlitzer was designed for what would have been the Granada Manchester by Harold Ramsay, modelled on the specification of the beautiful Tooting Wurlitzer. The sixteen-rank instrument was cut to fourteen with grand piano. Although similar to Tooting on paper, it was remarkably different - but one of the finest Wurlitzers in the UK. Gaumont-British brought Stanley Tudor up from the Gaumont Palace Hammersmith for its opening as the Gaumont in October 1935 and he was so popular that he remained at Manchester until 1953, apart from the war years, broadcasting regularly. He returned in 1959 for the run of *South Pacific*, followed by Doreen Chadwick. Two years after the Gaumont closed in 1974, the Wurlitzer was removed to storage. It has now returned to Granada, being installed in the Granada Studio Tours complex and looked after by the Lancastrian Theatre Organ Trust.

After Granada took full control of the Plaza Mansfield, they updated it and organ chambers were constructed from store rooms. Ramsay ordered a 190 Granada Special and opened it in

April 1936. The first resident was Watson Sleightholme, who wisely changed his name to Watson Holmes and became well known at the Blackpool Tower, Empress and Palace ballrooms where he remained for twenty-three years. After the Mansfield cinema closed as the Granada in 1973, the organ was purchased by former Granada organist John Madin. In the late Eighties it was installed in the former Methodist Church at Matlock Bank, beautifully converted into a concert/dance venue, and regular organ concerts are held.

Further 190 Granada Specials were installed at Wandsworth Road (opened there by Harry Farmer in 1936); East Ham (opened by Donald Thorne in November 1936); the superb Granada Woolwich (opened by the great Reginald Dixon from the Tower Blackpool on 20 April 1937); and Greenwich (opened by Donald Thorne in October 1937). The Wandsworth Road organ is in a private home in Northolt, Woolwich's is at the Neuadd Pendre (hall) at Tywyn in North Wales and used regularly for concerts and dances; East Ham's, having survived competition from a steam railway in a wild-life park, is in store, as is Greenwich's.

The next Granada, at North Cheam, had the first of a second batch of six Wurlitzers. Despatched from Tonawanda on 6 July 1937, it was simply described as a "three-manual organ" but it was basically the same as the specification for the 190 Granada Special, except for the substitution of English horn and saxophone for clarinet and vox humana, and stronger strings, i.e. gamba and gamba celeste instead of violin and violin celeste. This second batch of Wurlitzers was even more effective than the first and quite remarkable for their size.

Lloyd Thomas opened North Cheam. Further mark II Specials followed at Harrow (opened by Harry Farmer on 25 October 1937); Clapham Junction, a very effective organ in under-stage chambers (opened on 8 November by Donald Thorne); Greenford, opened only five days after Clapham, by Dudley Beaven; Welling (opened on 2 February 1938 by Robinson Cleaver, who had made a name for himself both on air and on wax at the neighbouring Regal Bexleyheath and was carried, shoulder-high, into the theatre on opening night); and Slough (opened on 25 March 1938 by Dudley Beaven).

Following call-up into the RAF, Reginald Dixon, who had been touring Granada theatres during the winter months, continued recording at Granada theatres, although this was not shown on the record labels. In the early years of the war, he recorded at Tooting, Clapham, Slough, Welling and Kingston-on-Thames.

Reginald Dixon also opened the Wurlitzer at Kingston on 3 November 1939, two months after war had been declared. As the scheme for Kingston had originally been for Gaumont Super Cinemas, the organ was transferred from the Picture House Edinburgh and enlarged from a 2/8 to a 3/10 with grand piano.

Granada organists. Clockwise, from top left: Reginald Dixon; John Madin; Harold Ramsay; Donald Thorne (at Tooting); Watson Sleightholme, later known as Watson Holmes. (All from the Tony Moss collection.)

*The Granada Woolwich
as a bingo hall in October 1982.
(Allen Eyles.)*

*The Granada Clapham Junction
as a bingo hall, seen in April 1983.
(Allen Eyles.)*

Four hanging cards from 1943. (Courtesy of Tony Duggan.)

The local press said that Reg liked Kingston so much he was staying for a month.

At Harrow, the organ remains at the time of writing in the closed Grade II listed theatre; the superb Clapham Junction Wurlitzer is in Switzerland; Greenford's went to a private home in Nottinghamshire; Welling's has been successfully reinstated at the Woking Leisure Centre, where concerts and dances are regularly held; Slough's is in store; and Kingston's is at a private home in Harrogate.

Some of the thirty-six-odd cinemas that Granada acquired possessed organs and, in some cases, they were overhauled and brought back into service. These included the Plaza Sutton, opened in 1934, with a fairly large Compton of ten ranks. Granadas supplied organists from the start, including Reginald Dixon as guest during one of his winter tours.

The Regal Kennington had, unusually, a Hammond LaFleur electronic organ with illuminated console, and this was brought back into use and visited by Reginald Porter-Brown and other members of the team.

Two of the Medway cinemas acquired in 1949 had small Compton organs – the State Grantham and State Dartford. Both organs were refurbished and used again after several years of silence.

The only one of the London and District cinemas, taken over in 1951, to be equipped with an organ was the Globe Clapham Junction. The small Compton had been damaged in the Blitz and the remains were removed with the refurbishment of the cinema to become the Century. The well-known Kenneth Stroud had appeared there at age fourteen as a "wonder boy organist".

Another acquired cinema was the Plaza Sevenoaks, renamed Granada. The small Compton was brought back into use and visited by the touring team.

The Elite Kingston had a straight organ brought from a mansion in Derbyshire which was removed for scrap in 1948. The Palace Slough no longer had one of only three theatre organs built by Spurden Rutt of Leyton: it had been removed to Gold Hill Baptist Church, Chalfont St. Peter, back in 1936.

Finally, the perhaps surprising purchase of the Adelphi Slough in 1953 brought in a Christie rebuilt by Compton in 1937.

In the thirty years or so that Granada employed organists on their books, they presented some fine musicians and outstanding showmen. In addition to their musical ability, they had to present interesting interludes and to look very smart at the console, the men usually in white suits. Many of them were regular broadcasters and some were recording artists. For example:

Dudley Beaven: joined Granada in 1936, remaining until 1945, apart from war service. He opened the organs at the Granadas at Greenford and Slough, and recorded at Clapham Junction.

Because of his outstanding talent and good micro-phone voice, he was invited to help Sandy Macpherson out on the air with a multitude of organ broadcasts at the outbreak of war.

Jackie Brown: joined Granada in 1940 at the age of seven-teen, playing at Willesden, Woolwich, Slough, etc. Did not return to Granada after the war but became arranger and conductor for Billy Cotton and appeared on TV in *Double Your Money*, *The Sky's the Limit* and *Take Your Pick*.

Doreen Chadwick: joined Granada at Tooting for the duration of the war. Later with ABC and Lyons' Corner House. Has been a regular broadcaster throughout her career.

Robinson Cleaver: joined Granada from Union Cinemas to open the Granada Welling. With Granada for nearly twenty years, he both broadcast and recorded from Welling and Tooting. The Theatre Organ Club was formed in 1938 in honour of this outstanding showman who often appeared with his wife Molly.

Nelson Elms: with Granada from 1936 to 1947, apart from war service, then with Gaumont-British, ABC and at the Empire Leicester Square. Played at children's matinees at Greenford in Fifties and sixties.

Harry Farmer: joined Granada at Bedford in 1934, opening Wandsworth Road and Harrow and broadcasting from both Bedford and Tooting. He toured with an electronic organ from 1939 and later went to Canada as musical adviser and TV producer.

Cyril Gell: joined Granada in 1937 and toured with Dudley Beaven (piano and organ show), broadcasting and recording. Later conducted the BBC Male Voice Choir in programmes like *Friday Night Is Music Night*.

John Madin: joined Granada from the Gaumont Finchley in 1937 and remained for twenty years, apart from RAF service. A regular broadcaster from Tooting. Gave the final official interlude on the Granada circuit at Welling, when he announced that he had got the "tick-tack". The "Wandering Minstrel" then joined the staff of RMS Queen Elizabeth and Queen Mary, regularly crossing the Atlantic.

Neville Meale: nephew of the famous Arthur Meale, he joined Granada in 1945, staying for nine years. Was very popular, billed as "Granada's Cheeky Chappie". Regular broadcaster.

Reginald Porter-Brown: with ABC in the Thirties and achieved fame with broadcasts from Torquay and Southampton. Joined Granada in 1944 and remained for ten years, broadcast-ing from Tooting and Clapham Junction. An outstanding musician.

Harold Ramsay: joined Granada in 1932 from Paramount in the USA, remaining for four years, broadcasting and recording. Had a strong influence on Granada organ policy, also with Union Cinemas which he joined in 1936.

Leo Rae: joined Granada in 1936 and remained until 1947, trans-ferring to management (as Leo Eales) at Sevenoaks, Crystal Palace, Welling, etc.

*More Granada organists. Above left, Dudley Beaven.
Right, Robinson Cleaver (in the organists' outfit).
Below, Lloyd Thomas at Woolwich.
(All from the Tony Moss collection.)*

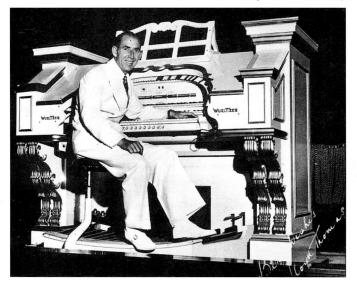

Bryan Rodwell: another outstanding musician, he joined ABC at age sixteen and Granada in 1951, playing for variety at East Ham until 1956. He later promoted electronic organs (Hammond, Rodgers, etc.) and was musical director to Edmund Hockridge. Broadcast from Granadas Clapham, Tooting and Rugby.

John Sharp: with Granada from 1936 to 1940, touring but for most of the time at Rialtos Leytonstone and Enfield. Commissioned a photograph of himself at the console, decided he could do better and became a professional photographer, later doing much work for Granada.

Kenneth Stroud: joined Granada at the age of eighteen. Later with ABC, Butlins, the Jan Ralfini Orchestra and Zetter's Enterprises.

Lloyd Thomas: joined Granada from Davis' Theatre Croydon in 1934, remaining until 1954 apart from RAF service. Opened the Granada North Cheam and was a regular broadcaster from Tooting, Clapham, North Cheam, Bedford, Harrow and Woolwich. He also recorded at Tooting.

Donald Thorne: having been a dance pianist and arranger for most of the famous dance bands in the early Thirties, he joined Granada in 1934, opening East Ham, Greenwich and Clapham Junction. He was a regular broadcaster and recorded at Willesden and Clapham Junction.

Bernard Worster: joined Granada in 1936, touring as an organist with Tony Lowry (piano). Resident for a while at Tooting in 2938 and married one half of an acrobatic act that he accompanied there. Accompanied variety acts with Bryan Rodwell (organ and piano) at the Granada East Ham for many years, also performing solo spots. As the last employed organist, he happily transferred to management, with Granada Poster Print and as relief manager, e.g. Clapham Junction, North Cheam and Crystal Palace, performing the occasional organ spot. Retired in 1970 after thirty-four years with Granada. A regular broadcaster.

After 1957, the organs were used only spasmodically, e.g. Reginald Porter-Brown played at Greenford on Sundays for some time. The organs continued to be broadcast and concerts continued to be arranged by The Cinema Organ Society and Theatre Organ Club, usually on Sundays. In the late Sixties and early Seventies, some of the organs enjoyed a renascence in connection with special films, e.g. Kingston with Robin Richmond and Sutton with Richmond and Ena Baga, but this was a local arrangement. The manager of Sutton Granada also featured the organ as a prelude to a variety show, John Mann presiding at the console.

At the time of writing (March 1998), only three of the circuit's organs remain *in situ*, at Tooting, Walthamstow and Harrow. Tooting remains on bingo, Walthamstow continues as an ABC cinema but Harrow is closed and its future looks most uncertain.

Granada Pantomimes And Other Christmas Shows

Dates are opening dates, usually for a week's run unless otherwise indicated. These are the shows that have come to light: they may have been others.

1936
Jack and the Beanstalk (*Violet Fields*) (with films): 6.1.36, Tooting

1938
Snow White and the Seven Dwarfs (with films): 8.8.38, Clapham Junction

1938/39
Dick Whittington and His Cat: 26.12.38, Maidstone; 2.1.39, Plaza Rugby

1947/8
Babes in the Wood (*Adele Dixon, Jean Colin, Jimmy Hanley*): Boxing Day 1947 – 10.1.48, Tooting; 12.1.48, Sutton; 19.1.48, Woolwich; 26.1.48, Clapham Junction
Cinderella (*Marie Bailey, Phyllis Terrell, Len Clifford, Granada Babes*): Boxing Day 1947 – 10.1.48, Shrewsbury; 12.1.48 (two weeks), Rugby
Aladdin (*Cyril Fletcher, Joan Turner*): Boxing Day 1947 – 10.1.48, Maidstone

1948/9
Aladdin (*Ralph Reader, The Smith Brothers*): 27.12.48 – 1.1.49, Tooting; 3.1.49, Sutton; 10.1.49, Woolwich; 17.1.49, Clapham Junction
Dick Whittington and His Cat (*Guy Fielding, Joan Winters*): 27.12.48 – 15.1.49, Shrewsbury; 17.1.49, Rugby

1949/50
Aladdin (*Joan Haig, Sirlani*): 26.12.49 (3 weeks), Shrewsbury
Dick Whittington and His Cat (*Jimmy Hanley, Radio Revellers, Low & Webster*): 26.12.49; 2.1.50, Sutton; 9.1.50, Woolwich; 16.1.50, Clapham Junction

1950/1
Cinderella (*Hal Monty*): 26.12.50 – 30.12.50, Tooting; 1.1.51, Sutton; 8.1.51, Woolwich; 15.1.51, Clapham Junction
Jack and the Beanstalk (*Benny Hill*): Rugby

1951/2
Jack and the Beanstalk (*Bonar Colleano, Susan Shaw*): 24.12.51 – 29.12.51, Tooting; 31.12.51 (*plus Josef Locke*), Sutton; 7.1.52, Woolwich; 14.1.52, Clapham Junction

1952/3
Robinson Crusoe (*Derek Roy, Joan Dowling*): 26.12.52 – 3.1.53, Tooting; 5.1.53, Sutton; 12.1.53, Woolwich; 19.1.53, Clapham Junction
Babes in the Wood (*Hal Monty*): 26.12.52 – 17.1.53, Shrewsbury; 19.1.53, Rugby
Jack and the Beanstalk (*Humphrey Lestocq, Peter Butterworth, Janet Brown*): 12.1.53, Walthamstow

1953/4
Cinderella (*Jimmy Hanley*) 26.12.53 – 16.1.54, Shrewsbury; 18.1.54, Slough Adelphi
Dick Whittington and His Cat (*Terry-Thomas*): 26.12.53 – 2.1.54, Sutton; 4.1.54, Woolwich

1954/55
Babes in the Wood (*Sally Barnes, Hal Monty, guest star Vera Lynn*): 27.12.54, Tooting; 3.1.55, Sutton; 10.1.55, Woolwich
Sim Sala Bim (*Kalanag and Gloria de Vos*) 27.12.54 (two weeks), Shrewsbury
Archie's Christmas Party (*Peter Brough, Archie Andrews*): 9-10.1.55, Shrewsbury

1955/56
Cinderella (*Tommy Trinder*): 26.12.55, Tooting; 2.1.56, Sutton; 9.1.56, Woolwich
Sleeping Beauty on Ice: 26.12.55 (two weeks), Shrewsbury; 9.1.56, Rugby
Rosaire's Christmas Circus: 26.12.55 – 31.12.55, Slough Adelphi; (shortened version in cine-variety show) 2.1.56, East Ham

1956/57
Aladdin (*Bill Maynard, guest star Alma Cogan*): 24.12.56 – 5.1.57 (two weeks) Brixton Empress; 7.1.57, Sutton; 14.1.57, Woolwich
Cinderella on Ice: Boxing Day – 12.1.57, Shrewsbury
Alice in Wonderland (*Mandy Miller*): Boxing Day (four weeks), Chelsea Palace

1957/8
Robin Hood (*David Hughes, Terry Scott*): 23.12.57, Tooting; (+ *guest star Winifed Atwell*) 30.12.57, Sutton; 6.1.58, Slough Adelphi; 13.1.58, Woolwich
The Big Christmas Show (*Al Read*): 26.12.57 – 11.1.58, Shrewsbury

1958/59
Where the Rainbow Ends (*Anton Dolin, Michael MacLiammoir*): 22.12.58 – 2.1.59, Sutton
Archie's Christmas Party (*Peter Brough, Archie Andrews*): 30-31.12.58, Bedford; 5-6.1.59, Mansfield

1959/60
Babes in the Wood (*The Mudlarks*): 11.1.60, Shrewsbury; 18.1.60, Woolwich

1960/1
Mother Goose (*Rosemary Squires, Peter Webster, Eddie Calvert*) 2.1.61 (two weeks), Shrewsbury; 18.1.60 – 23.1.60, Woolwich

1962/63
Cinderella (*Richard Hearne, Dagenham Girl Pipers*): 26.12.62 – 5.1.63, Shrewsbury; 7.1.63, Sutton; 14.1.63, Maidstone

1963/64
Aladdin (*Joe Brown and the Bruvvers*): 24.12.63 – 4.1.64, Shrewsbury; 6.1.64, Sutton; 13.1.64 – 25.1.64, Brixton

1964/65
Puss in Boots (*Richard "Mr. Pastry" Hearne, Davy Kaye*) 24.12.64 – 9.1.65, theatre not known
Once Upon a Fairy Tale (*Millie, Jess Conrad*): circa 1.65, theatre not known
Babes in the Wood (*Dick Emery, Sid James*): 24.12.64 – 9.1.65, Shrewsbury; 11.1.65, Sutton; 18.1.65, East Ham

1965/66
Christmas Crackers (*Norman Vaughan, Gerry and the Pacemakers*): 27.12.65, Shrewsbury

1966/67
Christmas Capers (*Hylda Baker, Clinton Ford, Fred Emney*): 26.12.66 (two weeks), Shrewsbury

1968/69
Hughie Green's Christmas Show (*Hughie Green, Monica Rose*): 26.12.68 – 11.1.69, Shrewsbury

1973/74
Cinderella (*Tony Blackburn, Anna Karen, Valentine Dyall*): 23.12.73 – 19.1.74, East Ham

It's Exclusive! And Other Widespread Bookings

These are the main films that from 1947 that have come to notice for being widely booked in preference to major circuit release programmes. They were occasionally exclusive to the Granada circuit, usually exclusive to the area of the Granadas which played them but taken up by independent cinemas elsewhere. 'B' features often varied from theatre to theatre and are listed (in brackets) if they were frequently attached to a particular main feature. Many supporting features were widely spot-booked on the circuit and not attached to a particular 'A' feature – these are not listed.

Dates are the first Granada showing that has come to light (but it has not been possible to check thoroughly). Most followed the normal release pattern, starting in the Northwest London area, but all played the Granada circuit less rigidly than major circuit releases. Many more features were spot-booked around the circuit and to the weaker cinemas. The general breakdown of rigid release patterns in the Seventies makes it difficult to pinpoint mainstream films which may have been taken up particularly by Granada (I have not attempted to track the vast number of sexploitation and dubbed horror releases). Distributors are given where known, and Associated British-Pathe, 20th Century-Fox, RKO Radio, United Artists and Warner Bros. have been abbreviated to AB-Pathe, Fox, RKO, UA and WB.

1947

Feb. 17: Beau Geste *Paramount revival*
Mar. 10: White Cargo *MGM revival*
  + King Kong *RKO revival*
Mar. 17: Rebecca *revival*
Apr. 14: The Arnelo Affair *MGM*
  (+ Split Face *RKO*)

Apr. 28: Gallant Journey *Columbia* [*with Gaumont circuit main feature* High Window]
May 28: A Tale of Two Cities *MGM revival*
June 2: The Jolson Story *Columbia revival*
June 9: Dangerous Moonlight *RKO revival*
July 14: Blaze of Noon *Paramount*
  + The Lady Eve *Paramount revival*
Aug. 4: State Fair *Fox*
Aug. 11: Green Hell *revival*
Aug. 18: Oh, Mr. Porter! *International*
Sept. 15: Angel and the Badman *British Lion*
  + Over the Moon *British Lion revival*
Oct. 6: Tarzan's New York Adventure *MGM revival*
Dec. 15: Tarzan Triumphs *RKO revival*
  + Trail Street *RKO*
Dec. 22: various + Old Mother Riley's Circus *revival*

1948

Apr. 12: The Four Feathers *British Lion revival*
July 5: Brief Encounter *ABFD revival*
  + The Rake's Progress *ABFD revival*
Aug. 2: Sign of the Ram *Columbia*
Aug. 9: The Way to the Stars *revival*
  + Getting Gertie's Garter *revival*
Aug. 9: The Unfinished Dance *MGM*
Aug. 22: If I Had My Way *Eros revival*
Sept. 6: If Winter Comes *MGM*
  (+ Trapped by Boston Blackie *Columbia*)
Sept. 20: If You Knew Susie *RKO*
  (+ West of the Pecos *RKO*)
Oct. 4: Berlin Express *RKO*
Oct. 11: Relentless *Columbia*
  (+ When a Girl's Beautiful *Columbia*)
Oct. 18: Killer McCoy *MGM*
Oct. 25: The Birds and the Bees *MGM*
  + Whistling in Dixie *MGM*
Nov. 15: Night Song *RKO*
Nov. 22: On Our Merry Way *UA*
  (+ Wreck of the Hesperus *Columbia*)
Dec. 6: Fury at Furnace Creek *Fox*
  (+ The Return of the Whistler *Columbia*)

1949

Jan. 24: Cry of the City *Fox*
  + Katina *Fox revival*
Feb. 7: The Street with No Name *Fox*
Feb. 14: Tarzan and the Mermaids *RKO*
  (+ Nevada *RKO*)
Feb. 21: The Emperor Waltz *Paramount*
  (+ Big Town Scandal *Paramount*)
Mar. 14: Rachel and the Stranger *RKO*
  (+ Dick Tracy's Amazing Adventure *RKO*)
Apr. 18: Black Arrow Strikes *Columbia*
Apr. 25: Sorry, Wrong Number *Paramount*
  (+ Lone Wolf and His Lady *Columbia*)
May 2: Tycoon *RKO*
  (+ Rusty Leads the Way *Columbia*)
May 16: Roadhouse *Fox*
  (+ Sword of the Avenger *UA*)
May 16: Bless 'Em All *Adelphi*
  + Fire Over England *Adelphi revival*
June 13: Drums Along the Amazon *British Lion*
June 27: Pitfall *UA*
  + Smuggler's Cove *AB-Pathe*
Aug. 8: Streets of Laredo *Paramount*
  (+ Golden Eye *AB-Pathe*)
Aug. 29: Blood on the Moon *RKO*
  + The Horns Blows at Midnight *WB*
Oct. 3: El Paso *Paramount*
Oct. 31: Black Bart, Highwayman *Eros*
  + Patrick the Great *revival*
Nov. 14: The Lost Tribe *Columbia*
Nov. 21: Red Canyon *Eros*
  (+ Vengeance Is Mine *Eros*)
Nov. 7: Command Decision *MGM*
  (+ Kazan *Columbia*)
Dec. 5: William Comes to Town *UA*
  + Buffalo Bill Rides Again *Exclusive*

1950

Jan. 2: The Red Shoes *GFD revival*
  + The Story Of Molly X *GFD*
Jan. 30: Tarzan's Magic Fountain *RKO*
  (+ Make Mine Laughs *RKO*)
Feb. 6: The Undercover Man *Columbia*
  + The Walking Hills *Columbia*

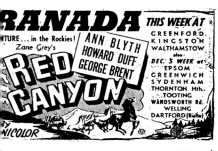

Feb. 27 (limited): Five Graves To Cairo
Paramount revival
Mar. 6: Gunga Din *RKO revival*
  + Return Of The Bad Men *RKO*
Mar. 27: Hounded *Columbia*
  + The Walking Hills *Columbia*
Mar. 27: For The Love Of Mary *Eros*
  (+ Massacre River *AB-Pathe*)
Apr. 24: Back To Bataan *RKO*
  + Down Dakota Way *British Lion*
May 15 Stromboli *RKO*
  (+ "C" Man *International*)
May 22: The Red Pony *British Lion*
  (+ Over the Garden Wall *Mancunian*)
May 29: Bomba, The Jungle Boy *AB-Pathe*
June 5: Not Wanted *International*
  (+ Skimpy in the Navy *Adelphi*)
June 19: The Boy with Green Hair *RKO*
  + Top Hat *RKO revival*
July 10: Northwest Mounted Police *Paramount*
  (+ The Higgins Family *Republic revival*)
July 17 Black Magic *UA* + Indian Scout *UA*
Sept. 18: Wagonmaster *RKO*
  + Miraculous Journey *International*
Oct. 30: Red Light *UA* + A Kiss for Corliss *UA*
Nov. 27: Tarzan and the Slave Girl *RKO*
  + The Fireball *Fox*

1951
Jan. 15: Bitter Rice *Lux*
  (+ Something in the City *Butcher's*)
Jan. 22: All Quiet on the Western Front *Eros*
revival
  (+ Drums of the Congo *Eros revival*
  + The Cure)
Feb. 12: Love That Brute *Fox*
  + Fighting Man of the Plains *Fox*
Apr. 2: Rio Grande *Republic*
  (+ Jungle Stampede *Republic*)
Apr. 30: City Lights *UA*
  (+ The Far Frontier *Republic*)
June 25: Roseanna McCoy *RKO*
  (+ The Harlem Globetrotters *Columbia*)
July 16: At War with the Army *Paramount*
  + Aloma of the South Seas *Paramount revival*
July 30: Tarzan and the Jungle Queen *RKO*
  + Susanna Pass *Republic*
Sept. 3: So Young, So Bad *UA*
  + Lucky Mascot *UA*
Oct. 1: Prehistoric Women *Eros*
Oct. 8: Valentino *Columbia*
  (+ Criminal Lawyer *Columbia*) *replaced after*
  two weeks by Lost Stage Valley *Columbia*
  + Fury of the Congo *Columbia*

Oct. 15: Highway 301 *WB*
  (+ Golden Stallion *Republic*)
Oct. 22: Across the Wide Missouri *MGM*
  (+ Madame Louise *Butcher's*)
Nov. 5: Sealed Cargo *RKO*
  + Fort Apache *RKO revival*
Nov. 26: Love Happy *Monarch*
  + The Hoodlum *Monarch*
Dec. 3: The Strange Door *GFD*
  + You Never Know *GFD*

1952
Jan. 14: The Prowler *UA*
  + The Tomahawk Trail *UA*
Feb. 18: Four in a Jeep *International*
  + Mr. Universe *International*
Apr. 7: Ten Tall Men *Columbia*
  (+ Beyond the Purple Hills *Columbia*)
June 9: Phantom of the Opera *Eros revival*
  + 13 East Street *Eros*
June 16: Loan Shark *Exclusive*
  + An Ideal Husband *revival*
July 14: Tarzan's Savage Fury *RKO*
  (+ The Pace That Thrills *RKO*)
Aug. 4: Dumbo *RKO revival*
  + Wonder Man *RKO revival*
Aug. 11 (limited): [Little Big Shot, *Gaumont
circuit release*]
  + Jet Men of the Air *Eros*
Aug. 25 (limited): My Six Convicts *Columbia*
  (+ Shadow of the Past *Columbia*)
Nov. 10: The Thing from Another World *RKO*
Nov. 24: Rainbow Round My Shoulder
Columbia
  (+ Last Train from Bombay *Columbia*)
Nov. 24 (limited): Thunder Across the
Pacific *Republic*
  (+ The Sea Hornet *Republic*)
Dec. 8: The Hour of 13 *MGM*
  + Fearless Fagan *MGM*
Dec. 15: My Wife's Lodger *Adelphi*
  [+ *Gaumont circuit co-feature* Yankee
Buccaneer]

1953
Feb. 9: The Narrow Margin *RKO*
  + Behave Yourself *RKO*
Feb. 23: One Minute to Zero *RKO*
  (+ Woman of the North Country *Republic*)
Mar. 2 (very limited): The Marrying Kind
Columbia
Mar. 9: *split week of* The Jolson Story
Columbia and Jolson Sings Again *Columbia*
May. 4: The War of the Worlds *Paramount*
  + Laxdale Hall *ABFD*

June 22 (limited): Small Town Girl *MGM*
+ Cry of the Hunted *MGM*
June 29: Tarzan and the She Devil *RKO*
+ Island of Monte Cristo *RKO*
Aug. 3: Crusin' Down the River *Columbia*
+ The 49th Man *Columbia*
Nov. 11: Pony Express *Paramount*
+ Gilbert Harding Speaking of Murder
Paramount

1954
Jan. 25: Life After Dark *GFD*
+ Abbott and Costello Meet Dr. Jekyll and
Mr. Hyde *GFD*
Mar. 3 (limited): Cease Fire *Paramount*
(non 3-D version)
Mar 22 (limited): Lost Treasure of the
Amazon *Paramount (non 3-D version)*
Apr. 12: Snow White and the Seven Dwarfs
RKO revival
+ The Man from Cairo *Exclusive*
+ Olympic Elk *RKO*
June 6: The Fortune Hunter *Republic*
+ Tobor the Great *Republic*
June 7: Flight of the White Heron *Fox*
July 7: Heidi *UA*
+ The Scarlet Spear *UA*
June 28: The Robe *Fox*
July 18: Beneath the 12 Mile Reef *Fox*
Aug. 8: King of the Khyber Rifles *Fox*
(+ Tournament of Roses *Fox*)
Aug. 15: How to Marry a Millionaire *Fox*
Sept. 5: Prince Valiant *Fox*
Sept. 19: 3 Coins in the Fountain *Fox*
Oct. 3: Hell and High Water *Fox*
Oct. 24: River of No Return *Fox*
(+ Child's Play *British Lion*)
Nov. 22: Night People *Fox*
Dec. 6 (limited): New Faces *British Lion*
Dec. 13: Modern Times *UA revival*
+ Go! Man! Go! *UA*

1955
Jan. 3: Demetrius and the Gladiators *Fox*
Jan. 31: Garden of Evil *Fox*
(+ Radio Cab Murder *Eros*)
Feb. 21: Long John Silver *Fox*
Feb. 28: The Egyptian *Fox*
(+ Jet Carrier *Fox*)
Mar. 7: Woman's World *Fox*
Mar. 14: Desiree *Fox*
Mar. 23: Broken Lance *Fox*
(+ African Conflict *Granada*)
Apr. 4 (very limited): That Lady *Fox*
Apr. 18: Carmen Jones *Fox*

Apr. 25: There's No Business Like Show
Business *Fox*
June 6: Black Widow *Fox*
June 13: A Man Called Peter *Fox*
July 4: Untamed *Fox*
(+ Thursday's Children *Republic*)
July 11: The Dark Avenger *Fox*
July 21 (very limited): Tarzan's Hidden
Jungle *RKO*
+ Hansel and Gretel *RKO*)
July 25: White Feather *Fox*
Aug. 15: Daddy Long Legs *Fox*
Sept. 4: Violent Saturday *Fox*
(+ What Every Woman Wants *Adelphi*)
Oct. 3: Such Men Are Dangerous *Fox*
Oct. 17: The Deep Blue Sea *Fox*
Oct. 24: Soldier of Fortune *Fox*
Nov. 14: The Seven Year Itch *Fox*
(+ Night Visitor)
Nov. 21: House of Bamboo *Fox*
Nov. 28: How To Be Very Very Popular *Fox*
Dec. 15 (limited): The Virgin Queen *Fox*
Dec. 19: The Tall Men *Fox*

1956
Jan. 9: Love Is a Many Splendored Thing *Fox*
(+ Treasure of Ruby Hills *AB-Pathe*)
Jan. 16: The Left Hand of God *Fox*
Jan. 30: The Girl in the Red Velvet Swing *Fox*
Feb. 20: Seven Cities of Gold *Fox*
Mar. 12: The Rains of Ranchipur *Fox*
(+ Laura *Fox "pocket edition"*)
Mar. 19: The Man Who Never Was *Fox*
(+ Christopher Bean *Fox "pocket edition"*)
Apr. 15: The Lieutenant Wore Skirts *Fox*
(+ Man on the Ledge *Fox*)
Apr. 22: Beyond the River *Fox*
May 20: Carousel *Fox*
(+ People and Places with Ronnie Waldman)
May 27: On The Threshold of Space *Fox*
(+ Gentlemen Prefer Blondes *Fox revival*)
June 25 (spot-booked – see below Oct. 29):
The Light Across the Street *Miracle*
+ The Winning Way *Rank*
July 2 (very limited): Secret Interlude *Fox*
July 9: Genevieve *Rank revival*
+ Doctor in the House *Rank revival*
July 16: Smiley *Fox*
July 30: The Proud Ones *Fox*
Aug. 20 (very limited): 23 Paces to Baker
Street *Fox*
Aug. 27 (limited): Hilda Crane *Fox*
Sept. 3: The Man in the Grey Flannel Suit (*Fox*)
Sept. 10: The Revolt of Mamie Stover *Fox*
(+ Gang Busters *Eros*)

Oct. 8: The King and I *Fox*
(+ Times Like These)
Oct. 22: D-Day The Sixth of June *Fox*
Oct. 29 (limited): Bigger Than Life *Fox*
(+ The Light Across the Street *Miracle*)
Nov. 19: Bus Stop *Fox*
(+ The Lyons in Paris *Exclusive*)
Nov. 26: The Last Wagon *Fox*

1957
Jan. 7: The Best Things In Life Are Free *Fox*
(+ The Hefferan Family *Fox*)
Jan. 14: Love Me Tender *Fox*
(+ Overnight Haul *Fox*)
Feb. 4: Between Heaven and Hell *Fox*
(+ The Desperadoes Are in Town *Fox*)
Feb. 11: Teenage Rebel *Fox*
(+ Stagecoach to Fury *Fox*)
Feb. 18: Three Brave Men *Fox*
(+ The Black Whip *Fox*)
Mar. 11: The Girl Can't Help It *Fox*
(+ Bitter Creek *AB-Pathe*)
Apr. 8 (spot-booked): Mam'selle Striptease
Miracle
Apr. 15: Anastasia *Fox*
(+ Time Out of War)
May 6 (spot-booked): The Creature Walks
Among Us *Rank*
+ The Mole People *Rank*
May 6: Sea Wife *Fox*
(+ The Quiet Gun *Fox*)
May 6 (spot-booked): Garden of Eden *Orb*
(local certificates)
May 26: The James Brothers *Fox*
June 3: Oh! Men Oh! Women *Fox*
(+ The Storm Rider *Fox*)
June 10: Boy on a Dolphin *Fox*
June 24 (very limited): The Way to the Gold
Fox
July 1: The River's Edge *Fox*
July 8: China Gate *Fox*
(+ Badlands of Montana *Fox*)
July : Smiley *Fox revival*
+ Broken Lance *Fox revival*
Aug. 5: Heaven Knows, Mr. Allison *Fox*
(+ The Empty Room *Fox*)
Aug. 12: His Other Woman *Fox*
Aug. 19: The Wayward Bus *Fox*
(+ Gun in His Hand *Fox*)
Aug. 26: Bernadine *Fox*
Sept. 9: Island in the Sun *Fox*
(+ Arrivederci Roma *Fox*)
Sept. 23: An Affair to Remember *Fox*
Oct. 14: A King in New York *Archway*
(+ Black Ice *Archway*)

Oct. 28 (spotbooked): Fantasia *RKO revival*
Nov. 4: Oh! For a Man *Fox*
Nov. 4 (limited): Godzilla King of the Monsters *Eros*
  (+ House of Dracula *Eros*)
Nov. 18 (limited): A Hatful of Rain *Fox*
  (+ The Wayward Girl *British Lion*)
Dec. 2: The Three Faces of Eve *Fox*
Dec. 30: The Sun Also Rises *Fox*

1958
Jan. 13: Stopover Tokyo *Fox*
  (+ Plunder Road *Fox*)
Feb. 3: Count Five and Die *Fox*
Feb. 17: The Enemy Below *Fox*
  (+ Escape from Red Rock *Fox*)
Feb. 24: The Naked Earth *Fox*
  (+ Morning Call *Astral*)
Mar. 10: Kiss Them For Me *Fox*
  (+ The Ride Back *UA*)
Mar. 31: A Farewell to Arms *Fox*
Apr. 7 (spot-booked): Gulliver's Travels *Orb revival*
  + Hoppity Goes To Town *Orb revival*
Apr. 14: April Love *Fox*
  (+ Ambush at Cimarron Pass *Fox*)
May 5: The Young Lions *Fox*
May 12: Smiley Gets a Gun *Fox*
  + Cattle Empire *Fox*
May 19: Sing, Boy, Sing *Fox*
+ Forty Guns *Fox*
June 9: The Long Hot Summer *Fox*
  (+ Thundering Jets *Fox*)
June 9 (limited): Rodan *RKO*
  + The Body Snatchers *RKO revival*
June 23: No Down Payment *Fox*
  (+ The Big Heat *Columbia revival*)
June 30: Ten North Frederick *Fox*
  (+ The Traitor *New Realm*)
July 28: Manhunt *Fox*
  (+ *various Bowery Boys comedies*)
Aug. 25: Harry Black *Fox*
Sept. 15: The Fly *Fox*
  (+ Gang War *Fox*)
Oct. 6: The Bravados *Fox*
Oct. 13: A Certain Smile *Fox*
  (+ Under Fire *Fox*)
Nov. 9 (spot-booked): It! The Terror from Beyond Space *UA*
  + The Curse of the Faceless Man *UA*
Dec. 26: The Sheriff of Fractured Jaw *Fox*
  (+ Men Against Speed *Fox*)

1959
May 11 (spot-booked): The Blob *Paramount*
  + I Married a Monster from Outer Space *Paramount*
June 22 (spot-booked): Quo Vadis *MGM revival*
Aug. 10: Doctor in the House *Rank revival*
  + Genevieve *Rank revival*
Dec. : The King and I *Fox revival*
  (+ We Are the Lambeth Boys)

1960
May 16: The Girl Rosemarie *Small*

1963
June: The Quick and the Dead *Grand National*
  + The 5th Battalion *Grand National*

1967
March 5: Psycho *Paramount revival*
  + War of the Worlds *Paramount revival*
circa September: Onibaba *Orb*
  + Nudist Paradise *Orb*
Oct. 22: For Whom the Bell Tolls *revival*

1968
Jan. 14 (spot-booked): Ulysses *British Lion*
June 2 (spot-booked): The Oldest Profession *Miracle*
circa July: Doctor Faustus *Columbia*
circa December: Belle de Jour *Curzon*
  (+ The Knack *UA*)

1969
Jan. 19: The Forsyte Saga *MGM*
  + High Society *MGM*
    (spot-booked): Charlie Bubbles *Rank*
Dec. 21: The Pure Hell of St. Trinian's *British Lion* + Blue Murder at St. Trinian's *British Lion* or The Belles of St. Trinian's *British Lion*

1971
Jan. 17: Woodstock *WB*
Feb. 21: There Was a Crooked Man *WB*
Mar. 7: Performance *WB*
circa March: The Virgin and the Gypsy *London Screenplays*
  (+ Rachel Rachel *WB*)
Nov. 2: Two Mules for Sister Sara *Rank*
  (+ Mr. Jericho *Rank*)
Dec. 26: Aladdin and His Magic Lamp *Target*
  + City Under the Sea *Warner-Pathe revival*

1972
Feb. 20: Gimme Shelter *Fox*
  (+ The Day The Fish Came Out *Fox*)

Granada Theatres From A To Z

This includes all cinemas operated by Granada and by the Bernstein family. It excludes cinemas where programmes were merely booked, cinemas operated only as bingo clubs, and (for lack of information) mobile cinemas. It includes some live theatres which had little or no cinema usage but excludes the Studio 7 Kingston which was acquired after closure solely as a property asset. Dates of take-overs refer where possible to when Granada assumed control, but may in some cases refer to the date of signing contracts. Dates of changes of name refer to the first press-advertised programme under the new name unless a special ceremony is known to have occurred. Information in brackets refers to periods outside of cinema operation by Granada. Accurate seating figures were not always available.

ACTON Northwest London

DOMINION High Street. (Opened 16.10.37 by Albert Bacal and N. Lee, architect: F. E. Bromige, 1500 seats.) Taken over 10.46. Renamed GRANADA 5.1.47. 1413 seats in 1955. 1198 seats in 1967. Bingo two nights weekly from 2.10.68. Closed 1.7.72. (Full time Granada bingo. Open in 1998.)

AYLESBURY Buckinghamshire

PAVILION High Street. (Opened 2.3.25 as Grand Pavilion, architect: C. H. Wright. 800 seats. Renamed Pavilion. Taken over by Wainwright circuit, later London & District Cinemas. Closed 10.36 for reconstruction, architect: Robert Cromie. Re-opened 4.1.37, 1234 seats.) Taken over 24.11.46. Renamed GRANADA 15.6.47. Closed 7.10.72. (Granada bingo. Taken over 5.91 by Gala, renamed Gala. Open in 1998.)

BEDFORD Bedfordshire

GRANADA 5/9 St. Peters Street. Opened 15.12.34 by Granada in association with local company, architects: (William T.) Benslyn, (James) Morrison & (R. Furneaux) Jordan, interior designer: Theodore Komisarjevsky, 1690 seats: 996 stalls & 694 balcony. Fully taken over by Granada. 1476 seats in 1973: 782 stalls & 694 balcony. Café converted to GRANADA 2, opened 29.7.74, 209 seats. (Taken over 1.89 by Cannon. Renamed Cannon. Closed 2.12.90. Demolished 2.91.)

EMPIRE 27 Midland Road. (Opened 27.5.12 by Ernest Blake, 534 seats: 374 stalls & 160 balcony.) Taken over 25.12.34, 682 seats. Closed 6.11.54 for improvements. Re-opened 22.12.54. 538 seats in 4.73: 378 stalls & 160 balcony. Closed 6.9.75. Re-opened 11.4.76 as GRANADA 3. Closed 19.6.77. (Demolished. Electricity Board showrooms.)

PALACE High Street, corner of Silver Street. (Opened 6.4.12, architects: Warner & Felce, 600 seats. Taken over 25.12.34. Closed 22.3.36. (Demolished 5.36 to 7.36. Shops and offices.)

PLAZA Embankment. (Opened 4.3.29, ex-function hall with some cinema use, part of former Castle skating rink, one floor. 1052 seats.) Taken over 17.2.69. Renamed CENTURY. 973 seats in 4.73. Closed 22.6.74. (Restaurant and nightclub. Closed. Demolished.)

BISHOP'S STORTFORD Hertfordshire

REGENT 11 South Street. (Opened 9.11.31 by Ernest E. Smith, architect: E. M. Allan-Hallett, 999 seats.) Taken over 23.8.65. Renovated and renamed GRANADA 30.1.67. 860 seats in 1973: 600 stalls & 260 balcony.

Closed 22.1.77. (Granada bingo from 14.7.77. Closed late 1982. Demolished by end 9.83. Marks & Spencer store on enlarged site.)

BOURNEMOUTH Dorset

ELECTRIC 23-27 Commercial Road. (Opened 22.12.21 by Capital and Counties Electric Theatres, architect: Cecil Masey, 1400 seats, replacing earlier Electric Theatre. Erected by Alexander Bernstein's building company. Sidney Bernstein was a director of the owning company, although no direct connection or booking arrangement with Bernstein Theatres is confirmed. Leased out to QTS from 9.27 to 1.4.29. Modernised and re-opened 14.7.30. Reconstructed and re-opened 12.7.37. 1187 seats. Closed 1967. Demolished.)

BOW Northeast London – see Mile End

BRIXTON South London

EMPRESS Bernay's Grove and Brighton Terrace. (Opened 26.12.98 as variety theatre, architects: Wylson & Long. Reconstructed, architect: Andrew Mather, and re-opened 9.31 as New Empress, with films shown on Sundays in 1930s. Reverted to name Empress. 1857 seats. Part of Variety Theatres Consolidated circuit.) Interest acquired 6.51. Managed from 1955. Closed 12.1.57 as live theatre. Re-opened 5.2.57 after alterations, architect: David E. Nye, designer: F. Mudd, as GRANADA cinema. Wrestling on Saturdays. Closed 10.2.67 (but wrestling on 11.2.67). (Granada bingo from 16.2.67. Closed. Demolished 11.92. Housing.)

CATFORD Southeast London – see Lewisham

CHARING CROSS ROAD London

PHOENIX THEATRE, Charing Cross Road and Phoenix Street. Opened 24.9.30 by Sidney L. Bernstein through Charing Cross Road Theatre Ltd., architects: Bertie Crewe, Cecil Masey, (Charing Cross Road facade) Sir Giles Gilbert Scott, interior designer: Theodore Komisarjesky, 1010 seats: 478 stalls, 280 circle & 252 gallery. Live theatre in cinema use from 22.4.31 to 23.5.31. Sold 3.32, but Bernstein Theatres continued to book film trade shows. (Public cinema from 8.2.39 briefly & for children's matinees in 1976 and 1977. Grade II listed building. Adjacent Curzon Phoenix cinema opened 20.3.87, entered through foyer of Phoenix Theatre. Both open in 1998.)

CHEAM South London
see also North Cheam

CENTURY Station Road [now Station Way], corner of Kingsmead Road, Cheam Village. Opened 22.3.37 by Granada, architect: James Morrison, 1001 seats: 768 stalls & 233 circle. Closed 3.41 by war damage. Re-opened 2.6.41. Closed 17.6.44 by bomb damage. Re-opened circa 5.45. Closed for improvements. Re-opened 16.8.48, new decorative scheme: John Armstrong. Closed 15.12.56. (Frontage demolished. Auditorium into car showroom, later demolished. Century House office block.)

CHELSEA West London

PALACE 232-242 King's Road, corner of Sydney Street. (Opened 13.4.03 as live theatre, architects: Wylson & Long, 2524 seats. Taken over 1925 by Variety Theatres Consolidated.) Interest acquired 6.51. Managed from 1955 as live theatre. 1641 seats in 6.56: 775 pits & stalls, 468 dress circle & boxes, 398 gallery. No cinema use. Renamed GRANADA 19.8.57. Leased 1.9.57 to Granada Television for television studio, modified internally, re-opened as GRANADA STUDIO 10. Sold. (Demolished 12.66.)

CHICHESTER West Sussex

EXCHANGE East Street, corner of Baffins Lane. (Opened 5.10 as the Corn Exchange following previous part-time film use. Taken over 1927 by Wainwright circuit. Closed

8.27 for major alterations, architects: G. S. Hall & G. de Wild. Re-opened 8.12.27 as the Exchange, 800 seats. Later part of Wainwrights' London & District Cinemas circuit. 740 seats.) Taken over 24.11.46. Closed 6.6.48 for alterations, architect: Robert Cromie. Re-opened 22.11.48 as the GRANADA EXCHANGE, 900 seats. Renamed GRANADA 15.1.50. 820 seats: 683 stalls & 137 circle. Closed 9.8.80. (McDonalds fast food outlet. Open.)

CLAPHAM JUNCTION South London

GRANADA St. John's Hill, corner of Plough Road. Opened 8.11.37 by Granada, architects: Leslie C. Norton & H. B. Horner, interior designer: Theodore Komisarjevsky, 2475 seats: 1542 stalls & 933 circle. 2135 seats in 3.73. Triple from 21.6.73, seating: 935 (former circle) + 191 + 187 (former rear stalls). Closed 5.7.80. (Detripled for Granada bingo club. Taken over 5.91 by Gala, renamed Gala. Closed 14.12.97. Grade II listed building from 29.4.98. Disused.)

GLOBE 15/17 Northcote Road. (Opened 8.30 by D. Mistlin, almost total reconstruction of old Globe cinema, architects: Bertie Crewe & Walter Gibbons, scenic artist: André Chaussent, 940 seats on one floor. Taken over by London & District Cinemas.) Taken over 24.11.46, 963 seats. Renamed CENTURY 2.7.51. Closed 17.10.64. (Tesco supermarket, opened 10.8.65. Kwik Save in 1998.)

CRYSTAL PALACE Southeast London – see Upper Norwood

DARTFORD Kent

GEM Spital Street. (Opened pre-World War One, part of Constitutional Club. Taken over by Medway Cinemas. 750 seats. Closed.) Taken over 2.47. Not re-opened. Sold.

SCALA THEATRE Kent Road, corner of Essex Road. (Opened 30.11.21, 800 seats. Balcony added, 972 seats. Taken over by Medway Cinemas. Live repertory theatre from 27.10.47. 1100 seats.) Taken over 18.4.49, continued as live theatre under lease to repertory company. (Put up for sale or lease 2.12.54. Ballroom from 4.3.63. Bingo from c1970. Nightclub from late 1978, later renamed Flicks.)

RIALTO Lowfield Street. (Opened 19.11.13 as New Theatre, 995 seats. Renamed The Cinema c1921. Renamed Rialto c1927. Taken over by Medway Cinemas. Reconstructed, architect: G. E. Bond, and re-opened 6.31, 995 seats.) Taken over 18.4.49. Renamed CENTURY 23.3.52. Closed 29.10.60. (Demolished. Supermarket.)

STATE Spital Street. (Opened 23.12.35 by Medway Cinemas, architects: J. Stanley Beard & Bennett, 1442 seats.) Taken over 18.4.49. Renamed GRANADA 2.10.49. 1292 seats in 1973: 828 stalls & 464 balcony. Closed 28.6.75. (Granada bingo club from 10.10.75. Taken over 5.91 by Gala, renamed Gala. Open.)

DEPTFORD Southeast London

BROADWAY Broadway/496 New Cross Road. (Opened 4.3.16, former live theatre with some films shown, 1300 seats. Taken over by A.O.C.) Taken over 5.48. Closed 16.10.49 for improvements, architect: George Coles. Re-opened 21.12.49. 1074 seats. Renamed CENTURY 15.8.55. Closed 30.4.60. (Demolished 3.63.)

DOVER Kent

GRANADA Castle Street. Opened 8.1.30 by Granada, architect: Cecil Masey, interior designer: Theodore Komisarjevsky, 1659 seats. (Leased 12.4.31 to Nat Lee. Sold 19.6.35 to ABC. Renamed ABC 4.60. Closed 6.6.70 for conversion to "luxury lounge" style. Re-opened 6.7.70, 610 seats, stalls only. Closed 30.10.82. Re-opened 6.84 as Images nightclub. Open in 1997.)

EAST FINCHLEY North London

REX 52 High Road, corner of Fairlawn Avenue. (Opened 1938 as reconstruction of existing cinema, architects: Howes & Jackman, 548 seats on one floor.) 320 seats in 4.73. Taken over 17.12.73. (Taken over by Contemporary Films 31.10.75. Closed for alterations. Re-opened 20.11.75 as Phoenix. Sold to independent. Open in 1998.)

EAST HAM Northeast London

EMPIRE Barking Road. Opened by 1915 by Alexander Bernstein, 1400 seats, one floor. Taken over 3.28 by Denman/Gaumont, operated by Bernstein/Granada, renamed

KINEMA. Improved by 28.7.28. 1416 seats in 10.34. Closed 23.5.36. (Demolished for Granada.)

GRANADA Barking Road (enlarged site of Empire). Opened 30.11.36 by Denman/Gaumont, operated by Granada, architect: W. E. Trent, interior designer: Theodore Komisarjevsky, 2468 seats. Closed 29.7.44 for three months by bomb damage. Fully acquired by Granada 3.65. 2248 seats in 1973: 1464 stalls & 784 circle. Closed Mondays and Tuesdays from 9.6.74. Closed 9.11.74. (Occasional live shows and Sunday Indian films. Granada bingo club from 16.1.76. Taken over 5.91 by Gala, renamed Gala. Open in 1998.)

EDGWARE ROAD North London

METROPOLITAN THEATRE 265-271 Edgware Road, Paddington. (Opened 22.12.87 as music hall, architect: Frank Matcham, re-build of earlier theatre. 1650 seats. Renamed Metropolitan Theatre of Varieties. Films shown on Sundays in 1930s. Part of Variety Theatres Consolidated circuit.) Interest acquired in 6.51. Managed by Granada from 1955. No film use. 1583 seats in 6.56: 623 stalls & pit, 460 circle & boxes, 500 gallery. Closed 19.7.58. Re-opened 6.10.58 as TV studio with invited audiences in balcony. Re-opened 7.9.59 as Irish music hall. Wrestling only on Saturdays from 7.60, plus occasional charity shows. Bingo added three nights per week. Closed 22.6.63. (Compulsory Purchase Order. Demolished for new road scheme.)

EDMONTON North London

EMPIRE 10 New Road, Lower Edmonton. (Opened 26.12.08, as music hall with some films, architect: Bertie Crewe.) Taken over 9.22 by Sidney L. Bernstein as music hall. 1290 seats. Closed end 3.27. Redecorated by Theodore Komisarjevsky and re-opened 18.4.27 as full-time cinema with variety. Taken over by Denman/Gaumont, operated by Bernstein/Granada. Closed 1.33 for reconstruction.

EMPIRE 10 New Road, Lower Edmonton. Opened 28.8.33 by Denman/Gaumont retaining walls of old Empire, architect: Cecil Masey, interior designer: Theodore Komisarjevksy, 1842 seats: 1165 stalls & 677

balcony. Renamed GRANADA c11.12.50. 1839 seats in 1964: 1162 stalls & 677 balcony. Fully acquired by Granada 4.65. Closed 13.7.68. (Granada bingo. Closed 27.7.69, taken over by local authority for redevelopment. Demolished 2.70. Car park.)

ENFIELD North London

RIALTO Burleigh Way (stalls entrance in Market Place, later closed). (Opened 8.11.20, former live theatre.) Taken over 5.25 by Bernstein. Improved and re-opened 23.8.27, architect: Cecil Masey, interior designer: Theodore Komisarjevsky, 1294 seats: 939 stalls & 355 balcony. Taken over 3.28 by Denman/Gaumont, operated by Bernstein/Granada. 1262 seats in 11.34: 901 stalls & 361 balcony. 1258 seats in 1951. Fully acquired by Granada 4.65. Renamed GRANADA 31.7.67. 1258 seats in 1970. Closed 17.7.71. (Granada bingo. Taken over 5.91 by Gala, renamed Gala. Closed 1997.)

FLORIDA London Road. (Opened 11.11.11 as Queen's Hall, 650 seats. Requisitioned during World War One. Balcony added in 1928: 1,300 seats. Closed 1940 by air raid damage. Taken over by Ministry of Food for store. Re-opened 19.5.47, renamed Florida, 878 seats. 827 seats in 4.73: 562 stalls & 265 balcony.) Taken over 17.12.73. 831 seats. Closed 12.6.76. (The Town House, banqueting hall and function suites. Open.)

EPSOM Surrey

CAPITOL Church Street. (Opened 30.12.29 by Wainwright circuit, architect: Robert Cromie, 1510 seats. Later part of Wainwrights' London & District Cinemas circuit.) Taken over 24.11.46. Renamed GRANADA 4.5.47. 1516 seats in 1955. Closed 15.10.60. (Sale completed 3.3.61. Demolished. Supermarket and Capitol House.)

GRANTHAM Lincolnshire

STATE 34 St. Peter's Hill. (Opened 4.10.37 by Wembley Cinemas [E. L. Manches], architect: J. Owen Bond, 1400 seats. Taken over by Medway Cinemas.) Taken over 2.49. Renamed GRANADA 13.2.50. Closed 1955 for improvments, architect: G. H. Dickinson. Part-week bingo from 5.66. 1298

seats in 3.72: 850 stalls & 398 balcony. Closed 9.4.73. (Full-time Granada bingo. Taken over 5.91 by Gala, renamed Gala. Closed. Demolished. National Westminster Bank on front of site.)

PICTURE HOUSE 38 High Street/St. Peter's Hill. (Opened 14.2.16 by J. A. Campbell, 980 seats: 800 stalls & 180 balcony. 886 seats in 1950.) Taken over 13.12.54. Closed 30.6.56 (Demolished. Tesco supermarket.)

EMPIRE George Street. (740 seats.) Taken over 13.12.54 as closed building. Not re-opened. Sold 1956.

CENTRAL. (Former Exchange Hall. 718 seats. Closed 5.51.) Taken over 13.12.54 as closed cinema. Not re-opened. Sold.

GREENFORD Northwest London

GRANADA Greenford Road (by Broadway). Opened 13.11.37 by Granada, architects: Charles Dixon & Henry Braddock, consultant: Cecil Masey, interior designer: Theodore Komisarjevsky. 1806 seats in 1955. Closed 15.9.66. (Tesco supermarket. Open.)

GREENWICH South London

GRANADA Trafalgar Road, between Vanbrugh Hill and Rodmere Street. Opened 30.9.37 by Granada, architect: C. Howard Crane, interior designer: Theodore Komisarjevsky, 1924 seats. Still 1924 seats in 1955. Partweek bingo from 1963. Closed 8.6.68. (Granada bingo. Closed. Stars nightclub. Closed and for sale in 1996.)

HARLESDEN Northwest London

HIPPODROME High Street. Taken over 3.9.27, reconstructed and re-opened 12.9.27 by Bernstein Theatres for cine-variety, former music hall known as Willesden Hippodrome. Managed from 3.28 as part of Denman/Gaumont group. 1979 seats in 3.28 but licensed for 1983: 864 stalls & pit, 517 circle & 602 gallery. Music hall use only from 28.1.29. Closed late 5.30. (Taken over c8.30 by ABC. 1900 seats. Closed 9.38. Re-opened as music hall, films on Sundays. Bombed 1940. Demolished 1957.)

HARROW North London

GRANADA Sheepcote Road/Station Road, corner of Bonnersfield Lane. Opened

25.10.37, architects: J. Owen Bond & Son, interior designer: Theodore Komisarjevsky. 1822 seats in 1973: 1192 stalls & 630 balcony. Triple from 26.11.73, seating 630 in old circle, 205 + 205 in former rear stalls. Grade II listed building from 4.8.88. (Taken over 1.89 by Cannon, renamed Cannon. Taken over 7.95 by Virgin. Taken over 3.5.96 by ABC. Renamed ABC 28.6.96. Closed 7.11.96.)

HOUNSLOW Northwest London

ALCAZAR Staines Road. (Opened 9.1.13, 959 seats. Part of London & District Cinemas circuit.) Taken over 24.11.46. Closed for modernisation, interior decorator: W. F. Mudd, and re-opened 21.12.51, renamed GRANADA. 1177 seats in 1955. Closed 29.10.60. (Demolished. Shops & offices.)

ILFORD Northeast London

EMPIRE Ilford Lane. Opened 4.13 by Alexander Bernstein, 960 seats. Improved & re-opened 1.3.22. (Taken over by Jacobson. Taken over 6.2.28 by Sam Martyn. Taken over c1932 by A. Maxwell and E. Josephs. Taken over c1934 by Ben Jay. 964 seats. Closed c1941.)

KENNINGTON South London

REGAL Kennington Road, corner of Princes Road. (Opened 17.11.37 by A.O.C., architects: Bertie Crewe & Henry G. Kay, consultant for Duchy of Cornwall estate: Louis de Soissons, 2000 seats. Closed during early World War Two. Re-opened 18.5.41.) Taken over 5.48. Renamed GRANADA 3.1.49. 1818 seats in 1955. Closed 15.7.61. (Granada bingo from mid-10.61 on Sundays, Tuesdays and Thursdays, then also Fridays. Wrestling on Saturdays from 28.10.61 or earlier. Bingo every night. 1762 seats in 9.62. Taken over 5.91 by Gala, renamed Gala. Closed 9.3.97. Added to local conservation area 7.97.)

KETTERING Northants

REGAL High Street. (Opened 26.12.36 by Cohen & Rafer, architect: George Coles, 1742 seats: 1164 stalls & 578 balcony.) Taken over 7.47. Renamed GRANADA 2.1.48. 1742 seats in 1955, 1967 & 1973. Closed 8.6.74. (Granada bingo from 20.2.75. Taken over 5.91 by Gala, renamed Gala. Open in 1998.)

KING'S CROSS North London

REGENT 37/43 Euston Road, corner of Tonbridge Street. (Opened 26.12.32, former Theatre of Varieties, original architect; W. G. R. Sprague, architect for alterations: Andrew Mather, 1200 seats. Taken over 14.10.35 by ABC. Taken over by independent after 24.12.49. Part of Variety Theatres Consolidated circuit.) Interest acquired through VTC in 1951. Managed by Granada as cinema from 7.52. Improved, architect: Leonard Allen, interior decorator: W. F. Mudd, and re-opened 13.9.54, renamed CENTURY. Renamed GRANADA 6.5.67, 853 seats. Closed 6.4.68. (Granada bingo from 1.5.68. Closed 1969. Demolished. Town Hall extension.)

KINGSTON Southwest London

ELITE London Road and Richmond Road. (Opened 21.5.21, architects: [James E.] Adamson & Kinns, 1369 seats.) Taken over 1.47. Improved and renamed CENTURY ELITE 4.51. 1237 seats. Closed 1.1.55. (Demolished. C&A Store, closed in 1996.)

GRANADA Richmond Road, now Clarence Street. Opened 3.11.39 by Granada, architect: George Coles, interior designer (uncredited): Theodore Komisarjevsky. 1758 seats in 1973: 1061 stalls & 697 balcony. Triple from 19.12.73, seating 975 (697 former circle & 278 front stalls) + 194 & 211 (former rear stalls). Closed 29.1.87. Grade II listed building from 30.1.87. Former circle area and front stalls converted to nightclub, two existing small cinemas in former rear stalls area retained and enlarged plus new cinema on upper floor. Re-opened as OPTIONS 11.12.87: 303 & 287 & 208 seats. (Taken over c1.89 by Cannon. Sometimes known as Cannon Options. Taken over by 7.95 by Virgin. Taken over 3.5.96 by ABC. Renamed ABC Options. Open in 1998.)

LEWISHAM Southeast London

HIPPODROME 135/7 Rushey Green, Catford. (Opened 13.2.11 as music hall, architect: Frank Matcham.) Taken over 5.27 as music hall. Cinema from 9.27. Renovated and re-opened 10.30 as live theatre. Closed 28.3.31 for alterations, architect: Cecil Masey, interior designer: Theodore Komisarjevsky. Re-opened 4.4.31 as cinema. (Taken over

c4.31 by ABC. Music hall with films on Sundays only by 1933. Closed 17.6.33. Taken over by independent, re-opened 16.10.33 as music hall. 2492 seats in 1937. Closed 1940 by bomb damage. Re-opened 12.5.52 by Hyams Bros. as Eros cinema. 1500 seats. Closed 14.11.59. Demolished 7.60. Eros House office block.)

LEYTON North London

KINGS Baker's Arms – High Road & Belmont Park Road. (Opened 26.3.10 as King's Hall cinema. Renamed King's. 969 seats. Part of Clavering & Rose circuit.) Taken over 4.49. Closed 28.10.51 for improvements, interior decorator: W. F. Mudd, & re-opened 17.1.52, renamed CENTURY. 995 seats in 10.54: 827 stalls & 168 balcony. Closed 27.7.63. (Tesco supermarket.)

LEYTONSTONE North London

RINK 821 High Road (through arcade) and Kirkdale Road. (Opened 4.11 as Rink, conversion of part of skating rink, 1550 seats on one floor.) Taken over 4.10.26. Closed 1.11.26 for major alterations, architect: Cecil Masey. Re-opened 6.1.27, renamed RIALTO, 1760 seats. Taken over 3.28 by Denman/Gaumont, managed by Bernstein/Granada. 1882 seats on one floor in 11.34. Closed 1.45 by bomb damage. Re-opened 1.10.45. 1760 seats in 1951. Fully acquired by Granada 3.65. Renamed GRANADA 25.6.67. 1418 seats in 1973. Closed 27.4.74. (Demolished.)

ACADEMY High Road, Harrow Green. (Opened 29.3.13 as Academy, 650 seats. Closed 26.8.33. Enlarged with new facade, architect: F. C. Mitchell, and re-opened 2.10.33, 1100 seats, stadium plan. Owned by Harry Hymanson.) Taken over 13.12.54 by Granada, 1016 seats. Closed 1.10.55 for renovations, architect: George Coles. Re-opened 21.11.55 as CENTURY. Taken over 28.7.57 by Denman (London), but continued to be operated by Granada. Bingo Thursdays from 8.11.62. Closed 5.1.63. (Granada bingo. Fully acquired by Granada 3.65. Closed 7.83. Demolished. Flats.)

LOUGHTON Essex

CINEMA High Road. (Opened 9.10.28, architect: Theodore E. Legg, 850 seats, one floor. Closed 23.6.34 for improvements. Re-opened 12.7.34, 700 seats.) Managed from 8.34. Closed 12.52 for modernisation. Re-opened 22.12.52, renamed CENTURY, 869 seats. Fully acquired 4.54. Closed 25.5.63. (Demolished. Shops.)

MAIDSTONE Kent

GRANADA Lower Stone Street, corner of Granada Street. Opened 10.1.34 by Granada, architect: Cecil Masey, interior designer: Theodore Komisarjevsky. 1684 seats in 6.34 and 1955. Closed 15.9.68 by flood damage. Re-opened 23.9.68, balcony only, 650 seats. Closed 24.4.71 for conversion, architects: George Coles & Partners, to Granada bingo in former stalls and two smaller cinemas with new side entrance. Re-opened 26.12.71 as GRANADA 1 & 2, seating 560 (old balcony) & 90 (former café). GRANADA 1 closed for twinning, re-opened 27.12.74 as GRANADA 1 & 3, 258 & 259 seats. (Taken over 1.89 by Cannon, renamed Cannon. Renamed MGM 21.5.93. Taken over 7.95 by Virgin. Taken over 3.5.96 by ABC. Renamed ABC 7.6.96. Open in 1998.)

MANCHESTER

HIPPODROME Oxford Street. Taken over 2.35 from Stoll as live theatre. Closed 2.3.35. Demolished for new Granada/Gaumont.

GAUMONT Oxford Street, corner of Great Bridgewater Street (site of Hippodrome). Built for Granada, architects: William T. Benslyn & James Morrison, interior designer: Theodore Komisarjevsky, 2300 seats: 1300 stalls & 1000 balcony. (Taken over on completion and opened 21.10.35 by Gaumont. Closed 28.1.74. Rotters nightclub. Closed. Demolished 1990. Site vacant in 1998.)

MANSFIELD Nottinghamshire

PLAZA West Gate. (Opened 4.8.30 by Oaksford Theatre group, architect: Alfred J. Thraves, 1523 or 1582 seats.) Taken over 9.34. Renamed GRANADA 20.4.42. 1530 seats in 1967 & 1973. Closed 26.5.73. (Demolished 8.73. Littlewood's store.)

HIPPODROME Midworth Street. Taken over 1.36. Renamed CENTURY 5.9.55. Part-week bingo by 11.62. Closed 27.5.61. (Granada

bingo by 7.67. Closed 5.73. Re-opened as extension of new Granada bingo club next door.)

MILE END Northeast London

EMPIRE 95 Mile End Road. (Opened as Paragon Music Hall.) Taken over & re-opened 11.5.12 by Alexander Bernstein & Harry Bawn, renamed EMPIRE and operated as cinema. (Taken over 1919 by Henry A. Goide. 800 seats. Taken over 1.28 by United Picture Theatres. Sold to independent 1934. Taken over c1936 by ABC. 2000 seats. Closed 3.4.38. Demolished for new Empire.)

ELECTRODROME 122 Eric Street (Fair Ground). (Previously known as Forrest's Electrodrome, operated by H. Forrest.) Operated by Bernstein in partnership with local owner from c1920. Taken over, leased out to independent 700 seats. Taken back c1933. Closed c1940.

MORECAMBE Lancashire

EMPIRE Promenade. (Opened 7.38 as live theatre, 1500 seats. Films from 9.38 to Summer 1939. Mixed later use. Re-opened 14.6.70 as two-screen cinema. 1200 + 250 seats. Converted to three screens from 28.5.72. Converted from 21.5.75 to quad: 260 + 240 + 350 + 350 seats. One screen closed.) Taken over 18.6.79. 362 + 360 + 276 seats. 4th screen re-opened by 9.79. Closed 24.9.83. (Demolished.)

ARCADIAN Promenade. (Opened 16.2.41, former live theatre, 1000 seats. Modernised 1970. Opened seasonally.) Taken over 18.6.79. Closed by 9.83. (Storage.)

NORTH CHEAM South London

see also Cheam

GRANADA 562 London Road. Opened 22.9.37 by Granada, architects: David E. Nye & James Morrison, interior designer: Theodore Komisarjevsky, 1668 seats. Closed 18.10.69. (Demolished. Sainsbury's super-market & offices. Wetherspoon's pub.)

NORWOOD South London – see Upper Norwood

OSWESTRY Shropshire

REGAL English Walls & Cross Street/Salop Road. (Opened 22.5.33, architect: Lionel A.

G. Pritchard, 1080 seats: 744 stalls & 336 balcony.) Interest acquired 11.34. Fully taken over 6.2.55, 1043 seats: 761 stalls & 282 balcony. Closed for improvements, re-opened 23.7.56, renamed GRANADA. 839 seats in 1973: 567 stalls & 272 balcony. Closed 14.6.75. (Taken over by independent and re-opened 25.2.76 as Regal. 839 seats. Twinned 1985, 261 + 261 seats. Third screen added 1987 on former stage, 66 seats. Converted to single screen cinema, 259 seats, and nightclub. Closed 16.6.94. Disused in 1998.)

KING'S THEATRE New Street (site of old King's Theatre). (Opened 17.4.33, architects: Bradley & Clarke.) Interest acquired 11.34. 1100 seats. Known as KINGS. Fully taken over 6.2.55, 954 seats. Modernised and re-opened 26.12.55, renamed CENTURY. Part-week bingo by 12.64. Closed 4.1.66. (Century bingo continued part-week, then full-time. Renamed Granada bingo by 9.77. Closed in 1998. Scheduled to become Wilkinson's hardware store.)

PITSEA Essex

BROADWAY The Broadway. (Opened 28.3.30, architects: A. J. Varndell & L. A. Green, 600 seats, one floor.) Taken over 28.6.54. Closed 2.1.55 for modernisation. Re-opened 15.2.55 as CENTURY. 670 seats in 1967. Bingo part-week by 7.67. Closed 31.10.70. (Granada bingo full-time from 1.11.71. Taken over 5.91 by Gala, renamed Gala. Open in 1998.)

PLUMSTEAD Southeast London

EMPIRE 81-93 High Street and Garibaldi Street. (Opened or taken over c11.13 by Alexander Bernstein, architects: Andrews & Peascod, 900 capacity.) Taken over 3.28 by Denman/Gaumont but operated by Bernstein/Granada. 1008 capacity (bench seats). Improved, architect: Cecil Masey, & re-opened 28.7.28 as KINEMA, 913 seats. Renamed CENTURY 3.3.52. Closed 24.9.60. (Training centre. Building stands, use unclear, in 1997.)

PLAZA 142/6 High Street. (Opened 7.9.11 as The Plumstead Cinematograph Theatre. Capacity 600. Altered and re-opened 1931 as Plaza, 528 seats. Part of London & District

Cinemas circuit.) Taken over 24.11.46. Closed 11.12.54. (Store from 9.61. Demolished. Woolworth's store.)

RUGBY Warwickshire

REGENT Bank Street. (Opened 22.5.20 as Picture House, architect: T. W. Willard, 1200 seats. Improved and renamed Regent 30.11.29.) Interest taken 12.12.32. Closed 17.7.38 for alterations. Re-opened 8.38. Acquired 9.44. Redecorated and refurbished, re-opening 20.8.53. Modernised & re-opened 25.7.55 as CENTURY. Closed 1.7.61. (Century Bingo Club from 19.7.61, initially part week. Closed 1976. Kwik Save supermarket. Closed 1990. Re-opened late 1997 as Chumley's café/bar – open in 1998.)

PLAZA North Street. Opened 30.1.33, architects: J. H. & R. B. Lyddington in association with Leathart & Granger, 1700 seats, under Granada management. Acquired 9.44. Renamed GRANADA 26.5.46. 1688 seats. 1678 seats in 1973: 1184 stalls & 494 balcony. Closed 28.2.76. (Granada bingo from 30.9.76. Taken over 5.91 by Gala. Open in 1998.)

REGAL Railway Terrace. (Opened 23.9.31, former Prince of Wales Theatre enlarged and redecorated, architect: W. T. Loveday.) Interest taken c7.33. 720 seats in 1935. Fully acquired 9.44. Closed 5.1.53. (Pickford's depository. Rite-Price Furniture Sales showroom in 1998.)

SCALA Henry Street. (Opened 9.13 as Empire Cinema De Luxe, architects: Eames & Jackson. Renamed Empire. Renamed Scala 9.3.23. 600 seats. Closed mid-1946 by fire.) Taken over 7.46, not re-opened. (Sold for live theatre use. Re-opened 5.12.49 as Rugby Theatre. Some films shown from 7.76. Open in 1998.)

RUSHEY GREEN Southeast London – see Lewisham

ST. PETERS PORT, Guernsey

LYRIC New Street. Listed with Bernstein Theatres c1921. (Taken over c1926 by PCT/Gaumont. Taken over by independent by 1940. Under enemy occupation during part of World War Two.)

SEVENOAKS Kent

PLAZA 152 High Street (site of former Electric/Cinema). (Opened 4.11.35, architect: David E. Nye, 1150 seats. Taken over by Lou Morris c4.37, renamed Plaza. Taken over 6.37 by Cohen & Rafer.) Taken over 7.47. Renamed GRANADA 28.11.48. Closed 22.10.60. (Demolished. New road.)

CARLTON St. John's Hill. (Opened as the New Picture Theatre. Closed 24.6.35 for modernisation. Re-opened 23.9.35, renamed Carlton. 382 seats in 6.41: 269 stalls & 113 balcony. Taken over 9.43 by Nathan Cohen. Operated by Cohen, Rafer and others from c4.46.) Taken over 7.47. 398 seats. (Taken over late 1949 by Miles Byrne. Renamed New Carlton Theatre 9.50 for live shows. Cinema again from 2.51. Renamed Embassy. Closed 14.2.54. Commercial use.)

SHREWSBURY Shropshire

EMPIRE Mardol. Opened 25.11.22 by Shrewsbury Empires in association with Bernstein Theatres, 903 seats. Closed part of 1931 for vestibule improvements. Taken over fully. 764 seats in 1967 & early 1973: 534 stalls & 230 balcony. Closed 12.5.73 for refurbishment, architect: George Coles, & re-opened 18.5.73, 509 seats. (Taken over 1.89 by Cannon. Taken over by 7.95 by Virgin. Taken over 3.5.96 by ABC. Renamed ABC 21.6.96. Closed 22.1.98.)

CENTRAL Castle Gates. (Opened 24.1.10 as Central Hall, former chapel.) Taken over c1930 by Shrewsbury Empires in association with Bernstein Theatres. Closed 21.3.31 by fire. (Retail use. Castle Hall, soft furnishings shop, in 1998.)

KINGS Wyle Cop. (Opened 12.3.14 as King's Hall, 750 seats. Re-opened 1.9.30. Known as Kings.) Taken over c1930 by Shrewsbury Empires in association with Bernstein Theatres. Taken over fully. 805 seats. Renamed CENTURY 9.1.56. Closed 11.6.60. (Century bingo from 14.6.61, initially two nights per week. Full-time bingo. Closed 4.73. Disused in 1996. Stalls area: retail store for kitchen equipment in 1998. Snooker club in former balcony in 1998.)

GRANADA Castle Gates. Opened 14.11.34 by Granada through Shrewsbury Empires,

architect: Cecil Masey, interior designer: Theodore Komisarjevsky, 1525 seats: 932 stalls & 593 balcony. Taken over fully. 1488 seats in 1972. Closed 31.3.73. (Granada bingo from 17.4.73. Taken over 5.91 by Gala, renamed Gala. Listed building from 17.11.95. Open in 1997.)

ROYAL COUNTY Shoplatch. (Opened 21.12.31, former Theatre Royal. Taken over c1933 by Regent/ABC.) Taken over 1936 by Shrewsbury Empires in association with Bernstein Theatres. Known as COUNTY. 500 seats. Closed 24.6.45 by fire. (Aston's furniture store. Newday furnishings. Poundstretcher discount store in 1998.)

SLOUGH Berkshire

GRANADA Windsor Road. Opened 23.3.38 by Granada, architect: C. Howard Crane, revisions: Cecil Masey, interior designer (uncredited): Theodore Komisarjevsky, 1710 seats: 1080 stalls & 630 balcony. 1370 seats in 3.73. Triple from 15.6.73, seating 624 (former balcony) + 239 & 187 (former rear stalls). Closed 19.11.87. (Demolished 1988.)

PALACE 127 High Street. (Opened c1921, 950 seats. Closed 3.7.37 for modernisation & setting back of proscenium arch, architect: Kenneth Friese-Greene. Re-opened 8.37, 1336 seats. Closed 8.45 by fire.) Taken over c1949, repaired, architect: George Coles, interior decoration: Howell Jones & W. F. Mudd, & re-opened 2.1.50 as CENTURY, 1400 seats. Closed 27.1.57. (Waitrose supermarket.)

ADELPHI THEATRE Bath Road. (Opened 17.2.30, architect: E. Norman-Bailey, 2014 seats: 1370 stalls & 644 balcony. Re-opened 29.5.33 by Southan Morris. Taken over c1933 by Union. Taken over 10.37 by ABC.) Taken over 31.3.53. Known as ADELPHI. Closed 21.1.73. (Granada bingo from 18.5.73. Taken over 5.91 by Gala, renamed Gala. Open in 1998.)

STRATFORD Northeast London

EMPIRE West Ham Lane, corner of Densham Road. (Opened 7.14 by Alexander Bernstein, architects: Andrews & Peascod.) Altered & re-opened 14.10.25. Reconstructed, architect: Cecil Masey, interior designer: Theodore Komisarjevsky, & re-opened

14.11.27 as KINEMA West Ham, 1659 seats on one floor. Taken over 3.28 by Denman/Gaumont but operated by Bernstein/Granada. 1594 seats in 11.34. Closed 7.9.40 by bomb damage. Re-opened 20.11.40. Renamed CENTURY 23.7.51. Styled Century Stratford from 13.7.53. Bingo one night weekly from c10.62. Closed 5.1.63. (Century bingo. Fully re-acquired 3.65. Renamed Granada bingo by 6.77. Taken over 5.91 by Gala, renamed Gala. Closed by 1994. Demolished 1996. Housing.)

SUTTON London

PLAZA Carshalton Road West, corner of Manor Park Road. (Opened 8.9.34 by Lou Morris, architect: Robert Cromie, interior designers: [Eugene] Mollo & [Michael] Egan, 2390 seats: 1641 stalls & 749 balcony.) Taken over 10.9.34 by Granada. Closed 20.9.40 by bomb damage. Re-opened 21.10.40. Renamed GRANADA 4.42. 2391 seats in 1955. 2041 seats in 1973 & 1975: 1290 stalls & 751 balcony. Closed 28.8.75 by fire at stage end. (Demolished. Office block.)

SWISS COTTAGE North London

EMBASSY Eton Avenue. (Opened 11.9.28 as live theatre, 678 seats. Closed 1955.) Taken over 6.55 as live theatre. 679 seats. (Lease sold c10.56 to Central School of Speech and Drama.)

SYDENHAM Southeast London

STATE 72/78 Sydenham Road, corner of Girton Road. (Opened 1.8.31, owner/architect: A. C. Matthews, 1484 seats [but plans of 11.30 show 1517 seats: 869 stalls & 648 circle]. Taken over 10.33 by Excelsior Super Cinemas. Part of Medway Cinemas circuit.) Taken over 3.49. Renamed GRANADA 3.10.49. 1433 seats. 1319 seats in 1967: 697 stalls & 622 balcony. 1270 seats. Closed 3.4.71. (Demolished 1971. Safeway Supermarket.)

THORNTON HEATH South London

STATE 793 London Road. (Opened 26.12.32, owner/architect: A. C. Matthews, 1893 seats. Taken over by Blue Halls 1938. Taken over 5.10.40 by A.O.C.) Taken over 5.48. Renamed GRANADA 1.1.49. 1885 seats in 1955. Closed 1.7.72. (Granada bingo from

13.10.72. Taken over 5.91 by Gala, renamed Gala. Open in 1998.)

TOOTING South London

GRANADA 50/58 Mitcham Road. Opened 7.9.31 by Granada, architect: Cecil Masey, interior designers: Theodore Komisarjevsky & (murals) Lucien Le Blanc, 3104 seats. 3086 seats in 1934. 3053 seats in 1962. 2909 seats in 1.68. 2,877 seats in 11.68 & 1973: 1552 stalls & 1325 balcony. Wandsworth Borough Council preservation notice issued 21.2.72. Grade II* listed building 28.6.72. Closed 10.11.73. (Disused. Re-opened for Granada bingo 14.10.76. Improved and relaunched 6.82. Taken over 5.91 by Gala, renamed Gala. Open in 1998.)

UPPER NORWOOD Southeast London

RIALTO 25 Church Road. (Opened 6.10.28, owner/architect: A. C. Matthews, 1393 seats. Taken over by Excelsior Super Cinemas. Part of Medway Cinemas circuit.) Taken over 3.49. Modernised, architect: George Coles, and renamed GRANADA 11.9.50. 1370 seats in 1955. Styled Granada Crystal Palace from 12.2.61. 1193 seats in 11.67. Part week bingo (discontinued). Closed 26.5.68. (Granada bingo from 27.6.68. Closed 7.69. Leased out 2.2.70 & re-opened as Lesleen Social Club for bingo 9.2.70. Closed. Re-opened by Granada for bingo. Taken over 5.91 by Gala, renamed Gala. Open in 1998.)

ALBANY 18 Church Road. (Opened 18.1.30, owner/architect: A. C. Matthews, 1250 seats on one floor. Taken over by Excelsior Super Cinemas. Remodelled, architect: C. Edmund Wilford, 970 seats on one floor. Part of Medway Cinemas circuit. Requisitioned for food store during World War Two. Re-opened 10.48.) Taken over 3.49. Closed for reconstruction. Re-opened 26.12.50, renamed CENTURY. Closed 30.5.58. (Car showrooms for Selhurst Park Garages, named Century House. Open in 1998 as S. G. Smith Century House car showroom.)

WALTHAMSTOW North London

VICTORIA Hoe Street. (Opened 19.8.07 as Victoria Hall. Remodelled and re-opened 2.9.21 as Victoria Picture Theatre.) Taken over 12.11.28. Closed 3.30. (Demolished for Granada.)

GRANADA Hoe Street (site of Victoria and adjoining property). Opened 15.9.30 by Granada, architect: Cecil Masey, interior designer: Theodore Komisarjevsky, 2697 seats. 2704 seats in 6.34. Closed 16/17.8.44 by war damage. Re-opened c24.11.44. 2680 seats in 1955. 2552 seats in 1973: 1608 stalls & 944 balcony. Triple from 16.10.73, seating 944 (former balcony)(+ 558 front stalls), 172 & 172 (former rear stalls). Minis 181 + 181 seats in 7.74. Front stalls seating removed. Grade II listed building from 24.2.87. (Taken over 1.89 by Cannon. Renovated and upstairs seating reduced to 592. Taken over by 7.95 by Virgin. Taken over 3.5.96 by ABC. Renamed ABC 28.6.96. Open in 1998.)

WANDSWORTH ROAD South London

CLOCK TOWER CINEMA 128/130 Wandsworth Road, Vauxhall. (Opened 5.8.21, former cadet training headquarters, 850 seats.) Taken over 30.4.34. 700 seats. Closed 28.3.36. (Demolished for new Granada on enlarged site.)

GRANADA 128/130 Wandsworth Road, Vauxhall, corner of Fount Street (partly on site of Clock Tower Cinema). Opened 13.10.36 by Granada, architects: E. D. Lyons, L. Israel and C. H. Elsom, decorative motifs: Frank Dobson, 2056 seats: 1320 stalls & 736 balcony. Closed 12.11.40 by enemy action. Repaired but severely damaged 5.41 before re-opening. Restored & re-opened 12.9.49. Monthly wrestling on Wednesdays from 1.2.60. 2008 seats in 1962. Bingo on Wednesdays from 25.7.62. Bingo on Wednesdays and Fridays from 14.12.62. Bingo on Mondays and Wednesdays from late 62/early 63. Closed 13.5.67. (Granada bingo five nights per week from 15.5.67. Closed by 4.77. Reconstructed internally as London South Bank Squash and Fitness Club, open in 10.96.)

WATFORD Hertfordshire

REGAL King Street, corner of Granville Road. (Opened 17.12.13 as Central Hall, architects: Norfolk & Prior, 1078 seats: 748 stalls & 330 balcony. Taken over D & M Cinemas. Taken over by Standard Cinema Properties, re-opened 30.9.29 as Regal.) Taken over by 6.32. Closed 21.11.32 for reconstruction, architect: George Coles, interior designer: Theodore Komisarjevsky, and re-opened 26.12.32, 1286 seats. (Taken over c1935. Improved and renamed New Regal early 1936. Taken over by Southan Morris. Taken over 26.8.54 by Essoldo. Renamed Essoldo 9.7.56. Closed 17.11.68. Essoldo bingo. Taken over by Ladbroke's, renamed Ladbroke's Social Club. Renamed Mecca. Open in 1998.)

WEST HAM LANE Northeast London - see Stratford

WELLING Southeast London

GRANADA Bellegrove Road. Opened 2.2.38 by Granada, architect: George Coles, interior designer (uncredited): Theodore Komisarjevsky, 1900 seats. 1480 seats in 1967. 1422 seats in 1973: 824 stalls & 598 balcony. Triple from 5.5.75, seating 598 (former circle) + 229 & 230 (former rear stalls). Closed 30.7.83. (Demolished. Shops.)

WELLINGTON Shropshire

GRAND Tan Bank. (Opened c1936, former theatre. 966 seats. Rebuilt 1938, 800 seats. Modernised 1968.) Taken over 17.3.75. 580 seats. Closed 25.10.75. (Granada bingo from 22.4.76. Demolished c1997.)

WILLESDEN Northwest London
see also Harlesden

EMPIRE 226 Church Road, corner of Ilex Road. (Opened 22.12.20 by Alexander Bernstein, architect: Cecil Masey, 1450 seats, one floor. Redecorated, director of colour scheme: F. L. Lyndhurst, & re-seated c9.24. Closed late 5.27. Reconstructed with balcony, architect: Cecil Masey, exterior sculptor: Frank Dobson, interior designer: Theodore Komisarjevsky, and re-opened 27.10.27, 1777 seats: 991 stalls & 786 balcony. Taken over 3.28 by Denman/Gaumont but operated by Bernstein/Granada. 1768 seats in 10.34: 1065 stalls & 703 balcony. Closed 11.7.36. Remodelled, architect: James Morrison, & re-opened 21.9.36 renamed GRANADA, 1694 seats. Closed 20.10.62. (Granada bingo. Fully acquired 3.65 by Granada. Closed. Re-opened 14.10.94 as The Comedy Empire, live theatre. Closed. Re-opened as Asian cinema, renamed Empire, circa 800 seats.

Closed 1997. Re-opened 13.7.97 by Miracle Signs and Wonders Ministries as church. Open.)

WOOLWICH Southeast London

GRANADA 174/186 Powis Street. Opened 20.4.37 by Granada, architects: Reginald H. Uren (frontage) & Cecil Masey (remainder), interior designer: Theodore Komisarjevsky, 2434 seats. Partweek bingo from 5.12.61. Bingo discontinued between 4.65 to 6.66. Closed 26.10.66. (Granada bingo, full-time from 30.10.66. Grade II listed building from 7.1.74. Taken over 5.91 by Gala, renamed Gala. Open in 1998.)

CINEMA 1 Beresford Square. (Opened 10.13 as Arsenal Cinema, 650 seats. Renamed The Cinema by 1915. Enlarged to 900 seats.) Taken over 11.52. Renamed CENTURY 9.53. 863 seats. Closed 27.5.61. (Century bingo from 8.61. Closed by 1966. Demolished late 1968.)

Bibliography

Articles

"Alone in the Dark: A Trick of the Trade as applied by Brian Gauntlett." (*Picture House*, No. 22, Summer 1997, pages 18-24). Recalls showmanship stunts at the Granada Tooting and elsewhere.

"CinemaScope and the Fox Circuit." By Allen Eyles. (*Picture House*, No. 2, Autumn 1982, pages 9-12.)

"Commerce – With Culture." By Tom Driberg. (*Leader*, 18 November 1944.) Short profile of Sidney Bernstein in series "Behind Their Faces".

"David Nye Cinema Architect." By Richard Gray. (*Picture House*, No. 22, Summer 1997, pages 41-54.) Covers Cinema (later Granada) Sevenoaks and Granada North Cheam, etc.

"Decorative Problems. How the Production of Harmonious Effects may be Achieved." By Theodore Komisarjevsky. (*Ideal Kinema*, 13 February 1930, pages 11-15. Describes his work on Dover.

"Ernest Wamsley Lewis: A Centenary Tribute." (*Picture House*, No. 23, Summer 1998.) Reprint of article "An Internationalist at Home" by Ernest Wamsley Lewis from *London Architect*, January and March 1972. Contains Sidney Bernstein's view of the New Victoria.

"Good Taste. Bernstein on Decorations." By Sidney L. Bernstein. (*Kinematograph Weekly*, 3 January 1924, page 123.)

"Granada Bedford: The Early Days." By John Squires. (*Picture House*, No.1, Spring 1982, pages 3-5.)

"Great Granada: The Pride of Tooting." By Tom Vallance. (*Picture House*, No.19, Winter 1993/4).

"Komisarjevsky in Britain." By Ralph Berry. (*Theatrephile*, Vol. 2, No. 5, Winter 1984/5.) Includes checklist of theatre productions.

"Mr. Granada." By David Leitch. (*Sunday Times Magazine*, 12 September 1965.) Profile of Sidney Bernstein.

"What The Film Trade Has Done. A Summary Of A Paper By Sidney Bernstein." (*Sight and Sound*, Winter 1936-37.) Paper delivered to the Conference on Films for Children in November 1936.

Books and booklets

All Pals Together. The Story of Children's Cinema. By Terry Staples. (Edinburgh University Press, Edinburgh, 1997.)

The British Film Industry. By Political and Economic Planning. (PEP, 1952.)

Cathedrals of the Movies: A History of British Cinemas and Their Audiences. By David Atwell. (Architectural Press, London, 1980.)

Cinemas in Britain: One Hundred Years of Cinema Architecture. By Richard Gray. (Lund Humphries, London, 1996.) Includes chapter on "The Granada Style".

The Cinemas of Croydon. By Allen Eyles and Keith Skone. (Keytone Publications/Croydon Public Libraries, 1989.) Contains fuller histories of Granada cinemas at Thornton Heath and Upper Norwood.

The Cinemas of Hertfordshire. By Allen Eyles and Keith Skone. (Hertfordshire Publications/ Premier Bioscope, 1985.) Contains fuller history of Granada Bishop's Stortford.

Cinema West Sussex. The First Hundred Years. By Allen Eyles, Frank Gray and Alan Readman. (Phillimore/West Sussex County Council, Chichester, 1996.) Contains fuller history of the Granada Chichester.

Gaumont British Cinemas. By Allen Eyles. (Cinema Theatre Association/BFI Publishing, Burgess Hill, West Sussex, 1996.) Includes the Denman (London) cinemas co-owned with Granada.

The Life of P. T. Barnum. Written by himself. (Sampson, Low, Son, & Co., London, 1855.)

London. By Ian Nairn. (1966.)

100 Years of Glasgow's Amazing Cinemas. By Bruce Peter. (Polygon, Edinburgh, 1996.) Refers to lawsuit over the name Granada.

Persona Granada. Some memories of Sidney Bernstein and the early years of Independent Television. By Denis Forman. (Andre Deutsch, London, 1997.) Presents a vivid portrait of Sidney Bernstein, disinterring fact from mythology, and has some valuable information on the family background.

The Picture Palace and other buildings for the movies. By Dennis Sharp. (Hugh Evelyn, London, 1969.)

Picture Palaces Remembered. An affectionate look at the Cinema Theatres of Dover, Deal and Folkestone. By John Roy and Tony Thompson. (Glenton Publications,1987.) Covers Granada Dover.

Red Roses Every Night. An Account of London Cinemas under Fire. By Guy Morgan. (Quality Press, London, 1948.) An account of London Granadas as typical cinemas in World War Two.

Sidney Bernstein. A Biography. By Caroline Moorehead. (Jonathan Cape, London, 1984.)

This Is Granada. (Granada Group, London, undated.) History of company given to new employees.